CLASSICAL MUSIC FUTURES

Classical Music Futures

Practices of Innovation

*Edited by Neil Thomas Smith, Peter Peters
and Karoly Molina*

https://www.openbookpublishers.com

© 2024 Neil Thomas Smith, Peter Peters and Karoly Molina

This work is licensed under a Creative Commons Attribution-NonCommercial 4.0 International license (CC BY-NC 4.0). This license allows you to share, copy, distribute and transmit the work for non-commercial purposes, providing attribution is made to the author (but not in any way that suggests that he endorses you or your use of the work). Attribution should include the following information:

Neil Thomas Smith, Peter Peters and Karoly Molina, *Classical Music Futures: Practices of Innovation*. Cambridge: Open Book Publishers, 2024, https://doi.org/10.11647/OBP.0353

Further details about CC BY-NC licenses are available at https://creativecommons.org/licenses/by-nc/4.0/.

All external links were active at the time of publication unless otherwise stated and have been archived via the Internet Archive Wayback Machine at https://archive.org/web.

Copyright and permissions for the reuse of many of the images included in this publication differ from the above. This information is provided in the captions. Every effort has been made to identify and contact copyright holders and any omission or error will be corrected if notification is made to the publisher.

Any digital material and resources associated with this volume may be available at https://doi.org/10.11647/OBP.0353#resources.

ISBN Paperback: 978-1-80511-073-6
ISBN Hardback: 978-1-80511-074-3
ISBN Digital (PDF): 978-1-80511-075-0
ISBN Digital eBook (EPUB): 978-1-80511-076-7
ISBN XML: 978-1-80511-078-1
ISBN HTML: 978-1-80511-079-8

DOI: 10.11647/OBP.0353

Cover image: Jean Pierre Geusens, *Focuss22* (2017)
Cover design by Jeevanjot Kaur Nagpal

Table of Contents

Notes on Contributors ... ix

Classical Music Futures: An Introduction ... 1
Neil Thomas Smith and Peter Peters

Whose Future?

1. Roundtable 1: Whose Future? ... 29
Neil Thomas Smith with contributions from Maria Hansen, Kirsteen Davidson Kelly, and George E. Lewis

2. Classical Music has a Diversity Problem ... 41
Brandon Farnsworth

3. Roundtable 2: Documenting Change: The Role of Best-Practice Guidelines ... 59
Neil Thomas Smith (MCICM) with contributions from Hannah Bujic (Sound and Music), Francine Gorman (Keychange), and Fiona Robertson (Sound)

4. Until George Floyd: An Afrofuturist Perspective on the Future of Classical Music and Opera ... 81
Antonio C. Cuyler

5. The Voice Party – A New Opera for a New Political Era ... 91
Lore Lixenberg

Future Musicians

6. Becoming a Classical Musician of the Future The Effects of Training and Experience on Performer Attitudes to Innovation ... 103
Stephanie Pitts, Karen Burland and Tom Spurgin

7. The Global Conservatoire: Towards an Integrated Approach to Developing Twenty-First-Century Artists ... 127
Diana Salazar and Christina Guillaumier

8. Meaningful Music in Healthcare: Professional Development and Discovered Identities of Classical Musicians Working in Hospital Wards   153
Krista de Wit and Beste Sevindik

Innovating Institutions

9. Roundtable 3: Orchestras in a Changing Climate   177
Neil Thomas Smith and Peter Peters with contributions from Teemu Kirjonen, Detlef Grooß, Georgina MacDonell Finlayson, and Jan Jaap Knoll

10. Is It Time for Brahms, Again? The Many Roles of Classical Music in the German-Speaking Lands in 2023   191
Jutta Toelle

11. The Environmental Sustainability of Symphony Orchestras: Challenges and Potential Solutions   205
Stine Skovbon

Learning from the Art Museum

12. The 'Museum Problem' Revisited: Learning from Contemporary Art Conservation   229
Denise Petzold

13. Futuring Classical Music through Contemporary Visual Art: Innovative Performance and Listening in the Works of the Artist Anri Sala   253
Noga Rachel Chelouche

Space and Proximity

14. Changing Rooms: A Diary of Spatial Innovation   277
Neil Thomas Smith

15. *Monsieur Croche* – Concerts at Eye Level   299
Tal Walker

16. Strategies of Proximity: Breaking Away from the Standard Classical Concert   315
Folkert Uhde and Hans-Joachim Gögl

17. Audiences of the Future – How Can Streamed Music
Performance Replicate the Live Music Experience?   333
Michelle Phillips and Amanda E. Krause

Artificial Intelligence

18. Artificial Intelligence and the Symphony Orchestra   355
Robert Laidlow

19. Ghosts of the Hidden Layer   379
Jennifer Walshe

List of Illustrations   401

List of Audio Files   403

Index   405

Notes on Contributors

Karen Burland is Professor of Applied Music Psychology in the School of Music, University of Leeds. She is University Academic Lead for Surfacing Skills and Student Futures and Faculty Lead for Employability, Opportunity and Ambition (Faculty of Arts, Humanities and Cultures). She researches musical identities and their role in musical participation in a variety of contexts. She is investigating the ways in which musicians create and support their work in music, and researching the role of music for wellbeing. She has recently been Academic in Residence at Opera North, working on an ethnographic study of the organisation, looking particularly at aspects of artistry, community, and identity. Her book *Coughing and Clapping: Investigating Audience Experience*, edited with Stephanie Pitts, was published in December 2014. https://orcid.org/0000-0003-0066-0132

Noga Rachel Chelouche is a doctoral student in musicology at Tel-Aviv University, Israel. In her dissertation she explores renewed modes of classical music in the twenty-first century, concentrating on contemporary multimedia works by various artists. She holds a bachelor's degree in musicology and humanities and a master's degree in musicology from Tel-Aviv University. In her MA thesis, she analyzed multimedia works by the contemporary artist Anri Sala, through which she suggested musicological research based on the juxtaposition of music and visual art. Noga works as a writer and editor in the program department of the Israel Philharmonic. https://orcid.org/0009-0007-5702-5363

Antonio C. Cuyler, Ph.D. (he/him/his) is Professor of Music in Entrepreneurship & Leadership in the School of Music, Theatre & Dance (SMTD) at the University of Michigan. He is the author of Access, Diversity, Equity, and Inclusion in Cultural Organizations: Insights from the Careers of Executive Opera Managers of Color in the U. S., editor of Arts Management, Cultural Policy, & the African Diaspora, and author or co-author of twenty-five peer reviewed articles that appear in journals including the *American Journal of Arts Management*, *International Journal of Arts Management*, and *International Journal of Social, Political and Community Agendas in the Arts*. Most recently, he co-authored the League of American Orchestras report 'Racial/Ethnic and Gender Diversity in the Orchestra Field in 2023'. He also founded Cuyler Consulting, LLC, a Black-owned arts consultancy that partners with cultural organizations to maximize their performance and community relevance through access, diversity, equity, and inclusion (ADEI). https://orcid.org/0000-0002-3221-2636

Krista de Wit, PhD, works at the Research group Music in Context of the Research Centre Art & Society and as a teacher at Prince Claus Conservatoire at Hanze University of Applied Sciences Groningen (NL). Her research focuses on live music and professional musicians in healthcare contexts. She received her doctorate in November 2020 from the University of Music & Performing Arts Vienna (AT). Krista's PhD-research focused on what live music practices can mean for the well-being and learning of care professionals both in elderly care homes and in hospitals, and how they can contribute to the work of the care professionals, hence to the quality of care. Previously, Krista has worked as a teacher at the Royal College of Music in Stockholm, and as a music educator, community music pedagogue and performing musician in Sweden and Finland. Krista's previous master's research into creating participatory music practices for elderly people with dementia in Stockholm was awarded with the Kerstin Eliasson Prize for Excellence in Research in 2013. In 2022, Krista received the Herta & Kurt Blaukopf Award for her PhD- research by the University of Music & Performing Arts Vienna. https://orcid.org/0000-0002-6836-6004

Brandon Farnsworth is a Swiss National Science Foundation postdoctoral researcher in musicology and music curator based at Lund University, Sweden. His current project, 'Another Break with Tradition?', is an ethnographic analysis of how diversity initiatives are changing an experimental music festival in Norway. After studying at the Zurich University of the Arts, he completed his PhD in Dresden with the publication 'Curating Contemporary Music Festivals' (2020, Transcript). As a music curator, Brandon has worked on projects with Ultima Festival Oslo, Montreal New Musics Festival, Sonic Matter Zurich, the Berlin New Music Society, and Malmö Konsthall. https://orcid.org/0000-0001-9095-2360

As a format author active at the point where art, social politics, and personal development meet, **Hans-Joachim Gögl** has gained insights from innovation research, religious rituals, and artistic strategies, all of which are elements found in many of his works. Together with the Berlin concert designer Folkert Uhde, he is the founder and artistic director of the 'Montforter Zwischentöne' in Feldkirch, Austria. The HUGO International Competition for New Concert Formats, developed by Hans-Joachim Gögl and Folkert Uhde as part of the festival, is regarded today as one of the foremost young awards for innovative performance practice in the German-speaking world. Since 2018, Hans-Joachim Gögl has been directing the series 'INN SITU – Photography, Music, Dialogue' at the BTV Stadtforum Innsbruck, which he conceptualized and initiated. Various teaching assignments and publications by Hans-Joachim Gögl can found at www.goegl.com

Christina Guillaumier, Reader in Music & Cultural Practice at the Royal College of Music (London), is a music historian and pianist with an early background in the dramatic arts. Dr Guillaumier is a highly sought after writer and broadcaster on music and the arts. She is a Fellow of the Royal Society of Arts (FRSA) and a Senior Fellow of the Higher Education Academy (SFHEA). She is also a peer reviewer for several academic journals and publishing houses. Dr Guillaumier is an editor for Baerenreiter publishing house, specializing in critical editions of piano music. https://orcid.org/0000-0001-7656-5735

Maria Hansen has worked in performing arts for almost thirty years. She was fundraiser and later executive director of Opera Liner Ottawa until 1985 and for eleven years Maria managed the Netherlands Bach society. In 2007 she became managing director of the municipal theatre and concert hall Philharmonie of Haarlem, and after ten years in Harlem she made the move to ELIA, the globally connected network of higher arts education based in Amsterdam.

Kirsteen Davidson Kelly was the Creative Learning Director of the Scottish Chamber Orchestra, which is based in Edinburgh, UK, until 2022. Kirsteen was a founder member of the innovative piano group Piano Circus and has a PhD in musicians' mental rehearsal strategies from the University of Edinburgh. She is now Chief Executive Officer of the National Youth Orchestras of Scotland.

Amanda E. Krause is a Lecturer (Psychology) in the College of Healthcare Sciences at James Cook University (Queensland, Australia). She also currently serves as President of the Australian Music & Psychology Society. As a music psychology scholar, she studies how we experience music in our everyday lives. Her research asks how our musical experiences influence our health and well-being. Dr Krause's research has made significant contributions to understanding how listening technologies influence people and how musical engagement impacts well-being. Recent publications and further information can be found on her website at www.researchaboutlistening.com. https://orcid.org/0000-0003-3049-9220

Robert Laidlow is a composer and researcher at the University of Oxford. His "gigantically imaginative" (BBC Radio 3) music is concerned with discovering and developing new forms of musical expression through the relationship between advanced technology and live performance. Laidlow's music exploring the intersection of classical music, artificial intelligence, and creativity includes Silicon (2022) for the BBC Philharmonic, Post-Singularity Songs (2023) for Stephanie Lamprea, and Tui (2024) for International Contemporary Ensemble. He is currently a Fellow in Composition at Jesus College, Oxford University. From 2018-22 he was the PRiSM PhD Researcher in Artificial Intelligence in association with the BBC Philharmonic. https://orcid.org/0000-0002-1585-723X

George E. Lewis is a composer, musicologist, technological artist, and trombonist. He is the Edwin H. Case Professor of American Music at Columbia University and is a fellow of the American Academy of Arts and Sciences, the American Academy of Arts and Letters, a Corresponding Fellow of the British Academy, and a member of the Akademie der Künste Berlin.

Lore Lixenberg is currently completing her PhD at the University of York. Alongside her interpretive and improvisational vocal practice, she has evolved a compositional practice focusing on the treatment of the voice, exploring extended vocal techniques in pieces such as 'BIRD' and 'Berberiana', also utilising socially engaged practices (PRET A CHANTER, THE VOICE PARTY) and digital technologies and apps for their operatic dramatic potential regarding the language of code as libretto, (SINGLR and VOXXCOIN). In 2021 she was nominated for the Centre Pompidou Prix Heidsieck for 'BIRD' and won the Phonurgia Nova prize for sound-art with 'theVoicePartyOperaBotFarm[myMuseIsMyFury]. She is also active as a mezzo-soprano specialising in new music in opera houses and festivals worldwide.

Karoly Molina is currently a researcher and support staff for the Maastricht Centre for the Innovation of Classical Music, a collaboration between Maastricht University, Zuyd University of Applied Sciences and the South Netherlands Philharmonic (philzuid). Karoly completed her BA in English literature at Texas A&M University and her MA at Maastricht University. Before her work at MCICM, Karoly taught English language and literature and worked as a translator.

Peter Peters is endowed professor in the innovation of classical music and associate professor at the Faculty of Arts and Social Sciences, Maastricht University. His current research combines a life-long passion for music with an interest in how artistic practices can be a context for doing academic and practice-oriented research. In previous years, he worked on an ethnography of a project at the Orgelpark in Amsterdam aimed at building a baroque organ for the twenty-first century. More recently, his research focuses on innovating classical music practices, especially symphonic music. Together with Stefan Rosu, director of Philzuid (South Netherlands Philharmonic), he developed the research lines in the Maastricht Centre for the Innovation of Classical Music: the role of classical music and its value for society; the ways in which the relationship between performers of classical music, such as symphony orchestras and their audience is mediated; and the ways in which classical music practices contribute to the preservation of our cultural and social sounding heritage. https://orcid.org/0000-0003-1009-7216

Denise Petzold (PhD) is an interdisciplinary researcher at the Maastricht Centre for the Innovation of Classical Music (MCICM), Maastricht University. In her doctoral research, she investigated what role artefacts and technologies play in the conservation of classical music's heritage and how this heritage is negotiated in practice. In doing so, she employed approaches from the field of contemporary art conservation to address the tension between 'conserving' and 'innovating' artistic heritage in highly professional and tradition-loaded communities of actors. Her research interests revolve around the role of science and technology in artistic practice, the conservation of ephemeral materials and artforms, as well as processes of craftsmanship and making.

Michelle Phillips is a Senior Lecturer and Deputy Head of Undergraduate Programmes at the Royal Northern College of Music, UK. Her research interests include music and time, perception of contemporary music, audience response to live and recorded music, entrepreneurship, and music and Parkinson's. She is co-investigator with Manchester Camerata for a study examining physiological, behavioural and neurological response to live and recorded music. Recent publications include a co-edited volume entitled 'Music and Time: Psychology, Philosophy, Practice' and an article on 'What Determines the Perception of Segmentation in Contemporary Music?' https://orcid.org/0000-0003-0933-3621

Stephanie Pitts is a Professor in the Department of Music, University of Sheffield, and director of the Sheffield Performer and Audience Research Centre (SPARC). She has research interests in musical participation, arts audiences, and lifelong learning, and is the author of books including *Chances and Choices: Exploring the Impact of Music Education* (2012), *Music and Mind in Everyday Life* (2010), and a co-edited volume on audience experience, *Coughing and Clapping* (2014). Her recent AHRC-funded project working with arts sector partners across four UK cities led to a new book, *Understanding Audience Engagement in the Contemporary Arts* (2021), and a downloadable handbook for arts practitioners: http://www.sparc.dept.shef.ac.uk/research/uaca/handbook/. https://orcid.org/0000-0003-1430-5801

Diana Salazar is Director of Programmes at the Royal College of Music, London, where she oversees learning and teaching strategy at junior, undergraduate and postgraduate levels. A conservatoire trained flautist and composer, her research interests combine practice research in electroacoustic composition with exploration of conservatoire pedagogies and technology-enhanced learning in higher music education. She is a founder of the Global Conservatoire, an international consortium of five conservatoires focussed on the development of innovative, transnational online teaching practices in the performing arts. Her compositions have been performed and broadcast internationally, with awards from the International Computer Music Association, Bourges, Musical Viva, and the Pauline Oliveros Prize among others. She is currenting co-editing a new edited collection, 'Inside the Contemporary Conservatoire: Critical Perspectives from the Royal College of Music, London' with Colin Lawson and Rosie Perkins.

Beste Sevindik is a researcher in the Lectorate Lifelong Learning in Music connected to the Kenniscentrum Kunst & Samenleving at the Hanze University. She studied violin at Hacettepe University Ankara State Conservatory in Turkey and completed her Master's degree at the Prince Claus Conservatoire in Groningen. As a chamber and orchestra musician, she has performed throughout Europe and Turkey. In addition to her work on stage, Beste regularly performs in socially engaged projects, such as working with patients and health care staff on surgical wards and with elderly people with dementia and their caretakers in residential homes as well as in virtual space. She is engaged in research in both these practices.

Stine Skovbon is a PhD candidate at the department of Arts and Culture Studies at the Erasmus University Rotterdam. She started writing her dissertation in 2021. Her research interests are classical music and sustainability, and her PhD focuses on environmental and social sustainability of symphony orchestras. The aim of her project is firstly, to investigate the current awareness and prioritising of sustainability within orchestras in areas such as travel activities, the well-being of musicians, and organisational, environmental and HR policies. A second aim is to map factors that create either constraints or possibilities for symphony orchestras to enhance sustainability.

Tom Spurgin is the Director of Learning and Engagement at the City of Birmingham Symphony Orchestra (CBSO), where he oversees all work related to participation, talent development, and community engagement. Prior to this, he was the Audience Development Manager at the Philharmonia Orchestra in London. With funding from AHRC, awarded via the White Rose College of Arts & Humanities (WRoCAH), Tom is undertaking a part-time Collaborative Doctoral Award with the University of Sheffield, University of Leeds, and Manchester Collective. The study aims to analyse Manchester Collective's alternative methods of audience development and offer a road map to a more relevant, sustainable, and socially engaged classical music sector in the UK. https://orcid.org/0000-0002-2227-4630

Neil Thomas Smith is a researcher and composer, teaching at the University of Edinburgh and the Open College of the Arts. Between 2018 and 2022 he was a postdoctoral researcher at the Maastricht Centre for the Innovation of Classical Music, where his research focussed on orchestras' attempts at spatial innovation, both inside the concert hall and beyond. Neil has also worked on German contemporary music and sociological examinations of 'emerging' composers, with articles appearing in journals including *Music & Letters, Cultural Sociology, Contemporary Music Review*, the *Journal of the Royal Musical Association, Tempo*, and the *British Journal of Sociology*. His first monograph, a critical companion to the composer Mathias Spahlinger, was published in 2021; while a debut disc of chamber music, Stop Motion Music, was released in 2023.

Jutta Toelle researches all aspects of a musical performance: musicians, audiences and the experience of live music and is Professor of Applied Musicology at the Gustav Mahler Private University of Music in Klagenfurt. She studied musicology and history in Berlin and Venice and did her doctorate at the Chair of Sociology of Music at Humboldt University Berlin (focusing on the economic and social foundations of the late-nineteenth-century Italian opera industry). She was a Visiting Scholar at the University of Chicago (2012/13) and a PostDoc at the Music Department of the Max Planck Institute for Empirical Aesthetics in Frankfurt am Main (2013-2019).

Folkert Uhde developed the term 'concert design' for his artistic work and established it as a theory in the discourse on new classical music concert formats. He is director of the Köthen Bach Festival and, together with Hans-Joachim Gögl, inventor and artistic director of the Montforter Zwischentöne in Feldkirch/Vorarlberg. The HUGO student competition for new concert dramaturgies was also created in the context of the Montforter. His own artistic projects range between concert design, direction and video. In addition to his artistic-conceptual work, the topic of regional development through culture has also become more and more central in recent years. Folkert Uhde teaches at various colleges and universities and advises institutions on artistic and strategic future issues. As artistic director of the international research project 'Experimental Concert Research', he and an interdisciplinary team examine the concert experience from the perspective of the audience.

Young Steinway Artist **Tal Walker** is an Israeli-Belgian pianist. Tal won a bronze medal at the Osaka Music Competition in Japan. He was invited to artist residencies in Italy and Canada and performed with orchestras in Belgium, Italy, and Poland. Tal graduated from conservatoires in the Netherlands and Belgium and attended the École Normale de Musique in Paris where he specialised in French repertoire. He is the founder of the Monsieur Croche concert series in Belgium and is currently pursuing his PhD at the Royal College of Music in London where he is focusing on French Piano Preludes from the early 1900s.

'The most original compositional voice to emerge from Ireland in the past 20 years' (*The Irish Times*) and 'Wild girl of Darmstadt' (*Frankfurter Rundschau*), composer and performer **Jennifer Walshe** was born in Dublin, Ireland. Her music has been commissioned, broadcast and performed all over the world. She has been the recipient of fellowships and prizes from the Foundation for Contemporary Arts, New York, the DAAD Berliner Künstlerprogramm, the Internationales Musikinstitut, Darmstadt and Akademie Schloss Solitude among others. Recent projects include TIME TIME TIME, an opera written in collaboration with the philosopher Timothy Morton, and THE SITE OF AN INVESTIGATION, a thirty-minute epic for Walshe's voice and orchestra, commissioned by the National Symphony Orchestra of Ireland. THE SITE has been performed by Walshe and the NSO, the BBC Scottish Symphony

Orchestra and also the Lithuanian State Symphony Orchestra. Walshe has worked extensively with AI. ULTRACHUNK, made in collaboration with Memo Akten in 2018, features an AI-generated version of Walshe. A Late Anthology of Early Music Vol. 1: Ancient to Renaissance, her third solo album, released on Tetbind in 2020, uses AI to rework canonical works from early Western music history. A Late Anthology was chosen as an album of the year in *The Irish Times*, *The Wire* and *The Quietus*. Walshe is currently professor of composition at the University of Oxford. Her work was profiled by Alex Ross in *The New Yorker*.

Classical Music Futures: An Introduction

Neil Thomas Smith and Peter Peters

The 'Problems' of Classical Music

Does classical music have a future? In fact it has many, in a manner similar to all art forms, technological enterprises and institutions. One future sees it slowly dwindle as its grey audience shuffles off this mortal coil one by one; another places its faith in the institutions of the concert hall, festival and orchestra to fight against the degradations of time; yet another projects the diversification and democratisation of the art form so that it takes a meaningful place in the lives of a greater portion of society. What these three visions have in common is that the future presupposes a significant challenge: the future is coming for classical music and it had best be prepared.

For there are various 'problems' to which the art form must respond. Rather than being purely the result of an academic critique – though these are far from absent[1] – the problems are the everyday backdrop to the work of classical music practitioners. They are felt every time a funding round is announced that focuses on finding new audiences, and whenever the 'elite world' of classical music is discussed in mainstream

---

1   To give some diverse examples: Lydia Goehr, *The Imaginary Museum of Musical Works: An Essay in the Philosophy of Music* (Oxford: Oxford University Press, 2007); Lewis Kaye, 'The Silenced Listener: Architectural Acoustics, the Concert Hall and the Conditions of Audience', *Leonardo Music Journal*, 22 (2012), 63–65; Anna Bull, *Class, Control, and Classical Music* (Oxford: Oxford University Press, 2019); Philip Ewell, 'Music Theory's White Racial Frame', *Music Theory Online*, 26/2 (2020).

media outside of the (dwindling) arts sections. These problems will be familiar to anyone even partially engaged in the field and the following is by no means an exhaustive list of their symptoms. The first, the *obsolescence problem*, is that classical music does not appeal to the young. It projects a future in which the art form slowly withers and dies if it cannot find greater relevance to younger people, families and people in employment. The second, the *demographic problem*, refers to the supposedly narrow sociodemographic appeal of classical music. Here, the music is seen as the preserve of the modern-day bourgeoisie, taking place in high-end locations, which present social as well as financial barriers. It is also racially homogenous to a significant degree. Finally, the *museum problem*, which describes a practice trapped in the past, unable to respond to contemporary currents in society and increasingly irrelevant to what is happening around it.[2] Suggested solutions to these problems do not merely tinker round the edges of this music practice, but can suggest radical revisions of how it is conceived and enacted. Yet, an old practice is like a large ship: difficult to turn in a hurry; while there is still a committed, active and vocal constituency willing to fight for the values that have sustained classical music over more than a century. When we use the term 'classical music practice', we understand this as covering the work of a whole range of music organisations, such as orchestras, festivals and music education institutes, as well as a professional field of musicians and other cultural workers. Yet, it is also a repertoire – a canon of musical works – around which particular rules, conventions and habits have emerged, such as performances that are true to the score and attentive listening in conditions that come as close as possible to silence. As such, the definition of the term 'classical music' has become contested, no longer only designating a certain genre, but also a context and approach to listening that is increasingly seen as high-brow and exclusive.

---

2   The research lines of the MCICM responded to the 'problems' of classical music by focusing on three main areas (see also www.mcicm.nl):
    The role of classical music and its value for society;
    The ways in which the relationship between performers of classical music, such as symphony orchestras and their audience is mediated;
    The ways in which classical music contributes to the preservation of our cultural and social heritage.

This is the context that saw the creation of the Maastricht Centre for the Innovation of Classical Music (MCICM), whose conference on 'Futuring Classical Music' in 2021 led to the present volume. The impulse for its foundation came not from a university or research institute but from an orchestra: Philzuid (South Netherlands Philharmonic). Its Intendant, Stefan Rosu, reached out to Maastricht University to initiate a collaboration: he wanted to open the orchestra up to researchers, rather like a teaching hospital is open to students and innovative medical practices. With this connection, two of the pillars of the MCICM were in place. The third came with the addition of the Zuyd University of Applied Sciences, which includes Maastricht Conservatorium. Orchestral music, Higher Music Education, and research were, therefore, all part of a structural collaboration, which then gained funding from the Province of Limburg, in which Maastricht is situated.

The collaboration at the MCICM is a sign of how classical music is an art form that is defined by a wide variety of people who are invested emotionally, spiritually and financially in its practice: festivals, ensembles, orchestras, and independent musicians all work to maintain its traditions; artistic leaders and support staff work tirelessly to create events of 'excellence' for a wider public; amateurs in orchestras, wind and brass bands, and choirs allow people to enact many of the conventions of the art form in their daily lives; music conservatoires and universities prepare their students for a world in which classical music might still be a potent force. The MCICM is built upon the belief that work within the institutions of classical music is vital to address some of the 'problems' identified above. Yet, there are also pitfalls here. It is easy to elide the future of classical music with the maintenance of its institutions. As such institutions are often significant barriers to change, this is by no means certain. For example, the people charged with addressing the demographic problem will most likely come from the very same privileged group from which classical music seeks to expand.

The problems of classical music and their associated futures are seen here as calls to action and reflection rather than any kind of neutral prediction of the art form's course. In this edited volume, we approach classical music futures and their practices of innovation and experimentation from various angles. The chapters in this book show how the future of classical music is made in the work of people all over the world engaged in transforming this practice. As such, the contributing authors represent a variety of voices, offering their perspectives and positions on issues and challenges that are at the heart of current debates and practices in and around classical music. This diversity of voices is reflected in the stylistic format of the chapters, ranging from conference roundtable transcripts, practice-based research papers, reflections on concert experiments by the organisers, diary entries, and polemics, through to fully worked-through academic research chapters.

The aim of this book is not only to present these innovative approaches from the sidelines, so to speak, but also to actively contribute in shaping new classical music futures. We hope to do so by achieving three goals: to show and share what insights may result from performing innovation; to show under what conditions innovation is able to thrive in academic and practical settings; and, following the MCICM example, to inspire scholars, music educators, and practitioners to collaborate and learn from each other by sharing experiences and practices. Before we introduce the theme of innovation and outline the book's chapters, we will first elaborate on how the question of whether classical music has a future is closely related to its past.

Unfinished Music?

How can we shape new futures for an art form that revolves around reiterating the past? When we debate if and why classical music is in crisis, and begin to address its problems, we need to acknowledge the 'pastness' of the practice. Classical music practice as we know it today originated in the nineteenth century. Following the example of museums, which assembled collections of timeless master works, musicians and music lovers constructed their own canon that has remained surprisingly intact right up until today. The ideal of romantic art focused on the resurgence of the past as a source of new art, on the one hand, and, on the other, on the creation of art for eternity. Whereas composers before him wrote their music for specific occasions, the later compositions of Beethoven, for example, were thought of as timeless masterworks.[3] As

---

3   Tia DeNora, *Beethoven and the Construction of Genius: Musical Politics in Vienna, 1792-1803* (Berkeley: University of California Press, 1996).

their musical language became more complex, composers developed a sense of progress in their art.[4] Musical romanticism required new instrumental colours and dynamic range. To synchronise the playing of large orchestras, conductors became more important. As the size of orchestras increased, concert halls became larger. Romantic aesthetic ideas materialised in buildings such as the Concertgebouw in Amsterdam, built in 1888.[5] Following examples in other European cities, the architect Van Gendt succeeded in creating a space in which music could sound as an isolated object of aesthetic admiration.[6] Audiences were disciplined to listen in silence and attentively.[7]

In the course of the nineteenth century, classical music became an art form that is defined in the 'romantic order', as the Dutch art philosopher Maarten Doorman calls it.[8] With other art forms, it shared the regulative idea of aesthetic autonomy: the self-regulation of art, independent of traditional morality, religion or politics, which allowed the performing and fine arts to become an independent domain in society. Autonomy thus related to the musical work itself, to the institutions responsible for performing these works, and to the place of art music in society.

Attempts to innovate classical music practice only seem to expose its roots in the romantic order. What is at stake is the value of timeless musical works and the skills to perform them, as well as the position of orchestras and ensembles as relatively autonomous art institutions. In her book *The Imaginary Museum of Musical Works* (1994), Lydia Goehr shows how any fixed philosophical definition of what a musical work is and how it exists has to establish a set of either essential properties

---

4   Charles Rosen, *The Romantic Generation* (London: HarperCollins, 1996). See also Maarten Doorman, *Art in Progress: A Philosophical Response to the End of the Avant-Garde* (Amsterdam: Amsterdam University Press, 2003).
5   Darryl Cressman, *Building Musical Culture in Nineteenth-Century Amsterdam: The Concertgebouw* (Amsterdam: Amsterdam University Press, 2016).
6   Two decades later, the new science of acoustics was able to explain the success of the building by showing how the shape and volume of the space resulted in a reverberation time that was perfect for large musical ensembles such as the symphony orchestra (Cressman, *Building Musical Culture in Nineteenth-Century Amsterdam*, p. 82).
7   James H. Johnson, *Listening in Paris: A cultural history* (Berkeley/Los Angeles/London: University of California Press, 1994). See also Cas Smithuijsen, *Een verbazende stilte: klassieke muziek, gedragsregels en sociale controle in de concertzaal* (Amsterdam: Boekmanstudies, 2001).
8   Doorman, *Art in Progress: A Philosophical Response to the End of the Avant-Garde*.

or identity conditions.⁹ This approach, she argues, does not take into account the historical, contingent, and possibly changing character of these properties and conditions. Goehr suggests that instead of describing what kind of *object* a musical work is, we should study how the *concept* of a work emerged in classical music and how it has functioned therein.¹⁰ Drawing on archival sources, she shows how the idea of the stable musical work only emerged around 1800. What Goehr calls the 'Beethoven paradigm' regulated how composers notated their music, how performers were expected to be true to the score to give authentic performances, and how audiences listened in silence to hear the beauty of the work itself.¹¹ The concept of the musical work shows the 'pastness' of this practice in two ways: it explains how music can be transmitted through time as a relatively stable and autonomous artwork;¹² and it also reveals the continuities in practice between the past and the present as traditions that are often difficult to change.

In everyday language, the word 'tradition' might suggest something that lies behind us, or that is repeated without reflection. For philosopher Hans-Georg Gadamer, however, it means that the past is actively handed over in our situated understandings and applications of it. It requires active questioning and self-reflection. Gadamer's conception of tradition is dialogical: rather than a form of antiquarianism, it is a continuing debate on questions, problems and issues to which we ourselves contribute. When we play works of art, we revisit the tradition that handed them down to us. In music and theatre, presenting works of art is thus not a matter of following earlier acts of presenting, but of interpretations that keep the future identity and continuity of the artwork open.¹³ This is

---

9   Goehr, *The Imaginary Museum of Musical Works*, p. 72.
10 Ibid. p. 4.
11 Ibid. pp. 205-243.
12 Although in different ways, consecutive performance styles all aimed at authentic renderings of the work. Bruce Haynes (2007) distinguishes between romantic, modern, and historically informed performance practice. Although very different in their aesthetic ideals, they share the centrality of the work concept. (Bruce Haynes, *The End of Early Music: A Period Performer's History of Music for the Twenty-First Century* (Oxford: Oxford University Press, 2007)).
13 These interpretations do not give the interpreter unlimited freedom, and on the other hand Gadamer sees canonizations of particular interpretations, e.g. a recording of a musical composition by its composer, as a simple imitation of a model that would deny the real task of interpretation. Interestingly, Gadamer seems to criticise what later became known as the historically informed

why playing works of art leaves the works themselves fundamentally unfinished: their meaning is never exhausted as long as we continue to play them in new situations.[14] If we think of classical music concerts in this Gadamerian vein, we are not only reconstructing a past meaning of the music, but we mediate the music with our own world.

Shaping new futures for classical music brings to the fore the practical work of mediating music from the past in the present. When we observe the current critical debates on the practice, however, a paradox is revealed. Whereas in Gadamer's line of reasoning the past renews itself under conditions of the present, in everyday practice classical music's pastness and traditions are often in significant tension with processes of innovation. Now that we know how to explain the obduracy of the practice by pointing to the romantic order that underlies it, we can also more clearly set the agenda for change. As will become evident in the following chapters, change will have to address the ways in which access to classical music's performances is organised, the values that are embodied in its dominant concert rituals, the institutions that are responsible for handing down its traditions, such as music education institutes, concert halls, and organisations, and finally the ways in which the practice relates itself to broader societal issues and challenges, such as new and emerging technological change, diversity and inclusion, and the climate crisis. The chapters in this book address these issues and challenges. Before we go into more detail about their content, we highlight moments of coherence between the chapters in the themes that they address.

The first theme is that of the existing inequalities that have been identified in fundamental facets of the classical music tradition, including its reliance on a restricted canon, the image of genius to which non-white males do not subscribe, and the entirely intentional and explicit exclusions that women and people of colour have faced in musical, as in many other, spheres of operation in Europe, North America and

---

performance practice movement: 'Thus, for example, historicizing presentations—e.g., of music played on old instruments—are not as faithful as they seem. Rather, they are an imitation of an imitation and are thus in danger "of standing at a third remove from the truth" (Plato).' (Hans-Georg Gadamer, *Truth and Method* (New York: Continuum, 1989[1960]), p. 118.)

14   For a more elaborate version of this argument, see Peter Peters, *Unfinished Symphonies* (Maastricht: Datawyse, 2019).

beyond. This topic is taken up in the chapters by Farnsworth, Cuyler and Lixenberg, as well as the first two round-table chapters. A vital question in these contributions is how to increase representation in terms of gender, race, and class.

Existing dominant concert formats embody the values that are central to the Beethoven paradigm: excellent performance of musical works by performers whose task it is to be true to the text, and audiences who allow themselves to reflect on the art character of the music by listening attentively and in silence. A second theme in the book is how attempts to change concert formats not only question the continued relevance of these values, but are also an invitation to explore new repertoires of qualities.[15] Performances are increasingly taking place in unconventional concert venues such as art galleries, museums, and cathedrals. Small venues with increased proximity to the artists can make these events intimate and exclusive – at eye level with the audience, as Walker writes in his chapter. The pandemic has accelerated the unprecedented (if enforced) explosion of experimentation in this area, whether online, outdoors, or in unusual buildings, as Smith explores in his chapter. Changing space alone, however, is unlikely to achieve the goals of improving classical music's value as an intrinsically meaningful and relevant cultural practice in society, as well as its demographic appeal. In their chapter on developing exceptional event concepts, Uhde and Gögl explore how music may provide the impetus for dealing with a particular social or political issue, as well as providing a resonating space for the spoken word. They describe this new curatorial attitude in their event conception as 'strategies of proximity'.

Addressing inequalities and expanding repertoires of qualities is a responsibility of the institutions that are embedding classical music in society. A third theme in the book concerns the ways in which these institutions respond to the significant changes in their external environment, notably the focus on generating a more sustainable future, the importance (and fragility) of global communities and the role of technology in the arts (Salazar and Guillaumier). Classical music institutions are often seen as struggling to react to contemporary events and developments, such as climate change. The third round-table

---

[15] Veerle Spronck, *Listen Closely: Innovating Audience Participation in Symphonic Music* (Maastricht: Maastricht University, 2022).

chapter summarises the discussion between four music professionals, each giving their own perspective on how their organisations are beginning to address the most pressing issue of our time. The topic of how orchestra institutions cope with the challenge of making their practices more sustainable is also taken up in the chapter by Skovbon. She gives examples of non-profit charity organisations trying to reduce their environmental footprint. Meanwhile Toelle argues in her chapter that where traditional classical music institutions are under increasing pressure due to budget cuts and the questioning of their societal relevance, the fact that classical music practices can actually play many different roles in a society makes the discussions about their future exciting.

The responsibility that higher music education institutes have for educating the musicians of the future is a fifth theme in the book. Current curricula for composers, musicians and music educators are often still restricted to the assertion of artistic excellence in the first place. Broadening the skillsets of the musicians of tomorrow is not just a challenge of funnelling more people through the same conduits, but presents fundamental questions for classical music education. In their chapter, Pitts, Burland and Spurgin present research in which musicians reflect on their training and the extent to which this prepared them for professional orchestral playing. This raises questions about the role of conservatoires in supporting or inhibiting innovation in the profession, highlighting the challenges of work-life balance that were altered by the pandemic, and showing how musicians themselves can be agents for change. The COVID-19 pandemic has intensified reflection on the merits and obstacles of online teaching. Salazar and Guillaumier propose that online teaching in the conservatoire has the potential to become an important vehicle equipping students to respond to changes in the external environment for all artists, notably the focus on generating a more sustainable future, the importance (and fragility) of global communities and the role of technology in the arts. In recognising the possibilities for online teaching, they move from a position of online 'replacing' or 'replicating' traditional conservatoire teaching to 'complementing' practice-led experiences.

As the experience in the MCICM suggests, reflecting on the benefits and challenges of cross-institutional collaboration as well as interdisciplinarity are crucial in attempts at innovating classical music. An example of this sixth theme is to be found in the chapter by De Wit and Sevindik on the emergence of an interprofessional community of practice between healthcare professionals and musicians in Groningen, the Netherlands. When professional, classically trained musicians play live music for patients and healthcare professionals inside hospital wards, their work is underpinned by interprofessional collaboration with these healthcare professionals, as well as the development of new professional skills of person-centred music-making. Interdisciplinarity between art institutions can induce learning. In her chapter, Petzold looks at an art institution that is related, yet very different from the orchestra: the contemporary art museum. She argues that classical music institutions and practitioners may gain new understanding from contemporary art museums about the ontology or existence of artworks, and this may inform institutional change. Visual art practices can also be a context for alternative performances of classical music, as Chelouche shows in her chapter.

Finally, a seventh theme in these chapters is the role of technologies and how they shape and are shaped by the practices of classical music. Reflecting on the ways that the COVID-19 pandemic introduced audiences to new ways of engaging with artistic performance in an online environment, Philips and Krause argue that 'liveness' involves not only such factors as the opportunity to share an experience and interact with other audience members and performers, but also the sense of atmosphere, immersion, sensory experiences, and being physically present. A salient development at the moment is the use of Artificial Intelligence in artistic practices, including classical music. As with any new technology, the discourse combines both utopian and dystopian expectations of how it will be used in practice. As Laidlow writes, classical music as an industry is well placed to answer salient questions that the age of artificial intelligence demands we consider, including: how this new technology affects, and will affect, the way an orchestra interacts with a composer, and how orchestral music can be used to explore technology that has an increasingly profound effect on all aspects of our day-to-day lives. As a composer, Walshe offers a wide-ranging discussion of her interactions with AI, showing how music can engage with it, particularly in terms of language and the voice.

The list of themes that we identify as connecting the chapters in this book is by no means exhaustive. As will become clear in reading, the chapters implicitly cross-reference each other in many ways. What they share is the notion that shaping new futures for classical music requires practical work and reflection. To further focus the agenda of innovation, we need to analyse the concept of the future in more detail. What role does it play when it comes to bringing the new into the world of classical music? How do futures become reality?

The Future as Innovation

Reflections on the future of classical music not only draw on music philosophy and sociology; they can also build on an established interest of the social sciences in the idea of the future. Emerging as an academic field in the 1960s, future studies sought to set up processes and approaches that might help government planning, particularly at first in terms of the military and industry. Yet confidence in our ability to predict accurately, and faith in progress more generally, waned during the later twentieth century and such attempts at looking into a crystal ball were replaced by a critical study of how the future functions in the present. Tutton, summarising Bell and Mau, states that the 'future is real in so far as social actors produce representations of the future which have an effect on others' actions in the present'.[16] Brown et al. highlight the 'resources' actors use to 'compete for the right to represent near and far term developments'.[17] Van Lente, in the linked field of studies of 'expectations', argues that 'expectation statements are not only representations of something that does not (yet) exist, they do something: advising, showing direction, creating obligations'.[18] The future, therefore, has no sense of the inevitable but is an unpredictable and contested field of possibility. Brown et al. point out that there is

---

16   Richard Tutton, 'Wicked futures: Meaning, matter and the sociology of the future', *The Sociological Review*, 65/3 (2017), 478–492 (p. 482); Wendell Bell and James Mau (Eds.), *The Sociology of the Future: Theory, Cases and Annotated Bibliography* (New York: Russell Sage Foundation, 1971).
17   Nik Brown, Brian Rappert and Andrew Webster, *Contested Futures: A Sociology of Prospective Techno-Science* (Aldershot: Ashgate, 2000), pp. 2–5.
18   Harro van Lente, *Promising Technology: The Dynamics of Expectations in Technological Developments* (Twente: University of Twente, 1993), 191.

little difference between discourses surrounding the future and the past in this sense, stating that the 'history of science as recounted in most textbooks gives little idea of the contested futures that once shaped the development of what is considered the "scientific canon" of today'.[19] The term canon used here is striking when looking at this sociological work from a cultural perspective. Work that calls into question the exclusions of the canon by arguing for a reorganisation of the problematic 'classical music museum' discussed above, is both making a different future for classical music while also revising its past.

On the question of how futures become 'reality', many authors point to the fact that futures need friends. For Little, futures are 'performative' in that they are 'understood as enacting a particular future (while also marginalizing alternative futures) in order to enrol actors in the present, who will, ideally, help realize the projected future in the future'.[20] Futures – either those to avoid or those to strive towards – are a means of building coalitions with others and it is this coalition-building that brings them closer to being realised. Harro van Lente, in the keynote address to the conference where this edited collection began, also argued for getting involved in 'creating your own futures': it behoves all who have a stake in classical music to shape it.[21]

At the same time, scholars of future studies do not believe there is an open field of possibility in which actors can blithely choose what the future will entail. Humans are not alone in creating their future, with the environment we work in and the materials we work with making certain paths more likely than others and creating particular limits. The limits of the natural world are the most obvious example of the

---

19 Brown et al., *Contested Futures*, p. 5.
20 Mike Michael, 'Enacting Big Futures, Little Futures: Toward an ecology of futures', *The Sociological Review*, 65/3 (2017), 509–524 (p. 513).
21 Images and expectations of the future are socially performative in that they structure decision-making and organise social actions and collaborations. Oomen et al. suggest that the concept of 'futuring' captures the active dimension of the future. Futuring is defined as 'the identification, creation and dissemination of images of the future shaping the possibility for action, thus enacting relationships between past, present and future.' See Jeroen Oomen, Jesse Hofman, and Maarten A. Hajer. 'Techniques of futuring: On how imagined futures become socially performative', *European Journal of Social Theory*, 25/2 (2021), 252-270 (p. 254). According to Oomen et.al. imagined futures can bring together various actors and serve as shared orientations for collaborative actions in futuring practices. Innovation of classical music thus requires 'techniques of futuring' (p. 254).

ways in which human activity is constrained. Yet such limitations and contexts are not all physical but also cultural.[22] As we have seen, the traditions of classical music and their roots in the romantic order create a significant obduracy in relation to change. Organisational approaches of institutions, as well as practices and rituals of concert-going and listening, create a barrier to any immediate and revolutionary change. A major theme of this future-orientated work is the sense – just as in the description of classical music above – that the future is ever closer at hand. This is captured in Helga Nowotny's description of the 'extended present' in which problems 'which could formerly be deferred into the future' now 'demand to be dealt with today'.[23] Chief among such issues are those of climate and sustainability, a discourse that has only increased in urgency since the publication of Nowotny's book in 1994. Barbara Adam argues that, rather than an 'empty' future, today 'the costs have to be paid, the disasters rectified, the cancers endured; our predecessors' glorious creations rebound as nightmares'.[24]

For Nowotny, two 'escape routes' from these issues are offered: either a 'non-existent idyllic past' or the 'next phase of technological innovation', but neither is effective and the future horizon becomes 'flat and motionless'.[25] The idyllic past is by no means absent in classical music discourse, with appeals to return to the 'core business' of performing music that is certain of its place at the pinnacle of Western culture: from this perspective the museum problem is no issue, but the art form's greatest asset. Nowotny's second point, which references technology, is taken up specifically in this volume in discussions of Artificial Intelligence but with the nagging feeling that it may create as many problems as it solves.

Concern over dwindling audience numbers and a withering of the art form evidently stems from a belief that classical music offers intrinsic value to society. Within classical music, any desire to return to a previous

---

22   See John Urry, 'Climate change, travel and complex futures', *The British Journal of Sociology*, 59 (2008), 261–279 (p. 275).
23   Helga Nowotny, *Time: The Modern and Postmodern Experience* (Cambridge: Polity Press, 1994), p. 11.
24   Barbara Adam, 'Future Matters: Challenge for Social Theory and Social Inquiry', Keynote Address to Italian Sociological Association Conference, Future Matters for Social Theory, Cagliari University, Sardinia (29 October 2009), p. 1.
25   Nowotny, *Time*, p. 49.

'normality' is a relatively straightforward call to maintain the conventions of concert events and the prized position of its cultural achievements within the canon. Far less discussed is the role of innovation, particularly within such a venerable art form. Innovation presupposes a particular relationship with the future as it assumes that what is to come may be radically different, and presumably better, than what has come before. It militates against a view of art forms as the concentrated preservation of a tradition, which can be seen in a 'traditionalist' reading of classical music as the performance of the great works of the Baroque, Classical and Romantic periods, as well as many traditional art forms around the world in which apprentices learn a seemingly fixed set of traditional practices from a master.[26] This links the current volume with another established area of scholarship: studies of innovation.

The dominant approach in innovation studies, according to Martin, has been to analyse radical technological innovation in the manufacture of products.[27] Take Schumpeter's now classic definition, in which he identifies four broad types:

> (i) a new or improved product; (ii) a new or improved process (new, at least, to that particular sector, but not necessarily entirely 'new' to the world); (iii) the opening of a new market (again 'new' for that sector and country); (iv) the acquisition of a new source of raw materials or semi-manufactured goods (irrespective of whether that source already exists); and (v) an organizational change (in the firm or the sector).[28]

The language of 'product', 'market' and 'raw materials' here is rather different from what we expect in the realm of culture, yet it still gives a sense of what people working within classical music expect from innovative practices: novel artistic approaches, reaching new people, achieving more through personal and organisational development. Such vocabulary may make some engaged in the arts uncomfortable,

---

26 The traditionalist reading is somewhat ironic considering symphonic music in particular grew up in a society shaped by capitalist expansion, colonial exploitation, and rapid technological progress.
27 Ben R. Martin, *Twenty Challenge for Innovation Studies* (Cambridge: Centre for Business Studies, University of Cambridge, 2015), p. 4; c.f. Paul Stoneman, *Soft Innovation: Economics, Product Aesthetics, and the Creative Industries* (Oxford: Oxford University Press, 2010), p. 1.
28 Thomas K. McCraw, *Prophet of Innovation: Joseph Schumpeter and Creative Destruction* (Cambridge, MA: Belknap Press, 2007), p. 73.

yet market forces have far more effect on cultural work than some would like to think.²⁹

At the same time, the specific values of cultural work should not be forgotten. Caves (2000) describes two fundamentals when considering creative industries: firstly that actors may not act in a purely economically rational fashion as an 'art for art's sake' agenda may still hold greater sway; and secondly, that the principle of 'nobody knows' is in play, which means that there is no way of knowing what will become commercially successful or useful to others.³⁰ While the latter applies to technology and the sciences far more than is often credited,³¹ there is a sense that logics of traditional innovation studies work against the practices of cultural workers. Peris-Ortiz et al. point to a paradox in that the 'wealth of novelty [in the creative industries] is fueled by tradition', with Jones et al. arguing that it is the depth of culture that sustains the capacity to innovate.³²

As with many western art forms, there has paradoxically been a simultaneous reliance on, but resistance to, artistic changes within the tradition. The museum problem describes an institution that is venerable but not entirely static. Famous scandals of the early twentieth century now only colour the programme notes of canonic works by the likes of Igor Stravinsky or Richard Strauss. Charles Rosen goes so far as to argue 'that tradition is often most successfully sustained by those who appear to be trying to attack or to destroy it'.³³ That these individuals are most frequently composers is not surprising. The roots of the Enlightenment, the industrial revolution and Romanticism give us the legacy of the

---

29 This is well-worn topic, with significant contributions by Howard S. Becker, *Art Worlds* (Berkeley: University of California Press, 1982); and Valentina Vadi and Hildegard E.G.S. Schneider, *Art, Cultural Heritage and the Market: Ethical and Legal Issues* (Berlin: Springer, 2014).

30 Richard Caves, *Creative Industries: Contracts Between Art and Commerce* (Cambridge, MA: Harvard University Press, 2000).

31 Most notably beginning with Thomas Kuhn, *The Structure of Scientific Revolutions* (Chicago: The University of Chicago Press, 1963).

32 Marta Peris-Ortiz, Mayer Rainiero Cabrera-Flores and Arturo Serrano-Santoyo (eds.), *Cultural and Creative Industries: A Path to Entrepreneurship and Innovation* (Cham: Springer, 2019), p. 2; Robert DeFillippi, Gernot Grabher and Candace Jones, 'Introduction to paradoxes of creativity: managerial and organizational Challenges in the Cultural Economy', *Journal of Orgnaizational Behavior*, 28 (2007), 511–521.

33 Charles Rosen, 'Culture on the Market', *The New York Review of Books*, 6 November 2003, https://www.nybooks.com/articles/2003/11/06/culture-on-the-market/

artist hero, who is a locus for innovative practices: struggling under the weight of their tradition, they push forward into unknown territory through a torturous inner struggle. Progress is to be found in the work, the 'musical material',[34] which adds another block to the pantheon of Western culture. In the case of artistic production, therefore, questions of innovation are far from new.

For some commentators, the composer is still the instigator of musical innovation par excellence. Certainly, there should be no study of musical innovation that leaves out their voices. Yet, the belief in the work and the composer as the only, or even primary, site of innovation within the art form can now be called into question. Berardi states that a lack of faith in the future, and in progress, has led the 'artistic imagination' into a situation in which it is 'unable to escape the territory of fear and despair'.[35] Certainly this volume is testament to the wide variety of actors who are engaged in what they see as classical music innovation, with composers being only one piece of the puzzle. Before we present our concluding thoughts on classical music innovation today, we will first give an overview of the sections and chapters of this book.

An Overview of the Book

This volume proceeds in five sections, each approaching the future and the problems of classical music from a specific thematic perspective. The first section, **Whose Future?**, addresses one of the most pressing challenges to the question of classical music demographics: the issue of representation and diversity. It describes some of the unique issues and baggage that classical music faces, such as its demarcation as a white space and the challenges associated with 'diversifying' its audience and practitioners. The first chapter presents snapshots on this theme from three different perspectives: Maria Hansen on Higher Education, Kirsteen Davidson-Kelly on creative learning in the orchestra, and George Lewis on new music. Inspiring change is at the centre of the second collaborative chapter looking at best-practice guidance in the classical music world. This focuses on three very recent guidelines

---

34 See Max Paddison, *Adorno's Aesthetics of Music* (Cambridge: Cambridge University Press, 1993), pp. 65–107.
35 Franco Berardi, *After the Future* (Edinburgh: AK Press, 2011), p. 17.

published by organisations working in new music. The first, the 'Fair Access Principles', were created by Sound and Music and outline what all competitions or competitive opportunities for composers should consider. The aim is to stop the exploitation of aspiring composers in the name of 'exposure' and to improve representation and diversity within new music. For the second set of principles, the internationally recognised organisation Keychange discusses their manifesto, which is focused on efforts to improve gender representation in the music industry. Finally, 'What we need to thrive' was created by Sound Scotland and concerns how to work with neurodiverse composers. Representatives from all three organisations contribute to the chapter and provide reflections on the principles themselves, a description of the process of their formation, and how such documents require 'buy-in' from partners and supporters: in other words, how their notional futures require friends. Antonio Cuyler reflects on this process of 'documenting change' through his research into Blacktivism in opera, asking how space can be made for people of African descent within classical music of the future.

The next contribution comes from Brandon Farnsworth, who continues the discussion of diversity by suggesting that classical music's chief problem is its tendency to universalise its practices and experiences, thereby invalidating other cultural activities. Farnsworth asks the question whether simply changing the people involved in the production of classical music is a way of challenging 'the field's fundamental contradictions', or whether rather more radical change is required. Just such radical change is the subject of the final contribution to the section, Lore Lixenberg's political-party-cum-participatory-opera, 'The Voice Party'. This party stood in the UK General Election with Lixenberg as its candidate on a manifesto that proposed putting music at the centre of everyday life in provocative and sometimes authoritarian ways. In exploring the connections between music and society, the Voice Party is a story of direct action with consequences impossible to predict.

The second section, **Future Musicians**, concerns itself with the future-readiness provided by musical education and professional development. Stephanie Pitts, Karen Burland and Tom Spurgin use survey responses from professional UK ensembles the Manchester Collective and the Philharmonia Orchestra to assess how well musicians feel their training prepared them for life in the profession. In particular, they ask how innovative practices impact on these professionals, raising questions both for how these practices are implemented and traditional conservatoire training. This is then followed by a reflective interview with the two orchestra directors on the role of professionals as catalysts and barriers to change. Musicians and their institutions are a key site of tension between renewal and tradition, as this contribution lays bare.

The issue of conservatoire training, its future and purpose, is also taken up by Diana Salazar and Christina Guillaumier in their study of the 'Global Conservatoire'. The pandemic has demanded significant changes to teaching and these authors consider their lasting impact and potential. They argue that the focus should now change from replication of in-person teaching experiences to 'complementing practice-led experiences'. Furthermore, the transnational nature of digital tools has the potential to deeply inform global artistic citizens and enable responses to the urgent issue of artistic relevance in classical music. In so doing, these tools provide the foundation for a reframing of classical music not as a superior art form in some Western-weighted hierarchy but as a practice that challenges and invigorates artistic action in multiple contexts.

The final contribution to the topic of musician training comes from Krista de Wit and Beste Sevindik, who use data from the Dutch Meaningful Music in Healthcare project to probe the navigation of professional identities when classically trained musicians are put in healthcare settings. Music in health is a growing area but little research considers the training needs for the musicians themselves, nor puts this in the wider context of training for greater societal relevance. The findings are important for this burgeoning area of practice, as well as other 'coal faces' in which classical musicians and practices meet with other societal partners. All three contributions examine the skills, training and approach required for musicians to look beyond their usual audiences and performance context, thereby addressing each of the 'problems' discussed above.

The third section looks at **Innovating Institutions** and their role in creating classical music futures. Jutta Toelle examines the sector at large to create a 'taxonomy of interventions': a catalogue of the types of things organisations do to innovate and reach new audiences. The chapter focusses on classical music practices in the German-speaking world. Several big questions are addressed, such as the advanced age profile of audiences and the seemingly old-fashioned canonic repertory. These two issues, coupled with the high subsidies that classical music receives, make classical music practices vulnerable. Alternatives are to be found in the concept-orientated performances by non-institutionalised performers, who are free from the burden of the big institutions but also responsible for providing their own income.

The section continues with two contributions on the issue of sustainability. The first is a roundtable, curated by the MCICM, in which an international array of representatives from ensembles and orchestras discuss classical music's responses to the climate emergency. The organisations include Germany's Orchester des Wandels, Scotland's Nevis Ensemble, and Finland's Lahti Symphony Orchestra.[36] They explore mainstays of the classical music scene, such as large orchestral tours, flying in star instrumentalists and conductors, musicians working two jobs in distant locations, and old and draughty concert halls, which are all potential areas of challenge in a sustainable future. More than this, however, the roundtable explores what classical music can offer *as an art form* in exploring the broader questions of engagement with the climate and nature. Finally, Stine Skovbon presents early findings from her research on orchestras and sustainability, mapping the challenges and arguing that sustainability goals must be at the heart of any future policy initiatives.

Approaching classical music innovation from the perspective of the arts is the topic of the section **Learning from the Art Museum.** Though the museum problem has been described here as an ill that haunts classical music practice, Denise Petzold argues that approaches to the conservation of contemporary art from Museum Studies provide useful perspectives for the preservation and presentation of classical works in the future. In particular, more recent approaches to performance art and time-based media from museum studies offer an area of scholarship that deals with similar 'ontological complexities' to music. Just like conservators, classical musicians and institutions are involved in a long-term effort to 'care for' the repertoire of the classical

---

[36] It is with sadness that the editors note that the Nevis Ensemble, who feature in the climate roundtable in this volume, have folded due to financial pressures.

tradition. Petzold seeks a new perspective on how this work might be understood and reveals new ways of caring for the classical canon. Noga Rachel Chelouche considers the presentation of classical music in the work of contemporary visual artist Anri Sala. Chelouche contrasts the experiences of the canonical compositions in Sala's work with their presentation in a traditional concert and, in so doing, confronts once again the museum problem by exploring a different way in which classical works can be experienced.

The format of the traditional concert is a key site in efforts to innovate classical music today, with changes large and small on the minds of institutions and individual practitioners alike. As one of the vital interfaces between the art form and its public – along with radio, records and streaming – these developments are primarily aimed at reaching new audiences in immersive ways, often in locations other than the concert hall. This is the focus of the contributions in **Space and Proximity**. In his chapter, Neil T. Smith explores attempts to innovate concert spaces. The chapter presents a diary of unconventional concert spaces, two pre- and four post-pandemic. The aim is to explore the effects of spatial innovation, providing insights for the future of performances outside the concert hall. Although he sees great potential in spatial exploration, which should be further exploited, the chapter is also a corrective to an approach that would imbue space with the ability to transform musical and social relations without the complicating factors of music's previous socialisations and the pre-existing complexities of the new spaces that are used.

The second chapter in this section describes the concert series Monsieur Croche, which is based in Antwerp, Belgium. The series seeks to present classical music in unusual concert venues in the city, thereby attempting to engage new audiences and to give a different sense of inclusion and interaction. It is part of an international effort to get classical music out of the concert hall and into people's lives. Walker describes the challenges of such a venture organisationally and artistically, providing a useful document for others engaged in similar efforts. In their contribution, Hans-Joachim Gögl and Folkert Uhde seek to move beyond discussions of dramaturgy, choosing instead to examine curatorial 'strategies of proximity': ways in which music can facilitate new types of interaction and experience with social and political themes. This they do using examples from their extensive curatorial practice, particularly in Austria. Michelle Phillips and Amanda Krause consider the legacy of the pandemic for live performance, reviewing recent literature on 'liveness' and the value of co-present versus online performance. While many classical music devotees were delighted to return to the concert hall, Phillips argues that there were benefits to the explosion of options for digital performance. This is a timely discussion of what the long-term benefits might be and if they offer tools that allow classical music to speak to a broader range of people.

As explored above, technological progress and musical progress appeared to be going in hand-in-hand for much of the nineteenth and twentieth centuries. Yet the impact of technological change on culture itself often occurs in a rather more subtle and complex fashion. In the **Artificial Intelligence** section, two contributors give their thoughts on how the questions of direct technological intervention – specifically AI – are displacing previous creative certainties, and opening up new creative possibilities. Robert Laidlow reflects on his own implementation of artificial intelligence in his works for orchestra, questioning the temporal relations between future and past that AI contains and the ideas of 'authenticity' that have been such a mainstay of classical music practice. He describes the 'benefits and limitations' of his approach as regards traditional compositional concerns such as the development of musical material and structure, as well as his own strategies for amplifying or mitigating the effects of this approach. In a personal reflection on the voice, its potential and the future role of AI, composer and performer Jennifer Walshe describes the challenge of the future as 'deciding what it means to make music when the machines can.' Walshe argues that the advent of AI will mark a turning point in human creativity that is both terrifying and enlivening. The future posited here is of a radical technological shift that requires an equally radical change in artistic consciousness.

Classical Music Innovation Today

Innovation in classical music today is a different animal from the often formalist and technical discourse that surrounded 'progressive' composers in the twentieth century. The concept has been fragmented and dispersed. Critiques of various concepts such as genius, linear views of musical progress, the work concept and the supposition of

Western supremacy are now mainstream. While there is undoubtedly still aesthetic and technical discourse in new music around value and experimentation, there is an increasing awareness that all musical activities are geographically situated and bear some relation to the market (whether through public funding or private philanthropy). Few within new music are (openly) claiming to be personally making great strides in advancing the western tradition in their works and, through this, bettering humanity at large. As discussed above, the future has become more uncertain and with it the belief in progress. What to add to the museum of great works is a fraught question, particularly when the contemporary music world has traditional drawn some of the most pointed accusations of elitism. For some, the answer is to try and change the idea of the museum altogether.

Rather than purely taking place in the world of composers and the avant-garde, the innovation that the MCICM has observed in classical music today is a case of self-reflection by individuals and organisations at all points within the network of classical music practitioners.[37] It is in the organisations seeking better representation amongst their artists and staff; in the individual musicians teaching stylistic diversity; and in unusual concert formats and series. It is taking place in all manner of locations: in schools, hospitals, car parks, and online; and we see it is as significantly dispersed, though by no means yet democratised due to the sociodemographic profiles of the vast majority of people in the classical music world.

Such dispersal is, however, no guarantee of its success. For, in these various locations, what constitutes innovation is highly dependent on various contextual factors, particularly on the default practice of whoever is involved. Thus, an outdoor performance for Pynarello (a Dutch conductorless orchestra) or the Nevis Ensemble (Scotland's 'Street Orchestra') is a very different beast compared to a more traditional, concert-hall-bound institution. This has the consequence

---

[37] Veerle Spronck, Peter Peters and Ties van de Werff, 'Empty Minds: Innovating Audience Participation in Symphonic Practice', *Science as Culture*, 30, 2 (2021), 216–236; Ties van de Werff, Neil Thomas Smith, Stefan Rosu and Peter Peters, 'Missing the Audiences. Online Musicking in Times of COVID-19', *Journal of Cultural Management and Cultural Policy*, 7, 1 (2021), 137–150; Neil Thomas Smith, 'Constructing the Public Concert Hall', *The Journal of the Royal Musical Association*, 146, 2 (2021), 255–281.

that certain 'innovative' ideas are continually being rediscovered and recirculated: playing outside or in an unusual location, performing to school groups, and accompanying films are all ideas that pop up in orchestral programmes with some regulatory, yet may all be identified as innovative by those involved. This rediscovery tells us about the situated nature of innovation but also about the difficulties faced in moving forward and learning from previous experiences elsewhere in the field. There is a danger of classical music innovation becoming the dog forever chasing its tail. Were this so, it would fit within a perspective that sees the 'innovations' of classical music institutions as tinkering at the edges of a fundamentally flawed model that many do not have the courage or wit to abandon. This is the tension that Brandon Farnsworth's chapter describes between 'reformist' and 'radical' critiques, the former working within the system to bring about change, the latter seeking to change the system. Certainly, there is a danger that the old contents are packaged in new ways and it is called progress. One purpose of this volume is to describe in some detail, and with a critical eye, certain common moves towards classical innovation so that the sector can break out of this repetitive loop.

Appeals to innovation can also be a powerful marketing tool: ensembles and performers can be made to 'look' experimental and disruptive despite offering the most common fare. Yet, any essential division between 'real innovation' on the one hand and 'marketing' on the other is problematic as innovative practices now involve reaching more, and more diverse, people, and marketing – who gets to hear about such events – has an important role in this. In trying to appeal to more people, however, marketing drives can often double down on the art form's elite nature, or the supposed 'genius' of its practitioners. In trying to solve one problem of classical music, another is encountered almost immediately. This is the basis of calls for rather more radical change.

There is, however, also a danger that a focus on innovative practices is part of a drive towards increased instrumentalization and marketisation of culture. For example, from a mainland European perspective, the United Kingdom appears a hotbed of innovative practice. This may be so, but these moves are tied to long-term decreases in state funding and an increased sense in government that the philanthropic model of the United States might be preferable to that of European social democracies since World War II. Economics defines artistic, or at least institutional, priorities to a significant degree and innovation in the UK context is partly a reaction to scarcity. One interpretation of this evidence is that such scarcity creates agile, innovative organisations, yet for innovative practices to take hold significant resource is required. The sector laments the often project-based nature of innovative interventions, which reach new people and places for a time but do not have the funding to be sustained, not to mention the knock-on effects of unstable employment for musicians of project-based work. Institutionalising innovative practice effectively is not, ultimately, a low-cost option, but if the only alternative is the future posited by the obsolescence problem – complete extinction – then practitioners have no choice. Such is the power of a convincing future with friends in the right places.

It is difficult to overstate the severity of critiques of the diversity of classical music. The problems listed above are not external to the way the art form has been understood, marketed and practised. The canon, orchestral discipline, the work of youth orchestras,[38] instrumental and vocal virtuosity, and the legacies of genius and artistic superiority are some of the most significant foundations on which the image and practice of classical music has been built. Removing them raises the question: what is left? At present there is a lack of overarching positive vision for the work of musicians and institutions within classical music, while efforts in this direction can too easily fall back on old (and continuing) exclusions. These are important considerations when considering how such exclusions in classical music might be subverted and transformed. As Bull and Scharff describe, 'discussing diversity means calling into question the boundaries of what counts as classical music.'[39] Starting again is not an option in a tradition this widespread, with such deep historical roots. The solutions, therefore, are to be found in conscious engagement and in playful experimentation. They are to be found in the diverse tools that are created in the work of people all over the world engaged in transforming this practice.

---

38 Bull, *Class, Control, and Classical Music*.
39 Bull, Anna, and Christina Scharff, 'Introduction' in *Voices for Change in the Classical Music Profession: New Ideas for Tackling Inequalities and Exclusions*, ed. by Anna Bull, Christina Scharff and Laudan Nooshin (Oxford: Oxford University Press, 2023), p. 13.

References

Adam, Barbara, 'Future Matters: Challenge for Social Theory and Social Inquiry', Keynote Address to Italian Sociological Association Conference, Future Matters for Social Theory, Cagliari University, Sardinia (29 October 2009).

Becker, Howard S., *Art Worlds* (Berkeley: University of California Press, 1982).

Bell, Wendell, and James Mau (eds.), *The Sociology of the Future: Theory, Cases and Annotated Bibliography* (New York: Russell Sage Foundation, 1971).

Berardi, Franco, *After the Future* (Edinburgh: AK Press, 2011).

Brown, Nik, Brian Rappert and Andrew Webster, *Contested Futures: A Sociology of Prospective Techno-Science* (Aldershot: Ashgate, 2000).

Bull, Anna, *Class, Control, and Classical Music* (Oxford: Oxford University Press, 2019). https://doi.org/10.1093/oso/9780190844356.001.0001

Bull, Anna, and Christina Scharff, 'Introduction' in *Voices for Change in the Classical Music Profession: New Ideas for tackling inequalities and exclusions*, ed. by Anna Bull, Christina Scharff and Laudan Nooshin (Oxford: Oxford University Press, 2023). https://doi.org/10.1093/oso/9780197601211.001.0001

Caves, Richard, *Creative Industries: Contracts Between Art and Commerce* (Cambridge, MA: Harvard University Press, 2000).

Cressman, Darryl, *Building Musical Culture in Nineteenth-Century Amsterdam: The Concertgebouw* (Amsterdam: Amsterdam University Press, 2016).

DeFillippi, Robert, Gernot Grabher and Candace Jones, 'Introduction to paradoxes of creativity: managerial and organizational Challenges in the Cultural Economy', *Journal of Orgnaizational Behavior*, 28 (2007). https://doi.org/10.1002/job.466

DeNora, Tia, *Beethoven and the Construction of Genius: Musical Politics in Vienna, 1792-1803* (Berkeley: University of California Press, 1996).

Doorman, Maarten, *Art in Progress: A Philosophical Response to the End of the Avant-Garde* (Amsterdam: Amsterdam University Press, 2003).

Ewell, Philip, 'Music Theory's White Racial Frame', *Music Theory Online*, 26/2 (2020). https://doi.org/10.30535/mto.26.2.4

Gadamer, Hans-Georg, *Truth and Method* (New York: Continuum, 1989[1960]).

Goehr, Lydia, *The Imaginary Museum of Musical Works: An Essay in the Philosophy of Music* (Oxford: Oxford University Press, 2007).

Haynes, Bruce, *The End of Early Music: A Period Performer's History of Music for the Twenty-First Century* (Oxford: Oxford University Press, 2007).

Johnson, James H., *Listening in Paris: A cultural history* (Berkeley/Los Angeles/London: University of California Press, 1994).

Kaye, Lewis, 'The Silenced Listener: Architectural Acoustics, the Concert Hall and the Conditions of Audience', *Leonardo Music Journal*, 22 (2012), 63–65. https://doi.org/10.1162/LMJ_a_00100

Kuhn, Thomas, *The Structure of Scientific Revolutions* (Chicago: The University of Chicago Press, 1963).

Lente, Harro van, *Promising Technology: The Dynamics of Expectations in Technological Developments* (Twente: University of Twente, 1993).

McCraw, Thomas K., *Prophet of Innovation: Joseph Schumpeter and Creative Destruction* (Cambridge, MA: Belknap Press, 2007).

Martin, Ben R., *Twenty Challenge for Innovation Studies* (Cambridge: Centre for Business Studies, University of Cambridge, 2015).

Michael, Mike, 'Enacting Big Futures, Little Futures: Toward an ecology of futures', *The Sociological Review*, 65/3 (2017), 509–524. https://doi.org/10.1111/1467-954X.12444

Nowotny, Helga, *Time: The Modern and Postmodern Experience* (Cambridge: Polity Press, 1994).

Oomen, Jeroen, Jesse Hofman, and Maarten A. Hajer, 'Techniques of futuring: On how imagined futures become socially performative', *European Journal of Social Theory*, 25/2 (2021), 252-270. https://doi.org/10.1177/1368431020988826

Paddison, Max, *Adorno's Aesthetics of Music* (Cambridge: Cambridge University Press, 1993).

Peters, Peter, *Unfinished Symphonies* (Maastricht: Datawyse, 2019).

Peris-Ortiz, Marta, Mayer Rainiero Cabrera-Flores and Arturo Serrano-Santoyo (eds.), *Cultural and Creative Industries: A Path to Entrepreneurship and Innovation* (Cham: Springer, 2019). https://doi.org/10.1007/978-3-319-99590-8

Rosen, Charles, *The Romantic Generation* (London: HarperCollins, 1996).

Rosen, Charles, 'Culture on the Market', *The New York Review of Books*, 6 November (2003), https://www.nybooks.com/articles/2003/11/06/culture-on-the-market/

Smith, Neil Thomas, 'Constructing the Public Concert Hall', *The Journal of the Royal Musical Association*, 146/2 (2021), 255–281. https://doi.org/10.1017/rma.2021.17

Smithuijsen, Cas, *Een verbazende stilte: klassieke muziek, gedragsregels en sociale controle in de concertzaal* (Amsterdam: Boekmanstudies, 2001).

Spronck, Veerle, Peter Peters and Ties van de Werff, 'Empty Minds: Innovating Audience Participation in Symphonic Practice', *Science as Culture*, 30/2 (2021), 216–236. https://doi.org/10.1080/09505431.2021.1893681

Spronck, Veerle, *Listen Closely: Innovating Audience Participation in Symphonic Music* (Maastricht: Maastricht University, 2022). https://doi.org/10.26481/dis.20220706vs

Stoneman, Paul, *Soft Innovation: Economics, Product Aesthetics, and the Creative Industries* (Oxford: Oxford University Press, 2010). https://doi.org/10.1093/acprof:oso/9780199572489.001.0001

Tutton, Richard, 'Wicked futures: Meaning, matter and the sociology of the future', *The Sociological Review*, 65/3 (2017), 478–492. https://doi.org/10.1111/1467-954X.12443

Urry, John, 'Climate change, travel and complex futures', *The British Journal of Sociology*, 59 (2008), 261–279. https://doi.org/10.1111/j.1468-4446.2008.00193.x

Vadi, Valentina, and Hildegard E.G.S. Schneider, *Art, Cultural Heritage and the Market: Ethical and Legal Issues* (Berlin: Springer, 2014). https://doi.org/10.1007/978-3-642-45094-5

Werff, Ties van de, Neil Thomas Smith, Stefan Rosu and Peter Peters, 'Missing the Audiences. Online Musicking in Times of COVID-19', *Journal of Cultural Management and Cultural Policy*, 7/1 (2021), 137–150. https://doi.org/10.14361/zkmm-2021-0107

1. Roundtable 1: Whose Future?

Neil Thomas Smith with contributions from Maria Hansen, Kirsteen Davidson Kelly, and George E. Lewis

This chapter looks at approaches to urgent issues around equality, inclusion and diversity within classical music today through the lens of this volume's main theme: the future. As Bull and Scharff state, 'musical innovation does not necessarily lead to social change, but can still entrench existing inequalities'.[1] As touched on in the introduction, these 'existing inequalities' have been identified in fundamental facets of the classical tradition, including its reliance on a restricted canon, the image of genius to which only white males belong, and the entirely intentional and explicit exclusions that women and people of colour have faced in musical, as in many other, spheres of operation in Europe, North America and beyond. These broader themes are not the topic of the conversation here, but they are an important backdrop to this conversation.

The discussion covers three arenas in which efforts to increase representation in terms of gender, race and – to a lesser extent – class are well underway, though with significant steps still to take for parity to be achieved. These are: music higher education, community projects undertaken by orchestras, and festivals of new music. Each author provides a snapshot of the issues at stake in these different areas of

---

1   Anna Bull and Christina Scharff, 'Introduction' in *Voices for Change in the Classical Music Profession: New Ideas for Tackling Inequalities and Exclusions*, ed. by Anna Bull, Christina Scharff and Laudan Nooshin (Oxford: Oxford University Press, 2023).

classical music practice, showing distinct challenges but also important areas of overlap. There is common ground in the attempt to broaden the profile of the students, participants and practitioners active in their various spheres and, in so doing, there is an implicit challenge to one or other of the tenets of classical music culture described above. Belief in 'excellence', for example, in contemporary music – that festivals will simply perform the best music – does not sit well with so-called affirmative action. Yet, the fact that the profile of composers is so restricted calls into question this assertion of excellence in the first place. A similar dynamic is at play in music education. Broadening participation, therefore, is not just a challenge of funnelling more people through the same conduits,[2] but presents fundamental questions for classical music practice. The discussion below originally took place as part of the Maastricht Centre for the Innovation of Classical Music's 2021 symposium that considered 'the Future'. The panel consisted of Maria Hansen, chief executive of ELIA, a Higher Education network; Kirsteen Davidson Kelly, formerly creative learning director of the Scottish Chamber Orchestra, now chief executive of the National Youth Orchestras of Scotland; and composer, improviser and scholar, George E. Lewis, who is the Edwin H. Case Professor of American Music at Columbia University.

In some ways our desired future is uncontroversial: all of us want a future in which everyone can reach their potential, a future in which all people are able to play and listen to all kinds of music and to make music part of their lives, throughout their lives, yet the route to this utopia is not so clear and requires critical reflection on the present, and on the structures in classical music that have been taken for granted for so long.

---

2   What is memorably described as 'add women and stir' in Roberta Lamb, Lori-Anne Dolloff, and Sondra Wieland Howe, 'Feminism, feminist research, and gender research in music education: a selective review', in *The New Handbook of Research on Music Teaching and Learning: A Project of the Music Educators National Conference*, ed. by Richard Colwell and Carol P. Richardson (Oxford: Oxford University Press, 2002), pp. 648–674: p. 666.

3 Key Issues in Conservatoire Education

Maria Hansen

ELIA is a globally connected European network of higher arts education institutions: we have 260 members, all of whom are art universities, art academies, or faculties of arts practice within larger universities. We are rooted in Europe but also have a sizable global membership. ELIA covers all disciplines of art practice, which makes us different from discipline-specific networks like the Association Européenne des Conservatoires (AEC), which many of you will know well. ELIA aims to provide a dynamic platform for the professional development and exchange of our members: talking about the future is what we do all the time. In fact, together with the AEC, we are currently part of an EU-funded project called FAST 45, which envisions higher arts education in 2045, together with partners from the arts education sector and the private sector.

Our work at ELIA is informed by a number of strategic priorities that are developed with our members, and the topic of diversity and inclusion is central to this. Discussions with colleagues at conservatoires and at the AEC confirmed that the topic of diversity and inclusion is complex but also central to their work.[3] I have three points to share from these amazing conversations: firstly, a key aspect of improving diversity and inclusion is the repertoire played and the context within which it is played. These are the two aspects that the AEC is addressing together with the higher music education sector. What is that body of work we call classical music? What is not part of it? Well, female composers to name only one category must be better represented but unearthing unknown composers through decolonization is another. There are already some great examples of this.

Sharing musical experience might be more important than a flawless performance. That means that taking performance out of the safe setting of the concert hall into the imperfect realm of the outdoors and the city is part of the answer at the conservatoire. This requires changes to the curriculum and many conservatoires are already addressing this,

---

3   The following benefits from discussions I, Maria, had with Stefan Gies from the AEC and also colleagues from Codarts in Rotterdam and Trinity Laban conservatory in London. So, thanks to Hans Leenders and David Bahanovich for their help (Codarts is an arts university in Rotterdam that specialises in music, dance and circus).

sometimes sending their musicians for weeks into cities to work together with artists from other disciplines and creating unexpected new work for new audiences. This is the case with the incubator program at Codarts in Rotterdam and also a new neighbourhood orchestra in The Hague.

The second point concerns the identity of musicians: they are being educated for a very specific role, like playing in an orchestra. Yet they are not being educated to become artists as citizens, nor artists as innovators. I've come across quite a number of conservatoires that are addressing this issue, now focusing on enabling musicians to figure out what their contribution to society could be for themselves.

Finally, and for me most importantly, conservatoires are part of an ecosystem that starts at the youngest ages and goes through secondary school into higher education, to work life and beyond. Every part of this ecosystem has to be part of this movement that will create a more diverse and inclusive classical music industry. In an ecosystem, everyone has to take care of each other and to relate to what is around them. I think, once you open up to that, certainly in the larger communities but also in the smaller ones, there are so many parts that you could connect to: the schools, the community centres. I think once you open up your mind, it's easy.

In Rotterdam, for instance, there is a music coalition of local music institutions, including the orchestra and Codarts, who are working together to improve access to music-making for children. We know it matters where a kid went to school and what opportunities they got at school. Trinity Laban has an intake of forty-three percent from state-funded schools, which is considered high. This, according to them, directly results in a much higher inflow of students from a BAME background, seventeen percent to be precise. They're embracing this challenge: it takes a lot to coach these kids through the pipeline in all sorts of ways and at the end they may have very different goals to playing in an orchestra. It takes teachers that understand this, with contact between student and teacher sometimes running for decades. Here lies a big challenge as many of you know: I asked everyone who their heroes were in this kind of 'ecosystem thinking' and I will just call out a few: the Kinshasa symphony was mentioned but also the Sphinx organisation in the US, which I know and admire. In the UK there is the Chineke! Orchestra.

My final thought is that sharing and moving together, across borders, in this is essential: learn globally, act locally. In my business, and in yours, every teacher matters.

Co-Creation in the Community

Kirsteen Davidson Kelly

I want to give you a whistle-stop tour of a recent Scottish Chamber Orchestra (SCO) project in the community and some of the thinking that underpins our community work. The SCO is an orchestra based in Edinburgh, which receives direct funding from the Scottish Government and has a remit to provide music to the entire country. This project is part of a community residency, which is a multi-year project in a specific Edinburgh neighbourhood, Wester Hailes. This community residency project was originally conceived as a series of school projects, but a local youth forum provoked us to engage with adults as well. So, we put out an open call for a series of 'music and visuals' workshops, leaving the framework as open as we possibly could so that the process and the output could be co-created.

The team consisted of a composer, a workshop leader, three SCO musicians and a visual artist. The initial aim was simply to articulate and amplify the experiences of local residents. The participants who came to the project didn't know each other beforehand. Some came from just having picked up leaflets in the community, some found out about it via social media, others were prescribed the project by their doctor or community link worker.

The group decided that they would create a piece to reflect a day in the life of Wester Hailes. They used a graphic in the workshop space of a twenty-four-hour timeline and at each session they explored just one window of time, working with the question 'what did you do today?'. Between the workshops, the participants used phones and cameras to capture sounds and images exploring their local environment and their everyday activities. As part of the process, the group went on visits to the Fruitmarket Gallery in the centre of Edinburgh and to SCO season concerts. The result of this process was that the composer and visual artist curated an audiovisual installation, capturing snapshots of daily life through found sound and workshop recordings, film and original music. The title *Incredible Distance* came out of conversations within the workshops.

We displayed the installation at the Royal Scottish Academy and at the Fruitmarket Gallery, both in the centre of town, as well as at WHALE Arts, which is where we were running the project. The installation took the form of a twelve-minute film with a hand-drawn score: https://www.youtube.com/watch?v=ifJWXjeGu7s. This included written text, snippets of conversations that happened during the process.

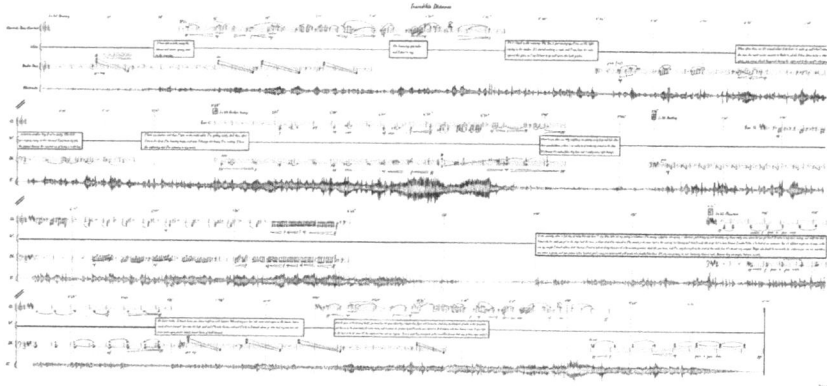

Fig. 1.1 Score of Incredible Distance.

We also displayed four images. These were accompanied by miniature sound representations of what participants deemed to be iconic Wester Hailes sounds. SCO musicians recreated the participants' recorded sounds for the piece.

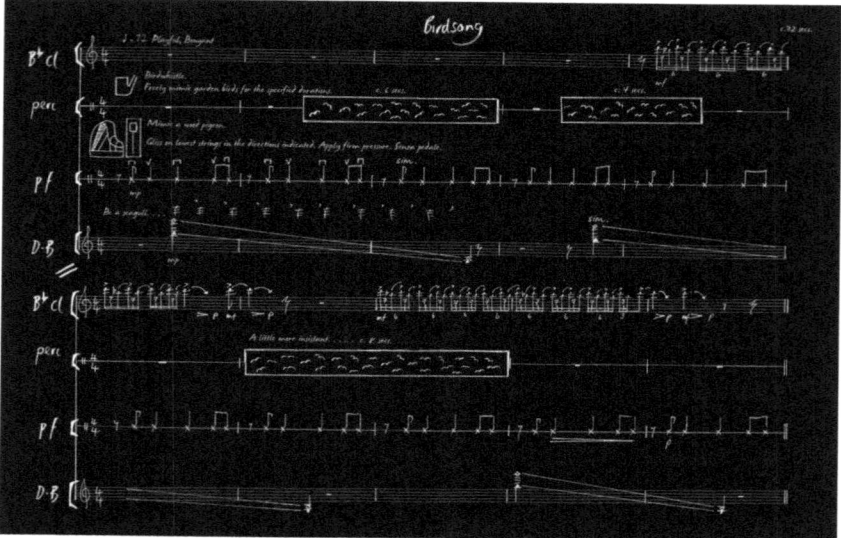

Fig. 1.2 Iconic Wester Hailes sound: Birdsong © Laura Baxter.

There is a particular kind of thinking and set of principles that underpins this inclusive work. I think we're continually needing to evolve our understanding of the civic role of funded organisations, our role in sustaining individuals and communities and our role in developing the art form. We focus on work that pays equal attention, and gives equal value, to both process and output, and we use co-created practice all the time. We treat music-making itself as a shared practice and a communicative tool and we deliberately create connections in order to unlock meaning. We share idea-generation and decision-making processes, and we understand that co-creation can be really messy, uncertain and challenging but, when it's done well, it is really innovative and rewarding for everyone involved. What we're doing is creating meeting points: we go out to people in their homes, and we invite them into ours. I mean this fairly literally in the sense that we are obviously going out to communities and welcoming people into our performance spaces, and I also mean it in the sense of the types of artistic process we use, which explore different perspectives, different types of music, different meanings, different processes.

It's really essential that we train musicians, and we include composers, in this collective practice – collaborative approaches and understanding co-creation – because it is difficult. It does take a lot of work and you need to grow teams very carefully in order for these things to be successful. So, in our community residency work, we link with all sorts of higher education institutions, we have students from, for example, the Royal Conservatoire of Scotland and the University of Edinburgh who come and work on projects with us quite often as part of their course.

I think one of the privileges of being a performing arts organisation that is core-funded by our government is that we do have a reasonable amount of time and resource to support these kinds of processes. We need to spend time in the room, we need to spend time with community partners understanding people's needs and the needs of the community. We need to get to know how to tread carefully, if you like, around what sensitivities there might be.

I think some of the tensions will be about bringing different practices together. So, for example, you can have a composer who is very highly skilled in working through a brief and working in great detail, organising and controlling material. And then you have a workshop process which is really messy, and nobody knows what's going on, where the purpose is largely to share information and to create human relationships. So again, you have to take care of those processes.

I hope I showed a little bit in that project in Wester Hailes what I mean when I say the outcomes of that project were not set: we didn't predict that we would be installing such an amazing piece of audio-visual art in a city-centre gallery. That came about because the process worked so well and the artists worked together so well, and the outcome was so beautiful.

For the artists, it extends their practice. It makes them think about it in new ways; it's innovation by default. For participants we had some very rich feedback and we had quite a bit of media attention around that particular project. The feedback basically said that they were blown away by how they were treated, how they were included, how they were part of the process and what it did for them. One participant said, 'I've lived in Wester Hailes for forty years and it was like an albatross around my neck until you came along … this project has made me look at the whole place with new eyes …we've all started to blossom as individuals.' Well, you don't get much better than that I suppose!

I thought I would finish this up with a quote from Nina Simon, who expresses it very well in her book, *The Art of Relevance*. She says that we are 'living in the creative tension between evangelising for the things you care about and listening with interest to what others care about. It's about radiating the inside out and inviting the outside in.'[4]

Steps Toward the Decolonisation of New Music Festivals

George E. Lewis

In a recent article of mine on decolonisation in new music I provide eight practical, albeit admittedly difficult steps toward forestalling what I see as the kind of impoverishment and devolution of the field that is resulting from the recirculation of the stereotype of exclusive whiteness

---

4   Nina Simon, *The Art of Relevance* (Santa Cruz: Museum 2.0, 2016), eBook, part 5.4.

around classical music's self-image.⁵ My basic question in this article was 'what would a decolonised curatorial classical music regime sound like?' Well, to some extent we know what it would *look* like: Okwui Enwezor was the first non-white curator of the famous contemporary art festival, Documenta 11, in 2002. This version of the festival presented contemporary art as 'a network in which New York, Lagos, London, Cape Town and Basel are all more or less equally important to a contemporary canon... as opposed to some centres being exotic margins and others more genuinely contemporary.'⁶

There's really no reason why festivals and other important institutions that support new music couldn't do the same. So why don't they do it? Sara Ahmed has written that institutional whiteness is about the 'reproduction of likeness'.⁷ For her, institutions are kinship technologies. For me, music, genre, race, gender and kinship are often co-present, and the naturalisation of these kinship-like discourses become obstacles to change. So my first step would be to move beyond kinship and invest in new populations.

Secondly, we might want to give up on meritocracy. Some ensembles, granting organisations, and festivals in the US have always achieved greater gender and racial diversity, while others have never given an award to or programmed the work of an Afrodiasporic composer. These decisions are always portrayed as being based on merit, but in fact there really isn't any such thing as the best composer. The impact of many years of essentially fake meritocracy – as well as decades of curatorial commissioning and academic employment and admissions decisions proceeding from what theorist bell hooks has called 'white supremacist capitalist patriarchy' – has resulted in whiteness becoming a form of unearned equity with a complementary *disinvestment* in other segments of the new music community.⁸

---

5   George E. Lewis, 'New Music Decolonization in Eight Difficult Steps,' *VAN Outernational*, https://www.van-outernational.com/lewis-en (English), https://www.van-outernational.com/lewis (German), https://www.van-outernational.com/lewis-fr (French).
6   Anthony Gardner & Charles Green, 'Post-North? Documenta11 and the Challenges of the "Global" Exhibition,' http://www.on-curating.org/issue-33-reader/post-north-documenta11-and-the-challenges-of-the-global-exhibition.html.
7   Sara Ahmed, *On Being Included: Racism and Diversity in Institutional Life* (Durham and London: Duke University Press, 2012), 38.
8   bell hooks, *Black Looks: Race and Representation* (New York: Routledge, 2014), 84.

I'm totally with Maria Hansen when she recommends talking about the diversification of school music programmes, and I'm thinking in particular about the production of composers in this case, even more than the production of performers. I'm thinking how university composition programmes, such as the one that I am currently the head of at Columbia University, are really (to use a US sports metaphor) like the farm teams for new music composers. So, if those cohorts are not diverse, the field experiences a kind of sensory deprivation in terms of what is being offered musically.

Another thing would be the internationalisation of music curation decisions. There's really no reason why major music institutions that tout themselves as international should continue to present all-white concert programmes, juries, faculties and the like. At the Ensemble Modern's November 2020 symposium on Afro-modernism in Frankfurt, one of the presenters was Björn Gottstein, then director of the Donaueschinger Musiktage, one of the most important in Europe and around the world. He said 'Well, I'm kind of part of the accused' or 'part of the problem', being a white man and a director of a European music festival, which in fact has programmed very few composers of colour in the past decades. Actually, there were in fact zero until 2020, at a festival that is a hundred years old.

So, one way around that might be to engage curators from non-majoritarian ethnicities, genders and regions that could allow audiences to hear a greater range of aesthetic and methodological directions. This is what they do at Documenta, for example, or what happened at Tanglewood's Festival of Contemporary Music 2022, where four curators created a programme that placed an unprecedented diversity of aesthetics, genders, ethnicities, and musical directions on the festival's table of contents. What we need now are new experts and new expressions of expertise.

Finally, I think a change of consciousness might be required. I've suggested that a mental envelope of creolization would allow contemporary music to think about a new 'we'. There is such a thing as inclusion, but the reason for including people is because you excluded them before. Why did you exclude them in the first place? What empowered you to enforce judgements regarding inclusion? And if race, gender, or other characteristics are part of the reasons for exclusion, this obviously has to be investigated and countered. Doing this sort of creolization is part of a technology of inclusion that would allow contemporary music to move beyond this celebration of a whiteness-based diaspora toward becoming a true world music that recognises historical, geographic, cultural and methodological cross-connections. The aim is not only to achieve diversity, but really, a new complexity that promises far greater creative depth.

I've been hearing about the irrelevance of classical music for most of my life. But I think there are some changes in the air. For one thing, throughout all the time we've been hearing about this irrelevance, people have continued to compose, people have continued to perform, people continue to produce things – and not all of it is supported by major institutions. People have made all kinds of grassroots efforts because they seem to find that there's something about this community and this music that they deem important.

Now the big issue, though, is that most of these people don't want to support exclusively whiteness-based diasporas. They don't want to be involved in the celebration of that, and people feel poorly when, in order to enter in a field, you have to give up your own identity, or you have to go through some sort of looking glass, a kind of 'decontamination filter' that winds up destroying who you are. Well, no one wants to do that, and I could see how that would result in people saying 'well…'. You see, when you do that – I don't care whether you do it in classical music or what happened in the eighties in jazz where people started doing that – the smart people leave and then the field devolves. I felt that my little eight steps were an attempt to forestall and counter that devolution.

The usual sort of binaries, this versus that, don't really work anymore because all of these fields, including classical music in my view, are inexorably becoming creolized. They're interpenetrating, so that there's no purity anymore. So people who are looking for that are generally going to be disappointed when they don't find it. So in this case, because classical music has asserted a purity narrative for so long, maybe that's a problem that could be fixed. I saw that my little end of it was to think about Afro-diasporic composers and the seemingly near-total absence of these people from institutional narratives, from books, from articles, and from critical reflection. It seemed at odds with what I was seeing in the community and in the world.

When you see these discrepancies, that's what I found there: a hole that could be filled. You can't fix every hole, but I felt that I could fix this one because I knew enough about it and I had some tools that I could bring to bear. I'm happy to help other people on fixing up the rest of the building.

References

Ahmed, Sara, *On Being Included: Racism and Diversity in Institutional Life* (Durham and London: Duke University Press, 2012). https://doi.org/10.1515/9780822395324

Bull, Anna and Christina Scharff, 'Introduction' in *Voices for Change in the Classical Music Profession: New Ideas for Tackling Inequalities and Exclusions*, ed. by Anna Bull, Christina Scharff and Laudan Nooshin (Oxford: Oxford University Press, 2023).

Gardner, Anthony and Charles Green, "Post-North? Documenta11 and the Challenges of the 'Global' Exhibition," *OnCurating*, http://www.on-curating.org/issue-33-reader/post-north-documenta11-and-the-challenges-of-the-global-exhibition.html

hooks, bell, *Black Looks: Race and Representation* (New York: Routledge, 2014). https://doi.org/10.4324/9781315743226

Lamb, Roberta, Lori-Anne Dolloff, and Sondra Wieland Howe, 'Feminism, feminist research, and gender research in music education: a selective review', in *The New Handbook of Research on Music Teaching and Learning: A Project of the Music Educators National Conference*, ed. by Richard Colwell and Carol P. Richardson (Oxford: Oxford University Press, 2002), pp. 648–674.

Lewis, George E., "New Music Decolonization in Eight Difficult Steps," *VAN Outernational*, https://www.van-outernational.com/lewis-en (English), https://www.van-outernational.com/lewis (German), https://www.van-outernational.com/lewis-fr (French).

Simon, Nina, *The Art of Relevance* (Santa Cruz: Museum 2.0, 2016), eBook, part 5.4. https://doi.org/10.1080/2159032X.2017.1346166

2. Classical Music has a Diversity Problem

Brandon Farnsworth

A recent profusion of statistics on classical music repertoire, performers, and education from across several countries have produced quantitative evidence confirming that it is primarily a musical tradition where white, middle-class European cis males succeed. This chapter examines how improving the inclusivity and equality of participation in classical music conflicts with its ideological investment in meritocracy and high musical quality. It argues that giving up on a belief in classical music's universalism and exploring instead the many situated entanglements and infrastructures that enable it to exist would allow for a new approach that does not fall back on the exclusionary categories that have historically supported classical music, while offering forms of engaging with it that better align with contemporary values of inclusivity and equality. I also argue that sustained statistical work is crucially important in continuing to address classical music's exclusions, but that in order not simply to facilitate surface changes to a problematic system (engaging in what I call a reformist critique), the goal must be to confound existing categorisations and help usher in new perspectives on the classical music tradition (a radical critique), which in turn requires statistical categories to be readapted. While structural problems will not disappear overnight, such an approach will reveal how classical music has always been entangled with its surroundings and been the site of many experiments and interactions with other musical genres, which it has marked as 'other' and has either forgotten, omitted or purposefully discarded.

Statistics

The following is an overview of recent statistical reports that have been produced about the lack of diversity in the institutions of classical music. Most statistics focus on the number of female composers who have been programmed in a particular orchestral season or at a specific festival over the course of its history. Some projects have been able to compile statistics at the national level, assembling data from several different kinds of institution, from chamber ensembles to symphonies, while others, in particular the DONNE Foundation report, have concentrated instead on international groupings of similar institutions, such as major symphony orchestras. Many of the studies only look at two gender categories, though some (increasingly) are including a third gender category, a race/ethnicity perspective, or an intersectional perspective. I have also included statistics on classical music education and working conditions, where statistics presenting intersectional relationships between categories of gender, race/ethnicity, class, and ability seem to be more common. The widespread production of statistics on this issue has only begun to take place in the past several years, though now that the picture has started to fill in, it is remarkable to see how pervasive the disparities are in the institutions of classical music.

The DONNE Foundation reported in July 2021 that among its sample of 100 orchestras across the world, 'only 747 out of the 14,747 compositions scheduled [...] throughout the 2020-2021 season, were composed by women – a total of 5%.'[1] Furthermore, 'only 1.11% of the pieces were composed by Black & Asian women and only 2.43% by Black & Asian men.'[2]

Panlasigui's 2021 research on professional German orchestras (*Berufsorchestern*) found that in the 2019/2020 performance season, only thirty-six female composers were performed, making up just 1.9 percent of works overall, with sixty percent of orchestras programming no works by women whatsoever.[3] Among contemporary music concert

---

1   Gabriella Di Laccio and others, *Equality and Diversity in Concert Halls* (DONNE: Women in Music, 2021), p. 3.
2   Ibid.
3   Melissa Panlasigui, *Women in High-Visibility Roles in German Berufsorchester* (Munich: musica femina münchen and Archiv Frau und Musik Sonderveröffentlichung), p. 11.

series, only thirteen percent of works were by women.[4] In institutions for contemporary classical music (*Neue Musik*, a classical music subgenre), research conducted in 2016 by Ashley Fure on the Darmstadt Summer Course archive found that ninety-three percent of compositions performed at the event between 1946 and 2014 were by men.[5] Statistics made by Gender Relations in New Music reported similar situations at other German contemporary classical music festivals: at the MaerzMusik festival in Berlin, from 2010 to 2018, just twenty-eight percent of pieces were by women, transmasculine or non-binary people, while at the Donaueschingen Musiktage between 2011 and 2017, this was only eighteen percent.[6]

The Danish Composers' Society's 2019 repertoire statistics report examined music played by symphony orchestras, opera houses, ensembles, and music festivals in Denmark in the 2015/16, 2017/18, and 2018/19 seasons. It found that, measured in minutes, 99.9 percent of the music that had been performed overall was composed by men. When limited to music composed after 1985, the figure was eighty-six percent.[7] A recent follow-up examining the period between 2020-2022 added categories for non-binary composers as well as collective compositions, and showed a small but significant improvement, with 9.5 percent of works performed by women, 0.12 percent by non-binary composers, and 2.22 percent by collectives.[8]

Two reports by Sweden's KVAST in collaboration with the Swedish composer's society FST (in 2015 and 2019) also examined the gender breakdown of repertoire statistics. The 2019 report found that across all music institutions in Sweden between 2016-2019, only 6.32 percent of

---

4   Ibid., pp. 14-15.
5   Ashley Fure, 'GRID: Gender Research in Darmstadt A 2016 HISTORAGE Project Funded by the Goethe Institute' (2016), https://griddarmstadt.files.wordpress.com/2016/08/grid_gender_research_in_darmstadt.pdf
6   Gender Relations in New Music, 'Donaueschinger Musiktage Statistics' (2017), http://grinm.org/20171020%20-%20Donaueschinger%20Musiktage%20Statistics%20GRiNM.pdf
7   Andreas Hastrup and Sine Tofte Hannibal, *Repertoirestatistik for danske symphoniorkestre, operaer, ensembler og musikfestivaler* (Dansk Komponistforening, 2018), p. 14.
8   Michelle Demant and Sine Tofte Hannibal, *Repertoirestatistik for danske symphoniorkestre, operaer, ensembler og musikfestivaler* (Dansk Komponistforening, 2023), p. 7.

works played were by women.⁹ According to Norway's Balensekunst, 'only 2 percent of the music played by Norwegian orchestras is written by women'.¹⁰

Finally, George Lewis has observed that until 2020, the prominent Donaueschinger Musiktage festival for new music in southern Germany had not programmed a single Black composer.¹¹ He has also pointed to what he calls the suspicious absence of Afrodiasporic composers in histories of twentieth-century modernism, a view that has led him to compile playlists of long-ignored music by these composers.¹² Agawu has also recently argued that scholarly work on African music tends to ignore art music on the continent, though he has not taken a statistical approach to do so.¹³

Looking at working conditions in classical music, Christina Scharff has examined the professional inequalities present in UK and German classical music, highlighting that 'the subjectivities required to work and succeed in the classical music profession are gendered, classed, and racialised.'¹⁴ She has compiled studies showing underrepresentation and pay gaps for women, BAME, and working-class musicians active in the field.¹⁵

Scharff also highlights gender and racial inequalities in UK music education, showing classical music education in the UK as being mainly for middle-class people and conservatoires as having

---

9   Swedish Association of Women Composers (Kvinnlig Anhopning av Svenska Tonsättare – KVAST); Swedish Society of Composers (Föreningen Svenska Tonsättare); Martin Jonsson Tibblin and others, (Föreningen Svenska Tonsättare and Kvinnling anhopning av svenska tonsättare, 2019), p. 14.
10 Balansekunst, 'What does Norwegian cultural life look like?,' https://www.balansekunstprosjektet.no/statistics
11 Kendall, Harald Kisiedu, and George Lewis, 'There are Black Composers in the Future,' in *Dynamic Traditions: A Text Collection on Behalf of Donaueschingen Global*, ed. by Elisa Erkelenz, Katja Heldt (Donaueschingen: Südwestrundfunk, 2021), pp. 143-157 (p. 143).
12 George Lewis, *African American Music after 1960*, 2018, mixed media installation, Darmstadt Summer Course (Schader-Forum), *Darmstadt*.
13 Kofi Agawu, 'African Art Music and the Challenge of Postcolonial Composition,' in *Dynamic Traditions: Global Perspectives on Contemporary Music, A Text Collection on Behalf of Donaueschingen Global*, ed. by Elisa Erkelenz, Katja Heldt (Donaueschingen: Südwestrundfunk), pp. 179-187 (p. 180).
14 Christina Scharff, *Gender, Subjectivity, and Cultural Work: The Classical Music Profession* (London: Routledge), p. 23-24.
15 Ibid., pp. 43, 50-57.

significant underrepresentation of BAME people on staff.¹⁶ A study of two Swiss music schools from 2016 showed how class-based exclusions were produced, as well as how the concept of diversity was understood only as equal opportunity within already-universalised categories, namely the specific technical virtuosity of (re)producing an uncritically reproduced white Eurocentric canon.¹⁷ In her 2019 book on music education in the UK, Bull argues that this kind of boundary-drawing and exclusivity is actively fostered in music education to preserve middle-class spaces, while the discourse of classical music's autonomy is used as a way of camouflaging this exclusivity behind musical rationalisations and classical music's narrative of excellence.¹⁸

When taken together, these statistics demonstrate that classical music is shockingly misaligned with notions of gender equality and the inclusion of minorities across its various institutions and in many different national contexts. The growing body of statistical work on this topic will continue to produce a clearer picture of this situation. Its increasing prevalence also means that future studies can build on existing work and focus on producing higher-quality data, as well as put its methodologies and results in dialogue with existing international counterparts. Lastly, the existence of this work will also make it easier to make the argument that statistics are an important tool for making inequalities visible.¹⁹

There remains, however, the question of how classical music should respond and move forward in light of these disparities of gender, race/ethnicity, and class. With the rest of this chapter, I want to sketch out an outline of what such a response could look like. In order to do this, I will first explore some of what I see as the key resistances to diversification reforms that exist in the classical music discourse.

---

16   Ibid., pp. 45-48.
17   Philippe Saner, Sophie Vögele, Pauline Vessely, *Schlussbericht Art.School.Differences: Researching inequalities and Normativities in the Field of Higher Art Education* (Zurich: Zurich University of the Arts, 2016), pp. 290-301.
18   Anna Bull, *Class, Control, and Classical Music* (Oxford: Oxford University Press, 2019), pp. 5-6.
19   Christina Scharff, *Gender, Subjectivity, and Cultural Work*, p. 42.

The Myth of Meritocracy

The first resistance that must be addressed is classical music's *myth of meritocracy*. This myth stems from some key beliefs that are deeply ingrained in classical music education and professional life. The most fundamental of these is the belief that classical music is ultimately a meritocratic system where everyone gets a chance to participate, but where the best musicians are rewarded for their skill and talent by rising to the top. Underpinning this is the belief that classical music is based on values of artistic excellence, and that achieving a high quality of musical production is the pinnacle of achievement. Removing any and all obstacles standing in the way of creating high-quality music is seen as the focus of much professional musical activity, from specialised education and rigorous auditioning requirements to reminding patrons to turn off their cell phones before a concert.

To suggest that creating high-quality music should not be the number one priority, or that additional, 'extra-musical' factors, as they are called, must also be taken into account, is seen as the ultimate betrayal of the classical music tradition. It is viewed as an affront to all the practice, hard work, money and sacrifice that has been invested in the pursuit of high-quality musical creation. Interventions in this system, for example through programming quotas, or blind-audition recruiting in orchestras, is viewed as potentially endangering the high-quality end product that elite orchestras strive for, a risk that, when put in these terms, simply cannot be tolerated by these organisations.

In short, resistance to change comes in the first instance from a framing of the debate as being about *diversity vs. high quality*, a false dichotomy that goes to the heart of classical music's self-understanding. To tackle the issue, we need to look at how classical music has come to focus on a specific definition of quality, one that is limiting, outmoded, and a central obstacle to change. Looking at its dictionary definitions, there are two: the first is 'the standard or nature of something as measured against other things of a *similar kind*'.[20] This is how quality is understood in classical music: there exists the notion of a clearly defined scale upon which music can be ranked using a standardised set of categories.

---

20 Emphasis mine. 'Quality,' in The Oxford English Dictionary [online], https://www.oed.com/view/Entry/155878?rskey=6PUTFJ&result=1&isAdvanced=false

This is seen for instance in the concept of *Werktreue*, where aspiring to achieve a musical result that is as close to the composer's intentions as possible creates an asymptotic but generally standardised set of ways to understand musical production.

The second definition of quality is 'an attribute, property; a special feature or characteristic'.[21] According to this second definition, quality no longer refers to a position on a predefined scale; rather it is a unique characteristic that is incomparable with anything else, at least along a clearly-delineated range. Whether banal or life-changing, such a quality is characterised by its singularity.

Classical music as a musical tradition focusing on notions of excellence lays prodigious value on the maintaining of a standardised framework by which high or low quality can be measured. Wrong notes, 'bad' style and unfaithful interpretations are therefore all foundational to classical music's self-understanding and the subject of meticulous discussion, justification and correction. This framework is constituted through its elaborate system of established tests that inculcate what these rights and wrongs are. Among performing musicians, these include tests to progress in music school, such as fluent knowledge of scales, arpeggios and a preselected musical repertoire, as well as determining orchestral hiring through auditions of orchestral excerpts and selected solo repertoire. Similar challenges face aspiring composers, though with the challenge of having both to succeed within the established system as well as write works that 'correctly' transgress its rules.

Another means through which classical music undermines an understanding of quality as singular and unique is through the work-concept and the musical canon. Goehr argues that the work-concept is the ideal (as opposed to prerequisite) of musical practice, which performance must try its best (but never fully be able) to live up to.[22] The canon, singular, is the policing of the historical and stylistic boundaries where this system is in effect.[23] Thus, the statistics above

---

21 Ibid.
22 Lydia Goehr, *The imaginary museum of musical works: an essay in the philosophy of music* (Oxford: Oxford University Press) p. 99ff.
23 On the stabilisation of the canon as a kind of 'musical museum', see Kirby's account of the attempts to exhibit music as part of 19th century international exhibitions for a very literal example of this stabilisation. Sarah Kirby, "'A mystery, and viewless / Even when present:" Exhibiting Music at International Exhibitions

create discomfort because they confront classical music with facts that force it to acknowledge that its definition of 'high quality' is not universal. It points out that classical music's meritocratic system clearly does not give equal opportunities to everyone and, perhaps even worse, that *addressing* such statistics to make the genre more equal might entail adapting the emphasis on high quality, or revisiting classical music's self-image as universal all together.

What makes doing this so difficult is the persistent belief in the universality of classical music itself: that it is somehow able to transcend the social context in which it is produced and exist as something beautiful for people of all different cultures around the world. This belief is maintained by de-emphasising the realities of working in and producing classical music. These are swept under the rug and are meant to fade into the background as the listener focuses on pure, acousmatic sound as detached as possible from any physical source.

Since how it is created is of secondary importance as long as it is of 'high quality', classical music erases the fact that success is gendered, raced, and classed, and then denies that this erasure has taken place, holding up the meritocratic values it promotes as universal and valid within any and all contexts. This is seen in the old joke where someone asks for directions to Carnegie Hall, and is told to 'practise, practise, practise'.

When these specific circumstances are taken to be natural and universal, then any argument about how they are situated, specific and trained, as well as how the conditions for success are tailored to white, middle-class European cis males, is construed as an attack on the core belief in the universality of classical music. This is the source of the fundamental resistance to addressing these statistics.

Corrective vs. Radical Changes

Despite the challenges just outlined of addressing social issues in a field focused on ignoring them, there have been many recent attempts to address gender and diversity issues in classical music, including increasing calls for gender-equal programmes in many countries, or,

---

in Nineteenth-Century Britain,' in *Institutionalization in Music History*, ed. by Saijaleena Rantamen and Derek B. Scott (Helsinki: DocMus Research Publications 19), pp. 107-126.

in the wake of the Black Lives Matter protests in the summer of 2020, orchestras trying to find ways, as Mitchener has put it, 'to present work that reflects the rich and varied musical voices in classical music today'.[24]

Now that the problem of the belief in the universality of classical music has been discussed, the second kind of response to statistics on the lack of diversity in classical music can be explored, namely attempts at changing and reforming the system. These responses can be broken down into two general approaches, *corrective* efforts and *radical* ones, borrowing from the terminology of Boltanski and Chiapello, who develop a theory of critique and its relationship to capitalism. While their categories could generally be applicable to many concepts, classical music's intertwinement with processes of capitalist extraction make the comparison all the more fitting.[25]

Corrective critiques are those that accept the underlying premise of the system, but demand reform because tests of the system's legitimacy are seen as imperfect or still unjust. This could, for example, involve measures such as enacting quotas to increase the number of female composers that are programmed in a given year and country, or changing aspects of how conservatory or orchestral tests are done in order to include more women and minorities in the sector. Such measures do not call into question the underlying notion of high quality; they only seek to adapt how that existing measure is achieved through concessions meant to increase the fairness of the current system.[26]

Radical critiques, also called revolutionary critiques, are by contrast those that call the fundamental principles of the system into question, here classical music and its normative canon, culture and performance practices.[27] A radical critique would address classical music's focus on high quality as a primary source of resistance by proposing to replace this paradigm with one focused on relativising classical music as one

---

24 Elaine Mitchener, 'How to Remove Earwax,' in *Dynamic Traditions: Global Perspectives on Contemporary Music, A Text Collection on Behalf of Donaueschingen Global*, ed. by Elisa Erkelenz, Katja Heldt (Donaueschingen: Südwestrundfunk), pp. 169-178 (p. 171).
25 Christina Scharff, *Gender, Subjectivity, and Cultural Work*; Marianna Ritchey, *Composing Capital: Classical Music in the Neoliberal Era* (Chicago: Chicago University Press).
26 Luc Boltanski and Ève Chiapello, *The New Spirit of Capitalism*, trans. Gregory Elliott (London: Verso), pp. 32-33.
27 Ibid.

musical tradition among many, and one whose notion of high quality can be better understood as a 'distinctive attribute' of this tradition, rather than a universal truth.

For Boltanski and Chiapello and their project of understanding critique in relationship to capitalism, what cuts across both approaches is that critique has accompanied the history of capitalism like a shadow.[28] They explore how adept capitalism has been at addressing and integrating critiques of its functioning into itself, arguing that this ability to adapt is why capitalism has succeeded in remaining a dominant force in our lives. Continuing the extended comparison between capitalism and classical music, criticism can be recontextualised as an act of support, and an expression of a will for classical music to continue in some form into the future. For this to happen, it must adequately address its critiques and integrate them into its functioning if it is to survive. Against this backdrop, I will present the case for both corrective and radical critiques. While corrective critiques are important in raising the issue of diversity within classical music, I argue that only a radical change presents a coherent way of responding to classical music's 'statistics problem,' but that this can be achieved while preserving much of what remains important to people who love and identify with this musical genre, and even reveal the works of many fascinating composers from around the globe and throughout history.

Critiquing Classical Music

As mentioned in Chapter 3, the Keychange Initiative began in 2015 in the popular music sector as an attempt to address gender equality problems in that sector by having organisations pledge to have 50:50 gender-equal programming by 2022. Since its founding, the number of organisations that have taken the Keychange pledge has rapidly grown to over 500, and the initiative's demands have accordingly become more differentiated. Their manifesto now makes a series of broad recommendations to the music industry, national governments, the European Parliament and the European Commission about how to systemically tackle gender equality by addressing working conditions for women in the music industry, investing in their empowerment, doing research to better understand

---

28 Boltanski and Chiapello, p. 36.

the nature of the problem, and educating their workforce about how to make the industry gender equal.[29]

While the initiative started with popular music festivals, its rapid growth has also attracted classical music institutions to take its pledge and join in its lobbying efforts. According to its website, the initiative now claims thirty-seven concert halls, eight conservatoires and thirty orchestras and ensembles as signatories, including major institutions like the Royal Philharmonic Orchestra, the Melbourne Symphony, and the Iceland Symphony Orchestra.[30]

Examining Keychange's manifesto, it is a clear example of a corrective, reformist approach to classical music. In addition to its central focus on a 50:50 gender balance within concert programmes, it recommends reforms that do not call into question the underlying legitimacy of the classical music system, suggesting, for instance, changes to the testing process: 'anonymise recruitment processes e.g. blind auditions in the classical sector, removal of gender/name information on job applications'.[31]

The reformist approach taken by Keychange is a form of popular feminism as defined by Banet-Weiser, especially when its size in the music sector is considered. Barnet-Weiser identifies three characteristics of popular feminism, defining it 'as media visibility and accessibility, as popularity, and as a struggle for meaning'.[32] Keychange is a coalition of 500 signatories in the music sector, run by the UK's PRS Foundation and supported by an EU Creative Europe grant, all representing a high degree of media visibility due to the institutions' influential role in the media industry, as well as popular support among a large group of people. Finally, in its core goal of gender equality, as well as its programmes empowering minority musicians, Keychange aligns with the struggle for visibility as a priority of this definition of popular feminism.[33]

---

29 PRS Foundation, *Keychange Manifestio: Recommendations for a Gender Balanced Music Industry* (London: PRS Foundation, n.d.), p. 6, https://www.keychange.eu/s/1052-keychange-A5-v15-web.pdf
30 Keychange, *Music Organizations*, https://www.keychange.eu/directory/music-organisations
31 PRS Foundation, p. 6.
32 Sarah Banet-Weiser, *Empowered: Popular Feminism and Popular Mysogyny* (Durham: Duke University Press, 2018), p. 6.
33 Ibid., p. 1.

Banet-Weiser argues that the problem with reformist critiques such as this one is that this form of empowerment is often based on a bare politics of visibility that does not challenge deeper inequities, nor offer a critique of the neoliberal thinking that produced the problems in the first place, contrary to classical liberal feminism.[34] The reformist critique addresses second-order effects and makes them instead into its primary concern. As she writes,

> Political categories such as race and gender have transformed their very logics from the inside out, so that the visibility of these categories is what matters, rather than the structural ground on and through which they are constructed.[35]

Looking at classical music and the example of participation in Keychange through the lens of this critique, we can see that further work to understand the nature of the problem and to educate people about it, or to adapt tests and working conditions for minority artists, are all measures that can take place without fundamentally addressing classical music's normative categories for success, or its fixation on high quality. The focus is instead on lowering barriers to entry to an existing labour market and thus increasing competition (and by extension raising the level of quality), or otherwise, as Banet-Weiser suggests, making categories such as race or gender into easily marketable visibilities for advertising departments. This illustrates how such a corrective critique is able both to demand reform, but still maintain support for the underlying system.

Due to the failure of this approach to address the fundamental causes of classical music's diversity problem, it should not be seen as an adequate response to the statistics that opened this chapter. As Charton has argued in relation to contemporary classical music (CCM), the work that must be done is rather to 'reflect on what is an unmarked default and what is a marked other in [CCM's] inherited infrastructures and institutions'.[36] In the best case, this more fundamental category work can avoid turning diversity initiatives into simple exercises in shifting visibilities that do not question underlying power structures. Instead,

---

34 Banet-Weiser, pp. 11-12.
35 Ibid., p. 23.
36 Anke Charton, 'Diversity and New Music: Interdependencies and Intersections,' *OnCurating*, 47 (2020), pp. 5-15 (p. 11).

such reflection on defaults can bring awareness to the historical and situated reasons for assumptions, and open the door to these being changed.

Despite these shortcomings, it is crucially important to acknowledge the importance of the work of Keychange, and of similar organisations engaged in awareness-raising and change. Activist work such as theirs, as well as that of creating statistics to quantify the dimensions of the problem, brings awareness and change to the lives of many who have been excluded from various forms of participation in classical music. Such activities also apply pressure and shift conversations happening among classical music's decision-makers. It would therefore be naïve to argue for some kind of idealised radical alternative to the real-world reformist example of Keychange.

Instead, I argue that diversity statistics and pledge initiatives are important tools that can form part of a radical critique of classical music provided they are properly framed. Rather than thinking about them as small correctives to restore the perfection of an otherwise unproblematic system, they must be understood as part of *ongoing* initiatives to situate classical music in relation to the social processes that maintain and underpin it, and that also underpin its musical neighbours entertaining audiences in other genres. Instead of continuing to chase a problematic notion of purity through superficial reforms, this reframes the debate on tracing the myriad ways that classical music has historically asserted its position as a universal music, erased the labour involved in producing and maintaining it, as well as demeaned the other musics of the world with which it co-exists, while continuing to extract ideas and inspiration from them.

Confounding Categories

To illustrate how statistical work can be part of a process of radical change, I will briefly discuss a data-harvesting workshop I organised as part of the activist group Gender Relations in New Music (GRiNM) in 2018 at the MaerzMusik festival in Berlin. The goal of the workshop was to produce data on the number of female and non-cis-male composers programmed at the MaerzMusik festival, the results of which have been included as part of the opening of this chapter.

The collective produced these statistics through crowdsourcing, inviting festival attendees to sit together with their laptops and go through old festival programmes together, entering data on a shared Google Sheet. The workshop thus produced a numerical percentage that was used to express inequality within a larger societal context focused on the language of statistics as 'the default code for being a serious person.'[37]

But in addition to making the very blatant inequalities in this field visible and sayable, providing quantifiable evidence of the problem in order for it to be taken seriously (which was not the case in 2018), there was great significance in *doing* these statistics collectively as an embodied and group practice. The data-harvesting activities gave a straightforward, informal, monotonously boring goal that led to people chatting, getting to know each other, and expressing their frustration as they entered row after row of male names over the years of the festival's existence.

Discussions speculating about root causes gave way to inevitable questions of categorisation such as assuming gender based on names, how to deal with composer/performers, collective compositions, or other non-standard or murky categories. These in turn led to equally productive discussions about the challenges of categorisation, intersectionality, and the nuance and complexity associated with achieving equal representation under real-world conditions. In many cases we were able to rely on the community's collective pool of knowledge about festival artists' self-identification to fill in (in terms of both gender identity and the spectrum between composing and performing). In others, we used the close collaborative situation to decide together on rules of thumb to apply consistently across the dataset.

The data unsurprisingly showed the severe lack of women and non-binary people in festival programmes in earlier years, but also that as the MaerzMusik festival (in part I believe thanks to earlier actions by GRiNM) made its programming more diverse and included different kinds of people and concert formats, the categories and tables we began with (female/non-binary/male composer) became less relevant,

---

37 Ben Davis, 'How We Ended Up in the Era of "Quantitative Aesthetics," Where Data Points Dictate Taste', *Artnet News*, 30 March 2023, https://news.artnet.com/opinion/quantitative-aesthetics-2276351

or otherwise no longer adequately reflected how the festival was programming music.

With this example in mind, the distinction between a reformist and radical critique could be connected to how we approach statistics about classical music's diversity problem. In a reformist approach, statistics are supposed to gradually change until they reflect the intended target that has been set out, as in the management adage 'what gets measured gets done', where deeper inequalities are allowed to go unmarked. However, in a radical approach, statistics could become the site for examining what is measured (and what is not), but also as the beginning of a collective conversation on how, together, we can confound existing categories, create new ones, and redefine the paradigms within which we operate.

Conclusion

Creating statistics about classical music's omissions will not be an immediate fix for its structural problems, as these are deeply rooted in beliefs about high musical quality and excellence. Statistics can however spark debates about classical music's exclusions, as well as demonstrate that the numerous in- and ex-clusions of the musical genre are the result of continually reaffirmed collective choices, not due to external, objective or material reasons that can be fixed through superficial reforms. But because of their ability to make visible the results of complex social patterns, statistics can be used as the beginning of a radical critique. Such a critique might begin with this making visible through numbers and charts, but must be carried out through collective dialogue and debate in order to address the underlying structures of inequality, rather than through a superficial politics of visibility that sidesteps engagement with underlying structural issues. What any such investigation of classical music would reveal is the thick web of entanglements with infrastructures that sustain and reproduce it. These connections are to individual people, but also to scores, instruments, conservatoires, events, concert halls, recordings, streaming music and to all the other ways in which 'the music itself' circulates.

Divestment from classical music's universalism is not a speech act or a pledge, it is a change in perception, one that involves no longer subordinating the role of contexts and infrastructures in producing music that claims to transcend them. Diving into interconnections, telling their stories, even simply investigating the ways in which classical music interacts (in the past, present, and future) with history, politics, or current affairs is how the deep inequities classical music has produced can be challenged. One such investigation could be into the globalised composition and distribution of art music since the twentieth century, or into art music in Africa, as mentioned in the introduction.[38] Another could be through critical explorations of classical music's role in colonisation, presenting artists who participated in the resistance to such processes but who have since fallen into obscurity, such as Ladislao Bonus' composition of the first Tagalog opera, intertwined with Filipino nation-building, or explorations of the specificities of Iberian (musical) colonialism and their appropriations by South American composers over the centuries.[39]

Doing so will reveal the many minorities that work in classical music today, and who have been central to the field historically, but whose stories are ignored or forgotten, as well as open up rich new possibilities for classical music programming and education. Such a shift would fundamentally transform many of the categories and statistics that opened this chapter, but would become the occasion for new statistics, new problems that must urgently be addressed, that must again be reconsidered by the entire community, and which will in turn lead to its transformation.

---

38 Utz, Christian, *Musical Composition in the Context of Globalization: New Perspectives on Music History in the 20th and 21st Century* (Bielefeld: transcript, 2021); Agawu, Kofi, 'African Art Music and the Challenge of Postcolonial Composition,' in *Dynamic Traditions: Global Perspectives on Contemporary Music, A Text Collection on Behalf of Donaueschingen Global*, ed. by Elisa Erkelenz, Katja Heldt (Donaueschingen: Südwestrundfunk, 2021), pp. 179-187.

39 yamomo, meLê, *Theatre and Music in Manila and the Asia Pacific, 1869-1946: Sounding Modernities* (Cham: Palgrave Macmillan, 2018); Illari, Bernardo, 'Music to Empower the Colonized Self: Reverse Assimilation in South America (to 1920)', unpublished paper delivered at the conference 'Music's institution and the (de) colonial' (Lund University, 4-5 May 2023), https://portal.research.lu.se/en/activities/musics-institution-and-the-decolonial

References

Agawu, Kofi, 'African Art Music and the Challenge of Postcolonial Composition,' in *Dynamic Traditions: Global Perspectives on Contemporary Music, A Text Collection on Behalf of Donaueschingen Global*, ed. by Elisa Erkelenz, Katja Heldt (Donaueschingen: Südwestrundfunk, 2021), pp. 179-187.

Balansekunst, 'What does Norwegian cultural life look like?,' https://www.balansekunstprosjektet.no/statistics

Banet-Weiser, Sarah, *Empowered: Popular Feminism and Popular Mysogyny* (Durham: Duke University Press, 2018).

Boltanski, Luc, and Ève Chiapello, *The New Spirit of Capitalism*, trans. Gregory Elliott (London: Verso, 2005).

Bull, Anna, *Class, Control, and Classical Music* (Oxford: Oxford University Press, 2019), https://doi.org/10.1093/oso/9780190844356.001.0001

Charton, Anke, 'Diversity and New Music: Interdependencies and Intersections,' *OnCurating*, 47 (2020), 5-15.

Davis, Ben, 'How We Ended Up in the Era of "Quantitative Aesthetics," Where Data Points Dictate Taste', *Artnet News*, 30 March 2023, https://news.artnet.com/opinion/quantitative-aesthetics-2276351

Demant, Michelle and Sine Tofte Hannibal, *Repertoirestatistik for danske symphoniorkestre, operaer, ensembler og musikfestivaler* (Dansk Komponistforening, 2013).

Di Laccio, Gabriella and others, *Equality and Diversity in Concert Halls* (DONNE: Women in Music, 2021), https://donne-uk.org/wp-content/uploads/2021/03/Equality-Diversity-in-Concert-Halls_2020_2021.pdf

Fure, Ashley, 'GRID: Gender Research in Darmstadt A 2016 HISTORAGE Project Funded by the Goethe Institute' (2016), https://griddarmstadt.files.wordpress.com/2016/08/grid_gender_research_in_darmstadt.pdf

Gender Relations in New Music, 'Donaueschinger Musiktage Statistics' (2017), http://grinm.org/20171020%20-%20Donaueschinger%20Musiktage%20Statistics%20GRiNM.pdf

Hastrup, Andreas and Sine Tofte Hannibal, *Repertoirestatistik for danske symphoniorkestre, operaer, ensembler og musikfestivaler* (Dansk Komponistforening, 2018).

Illari, Bernardo, 'Music to Empower the Colonized Self: Reverse Assimilation in South America (to 1920)', unpublished paper delivered at the conference 'Music's institution and the (de)colonial' (Lund University, 4-5 May 2023), https://portal.research.lu.se/en/activities/musics-institution-and-the-decolonial

Kendall, Hanna, Harald Kisiedu, and George Lewis, 'There are Black Composers in the Future,' in *Dynamic Traditions: A Text Collection on Behalf of Donaueschingen Global*, ed. by Elisa Erkelenz, Katja Heldt (Donaueschingen: Südwestrundfunk, 2021), pp. 143-157.

Keychange, *Music Organizations*, https://www.keychange.eu/directory/music-organisations

Lewis, George, *African American Music after 1960*, 2018, mixed media installation, Darmstadt Summer Course (Schader-Forum), Darmstadt.

Mitchener, Elaine, 'How to Remove Earwax,' in *Dynamic Traditions: Global Perspectives on Contemporary Music, A Text Collection on Behalf of Donaueschingen Global*, ed. by Elisa Erkelenz, Katja Heldt (Donaueschingen: Südwestrundfunk), pp. 169-178.

Panlasigui, Melissa, *Women in High-Visibility Roles in German Berufsorchester* (Munich: musica femina münchen and Archiv Frau und Musik Sonderveröffentlichung, 2021).

PRS Foundation, *Keychange Manifestio: Recommendations for a Gender Balanced Music Industry* (London: PRS Foundation, n.d.), https://www.keychange.eu/s/1052-keychange-A5-v15-web.pdf

'Quality,' in The Oxford English Dictionary, https://www.oed.com/view/Entry/155878?rskey=6PUTFJ&result=1&isAdvanced=false

Saner, Philippe, Sophie Vögele, Pauline Vessely, *Schlussbericht Art.School. Differences: Researching Inequalities and Normativities in the Field of Higher Art Education* (Zurich: Zurich University of the Arts, 2016).

Scharff, Christina, *Gender, Subjectivity, and Cultural Work* (London: Routledge, 2018).

Ritchey, Marianna, *Composing Capital: Classical Music in the Neoliberal Era* (Chicago: Chicago University Press, 2019).

Utz, Christian, *Musical Composition in the Context of Globalization: New Perspectives on Music History in the 20th and 21st Century* (Bielefeld: transcript, 2021), https://doi.org/10.14361/9783839450956

yamomo, meLê, *Theatre and Music in Manila and the Asia Pacific, 1869-1946: Sounding Modernities* (Cham: Palgrave Macmillan, 2018), https://doi.org/10.1007/978-3-319-69176-3

3. Roundtable 2: Documenting Change: The Role of Best-Practice Guidelines

Neil Thomas Smith (MCICM) with contributions from Hannah Bujic (Sound and Music), Francine Gorman (Keychange), and Fiona Robertson (Sound)

Visions for the future of classical music usually contain an implicit critique of the present. Getting from 'here' to 'there' requires a process of change, yet starting to change a practice with such seemingly well-worn grooves of activity can seem an insurmountable challenge.

This chapter considers three recent sets of best-practice guidelines that address urgent areas requiring change within the UK classical music sector and beyond: the way that organisations work with composers; the representation of women at all levels of the music industry; and the way organisations work with neurodiverse artists and participants. Each document seeks to crystallise practical steps that organisations can take to begin bringing about change in these areas. At the same time, the documents themselves become vital parts of the efforts to make change happen. The authors describe both the contents and the goals of their documents, as well as the way in which they were created. The aim is to provide a practical insight for people who may wish to create or use such guidelines, but also to critically assess the role of such documents in processes of change. Guidelines are a useful tool for considering what it takes for real change to embed in a practice, as well as the challenges and barriers that exist.

The chapter begins with a summary of each document and the process of its creation. Hannah Bujic from the national new music charity in the UK, Sound and Music, discusses the creation of their Fair Access Principles, which outline practical steps towards dismantling barriers that composers face when accessing opportunities for performances and professional development. Francine Gorman from Keychange – an organisation promoting better gender representation within all music sectors – describes the evolution of the organisation and their pledge and manifesto, which are used to help initiatives of all kinds work towards more equal representation in their activities. Finally, Fiona Robertson from the new-music incubator, Sound, based in North-East Scotland, discusses the process of creating 'What we need to thrive: working with neurodiverse composers', which illuminates the sometimes surprising facets of participants' experiences that promoters must consider to make their work open to autistic artists.

The chapter ends with a brief discussion of these documents with all four authors, highlighting their benefits and limitations, as well as the requirements for long-term change to really take place. Though the documents explored here have specific aims in particular sectors, much of the process of engaging with stakeholders and promoting the findings is easily transferrable to radically different contexts, while the recommendations that came out of their creation are often highly relevant for other parts of the music industry, and other sectors entirely. What emerges as a theme is that these documents are never the end of a process. Rather, for their effect to spread within the sector, consistent work is required to talk with stakeholders to keep the recommendations relevant.

At the same time, it is clear that all three find such documents are extremely useful tools to help people take first steps to address what can feel like overwhelming, systemic issues. In the concluding discussion the authors stress the importance of offering a positive vision of change, one that others can engage with and get behind. This relates to an important theme in this volume regarding change within and outwith the systems and organisations in which we find ourselves. This is picked up further in the reflection on this chapter by Antonio Cuyler, whose work on blacktivism amongst opera administrators is the basis for considering the issues raised below.

1. The Fair Access Principles

Hannah Bujic

Traditional approaches to talent development within the music industry have relied on an assumption of equity, that open call processes are, by their nature, open to all, and therefore theoretically should achieve equality: that it is the best music, the best applicant, who will be offered a potentially career-changing opportunity. However, when we look at progress in terms of how representative the music industry is – across gender, ethnicity, socio-economic background and disability – there is still a fundamental problem. The point in the pipeline where artists are accessing talent development opportunities often excludes those who face other barriers in their work and practice. This can be due to application and selection processes, financial barriers, or inflexibility in what is on offer, meaning those with particular needs cannot access an opportunity.

The new-music charity Sound and Music has been capturing evidence of these inequalities for many years through data from equal opportunities monitoring of applicants to our programmes and those who are selected. In the 2018-19 financial year, thirty-four percent of applicants to our programmes were women, and nine percent disabled. For selected applicants, those figures were forty percent and five percent—which for gender diversity was still short of our target of fifty percent, and very poor for disability given that the percentage of working-age adults identifying as disabled is nineteen percent.[1] We also had anecdotal evidence from composers within our networks that barriers were consistently preventing them from applying to opportunities across the industry. We started work on a set of best-practice guidelines, to act as a manifesto for change. This became the Fair Access Principles, which launched in February 2020 with a group of six partners from across the UK (including Sound, who have also contributed to the present chapter).[2]

---

1 Office of National Statistics, UK, *Family Resources Survey, Financial Year 2019 to 2020*, https://www.gov.uk/government/statistics/family-resources-survey-financial-year-2019-to-2020/family-resources-survey-financial-year-2019-to-2020

2 Sound and Music Website, 'Fair Access Principles', https://soundandmusic.org/our-impact/fair-access-principles

The first step in this process was pooling our collective knowledge within the organisation with brainstorming sessions. This relied on our experience of running artist development programmes including the experimental Pathways programme (2016; open to disabled composers and composers from minority ethnic backgrounds), and New Voices (2018 onwards; open to any composers). Managing application and selection processes for a large number of composer calls across many years had given us a wealth of insight into common barriers, such as caring responsibilities, work commitments and difficulties with written applications. We had been progressively working to break many of these down, for instance ensuring we brought inclusive, fresh perspectives into selection panels by rotating external panellists.

It was important to us that we did not produce the Fair Access Principles in isolation, that this was a collaborative process both internally and externally. Externally we began a consultation process with partners and composers, to ask advice and further explore the need for a set of best-practice guidelines. From this external consultation, we quickly gathered a list of common 'dos and don'ts' for artist development programmes. We used an iterative approach of asking for feedback on draft sets of guidelines, including via Composer Advisory Group meetings,[3] constantly refining and improving the material. A key principle of our approach was taken from the way we had already started to publicly share our equal opportunities monitoring data, presenting it not because we have all the answers as an organisation but because we want to start conversations and enable change.

Our goal was to produce something streamlined, memorable and powerful. A long and impenetrable set of guidelines would be counterproductive, so we worked to build a set of concise principles. It was also important to us that, as far as possible, they were framed positively – so turning 'don'ts' into 'dos' to reinforce the positive actions they contained. Themes emerged that helped us to streamline the Fair Access Principles into key headings: Application, Selection, Money and Conversation. Talking with composers, we realised how regularly these barriers were encountered, though we were certain that the vast majority

---

3   The Composer Advisory Group includes a diverse range of composers who inform the work of the charity.

were in place unintentionally and that the problems were caused by lack of knowledge rather than intentionally excluding composers.

One of the principles which continues to prove most challenging to explain is 'do not use anonymised selection' (interestingly our only 'negative' principle). In recruitment and some areas of the music sector, such as orchestral auditions, anonymised selection is considered best practice, with evidence to back up its effectiveness in removing barriers for under-represented groups. In talent development however, where what is being assessed is as much (or even more) about potential as what someone has already achieved, having the full picture of an applicant's background and any challenging circumstances makes for a fairer process. The playing field for composers is not level in terms of access to opportunities, but anonymised selection assumes that it is.

The Fair Access Principles launched in February 2020 with a group of six launch partners: Drake Music Scotland, Opera North Projects, Sage Gateshead, Sound Festival, Tŷ Cerdd-Music Centre Wales and Unlimited. We also received endorsement from the Performing Rights Society for Music Foundation.[4] The launch was in the form of a press release and social media campaign with new video content released over a number of weeks, including short interviews with composers talking about the importance of the Fair Access Principles to them. It was important to us that we had partners on board at the point of launching, to give weight to the principles as well as national reach across England, Scotland and Wales. Our primary audience was other organisations and gatekeepers of talent development opportunities, with a secondary audience of composers in order to raise awareness of Fair Access as a 'kitemark'. Organisations who sign up to the network can display the Fair Access logo on their websites, which acts as a public statement of their commitment to removing barriers to participation in their programmes.

The commitment we ask from organisations who sign up is that within two years they adhere to all of the principles, and in addition that they contribute to an annual assembly to share learning and challenges. Now that we are two years on from the launch, we are in the process of

---

4   The Performing Rights Society is the licensing and collection agency for the UK. The PRS for Music Foundation is a charity supporting grassroots music that benefits from a significant PRS grant.

designing a data-sharing platform to gather data on the impact of the principles, which will allow signatory organisations to share anonymised applicant data. Anecdotally, we know that most organisations within the network have made significant changes to their composer development programmes. At Sound and Music this has included standardising the option for video applications across our programmes, adding budget lines for access costs (such as paying support workers to put together applications), and offering 'Infrequently Asked Questions' zoom sessions about programmes for d/Deaf, disabled and neurodiverse composers.

The annual assemblies (of which we have now run two) have allowed us to share learning across the network, in particular our most recent one in February 2022 which focussed on breaking down barriers faced by composers for socio-economic reasons. As this is arguably an area of disadvantage that is least discussed in the music sector, our aim for the assembly was to accelerate our collective understanding in order to enable action. As organisations we have all made changes to the way we work and as a network are more powerful than the sum of our parts.

The chief lesson from this process is best condensed in the following three points:

- Assume you do not know everything: the Fair Access Principles originated for Sound and Music as a way of starting positive conversations within the music sector, with the aim of increasing our understanding about the difficulties composers face in accessing opportunities. We started from a position of knowing quite a lot, but this knowledge increased dramatically with every conversation we held in the initial stages of putting the principles together.

- Keep assuming you do not know everything: if you have put work into researching best-practice guidelines, be prepared that circumstances and knowledge will keep developing. An example of this is the research we did recently to put together an open call for an award specifically for composers from low socio-economic backgrounds. Over the course of a few conversations our understanding had transformed and allowed us to put out a much fairer, inclusive call than the one we had initially conceived.

- Be generous and curious: think about who you are including in the conversations you're having, and in particular bring in the voices of those you're aiming to support with your best-practice guidelines.

In the work of Sound and Music we have seen that women and minorities are more likely to be adversely affected by the barriers explored above and, therefore, more likely to benefit from fair access. As such, we have been an enthusiastic supporter of Keychange and its mission, which is explored further in the next section.

2. The Keychange Manifesto

In conversation with Francine Gorman of Keychange

Keychange started in 2017 after conversations between the Performing Rights Society for Music Foundation (PRSF), headed at that time by Vanessa Reed; Reeperbahn Festival (Germany); and the Swedish music information centre Musikcentrum Öst. Up to that point, these conversations had been quite informal, mainly focusing on how best to represent women in the music industry. It was a subject that had been around for years but was becoming more significant in various arenas, such as scrutiny of festival line-ups, studio spaces and representation panels. PRS's Women Make Music fund was an important jumping-off point. It was created because the membership of women and gender minorities within PRS's membership scheme was so low. We knew there were many more music creators out there than were registered, so this fund was put together to encourage women creators to apply for funding, to register for PRS, to enter into the royalty and collections ecosystem, and to gain all the benefits, experience and access that they could from that. It provided a lot of important data that we could use for the Keychange project.

The original Keychange focus was talent development: a Europe-wide programme that would help artists and music industry professionals access opportunities in different territories. Quite quickly, however, the feedback received from peers, friends and colleagues was that more industry-wide action needed to take place. This was where the Keychange pledge idea was initiated, with the manifesto following soon after. We define the manifesto, launched in 2018, as a statement of the ambitions of the full Keychange programme, while the pledge is a set of guidelines to help people realise these aims.[5] We are now gathering data from all the pledge signatories and are looking at best practices to feed into an updated manifesto at the end of the current phase of the project (2024).

The Keychange pledge was created in response to the industry requiring some practical steps that could assist people who had the ambition of changing the gender representation of their set-up but who did not necessarily know where to start. It is very much an outreach tool, a flexible framework to put in front of a music organisation to help begin what are sometimes difficult conversations. When the pledge first started it was very much about festivals with the initial headline: '50/50 by 2022', while the pledge document that supported it created a space to say in which area an organisation wanted to improve their representation and what they wanted to achieve. Festivals and conference panels were the main target at that time. The aim was: fifty percent of speakers in panels, fifty percent of moderators, and fifty percent of artists on stage should be women. After going out with '50/50 by 2022' in festivals and conferences we got a lot of feedback from the wider industry to say that this framework could be applied to so many other areas and we were asked to look into a possible expansion.

In late 2018, therefore, we opened up the Keychange pledge to any music organisation and we changed the phrasing from '50/50 by 2022' to 'at least fifty percent representation within your chosen area'. And since we opened up the scope of the pledge, we have had all sorts of different people signing up. We currently have 565 signatories and they range from conservatoires to orchestras, from booking agents to record labels and music magazines.

There was initially some pushback from people who took the word 'quota' as being quite a legalistic term. This is a global project and the term has a very different weight in different languages. We were always clear that people should not be booking or commissioning things based on quotas, it should always be based on talent. What Keychange does

---

5   Keychange, 'Keychange Manifesto', https://static1.squarespace.com/static/5e3ac2fecd69e2663a9b793c/t/5f0324b481fcf002f4f702c9/1594041527239/1052-keychange-A5-v15-web.pdf

with this fifty percent is to encourage people to look at *why* the pool that they are booking from does not already contain the brilliant female talent that we know is out there. As a pledge organisation, I have to ask myself: what is the gender representation of my current line-up? If it's twenty percent women, am I actively saying that there is only one woman artist to four men who is of equal talent or is it because I am just booking from the same old pools? There is a lot to be gained from internally asking questions about whether an organisation is actively changing the landscape or passively letting it continue to exist.

Becoming a pledge signatory is a very involved process, so it is not just a case of signing up on a website and then sticking a logo on your poster. It is a real conversation with us to look into and examine the various facets of an organisation and to have a chat about the actions that could be put in place. The document is then completed in collaboration with the Keychange team, with us offering resources and support as they try and meet the criteria.

The three core partners of the project were responsible for writing the original manifesto, with PRSF and Vanessa Reed leading. The project is now at an exciting moment in that we are moving towards the next manifesto. Everything we do at the moment is gathering information to inform and inspire what the project will do after our Creative Europe funding ends in 2024. When we first started the project, gender equality was the absolute heart and soul of what we were working on and, even at that time, there were many other considerations and barriers people were experiencing in accessing the industry. We decided to focus on one. However, we know from our experience of the past couple of years, and the feedback from our participants on the programme, that we need to be much more intersectional in our focus. What we know is that being a woman in the music industry is one barrier, being a black woman in the music industry is a second barrier, being a queer black woman in the music industry just adds further dimensions to this. The next stage is to consider what can we put in place to make this industry as safe and accessible as it can be for anybody experiencing one or more of these barriers.

Our key message was about positive action to inspire change. The idea was never to call people out for not being representative in the work they were doing but to encourage people to look internally at the representation in their teams and on their stages and to put some actions in place to change that. If they wanted to be very public about that then they were in their rights to do so, but quite a number of the signatories wanted to keep their actions to themselves and put frameworks and structures in place to create change. This is also important because it means that these conversations are still happening, though not necessarily out in the open.

To sum up, we really try to put the responsibility of change, of action, into the hands of those who are working on the project and our best legacy would be to have educated and inspired many different people and many different areas of the industry. The responsibility is with everybody in the music industry to make change, from the CEOs to the musicians stepping into a club for the very first time. After achieving their first goals, there are likely other areas that organisations can work on. Quite a few people who have signed the pledge have come back with additional goals. After all, we want security to be representative, stage hands, performers, organisers, promoters: everybody in the room. A big part of what we do is to keep the conversation going, to make sure that post-pandemic (or wherever we are), that gender equality is still a huge subject on the agenda and that we have not forgotten it, that it still needs to be front and centre of every single action that we are taking and everything we do.

3. 'What We Need to Thrive: Working with Neurodiverse Composers'

In conversation with Fiona Robertson of Sound

'What we need to thrive: improving collaboration with autistic composers' was created for Sound as well as other promoters and ensembles to give them a helping hand working with neurodiverse people.[6] The impetus came from conversations with other talent development organisations around disabilities. I realised we generally fell into the habit of talking about people with physical disabilities, and not people with hidden challenges such as autism. There is no obvious sign that someone is

---

6 Sound Website, 'What we need to thrive: improving collaboration with autistic composers', https://sound-scotland.co.uk/news/what-we-need-to-thrive

autistic so it seemed like there was a useful piece of work to do on this issue.

We did not embark on this journey without any background of working with neurodiverse composers. We had already been working with individuals who we knew were on the autism spectrum. We first met up with two of these composers in June 2018, who then identified Ben Lunn, a prominent young autistic composer, as an important contact to take the project further. An open call was put out for neurodiverse composers, contact was made with Ben, and personal invites were sent out to composers for a specific day-long workshop on neurodiverse needs. In the end, six composers joined Sound and disability charity Drake Music Scotland to discuss their access needs, which gave us the basis for the guidelines as they exist now. It is worth noting that all the composers were invited rather than responding to the open call.

Organising such a day is not without challenge. Everything you do, you have to think about harder: the space, the time allocated, and certain facilities the need for which can be surprising for 'neurotypicals'. For example, Ben Lunn, who was now a key contact in organising the event, suggested having soft toys to hold if the participants got tired and, later in the afternoon, we could see them making use of these. Organisers have to accept the need to leave time because you do not want to be stressing people out: you cannot blast through your agenda but have to be more thoughtful. The process of talking to these composers and organising these events fed directly into the guidelines, indeed we almost needed the guidelines at the beginning of the process of their own creation.

The main team who took the document further was in place after that meeting: Ben Lunn; Fiona Robertson and Ellen Thomson from Sound; and Pete Sparks from Drake Music Scotland. Sharing and collaboration were very important to the writing process. At one point, Sound was going to write the guidelines, at another there was meant to be a communal writing process on the part of the composers. In the end, we commissioned Ben Lunn to write the document, partly because the communal process was not progressing, and partly because we did not want to be putting unnecessary pressure on individuals who might easily be overwhelmed. The whole process took much longer than initially thought, with Ben doing the writing and much to-ing and fro-ing taking place between the other team members so that it reflected autistic composers' needs but was also understandable to a wide audience.

My erroneous preconception was that the challenges faced by autistic composers would be primarily around social contact and networking. All composers can find this a difficult facet of the music world but autistic people face even greater barriers. Instead, what came across from talking with the composers was the potential for small changes or setbacks to be amplified and become overwhelming, as well as the huge variety of aspects that feed into participants' experiences when working with an organisation. We were looking with them from the beginning of the commissioning process to the end: how to make rehearsals easier; how to make social interaction easier; how to communicate; trains, bedsheets and hotels – each can make a situation manageable and a collaboration successful.

The main takeaway was that *all* of this is relevant, all of this is important—not necessarily for every composer, but promoters need to understand that all of this *may* be relevant to a composer they are working with. It is not about how composers communicate with us but how we communicate with them and the information we need to know to make their journey with us as easy as possible.

We organised a conference in January 2021 (naturally delayed due to COVID-19) with ensembles, organisations, neurodiverse composers and creators. This was linked to Sound's annual festival in North-East Scotland. We used that conference as a soft launch for the guidelines, asking everyone to go home and read a draft. We contacted as many organisations as possible, focusing primarily on Scottish festivals, ensembles, and promoters involved in new music, as well as (inter)national networks through Sound and Music, personal networks and social media. Similarly, when it came out as a finalised document, it was sent out to these same people. One misstep occurred during the conference, when we programmed a piece by Siobhan Dyson, which sought to portray the feeling of being neurodiverse and was, therefore, something of an assault to the senses. We should have thought about this and warned the audience in advance, and although one or two people had to leave for the performance, they were able to come back in for the rest of the conference.

When we started the guidelines, it felt like we were on the cusp of something, but by the time we finished things had moved on. You start out on these journeys thinking you are doing something unique, only to find lots of other people are doing something similar. It is rather like giving your children names you think are original without realising everyone else has chosen the same original names. You are not alone in being in that flow. Raising these issues is not necessarily new but hopefully these guidelines help bring the ideas to a wider audience.

Perhaps the main lesson to draw from working with neurodiverse composers, and people in general, is taking time to think about how you interact with people. Occasionally we do not have time to think about our interactions enough due to the pressures of being an arts organisation today, such as limited capacity and financial economy. We need to make time to think about that better, to work with neurodiverse composers and, really, any other collaborators.

Discussion

The authors met in April 2022 to discuss themes that emerged from comparing their experiences in working on these documents. It is clear that such processes are not to be undertaken lightly, both in terms of creating the documents through stakeholder engagement and then publicising the ideas once they are created. The process of their creation, however, has also led to wide ranging reflection on the authors' professional practice, starting with the time and care they give to artists and professionals in their daily work.

Time and Care

Neil T. Smith (NTS): What resonated with you reading the other contributions?

Fiona Robertson (FR): It all reinforced for me the need for time and care. *Anything* can make it really difficult for people to access opportunities, to go through those processes and to manage them and I think for us it's going from 'under-represented groups are really important' to actually being caring throughout the whole process.

Hannah Bujic (HB): That also resonated with me, especially how we should be taking the time to have these meaningful interactions with everybody we're engaging with. That then opens up the possibilities of making opportunities available to people and increasing our own learning at every stage of these conversations.

NTS: That's pretty challenging, I imagine. For an organisation reading this, what is their first step for trying to make this a habit rather than something you do on special occasions?

FR: We're just addressing that at the moment. We're going to focus more on time, taking time to evaluate properly, taking time to improve everything rather than doing it all in a rush because we're all too stressed. Not that it is necessarily going to work...

Reading Francine's contribution, though, I have no worries about female representation because it's so embedded in what we do. It has become absolute second nature. We did a plus fifty percent festival in 2017, so we've been doing it for a while and it just seems natural now. And I think if you take the time to do it, then it will eventually take less time because it becomes embedded in the process and the system.

Francine Gorman (FG): I completely agree, what you've just said there is a really good example of what we try and encourage people to do through Keychange, which is to make changes to their own set-ups and systems. Hopefully in the incremental steps that are made to reach their targets there is sustainable change being made because it does become second nature to look at your programming and do a quick tally of what the gender balance looks like.

Learning to Improve

NTS: Has any one organisation that you have worked with ever slid back? Do you find that this process of learning is cumulative and that people do keep on improving?

HB: I wouldn't say it's linear. I suppose there are two sides to that: there's the stuff that we can take responsibility for as an organisation and there are things outside of your control. Because we're relying on people applying to our programmes and talent development we are having to make changes that will encourage people to apply to our programmes. We can look at who we are selecting but we rely to a degree on who is actually applying to our programmes. That is not something we can actually strongly affect in that we can say we are definitely going to have fifty percent women this year, for example.

That is where the non-linear part comes in because we are doing everything we can to encourage under-represented groups to apply to our programmes but there are external factors that come into play that increase or decrease those numbers. Covid has had a huge impact, I think, on who feels they can apply to our programmes, who has the time, and the financial position to actually make the time to engage. I'd like to say we're heading towards equal representation but, in terms of people applying to our programmes, we're going through a bit of a wavy cycle. It's not all uninterrupted progress.

FR: At the Royal Conservatoire of Scotland it feels as if there is a good bunch of young women and gender-diverse people coming through. But we struggle with ethnic minorities, there seems to be hardly anyone coming through the pipeline so how do you manage those other under-represented groups when it is difficult to have an impact directly? And that probably means going back to schools. We do encourage young people but it's going to be a while before that has an impact and they come out the other end.

NTS: Francine, have people struggled to maintain the changes?

FG: I wouldn't say so with the pledge signatories because these are people who have gone through the process to really make this a target and an ambition for their organisation. But I'm sure there have been festivals or organisations that we've been in touch with, who have not signed the pledge who may have experienced some of what you described.

In terms of the pipeline, there need to be changes at every single level. Things like the Fair Access Principles being applied to all these different levels – school spaces, education spaces all the way through – things like that are so important just to make sure that the pipeline is open for musicians coming through and that gender balance is considered at every stage.

How Caring Can Classical Music Be?

NTS: Care and attention is not really what classical music is known for if you look from the outside. It is often hyper-competitive, rewards 'talent', 'excellence' and 'skill'.

FB: I think there is a tension as well, certainly when you're working with composers and creating new pieces. Ensembles are so good: they come in, read the music and power through to the other side. It's not often that they've got an enormous amount of time to rehearse and spend with whichever composer you have given a commission or opportunity. There are opportunities to space things out a bit more and give more time and care to the composers so that they are meeting the players before the first rehearsal, for example. The other thing we've found really successful is that we have a local new music ensemble, Any Enemy, and they're all teachers and students up here and they do this as volunteers – they get paid for gigs, minorly – but they do it basically as a voluntary ensemble because they want to. In programmes we do with them we find there is a lot more care, time and nurturing when we have young composers working with them.

HB: I think there's a slight backlash about the language of talent and excellence – in the field of talent development ironically. That in itself is exclusionary language as it is less likely that someone who has not been able to access opportunities will identify themselves as talented. And so using a word like 'potential', or just leaving that out altogether, or making sure that it is understood that it is as much about looking at where someone can get to as opposed to where they are right now is so crucial in all of what we did for putting together the Fair Access Principles. Classical music in particular is guilty of laying a lot at the door of 'this is about talent', 'this is about excellence', when really we need to look at why somebody could be considered talented or excellent. What access have they had to resources and opportunities, in terms of their upbringing and education that allows them to step foot into those opportunities and progress through the pipeline?

FR: One of the questions is why the UK seems to be taking a lead on these issues. I worked in France for years and started off in the music sector. Where the arts in the UK tends to have fairly left-wing people working for it (*Guardian* reading), in France it can be very different. I worked in an office where everyone read *Le Figaro*. I have seen tour proposals from France going round with ten male composers and there is certainly a different level of understanding, but that is evolving now. And probably it is completely different in Scandinavia.

FG: This is definitely the experience we've had with the pledge. We were having such different conversations in Scandinavia to those we were having in Southern Europe, for example. But what was really interesting at that point was that in Scandinavia, because gender representation and equality has been so ingrained in their society for such a long time, they felt that they didn't want to go out publicly and say they were actively giving these issues thought or working on them because it would give the impression that they had not been thinking about it before the pledge. Whereas in Southern Europe, it was about starting a fresh conversation. But now, five years into the project, we're seeing that in Italy, for example, where we really did have to knock on doors at the start to get the project rolling, there is a huge number of gender-focused initiatives that are happening throughout the music industry.

Making Change Happen

NTS: There seems to be an assumption that exclusions are happening unintentionally and the guidelines discussed above all focus on positive action. Are we going too easy on the music industry? Can some of these exclusions be rather more deliberate?

HB: Firstly, I have genuinely not yet come across someone who is at least willing to say 'no, we really do want to exclude certain people and we'll carry on doing that, thank you very much'. Every conversation that I've had is around people wanting to find out more about how to be more inclusive. There is an assumption with the question that there are more effective methods of making change happen other than positive action, that by preaching or cracking a whip you'll get more change happening. The idea that positive action is a way of enacting change is a viewpoint that goes beyond music. Negative arguments are rarely as effective as persuasive as positive ones and using the psychology of collaboration and support is more effective than preaching. Everything we have found with the Fair Access Principles doesn't mean we're avoiding difficult conversations. In fact, the whole idea, as Francine mentions, is creating a framework for difficult conversations. We didn't want to get into Twitter spats saying 'we're not going to publicise your call because we don't think what you're doing is right'. That shuts down conversations and using best practice guidelines as a framework for opening up difficult conversations allows them to happen in a way that helps everybody progress to more positive outcomes.

FR: We work quite closely with smaller organisations. The local music clubs etc. There *are* some real dinosaurs there. I'm not sure it's entirely unconscious but there are one or two organisations where the board are all middle-aged blokes, and they're all volunteers because it's a volunteer organisation more or less and they're programming classical music concerts. But those things matter because they're part of the landscape and some of them are commissioning composers and some of them are performing all-male programmes. I don't think it's actively misogynistic, but I certainly have heard jokey comments about the 'nonsense, of having to have female composers' or 'us white, male composers aren't going to have any work left!'. It could just be individuals, but I think it is a little more ingrained than that. And I'm wondering: we all communicate well among ourselves because we're all organisations with a fairly national outreach, but what about the local ones? The guidelines we've all prepared are perhaps too big for them, it would have to be something much simpler.

FG: I fully support everything Hannah said about positive action and that is the experience we had throughout this project. You're never going to start a useful conversation by shouting at somebody. Our approach has always been to invite people to self-reflect, meaning that by looking at their workspace and organisation then letting them engineer change.

NTS: One theme that emerges is that guidelines, once written, need support and attention to make their way in the world. Completing them is by no means the end of the story.

FG: It's important that any project or plans or principles that we're putting in place have a fairly long life after the launch time because it does take people a long time to get the idea, or to understand the conversation, or to see how it applies to their own context. I do think there has to be some kind of plan and sustained activity for whatever guidelines are coming out to keep the conversation active: if after three months it slips off the agenda, then you need something to happen that keeps it fresh and in mind.

NTS: I think that's useful for anyone thinking about writing these, that finishing them is not the endpoint but the beginning of a different process.

HB: The idea that best practice guidelines and work around equality and inclusion is just going to continue, is disheartening. I think in reality there will always be some level of work required around developing understanding and that curiosity that allows us to understand what other people are going through, whether that's underrepresented groups or just anybody that we're having conversations with. But the idea that this current push that we're all part of will have to be sustained for quite a long time, I find that quite depressing. I would hope, though, at some point in the future when the landscape has changed for the better that the conversations we're having are more about the nuances: about being curious and including people in conversations because we understand the issues and the challenges and we want to include their viewpoints, rather than because there is such a bleak lack of representation within the industry.

FR: I'd hope that certainly for some aspects it would go away. You'd hope that for gender and ethnic minorities once we get to fifty percent, or the representative proportion, that that would go away and that we would not need guidelines. I'm slightly less optimistic about neurodiversity because it is so complicated the whole way through the whole thing, even if you get them through there is so much to deal with and so much to take into account and every person is so different, it will just need ongoing attention and will not disappear.

Socio-Political Factors

NTS: We're talking about equity and there's a wide range of factors that affect this. Is there a danger that guidelines tend to work within a system or political horizon and that true equity may need to overstep these bounds?

FR: I think socio-economic background is becoming a major issue and will become even more important. The way music education is going and things are going post-COVID, there's going to be less and less opportunity. I know a lot of players now from working-class backgrounds but I don't think you'll get the same thing in ten years' time. It becomes very much about 'haves' and 'have-nots'.

HB: And as you said earlier Fiona about what is happening further downstream, where we perhaps have less impact: we have less impact because of the socio-political factors that are at play there. We can do what we can in our areas but if opportunities are being lost for children and young people to enter the arena and become aware of the opportunities, let alone to then access them, then what we're doing is going to continue to be a struggle.

Concluding Remarks

The documents described in this chapter did not emerge from nothing. It is clear that there are currents in society that gain momentum, forming an important backdrop to these ideas, while the change sought by these three examples requires partners and allies to be effective: people who are passionate about the cause in question and with a shared sense of direction. Yet, it is difficult to imagine these networks being created without the documents discussed above, making them a vital part of the process of real-life change. They do not merely reflect the concerns of an area of artistic practice, but define these concerns to a significant degree. The changes of approach they seek can then snowball as the themes and actions explored are picked up in other sectors and locations. For organisations and individuals, the first step in the face of huge social issues can be the most difficult to take and these guidelines can clarify people's thinking and make such a first step possible. Work in equalities is also obviously vulnerable to a whole range of other societal issues, including access to education, healthcare, musical opportunities and care provision. Documents such as these cannot always acknowledge this interconnectedness, as their remit must be specific enough to inspire concrete, practical steps. Yet, it is clear that work here can never be fully divorced from political activity in the wider world, both in the sense that access to the arts is influenced by all these other societal factors, and in the sense that work within an artistic field promoting equalities is a political act that can resonate throughout wider society. The change described here requires consistent care and work to communicate and promote the ideals these documents embody. In many ways such guidelines can only become as strong as the networks that are built around them.

References

Keychange, 'Keychange Manifesto', https://static1.squarespace.com/static/5e3ac2fecd69e2663a9b793c/t/5f0324b481fcf002f4f702c9/1594041527239/1052-keychange-A5-v15-web.pdf

Office of National Statistics UK, *Family Resources Survey, Financial Year 2019 to 2020*, https://www.gov.uk/government/statistics/family-resources-survey-financial-year-2019-to-2020/family-resources-survey-financial-year-2019-to-2020

Sound Website, 'What we need to thrive: improving collaboration with autistic composers', https://sound-scotland.co.uk/news/what-we-need-to-thrive

Sound and Music Website, 'Fair Access Principles', https://soundandmusic.org/our-impact/fair-access-principles/

4. Until George Floyd: An Afrofuturist Perspective on the Future of Classical Music and Opera

Antonio C. Cuyler

> In the World through which I travel, I am endlessly creating myself.
> —Frantz Fanon[1]

The previous chapter advanced discourses about practical solutions to classical music's exclusion problem relative to women, neurodiverse people and cultural workers from low socioeconomic backgrounds. In 'Moving Beyond @operaisracist: Exploring Blacktivism as a Pathway to Antiracism and Creative Justice in Opera'[2] and '(Un)Silencing Blacktivism in Opera: A Conversation about the Letter to the Opera Field from Black Administrators',[3] I documented how the Black Opera Alliance and Black Administrators of Opera have compelled opera companies to sign a pledge for racial equity as the first step towards racial justice in classical music following George Floyd's state-sanctioned murder in May 2020. The pledge compels opera companies to (1) hire Black artists, (2) require staff, orchestra members and independent contractors to reflect the racial demographics of our most diverse communities, (3)

---

1   Frantz Fanon, *Black Skin, White Masks* (London: Pluto Press, 1967), p. 229.
2   Antonio C. Cuyler, 'Moving Beyond @operaisracist: Exploring Blacktivism as a Pathway to Antiracism and Creative Justice in Opera,' in *Music as Labour: Inequalities and Activism in the Past and Present*, ed. by Dagmar Abfalter and Rosa Reitsamer (London: Routledge, 2022), pp. 204-218, https://doi.org/10.4324/9781003150480
3   Antonio C. Cuyler, '(Un)Silencing Blacktivism in Opera: A Conversation about the Letter to the Opera Field from Black Administrators,' in *Voices for Change in the Classical Music Profession: New Ideas for Tackling Inequalities and Exclusions* (Oxford: Oxford University Press, forthcoming).

©2024 Antonio C. Cuyler, CC BY-NC 4.0   https://doi.org/10.11647/OBP.0353.04

program and prioritise works by Black composers, (4) hire more Black creatives and production personnel, (5) require that visual artists undergo training in successfully preparing Black artists for the stage, (6) review the organisation's hiring practices and policies for racism, (7) review the board's recruitment culture, (7) and include within the company's official code of conduct a commitment to anti-racism, and anti-oppression. Furthermore, the Black Administrators of Opera suggested that opera companies (1) commit to equity in salaries and promotion opportunities, (2) commit to company-wide racial equity education and professional development, (3) commit to equitable hiring and recruitment practices, (4) commit to company-wide intentional inclusion in the execution of mission and programs, and (5) commit to adequately funding company diversity, equity, and inclusion initiatives and working groups.

Documenting the ways in which people of African descent write themselves into classical music's future today is critical for comprehensively addressing those who have historically and continuously faced exclusion and oppression because of their race when pursuing their creative justice in classical music. Furthermore, documenting these practices holds significant value in countering a belief expressed by conservative critic and author of *The Diversity Delusion: How Race and Gender Pandering Corrupt the University and Undermine Our Culture*, Heather Mac Donald, and held by far too many White people that 'classical music is under a racial attack. Orchestras and opera companies are said to discriminate against Black musicians and composers. The canonical repertoire, the product of a centuries-long tradition of musical expression, is allegedly a function of white supremacy.'[4]

A voluminous amount of evidence exists documenting the historic exclusion from the classical music industrial complex that continues to characterise the lived experiences of people of African descent. In *Anti-Black Discrimination in American Orchestras*, Aaron Flagg documented for the League of American Orchestras – a US-based trade association for orchestras whose mission is to 'advance the experience of orchestral music, support the people and organisations that create it, and champion the contributions they make to the health and vibrancy of

---

4   Heather Mac Donald, 'Classical Music's Suicide Pact (Part I),' *City Journal*, Summer 2021.

communities,' – the ways in which the orchestral field has systematically and systemically undermined the participation of people of African descent in orchestral music. He wrote, 'the field has never effectively engaged a fair representation of the racial and ethnic talent in the country. One might ask: In 2020, are the musician, staff, and board roles equally accessible to everyone interested in this music? Sadly, the simple answer is no.'[5] Flagg's summation remains true of opera, too.

Although opera has and continues to tokenise some artists of African descent; artists, audiences, board trustees, executives, managers and volunteers of African descent do not reflect the thirteen percent of the Black population living within the US.[6] In *Access, Diversity, Equity, and Inclusion in Cultural Organisations: Insights from the Careers of Executive Opera Managers of Color in the US*, I documented the ways that opera has struggled to embrace the executive leadership and talent of people of African descent. In fact, since 1735, when opera first appeared in the US, only five people of African descent have held executive-level positions with major opera companies.[7]

In addition, since its 1883 founding, and even though William Grant Still submitted operas for its consideration,[8] only as recently as 2021 did the Metropolitan Opera (MET) programme its first and only opera by a Black composer, *Fire Shut Up in My Bones* by Terrance Blanchard. The MET appears poised to continue its practice of programming operas by Black composers. In its 2022-2023 season, presented *Champion*, another opera by Blanchard.[9] Even in my own more than thirty-plus-year history of attending classical music and opera performances, I have heard and

---

5   Aaron Flagg, 'Anti-Black Discrimination in American Orchestras,' League of American Orchestras.
6   U. S. Census, *Quick Facts*, 2022, https://www.census.gov/quickfacts/fact/table/US/PST045221; OPERA America, *2021 Field-Wide Opera Demographic Report*, 2022, https://www.operaamerica.org/r/business-research/8569/2021-field-wide-opera-demographic-report
7   Antonio C. Cuyler, *Access, Diversity, Equity, and Inclusion in Cultural Organisations: Insights from the Careers of Executive Opera Managers of Color in the U. S.* (London: Routledge, 2021).
8   Zachary Woolfe, 'A Black Composer Finally Arrives at the Metropolitan Opera,' *New York Times*, 23 September 2021, https://www.nytimes.com/2021/09/23/arts/music/terence-blanchard-met-opera.html
9   Joshua Barone, 'More Terrance Blanchard Coming to Met Opera After Success of Fire,' *New York Times*, 7 December 2021, https://www.nytimes.com/2021/12/07/arts/music/met-opera-terence-blanchard-champion.html

seen more compositions and operas programmed by composers of African descent after George Floyd's murder than before. For example, in 2004, I saw Nathan Davis' Jazzopera, *Just Above My Head*, based on the James Baldwin novel.[10] Over the last year, I have seen Dave Ragland's *One Vote Won*, *Fire Shut Up in My Bones*, Joel Thompson's *The Snowy Day*, Anthony Davis' *X, the Life and Times of Malcolm X*, Rhiannon Giddens & Michael Abels' *Omar*, and William Menefield's *Fierce*.

Given this irrefutable body of evidence, an examination of the cognitive acrobatics Mac Donald performed to come to her erroneous and intellectually dishonest conclusion remains beyond the scope of this reflection. However, she is correct about one point. The canonical repertoire is, indeed, a function of White supremacy culture, and as Okun pointed out,[11] 'White supremacy's aim is the annihilation and destruction of all people of the global majority', but especially people of African descent and specifically the erasure of their contributions to classical music.

Still, it might tempt one to ask, why has this progress taken so long? In addition, why did a Black man have to have his life taken so mercilessly, publicly, shamefully, and violently to bring classical music to the point of seemingly recompensing for its historic and continuous anti-Black racism? Has invoking George Floyd's name and the memory of his brutal murder finally compelled real transformation in classical music? The answer to these questions lies in an enduring observable truth. Clearly, anti-Black racism exists in classical music. Given this truth, in this chapter I contemplate two questions: (1) in the future, will people of African descent fully participate in classical music, and (2) if yes, by what means? To address these questions, I use Afrofuturism as the theoretical lens to examine the phenomenological real-world ways in which people of African descent currently create and write themselves into classical music's future as a result of the racial reckoning of the summer of 2020.

---

10 University of Pittsburgh Department of Music, 'Professor Nathan Davis's Jazzopera: Just Above My Head received its premiere performances by the Pittsburgh Opera Theatre on June 9-13', https://www.music.pitt.edu/blog/professor-nathan-daviss-jazzopera-j040609

11 Tema Okun, *White Supremacy Culture Characteristics*, (2021), https://www.whitesupremacyculture.info/characteristics.html

Afrofuturism

In 2016, Dean and Andrews described Afrofuturism as an evolving field of study in Black cultural studies: 'Its theories and scholarship are heavily influenced with particularities in science fiction, speculative fiction, new media, digital technology, the arts, and Black aesthetics all situated and focused on the continent of Africa, the Diaspora, and its imaginaries.'[12] Observing these phenomena, Mark Dery coined the term Afrofuturism in the mid 1990s.[13] A key aspect of Afrofuturism is that it pays close attention to the methods, narratives and theories that position Black identity in the present and into some futurity of the imaginary. Practically, then, Afrofuturism is about finding safe spaces for Black life to freely exist.[14] Doing so remains critical because of the potential overdetermination of the past, specifically apartheid, colonialism, imperialism, Jim Crow, forced migration, racism and the trans-Atlantic slave trade on Black future spaces. Thus, Afrofuturism remains a product of the de-colonised imagination and mind.

As Hamilton suggests,[15] the Afronauts – classical music artists, audiences, board trustees, executives, managers and volunteers of African descent – make definitive statements about the current status of their freedom, liberation and oppression while simultaneously referencing the past and staking out a place for Black life within classical music's future. In *Afrofuturism + Detroit*,[16] Ingrid LaFleur reminded attendees of the Detroit Opera's production of *X, the Life and Times of Malcolm X*, that the city of Detroit gave the jazz musician, Sun Ra, the key to the city in 1980. The self-proclaimed Martian made music and poetry that spoke of Black liberation, and he believed the music that he made with his band, the Arkestra, could transport all Black people

---

12   Terrance Dean and Dale Andrews, 'Introduction: Afrofuturism in Black Theology – Race, Gender, Sexuality, and the State of Black Religion in the Black Metropolis', *Black Theology*, 14 (2016), 2-5, (p. 2).
13   Ingrid LaFleur, 'Detroit + Afrofuturism' (2022). *Detroit Opera Digital Production Book for X, the Life and Times of Malcolm X*.
14   Elizabeth C. Hamilton, 'Afrofuturism and the Technologies of Survival, *African Arts*, 50 (2017), 18-23, (p. 18).
15   Ibid.
16   Ibid.

to Mars, a place where Black people could finally live free from the incessant, infectious and insidious disease of White supremacy.[17]

LaFleur maintained that Sun Ra's type of mythmaking during ongoing times of racial discord and deep oppression presented a radical form of resistance.[18] Through the musical creation of alternative histories and mythmaking, people of African descent empower themselves by granting themselves the permission to imagine their lives beyond their current circumstances, which include mass shootings while attending church or grocery shopping, and individual killings while performing the most mundane of everyday activities that some people not of African descent take for granted. She further argued that as a liberation movement, Afrofuturism emboldens people of African descent to craft destinies and realities of health, inclusion, joy and prosperity using imaginative modalities such as cosmology, fantasy, horror, magical realism, science fiction and surrealism.[19]

For LaFleur, then, a practical application of Afrofuturism explores the intersections of race with emerging economics, politics, sciences and technologies in order to map the future. In classical music, the emergence of several collectives by and for people of African descent during the 2020 'summer of racial discontent' such as the Black Administrators of Opera,[20] Black Classical Music Educators,[21] Black Music Action Coalition,[22] Black Opera Alliance,[23] Black Opera Research Network[24] and Black Orchestral Network[25] also serves as real-world examples of people of African descent creating and writing themselves into classical music's future. LaFleur further identified ancestral grounding, co-creation, cooperative economics, love, non-linear time, pleasure and joy, and resilience as technologies of liberation,[26] while Hamilton might argue

---

17   Ibid.
18   Ibid.
19   Ibid.
20   Black Administrators of Opera. 'Letter to the Opera Field from Black Administrators,' (2020), https://blackadmofopera.medium.com/, https://blackadmofopera.medium.com/
21   Black Classical Music Educators, https://blackclassicalmusiceducators.com/about
22   Black Music Action Coalition, https://blackadmofopera.medium.com/
23   Black Opera Alliance, https://www.blackoperaalliance.org/home
24   Black Opera Research Network, https://blackoperaresearch.net/about/
25   Black Orchestral Network, https://www.blackorchestralnetwork.org/
26   Ibid.

that these are also tools critical for the survival of people of African descent in and beyond classical music.[27]

Closing Thoughts

I began this chapter with the Frantz Fanon quote, 'In the World through which I travel, I am endlessly creating myself.'[28] Though Fanon lived long before the naming of Afrofuturism, the ancestral grounding that LaFleur spoke of aligns brilliantly with the possibilities that unfold when people of African descent own the responsibility of endlessly creating themselves into the future. People of African descent will fully participate in all aspects of classical music's future. In fact, because of the ways people of African descent have responded to the 2020 summer of discontent by establishing collectives that will communally hold classical music accountable for offering more than rhetorical commitments to racial justice, we will lead the actualisation of a dynamic and vibrant future for classical music. The previous chapter posed the question: how caring can classical music be? Classical music needs to exhaust the possibilities of its caring because it cannot ethically and financially afford to continue excluding people of African descent. According to the United Nations, by 2050 one in four people on Earth will identify as of African descent.[29] In addition to the best practices described in the pledge for racial equity, to exhaust the possibilities of its caring when it comes to Black Americans specifically, the classical music industrial complex should activate the Black community's aspirational capital, and celebrate its creativity, support their self-care, work to earn their trust and create a sense of belonging.[30]

In closing, I contemplate the second question I posed in this chapter: if people of African descent are to participate in classical music, by what

---

27 Ibid.
28 Ibid.
29 United Nations, *World Population Prospects: Key Findings and Advance Tables*, 2015, chrome-extension://efaidnbmnnnibpcajpcglclefindmkaj/https://population.un.org/wpp/Publications/Files/Key_Findings_WPP_2015.pdf
30 Melody Dawkins, Ciara Knight, Tanya Treptow, and Camila Guerrero, *A Place to be Heard; Black Perspectives on Creativity, Trustworthiness, Welcome, and Well-Being- Findings from a Qualitative Study*, 2022, https://wallacefoundation.org/report/place-be-heard-space-feel-held-black-perspectives-creativity-trustworthiness-welcome-and

means? Although we have taken ownership of creating and writing ourselves into classical music's future in the now, I have concerns about the fragmentation of how the creating and writing takes place. If Kimberle Crenshaw is correct in her theorising of intersectionality,[31] and specifically that oppression compounds when a person has two or more oppressed social identities, then perhaps power, too, compounds. To amplify this power, however, unity must also become a technology of the liberation of people of African descent and their participation in the future of classical music's future. In doing so, the collectives might acknowledge and identify the other voices currently missing in the creating and writing of people of African descent into classical music's future. For example, where is the collective for classical music audiences of African descent? We need their perspective and power, too, to compel transformation. In addition, similar to the Black Trustee Alliance for Art Museums,[32] where is the Black Trustee Alliance for Classical Music? Imagine how each collective's power could magnify through unity. If people of African descent will have a future in classical music, it will surely and unequivocally come as the result of endlessly creating and writing ourselves into classical music's future together.

References

Barone, Joshua, 'More Terrance Blanchard Coming to Met Opera After Success of Fire,' *New York Times*, 7 December 2021, https://www.nytimes.com/2021/12/07/arts/music/met-opera-terence-blanchard-champion.html

Black Administrators of Opera, 'Letter to the Opera Field from Black Administrators', (2022), https://blackadmofopera.medium.com/letter-to-the-opera-field-from-black-administrators-240977b355e5

Black Classical Music Educators, 'About', (2022), https://blackclassicalmusiceducators.com

---

31 Kimberle Crenshaw, 'Demarginalising the Intersection of Race and Sex: A Black Feminist Critique of Antidiscrimination Doctrine, Feminist Theory and Antiracist Politics', *University of Chicago Legal Forum* 1 (1989), 139-167.
32 Black Trustee Alliance for Art Museums, https://blacktrusteealliance.org/about/overview/

Black Music Action Coalition, 'Home', (2022), https://www.bmacoalition.org/

Black Opera Research Network, 'About', (2022), https://blackoperaresearch.net/about/

Black Orchestral Network, 'Home', (2022), https://www.blackorchestralnetwork.org/

Black Trustee Alliance for Art Museums, 'Home', (2022), https://blacktrusteealliance.org/

Crenshaw, Kimberle, 'Demarginalising the Intersection of Race and Sex: A Black Feminist Critique of Antidiscrimination Doctrine, Feminist Theory and Antiracist Politics', *Legal Forum*, 1 (1989), 139-167.

Cuyler, Antonio C., 'Moving Beyond @operaisracist: Exploring Blacktivism as a Pathway to Antiracism and Creative Justice in Opera,' in *Music as Labour: Inequalities and Activism in the Past and Present*, ed. by Dagmar Abfalter and Rosa Reitsamer (London: Routledge, 2022), pp. 204-218, https://doi.org/10.4324/9781003150480

Cuyler, Antonio C., '(Un)Silencing Blacktivism in Opera: A Conversation about the Letter to the Opera Field from Black Administrators,' in *Voices for Change in the Classical Music Profession: New Ideas for Tackling Inequalities and Exclusions*, ed. by Anna Bull and Christina Scharff (Oxford: Oxford University Press) (forthcoming).

Cuyler, Antonio C., *Access, Diversity, Equity, and Inclusion in Cultural Organisations: Insights from the Careers of Executive Opera Managers of Color in the U. S.* (London: Routledge, 2021).

Dawkins, Melody, Knight, Ciara, Treptow, Tanya, and Camila Guerrero, *A Place to be Heard; Black Perspectives on Creativity, Trustworthiness, Welcome, and Well-Being-Findings from a Qualitative Study*, (2022), https://wallacefoundation.org/report/place-be-heard-space-feel-held-black-perspectives-creativity-trustworthiness-welcome-and

Dean, Terrance and Dale Andrews, 'Introduction: Afrofuturism in Black Theology – Race, Gender, Sexuality, and the State of Black Religion in the Black Metropolis', *Black Theology*, 14 (2016), 2-5, https://doi.org/10.1080/14769948.2015.1131499

Fanon, Frantz, *Black Skin, White Masks* (London: Pluto Press, 1967).

Flagg, Aaron, 'Anti-Black Discrimination in American Orchestras,' League of American Orchestras.

Hamilton, Elizabeth C. 'Afrofuturism and the Technologies of Survival, *African Arts*, 50 (2017), 18-23.

LaFleur, Ingrid, 'Detroit + Afrofuturism', Detroit Opera Digital Production Book for *X, the Life and Times of Malcolm X*, 2022.

Mac Donald, Heather, 'Classical Music's Suicide Pact (Part I),' *City Journal* (2021).

Okun, Tema, *White Supremacy Culture Characteristics*, (2021), https://www.whitesupremacyculture.info/characteristics.html

OPERA America, *2021 Field-Wide Opera Demographic Report*, (2022), https://www.operaamerica.org/r/business-research/8569/2021-field-wide-opera-demographic-report

United Nations, *World Population Prospects: Key Findings and Advance Tables*, (2015), https://population.un.org/wpp/publications/files/key_findings_wpp_2015.pdf

University of Pittsburgh Department of Music, 'Professor Nathan Davis's Jazzopera: Just Above My Head received its premiere performances by the Pittsburgh Opera Theatre on June 9-13', (2004), https://www.music.pitt.edu/blog/professor-nathan-daviss-jazzopera-j040609

US Census Bureau, *Quick Facts*, (US Census Bureau, 2022), https://www.census.gov/quickfacts/fact/table/US/PST045221

Woolfe, Zachary, 'A Black Composer Finally Arrives at the Metropolitan Opera,' *New York Times*, 23 September 2021, https://www.nytimes.com/2021/09/23/arts/music/terence-blanchard-met-opera.html

5. The Voice Party – A New Opera for a New Political Era

Lore Lixenberg

'Fed-up with the blah blah blah? VOTE VOICE FOR SOME LA LA LA!!

THE VOICE PARTY IS A PARTY FOR VOICES! And the only political party that promises you nothing at all.'

—The Voice Party election slogan 2019

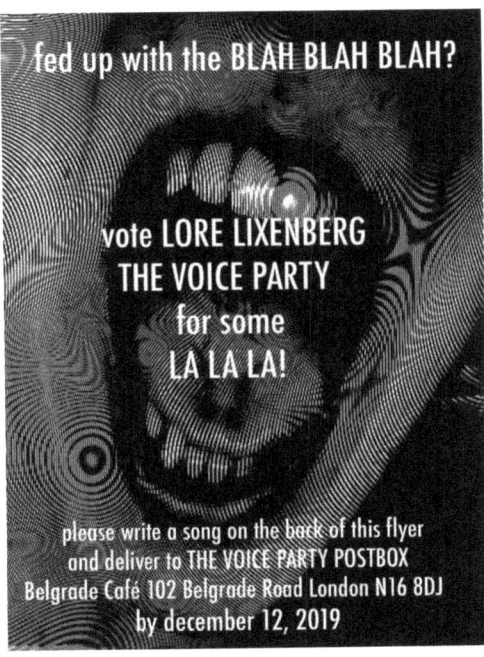

Fig. 5.1 Lore Lixenberg, The Voice Party election flyer for the 2019 UK Election (2019) © Lore Lixenberg.

The Voice Party is a political party and also an experimental opera, born out of the trauma of Brexit in 2016 and launched in Berlin at the Hamburger Bahnhof during the German elections of 2017. It also stood in the UK General Election in 2019, in the constituency of Stoke Newington and Hackney North, against Labour MP Diane Abbott among others. The entire election campaign was conducted in song and in vocalisations, including the hustings, election-night interviews, door-stopping and interaction with the public generally. The leaflet that was handed out by the voice party had, on one side The Voice Party logo and manifesto, while the other consisted of manuscript paper where people were encouraged to write music, a song, a drawing, a recipe or a poem, or anything they wanted to express in whatever form that came to them.

What then is The Voice Party, and what was the inspiration to start a new political party? What is it about the mainstream and even the alternative political parties that leaves one with the feeling that there is a big void at the heart of politics and society and how does this relate to music-making? Arguably, this metaphysical vacuum could be the result of music and the arts in the UK being for some time in deep crisis. The state of the arts can be seen to reflect society as a whole and the overall health of the society in many different ways. There are drastic cuts to free music education in schools, and professional musicians are legally robbed by unscrupulous streaming platforms. Many music departments in Higher Education have been axed completely or had their funding cut by a massive fifty percent.[1] The COVID-19 pandemic has also revealed seismic inequalities and stratifications in our societies that were already exacerbated by the financial crash of 2008 and a ten-year programme of brutal austerity. Music and cultural activities generally have always been regarded in the UK as a frivolity, something outside the mainstream of society, not to be taken seriously, financially non-viable and a soft force not worthy of serious study. Indeed, even as far back as 1914, Oscar Schmitz referred to England rather unflatteringly as 'Das Land ohne Musik' (The Land Without Music).[2] By other countries in mainland

---

1   Bethan Staton, 'Funding for arts courses and London universities to be slashed', *Financial Times*, 20 July 2021, https://www.ft.com/content/937ee941-a808-40ac-b83e-429d0a7ae5d8

2   Oscar A. H. Schmitz, *Das Land ohne Musik: englische Gesellschaftsprobleme* (Munich: G. Muller, 1904).

Europe, the UK has also been called a nation of shopkeepers; arguably that should now be changed to a nation of online shoppers.

Fig. 5.2 Frederic Acquaviva, *The Election Night Count*, Hackney Britannia Centre © Lore Lixenberg (2019).

Rishi Sunak, Chancellor of the Exchequer,[3] stated rather surprisingly [4] that as music is a financially non-viable activity, musicians should seek alternative income streams. This is in spite of the fact that in 2018 alone, music as an industry added 5.2 billion pounds to the national purse. It would be useful if the current government at the very least knew the price of everything and the value of nothing, but they don't even seem to know that. However, more worrying is the huge disconnect between political and everyday life in the UK and, following on from that, everyday life and music and creativity. It's as though we have bred a nation of cap-doffing, class-conscious super-consumers with

---

3 Correct at the time of writing, though Rishi Sunak has gone on to become Prime Minister.

4 ITV, 'Covid: Rishi Sunak says people in "all walks of life" are having to adapt for employment', 6 October 2020, https://www.itv.com/news/2020-10-06/rishi-sunak-suggests-musicians-and-others-in-arts-should-retrain-and-find-other-jobs

an imprisoned slave mentality who have been taught to know their place and stay there and who don't really view themselves, their lives or communities as inherently creative. In fact the idea of an autonomous organic community, where different people work together for the common good, seems to be actively discouraged, resulting in an increased sense of isolation and polarisation. The result of this is that many people don't see themselves as creators, and can only relate to music and cultural activity as customers. The relationship to music is commodified along with everything else; music is once again something to be bought and passively ingested. Understandably, if you have been running around an Amazon warehouse all day, obliged to urinate into a plastic bottle because your employer even sees attending to basic bodily functions as a time-wasting drain on the corporate purse, the energy and will to create is bled out of the individual.[5]

In order to satisfy the needs of an exhausted populace, genres broadly referred to as pop and folk music, and other styles of vernacular music, have been appropriated by government-funded institutions, whereas these styles used to be rebellious alternatives outside the institutions. It's hard to imagine for instance, Jimi Hendrix considering something like a Snape Malting Residency or a PRS-funded album launch or ACE 'Develop Your Practice', to create their sound. Groups like Rudimentary Peni and The Dead Kennedys thrashing through their ugly, raw, beautiful and rude sound also spring to mind. There is certainly a general lurch toward a more soothing, bland, unchallenging, pre-chewed music.

With this in mind, as both an operatic form and a political party, how would The Voice Party conduct itself? Whilst it is arguable that world politics have become absurd and operatic enough already (we have the example of the Trump administration and also Vladimir Putin, who hired an experimental theatre director, Vladislav Surkov, with the express intention of encouraging a post-truth era: confusing, manipulating and exhausting world populations), arguably art, music, operatic structure and life have become entwined in a duplicitous, twisted way. It is important then that The Voice Party remedies this in

---

5   Colin Drury, 'Amazon workers "forced to urinate in plastic bottles because they cannot go to the toilet on a shift"', *Independent*, 19 July 2019, https://www.independent.co.uk/news/uk/home-news/amazon-protests-workers-urinate-plastic-bottles-no-toilet-breaks-milton-keynes-jeff-bezos-a9012351.html

an authentic and sincere way, utilising operatic and quotidian structures to infuse each other and explore different modes of musical creation by putting musical creativity at the very centre of politics and daily life.

This being said, The Voice Party also has its own dedicated Twitter bot farm, utilising social media to create a musical disseminating structure. A dedicated Twitter developer account was set up @TheVoiceParty1 (theVoicePartyOperaBotFarm) as a bot account that only follows @10DowningStreet and @BorisJohnson,[6] and automatically answers these accounts in opera, or rather heightened vocalisations. The bot is linked to a SoundCloud account that acts as a repository of bot material. Created purely for Twitter, this store of material is used by the main protagonist in this Twitter opera, the 'Twitter Troll'. These trolls usually hide behind anonymous Twitter handles and are often created in bulk for operabot farms. Whether the troll is human or a programmed bot, they can be seen as vengeful (or simply mercenary) characters who amplify extreme political thought and fake news of many different persuasions. There is a parallel between the function of these botfarms and that of the chorus of the ancient Greeks, whose function it was to echo and comment on the main action unfolding onstage, the actors being anonymised by the use of masks. The plot is very simple: every time @10DowningStreet or @BorisJohson tweets, the bot replies in opera. Some of the bot content was built by simple voice-multitracking and collage techniques, some of the bot 'arias' were made by AI taking on the distinctive voice of Boris Johnson and autogenerating material. There are two sorts of bot aria; one is a simple repeated module such as 'Liar' and 'Fuck You', that are formed of multi-tracked vocal loops. The second structure is composed in response to a particular event, such as 'Not Father Christmas', which is a retort to Boris Johnson's remarks in the autumn of 2020 (the middle of the COVID-19 pandemic) that we would all have a normal family Christmas and how important that is. These utilise collage and also, in some cases, AI voice analysis of Boris Johnson's speeches to pick out repeated vocal tropes and tics and interactions such as 'ping pong', 'wowzers' and various Churchillian quotes. This opera uses Twitter as its stage, in the way Goffman states that in the 'theatre play where

---

6   At the time of writing, Boris Johnson was Prime Minister; he was replaced in 2022 by Liz Truss whose premiership lasted forty-nine days, after which Rishi Sunak took the position.

I conduct a performance, I play a role' only showing the 'front stage and not the backstage.[7] Social media, especially Twitter, is in some ways diametrically in opposition to Rancierian thinking as presented in *The Emancipated Spectator*, or Debordian critique, as Twitter is in some ways the heart and soul of exteriority. 'Theatre accuses itself of rendering spectators passive and thereby betraying its essence as community action'.[8] Twitter users often mask themselves behind obscure usernames. In fact Twitter bots always do, and users who use their actual names rarely present a full and authentic picture of themselves. Social media platforms have been utilised to wreak havoc on democracies and the idea of political truth. There is a dichotomy and dramatic tension between a platform that purports to be representative of the everyday, encouraging people to connect via microblogs and tiny interactions, but is in fact the opposite of that, often creating an alternate reality.

As an operatic structure, The Voice Party proposes to subvert Twitter's propensity to twist the truth and go beyond the mere representation of character and situation, something one also often finds in contemporary opera as well as Twitter: characters are continually presented to us in opera houses as a parade of quasi trans-humanist-pre-post-cyborg avatars, extensions of neurotic backstories inherited from redundant social structures designed to keep people in their place. The Voice Party proposes opera and operatic character as pure, truthful embodiments of oneself, of fantasies and creations, and of present and future potentialities, completely free of these outmoded, patriarchal, colonialist paradigms. We as humans could become as free as the birds. This would automatically address ideals of inclusivity as this quality is inbuilt into the very structure of the piece.

The Voice Party would completely reverse the current situation where musical activity occurs on the sidelines of society, grateful for any crumbs of financial support that fall from the table, for which it must conform and castrate itself to receive. Music would proudly stand at the very centre of all decision-making in all aspects of daily life, and politics would be informed and guided by the beautiful, elegant laws of music,

---

7   Erving Goffman, *The Presentation of the Self in Everyday Life* (Edinburgh: University of Edinburgh Social Sciences Research Centre, 1956), p. 53.
8   Jacques Rancière, *The Emancipated Spectator*, trans. by Gregory Elliot (London; New York: Verso Press 2009), p. 7.

unencumbered by corporate and state interference. The Voice Party, as a participatory operatic political structure, asks what the outcome would be if participatory musical performance principles were actually placed at the centre of daily life and politics. Needless to say, The Voice Party would prioritise music lessons, inclusive and decolonised for each and every child, but for this to really work we need to go much further than that. The entire fabric of society needs to be radically musicalised, which means supporting parents and musicalising the structures that parents operate within. The cost of instruments and instrumental lessons and voice lessons are not the only barriers to music education, but also the atmosphere in which children grow up. How can you practise or simply play or sing if there is no physical or sonic space, and if your surroundings are unsympathetic to musical activity?

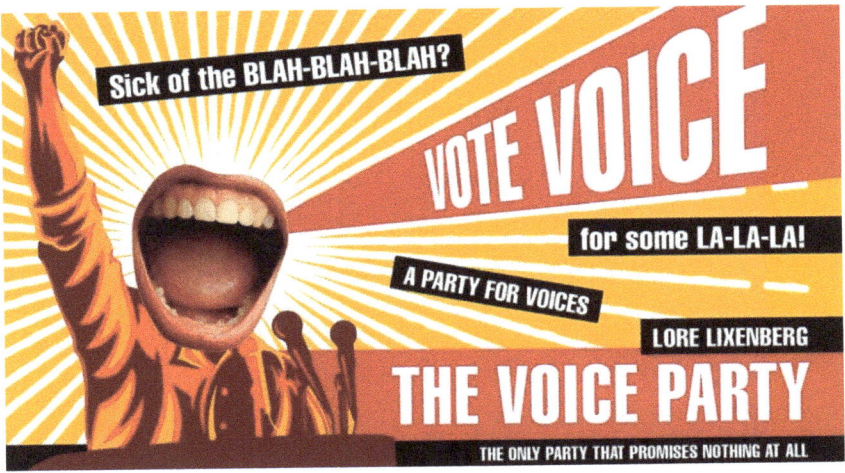

Fig. 5.3 Jeremy Richardson, Election window banner design © Lore Lixenberg.

Musical activity has a profound impact on the way in which the human brain functions. It makes the left and the right brain more integrated, and better at connecting thoughts, memories and emotions.[9] It has a calming and invigorating effect on the brain, encouraging both independence and social cohesion, resulting in an individual being equipped to think for themselves, possibly immunising them against lies and media

---

9   Nigel Osborne, 'Neuroscience and "real world" practice: music as a therapeutic resource for children in zones of conflict', *Annals of the New York Academy of Sciences* 1252 (2012), 69–76.

mendaciousness, making that person more confident.[10] Little wonder then, that music is banned or at least controlled in totalitarian states. This quality of social cohesion coupled with individual free thinking is the last thing that budding authoritarian regimes and corporations want to encourage. Can you imagine an Amazon delivery truck driver orchestra or the Walmart Community Choir? Can you imagine the outcome if such things existed?

The Voice Party has a manifesto that can be summed up by the following main points:

1. The Voice Party is the only party you cannot join; it joins you.

2. The Voice Party aims to put music at the centre of UK politics by using musical forms as templates for social structures and by making musical activity mandatory for all institutions and businesses. Any organisation failing to implement this will be heavily fined via the Voxxcoin system (see below).

3. The fiscal policy: the Voice Party is not anti-capitalist or hyper-capitalist, rather it is a-capitalist. It is beyond capitalism. It has a specific fiscal policy and economic system and would put in place its own currency, the Voxxcoin.

4. The housing policy is that everybody should have one, and all new architectural structures would include acoustic planning as a priority. A building that has a wonderful acoustic as its primary objective will automatically enhance the health and wellbeing of the population. These buildings would also have mandatory dedicated rehearsal and practice spaces.

5. The Voice Party education policy is that all lessons of all subjects will be vocalised and history will be taught largely via the musical history of all cultures. Science will be taught through the prism of music, acoustics, psychoacoustics and sound generally.

6. Children would be encouraged to create and not consume. They would be encouraged to find themselves through

---

10 François Matarasso, 'The Parliament of Dreams: Why everything depends on culture', Version 2.5 (2013), 2. This text was originally given at Junction 2010, the Regional Arts Australia conference in Launceston, Tasmania on 27th August 2010.

meaningful artistic pursuits and not by buying their way into a particular look, tribe or identity.

7. The health policy states simply that everyone gets treatment when they need it and music therapy is a daily practice. Space would be made in all workplaces for musical meditation, and small ailments would be attended to before they escalate. Also, more funding would be dedicated to preventative medicine, and cutting-edge treatments would be available to all and not only the very rich.

8. The foreign policy simply states that it is mandatory for all visitors, imFmigrants and refugees, to contribute to the musical activities of the UK on arrival, in any way they wish. The Voice Party aims for orchestral and choral communities within open borders.

9. Defence policy: we shall sing our enemies into submission. We will destroy them with the power of our voices.

Fig. 5.4 Frederic Acquaviva Election night: 3am exhaustion with the obligatory flask of hot whisky todd © Lore Lixenberg (2019).

The Voice Party has already made additions to its front bench: a cabinet of advisors picked from a cohort of musicians, with the proviso that anyone who is on the front bench of The Voice Party must be a musician of some discipline. In addition to this, the Voice Party insists if it were to be in power, all politicians of all parties would go through a stringent anonymous audition, to be allowed to serve and must also be proficient in at least two languages as well as their mother tongue. They must also have lived in another country for at least three years. The front bench at the time of the UK election of 12 September 2019 was:

1. Party Leader: Lore Lixenberg.
2. Minister of Fluids and Fluidity: Bill Banks Jones.
3. Minister of Voxxcoin, Shadow Chancellor of the Exchequer: Natalie Raybould.
4. Minister of Vintage Clothing, Environment, Farming and Fisheries: Heloise Werner.
5. Minister of Knowledge and Mental Pleasures: Martina Schwarz.
6. Shadow Home Secretary, or Minister of Flirtatiousness and Charm: Elise Lorraine.
7. Minister of Earth, Wind, Fire, Transport: Joost de Krammer.
8. Minister of Gatherings, Parties, Weddings, Funerals, End-of-the-World Soirees: Richard Thomas.
9. Department of Communications and Visual Representation: Jeremy Richardson.
10. Department of Compositional Technique and Art Curation: Frederic Acquaviva.

The Voice Party as opera and politics is, in some ways, an act of resistance in the same way that post-World-War-One Dadaism and post- World-War-Two Lettrism were an antidote to a time when words were twisted into lies by the political classes, leading to the horrors of the trenches and the holocaust. On top of this, in the twenty-first century we have a world of AI deep-fakes and increasingly sophisticated, yet woefully unoriginal chatbots, where you cannot even be sure that the person who appears to be saying something is actually saying it. We also have a cacophony of art as entertainment: Netflix, opera houses and theatres dealing in dumbed-down, corporate cultural crack cocaine, and Society of Spectacle soylent green junk food. The only answer is to scream complex raw vocalisations in any way other than speech.

Maybe this all comes across as insane and non-implementable. But I ask you, why not dream up completely new systems of organisation? After all, what could be more insane than what we have in the UK right now? What could be more insane than spending billions on unusable personal protective equipment in a pandemic? What could be more insane than spending billions on a track-and-trace system that did not work? What could be more insane than the several tonnes of lobster rotting on a quayside in Scotland because the government could not get the Brexit paperwork together in time? What could be more insane than the blatant national self-harm that is Brexit? What could be more insane than Boris Johnson's haircut?

Fig. 5.5 Lore Lixenberg, The Voice Party Election street poster Berlin (2017) © Lore Lixenberg.

References

Drury, Colin, 'Amazon workers "forced to urinate in plastic bottles because they cannot go to the toilet on a shift"', *Independent*, 19 July 2019, https://www.independent.co.uk/news/uk/home-news/amazon-protests-workers-urinate-plastic-bottles-no-toilet-breaks-milton-keynes-jeff-bezos-a9012351.html

Goffman, Erving, *The Presentation of the Self in Everyday Life* (Edinburgh: University of Edinburgh Social Sciences Research Centre, 1956).

ITV, 'Covid: Rishi Sunak says people in "all walks of life" are having to adapt for employment', 6 October (2020), https://www.itv.com/news/2020-10-06/rishi-sunak-suggests-musicians-and-others-in-arts-should-retrain-and-find-other-jobs

Matarasso, François, 'The Parliament of Dreams: Why everything depends on culture', Version 2.5, *A Selfless Art*, (2013), https://arestlessart.files.wordpress.com/2018/09/2013-the-parliament-of-dreams.pdf

Osborne, Nigel, 'Neuroscience and "real world" practice: music as a therapeutic resource for children in zones of conflict', *Annals of the New York Academy of Sciences* 1252 (2012), 69–76.

Schmitz, Oscar A. H., *Das Land ohne Musik: englische Gesellschaftsprobleme* (Munich: G. Muller, 1904).

Staton, Bethan, 'Funding for arts courses and London universities to be slashed', *Financial Times*, 20 July 2021, https://www.ft.com/content/937ee941-a808-40ac-b83e-429d0a7ae5d8

Music for Nothing, *The New Republic*, https://newrepublic.com/article/162542/music-streaming-services-musicians

Interview with Chancellor of the Exchequer, Rishi Sunak during the Covid 19 pandemic. https://www.itv.com/news/2020-10-06/rishi-sunak-suggests-musicians-and-others-in-arts-should-retrain-and-find-other-jobs

6. Becoming a Classical Musician of the Future
The Effects of Training and Experience on Performer Attitudes to Innovation

Stephanie Pitts, Karen Burland and Tom Spurgin

Introduction

The classical music sector changes slowly, and usually with the audience at the heart of decisions, whether driven by concerns over diversity (or its lack) or the simple bottom line of needing to increase ticket sales and income. Recent innovations include shifting the concert location to an informal or unusual venue,[1] increasing the interaction between performers and audiences,[2] and making changes to the marketing, programme notes and presentation.[3] Performers are hugely impacted by these decisions, but have little agency over the direction of their organisations, and little training for the adapted roles and settings in which they might find themselves.

---

1   Julia Haferkorn, 'Dancing to Another Tune: Classical Music in Nightclubs and Other Non-traditional Venues', in *The Classical Music Industry*, ed. by Christopher Dromey and Julia Haferkorn (New York; London: Routledge, Taylor & Francis Group, 2018).
2   Stephanie E. Pitts, 'What Makes an Audience? Investigating the Roles and Experiences of Listeners at a Chamber Music Festival', *Music & Letters* 86:2 (2005).
3   Pitts, Stephanie E. and Sarah M. Price, *Understanding Audience Engagement in the Contemporary Arts* (Abingdon, Oxon; New York, NY: Routledge, Taylor & Francis Group, 2021).

The impact of innovation in classical music on performers' experiences and wellbeing is currently under-researched, with insufficient focus on the resultant changes that might be needed in conservatoire and university music education to equip performers for this new age.[4] In our collaboration between the Sheffield Performer and Audience Research Centre (SPARC), Manchester Collective and the Philharmonia Orchestra, we are raising questions about how performers in heritage and alternative classical music organisations are adapting to changing circumstances.

Our chapter draws upon twenty-seven survey responses and four interviews with musicians from our two partner ensembles, in which the musicians reflect on their training and the extent to which this prepared them for professional orchestral playing. We shared our findings and analysis with the then Manchester Collective Chief Executive, Adam Szabo, and his responses are included towards the end of the chapter, helping to set the agenda for future research and innovation. These exploratory findings raise questions about the role of conservatoires in supporting or inhibiting innovation in the profession, and highlight the challenges of work-life balance that were altered by the pandemic. We consider the implications of these findings for orchestras as workplaces, and for musicians as agents for change in the classical music industry.

Literature Review: Foundations for Classical Music Careers

The transition from training to working as a musician is widely considered to be complex and unpredictable,[5] and while this is true of career transitions more generally, this is particularly pronounced for

---

[4] Karen Burland and Dawn Bennett, 'Creating a Sustainable Performance Career', in *The Oxford Handbook of Music Performance: Insights from Education, Psychology, Musicology, Science and Medicine*, ed. by Gary E. McPherson (New York: Oxford University Press, 2022), pp. 135–153.

[5] Burland and Bennett, 'Creating a Sustainable Performance Career'; Andrea Creech, Ioulia Papageorgi, Celia Duffy, Frances Morton, Elizabeth Haddon, John Potter, and others, 'From Music Student to Professional: The Process of Transition', *British Journal of Music Education*, 25:3 (2008), 315–31; Jerry C. Middleton and Jason A. Middleton, 'Review of Literature on the Career Transitions of Performing Artists Pursuing Career Development', *International Journal for Educational and Vocational Guidance* 17:2 (2016), 211–32.

performing artists who face diverse pathways through protean and portfolio careers.[6] Even before the global COVID-19 pandemic which began in 2020, the music industry was associated with precarity,[7] financial insecurity[8] and threats to work-life balance.[9] The pandemic has undoubtedly caused a great deal of anxiety for professional and aspiring musicians, particularly in relation to their working lives and the future shape of the music profession.[10] The suspension of live performance during lockdowns also became a source of identity threat to the musicians affected, whose sense of self is so intertwined with their musical activities,[11] particularly because music usually has been a dominant feature of their lives from a relatively young age.[12]

Such extreme disruption to the working lives of musicians is thankfully rare, and has never occurred before on the scale experienced during the pandemic. The new insights this collective disruption has provided into the impact of change within the music profession echo work which has considered the experience of redundancy for opera singers;[13] the psychological challenges faced by pre-elite, transitioning-elite and established-elite performers;[14] and the 'hidden injuries' experienced by rock-and-roll musicians frustrated by, and eventually

---

6   Jerry C. Middleton and Jason A. Middleton, 'Review of Literature on the Career Transitions of Performing Artists Pursuing Career Development', *International Journal for Educational and Vocational Guidance* 17:2 (2016), 211–32, https://doi.org/10.1007/s10775-016-9326-x

7   Norma Daykin, 'Disruption, Dissonance and Embodiment: Creativity, Health and Risk in Music Narratives', *Health: An Interdisciplinary Journal for the Social Study of Health, Illness and Medicine* 9:1 (2005), 67–87.

8   Melissa C. Dobson, 'Insecurity, Professional Sociability, and Alcohol: Young Freelance Musicians' Perspectives on Work and Life in the Music Profession', *Psychology of Music* 39:2 (2011), 240–60.

9   Charles Umney and Lefteris Kretsos, 'That's the Experience', *Work and Occupations* 42:3 (2015), 313–34.

10   Susanna Cohen and Jane Ginsborg, 'The Experiences of Mid-Career and Seasoned Orchestral Musicians in the UK During the First COVID-19 Lockdown', *Frontiers in Psychology* 12 (2021), 645967–645967.

11   Glynis M. Breakwell and Rusi Jaspal, 'Identity processes and musicians during the COVID-19 pandemic', *Musicae Scientiae* 26:4 (2022), 777-798.

12   Middleton and Middleton, 'Review of Literature'.

13   Jane Oakland, Raymond MacDonald and Paul Flowers, ''Identity in Crisis: The Role of Work in the Formation and Renegotiation of a Musical Identity', *British Journal of Music Education* 30 (2013), 261–276.

14   Ellis Pecen, David J. Collins and Áine MacNamara, '"It's Your Problem. Deal with It." Performers' Experiences of Psychological Challenges in Music', *Frontiers in Psychology* 8:2374 (2018).

unsuccessful in achieving, their ambitions and attempts to work in music.[15]

The working lives of musicians have always demanded a certain amount of flexibility, requiring individuals to possess openness and agency in embracing change and seeking opportunities.[16] However, over the past two decades there has been a step-change in the ways that organisations have responded to demands to diversify, maintain relevance, attract new audiences, and meet the changing expectations of funders and the public more broadly.[17] Innovation often focuses on enhancing audience experience, by offering closer connection to the performers or curating performances in non-traditional venues, for example; research highlights the impact of such audience development strategies on the audience,[18] or the intended impact from the perspective of producers,[19] but rarely considers the players' perspectives.

Training as a musician has traditionally been associated with developing technical expertise alongside competitive distinctiveness[20] which means that as the music profession develops and transforms, some musicians may not feel equipped to take on new tasks such as leading education projects, talking to audiences or performing in a wider range of musics. Musicians, particularly those who have more recently completed their training, increasingly recognise the value of developing entrepreneurial skills in order to identify opportunities to be

---

15 George Morgan and Julian Wood, 'Creative Accommodations: The Fractured Transitions and Precarious Lives of Young Musicians', *Journal of Cultural Economy* 7:1 (2014), 64–78.

16 Sini Juuti and Karen Littleton, 'Tracing the Transition from Study to a Contemporary Creative Working Life: The Trajectories of Professional Musicians', *Vocations and Learning* 5:1 (2011), 5–21.

17 Hilary Glow, Anne Kershaw and Matthew Reason, 'Leading or Avoiding Change: The Problem of Audience Diversification for Arts Organisations', *International Journal of Cultural Policy* 27:1 (2021), 130–148; Steven Hadley, *Audience Development and Cultural Policy* (London: Palgrave Macmillan, 2021).

18 Pitts, 'What Makes an Audience?; Pitts and Price, *Understanding Audience Engagement in the Contemporary Arts*

19 Christopher Dromey and Julia Haferkorn, *The Classical Music Industry* (New York; London: Routledge, Taylor & Francis Group, 2018).

20 Paul Hager and Mary C. Johnsson, 'Learning to Become a Professional Orchestral Musician: Going Beyond Skill and Technique', *Journal of Vocational Education & Training* 61:2 (2009), 103–18.

creative or innovative in ways that align with their identities and values.[21] Such individuals may embrace change and challenge as an exciting opportunity.[22] However, other individuals, perhaps those without this kind of 'growth mindset',[23] may feel increasingly disconnected from their co-workers and organisation when trying to align with new expectations; they may become insecure about their abilities, or experience an unwelcome threat to their identity as a musician.[24] There are therefore potential negative psychological risks for individuals who are unable to meet changing expectations, particularly where there are low levels of perceived control and support.[25]

In their study exploring the psychological challenges experienced by aspiring and established musicians, Pecen et al. highlight that their elite performers demonstrated a range of positive behaviours towards their work, including those relating to health habits, strategies for coping with anxiety, and a reflective attitude towards performance, suggesting that these characteristics are essential in order to sustain work as a music performer.[26] In addition, all of their participants recognised the need for a range of professional skills relating to organisation, communication, and managing a business. This aligns with Vaag et al. who highlight that 'having adequate personal resources such as entrepreneurial skills, value-anchored flexibility, tolerance for ambiguity and dedication to music making were described as important for managing life as a freelance musician'.[27]

The evidence of the workplace challenges faced by professional musicians points to the need for greater understanding of how training can best equip players to be agile, resilient and open-minded without

---

21   Staffan Albinsson, 'Musicians as Entrepreneurs or Entrepreneurs as Musicians?', *Creativity and Innovation Management* 27 (2017), 348–357; Jonas Vaag, Fay Giæver and Ottar Bjerkeset, 'Specific Demands and Resources in the Career of the Norwegian Freelance Musician', *Arts and Health* 6:3 (2014), 205–222.
22   Karen Burland, 'Becoming a Musician: A Longitudinal Study Investigating the Career Transitions of Undergraduate Music Students' (Unpublished doctoral thesis, University of Sheffield, 2005).
23   Carol S. Dweck, 'Motivational Processes Affecting Learning', *American Psychologist* 41:10 (1986), 1040–48.
24   Creech and others, 'From Music Student to Professional'.
25   Daykin, 'Disruption, Dissonance and Embodiment'.
26   Pecen and others, '"It's Your Problem. Deal with It."'
27   Vaag and others, 'Specific Demands and Resources in the Career of the Norwegian Freelance Musician', p. 205.

losing the core values of classical music-making (usually assumed to include technical excellence and expressive performance). Pecen et al. highlight the importance of acknowledging the challenging reality of pursuing work as a musician, encouraging engagement with extra-curricular activities and raising awareness of sources of self-help.[28] A student-centred approach, which enables individuals to understand what future success looks like to them, is also vital. Other research highlights that students would benefit from exposure to a mixture of informal and formal learning opportunities,[29] as well as the 'provision of many and varied performance opportunities and support for developing self-discipline and autonomy in relation to the acquisition of musical expertise';[30] such activities may help to foster a more flexible approach towards music-making and the confidence to adapt to new challenges.

Social support from friends, family and peers during periods of transition and change is also important for managing the hurdles associated with trying to become established in the music profession and for managing life as a freelance musician.[31] Valuable support also comes from access to mentoring or multi-genre peer networks during periods of transition,[32] as well as opportunities to experience 'guided contextualising' through situated learning (e.g. the professional orchestra).[33]

It is clear that in order to best support the complex process of acquiring and sustaining work in a changing and opaque music profession, greater insight into the challenges and opportunities it affords for established and aspiring musicians is now needed. Our study aims to begin this work, considering the implications for music organisations and training institutions, and of course, for the musicians themselves.

---

28 Pecen and others, '"It's Your Problem. Deal with It."'
29 Susan Coulson, 'Getting "Capital" in the Music World: Musicians' Learning Experiences and Working Lives', *British Journal of Music Education* 27:3 (2010), 255–70.
30 Creech and others, 'From Music Student to Professional', p. 315.
31 Umney and Kretsos, 'That's the Experience'; Vaag and others, 'Specific Demands and Resources in the Career of the Norwegian Freelance Musician'.
32 Creech and others, 'From Music Student to Professional'.
33 Hager and Johnsson, 'Learning to Become a Professional Orchestral Musician'.

Research Methods

The data for this study were collected from musicians working with two classical ensembles based in the UK with whom we had existing contacts: the Philharmonia Orchestra, a symphony orchestra based in London, and Manchester Collective, a smaller, flexible chamber ensemble. Both ensembles work with freelance musicians and so some of our participants had experience of working with both the smaller and larger classical music ensembles represented in this study.

The research was split into three stages:

1. *Survey:* An online questionnaire sent to all player members of the Philharmonia Orchestra and musicians who had performed with Manchester Collective during 2019, 2020 and early 2021. The survey sought responses on musicians' experiences of education and training, and the relevance of this training to their current practice; the effects of COVID-19 on their work; how the classical music profession has changed over their time in the industry; reflections on what they would do differently if they were to train again; and what skills they anticipate being required of classical musicians in the next twenty years.

2. *Interviews:* Follow-up interviews were conducted with four survey participants who had expressed a willingness to talk in more depth about their experiences. The interviews focused on participants' experiences of training and their willingness to engage in activities outside of their formal training curricula.

3. *Sector response:* Having analysed the survey results and interview transcripts, key themes and quotes were posed to Adam Szabo, the then Chief Executive of Manchester Collective, to gain his reflections on the findings to date. (We had originally intended this conversation to take place between the Artistic Directors and Chief Executives of both ensembles, but this proved difficult to schedule due to personnel changes and diary clashes.)

The survey received twenty-seven responses in total, of which thirty percent (n=8) were named participants from the Philharmonia

Orchestra and thirty-three percent (n=9) were named participants from Manchester Collective. A further thirty-seven percent (n=10) were unnamed participants. The surveys and interviews were all collected between March and April 2021. Four interviews took place, three with musicians working regularly with the Philharmonia Orchestra and one with a Manchester Collective player. Interviews were conducted online by Tom Spurgin, then Audience Development Manager at the Philharmonia Orchestra and currently undertaking a PhD in collaboration with Manchester Collective, supervised by Stephanie Pitts and Karen Burland.[34] Responses from the surveys and interviews were analysed by all three authors using Interpretative Phenomenological Analysis (IPA). They are presented anonymously in the discussion that follows, using participant codes for the surveys (S1-S27) and player interviews (P1-4).

The first two stages of data collection and analysis took place in 2021 ready for the paper's presentation at the Maastricht Centre for the Innovation of Classical Music (MCICM) 2021 symposium, and the final stage was completed in March 2022 in preparation for this chapter. Our data collection was therefore affected by the COVID-19 pandemic, taking place online and coming at a time in which participants were in a heightened state of reflection on their career choices and job security. The participant sample is small but the data generated was rich and detailed. Key themes were evident in the analysis of interviews and surveys, relating to the research topics of the future of classical music and the training required to support musicians' preparedness for sector change. We discuss these thematic findings in turn below, before presenting our discussion with Adam Szabo and the implications of the study for the classical music industry and for future research.

Research Themes and Findings

Undertaking this research after the pandemic lockdowns of 2020 and 2021 meant that our participants were facing uncertainty and anxiety about their futures, as freelance musicians suffered a devastating loss

---

[34] Tom Spurgin's PhD is undertaken with funding from the Arts and Humanities Research Council (AHRC), awarded via the White Rose College of Arts & Humanities (WRoCAH).

of income and lack of support.³⁵ In the survey and interviews, they gave detailed responses about the experiences of being an orchestral musician, including their preparedness for the profession, their understanding of the orchestra as a distinctive work environment, and the impact of these training and employment experiences on their musical identities. Woven throughout these discussions was a consideration of the purpose of orchestras and of classical music more widely, as participants' individual struggles to find a secure place in the classical music world were coupled with doubts about how that world might – or should – change in the future.

Preparedness for the Profession

The majority of our participants had taken a conventional route to becoming a classical musician, and reported having instrumental lessons privately (sixty-three percent; n=17) or through school (fifteen percent; n=4), and then progressing to undergraduate music degrees at a conservatoire (fifty-six percent; n=15) or university (fifteen percent; n=4), often followed by postgraduate study (conservatoire seventy-four percent; n=20; university eight percent; n=2).³⁶ For some, the route into professional playing had been similarly traditional: eight people had worked their way into an orchestral position through 'gain[ing] enough orchestral experience to audition and go for principal positions' (S24), while another seven had undertaken freelance work, such as in

---

35 C.f. Paul Chamberlain and David Morris, *The economic impact of Covid-19 on the Culture, Arts and Heritage (CAH) sector in South Yorkshire and comparator regions* (University of Sheffield, 2021), https://www.sheffield.ac.uk/city-region/enhancing-cultural-vibrancy/covid-research-0; Ben Walmsley, Abigail Gilmore, Dave O'Brien and Anne Torreggiani, *Culture in Crisis: Impacts of Covid-19 on the UK cultural sector and where we go from here* (Centre for Cultural Value, 2022), https://www.culturehive.co.uk/CVIresources/culture-in-crisis-impacts-of-covid-19/

36 Participants were asked to 'tick all that apply' from a list of multiple-choice options, but the increase in numbers towards postgraduate degrees suggests that many had reported only their highest qualification, and therefore numbers receiving instrumental lessons in childhood were much greater in reality. All four of those who began their instrumental lessons in school subsequently had privately funded tuition. This of course raises questions about access and privilege in professional music careers, which are beyond the scope of this chapter; for further discussion see Anna Bull, *Class, Control and Classical Music* (New York, NY: Oxford University Press, 2019).

'numerous part time orchestras, slowly working up' (S5). In six other cases, the 'portfolio career' description was more apt,[37] and often viewed positively as a way of gaining a broader repertoire of musical skills: 'my diverse experience such as chamber musician, modern ensemble player, soloist and orchestral musician helped me in many ways when I was on trial' (S16).

While these participants had followed the expected educational route into the classical music profession, they were often critical of the extent to which it had prepared them for their working lives. The interviewees described the 'very narrow discipline' (P4) of the conservatoire curriculum and, like the survey respondents, felt that the emphasis on their instrument had been a limiting factor in their training:

> Often today's students prepare technically and musically but lack cultural awareness and exposure to the influences which could single them out for a successful career. (S2)

Some participants had taken musicianship or orchestral training classes, but still felt that they had been left to learn much of the craft of orchestral playing 'on the job', such as how to relate to other members of an orchestral section, both socially and musically. The most common mode of learning new skills was to 'make it up as you go along – watch what other people do and imitate them' (S17). While a few players lamented the lack of professional development offered by their ensembles, others felt this would be superfluous: 'It's common sense, and everyone should find their own way' (S2). This latter attitude highlights the qualities of being 'versatile and adaptable' (S3) that were felt to be essential for success in the classical music procession, but it also positions the need for help or training as a weakness, thereby creating a barrier to seeking such help.[38] Respondents were more likely to regret an absence in their initial training – such as the provision of improvisation lessons, recording technique, or guidance on how to avoid injury – than to express a desire for future development, reiterating that being a classical musician is 'a job you can only learn by doing' (S17).

---

37   Brydie-Leigh Bartleet and others, 'Building Sustainable Portfolio Careers in Music: Insights and Implications for Higher Education', *Music Education Research* 21:3 (2019), 282–94.
38   C.f. Daykin, 'Disruption, Dissonance and Embodiment'.

Experience of Being in an Orchestra

Gaining a place in an orchestra had been the clear ambition for many participants throughout their training, and performing with others was at the heart of responses to the question 'What do you enjoy most about your job?':

> I love working with people to create something powerful in that one moment. Putting together programmes that have a gripping emotional arc and then giving everything to get as much of that across in performance as possible. It's about making the art come alive. (S13)

This deeply-felt satisfaction did not alter the fact that orchestras were seen as frustrating and problematic workplaces by many of the respondents, and the interviewees spoke in detail about not feeling heard by their section leaders or orchestral management. Taking on membership of committees was interesting but additional work, such that 'balancing [the] artistic process with meetings and admin can be tricky' (S13). Outside those official forums, where players could feel 'listened to in a way that might meaningfully alter the work' (P4), the mechanisms for influencing change were perceived as difficult or risky: 'often there is no opportunity to question without the risk of losing work' (S20). Likewise, the emotional labour[39] of ensuring smooth interpersonal relations within the orchestra and making new members feel welcome was acknowledged as an effort, and not always evenly distributed among the players: one interviewee felt the need for 'some kind of personal development workshop like how to deal with people you disagree with' (P3), while another had 'made a pact with myself to work harder to include people that I didn't know or that were new to the orchestra' (P1). These frustrations show that the players have insights on the orchestral workplace that are under-represented in decision-making, so diminishing their willingness to engage in conversations about the future direction of the ensemble.

Other challenges of pre-pandemic orchestral working life mentioned frequently were travelling, unsociable hours and relentless schedules, with several survey respondents describing the negative effects of

---

39 C.f. Arlie Russell Hochschild, *The Managed Heart: Commercialization of Human Feeling*, 3rd edition (Berkeley: University of California Press, 2012).

exhaustion, which can make it 'easy to stop caring' (S24). As the players resumed ensemble performance after the pandemic lockdowns, some described the pressure as even higher, with fewer performances meaning that 'the increased adrenaline is felt more keenly when it is not experienced regularly' (S10). The mental and physical strain of a busy performance schedule was mentioned by the majority of participants, and yet there was a high level of acceptance that these pressures were an inevitable part of the job:

> Sometimes (pre-pandemic) we could work for a month or longer without a day off (unless one deliberately takes work off to create free days), the working hours are somewhat unsociable (i.e. mostly when 'normal' people are free), and there can be a lot of travelling, both in the UK and abroad. But because I absolutely love my job, I don't necessarily see these challenges in a negative light! (S7)

In accepting the social challenges and working conditions of the orchestra, there was a strong sense of fitting into 'the way things are' (P2), showing an inertia about changing the culture. This could be related to the risks of questioning practices and therefore potentially losing work to a player seen as easier to deal with, but some participants noted the negative effects of being part of organisations whose success is directed by external markers of 'prestige and funding' (S20), meaning that 'as classical musicians we are in danger of our voice and creativity being stifled by the confines and traditions of the profession' (S26).

The pandemic had disrupted the routine of orchestral playing, and while some participants were eager to get back to 'normal' orchestral life, others had undergone a reappraisal of priorities and were aiming 'to strike a better balance in the future, post-pandemic' (S1). While the majority of the survey participants talked mainly about the loss of work caused by the cancelling of concerts, others identified new sources of income, including online teaching, and five gave examples of enjoying having family and leisure time that was usually unavailable to them: 'I'm a better and more spontaneous cook, know considerably more about Bordeaux and Burgundy wines, and the garden looks great!' (S2). Having interests beyond music was evidently a novelty to some of these players, and in some cases had helped them to cope with the losses and challenges of the pandemic lockdowns.

Whether the respondents were able to keep their resolutions to maintain these new interests once the pace of rehearsal and performance schedules quickened again was beyond the scope of our data collection, but some responses indicated that this was considered important, not only to personal wellbeing, but to the effective functioning of the classical music sector. Lack of cultural awareness and 'an interest in other parts of life' (S2) were noted as limiting factors for more traditional classical musicians, for whom 'the tunnel vision and specialisation of classical music can be limiting when diversifying one's portfolio' (S17). Some respondents hoped for change as the next generation of graduates joined their ranks: 'I think it will no longer be enough to be able to play your instrument very well, do a good audition, and settle into a comfortable job for life' (S26).

Musical Identity

The interviewees were all highly reflective about how their personalities and characteristics were bound up with their experiences of being classical musicians. The importance of emotional intelligence in the orchestral workplace (see 4.2) was evident in their descriptions of themselves as an 'over-thinker' (P3) or 'hypersensitive' (P4), with a capacity to 'read situations' (P4) that could be both helpful and obstructive to performance focus.

Participants also expressed views about which parts of their work were most important to their musical identity, with particular sensitivities around how they adapted to tasks for which they felt they had not been trained, notably learning and participation work with young people. This was often seen as an extra demand on players, who might 'never want that to be my job' (P3), though one survey respondent had identified the way to avoid this problem: 'I don't often agree to do work which I feel I haven't trained for, so I don't get asked for that very often any more' (S7).

There was some resistance from interviewees to describe themselves as a 'classical musician', since playing in other genres was also important to them, personally if not financially: 'that's not a majority of my income; that's probably quite a small amount but I see that as a big part of my identity as a musician' (P2). For this interviewee, having skills beyond those of an orchestral player set them apart as having 'a different kind of flexibility that maybe classical musicians don't always have' (P2), so echoing some of the sentiments on managing people, which was felt to be an unevenly distributed skill (see 4.2). The fragility of musical identity is evident in the way that interviewees evaluate themselves – favourably or otherwise – against other orchestral players and assert their individuality. Alongside this fragility, however, the sense of being committed to the role was also present: 'you keep doing it because the thought of not doing it is a major life decision' (P4).

The Purpose of Orchestras

The focus of our questions was mainly on participants' own experiences as performers, but this prompted a number of spontaneous reflections on the larger purpose of their work, in relation to reaching both new and loyal audiences and promoting classical music in contemporary society:

> I think the ability to be a passionate advocate for our art form is important. We need to be evangelical about the relevance of the music we love. (S4)

Being an 'advocate' for classical music increased the connection between education work and performance for some players, with several interviews noting that the qualities of effective workshop leading were close in purpose and approach to effective performing:

> I think people think classical music is really serious, and it is but it's also fun and music should be fun and enjoyable and I always come from that perspective. It's also the way I play [my instrument] as well as like, you're not just playing it for yourself, you're trying to communicate something, so it's all about communication. (P1)

These qualities of fun, enjoyment and communication underpinned other responses that were concerned with advocating for classical music, and reaching audiences who might otherwise think it was not for them. Responses that talked of 'sharing a passion' for classical music were frequent, and showed a strong emotional drive: 'I genuinely have a deep, deep love of music and the fact that I get to hang out with music, think about music, hear and create music every day is a great privilege'

(S15). For P3, fostering new audiences for classical music was an important source of satisfaction in the player role: 'you often get a sense of bringing music out into the world which is really, really amazing, and reaching audiences who you probably wouldn't see in a concert hall, which is just really great.'

There were several mentions in the survey responses of a shift in attitudes towards diversity and inclusion, with it becoming 'less and less acceptable to programme solely music by dead, white men (and rightly so)' (S15). While individual players might feel relatively powerless to tackle the concerns that they mentioned in their responses, including a lack of racial diversity or support for female conductors, they welcomed the general shift of 'organisations [who] are starting to understand the importance in their role for change rather than always just passing the buck to education like they don't have any influence' (S10). As one player noted, however, the pace of change was slow and relied upon 'a small number of artists, ensembles and institutions who deliberately and outspokenly challenge the old norms and traditions' (S26).

A similar overview of the sector was offered by another survey respondent:

> It's much more open and adventurous now. I feel like I can see the chasm between the old school and new school deepening – there are some people that are very set in their ways, certain parts of orchestral culture that appear very unhealthy to me. I think it's only a matter of time until these cultures eat up these institutions unless something radical changes. There are also some really inspiring groups and people who are challenging the norm and forging new paths. (S13).

Manchester Collective are explicitly on the forward-thinking side of this 'chasm', with the stated aim on their website being to 'create radical human experiences, inspired by the music that we love' (manchestercollective.co.uk). In seeking responses to our findings from their Chief Executive, Adam Szabo, we revisited the themes of preparedness for the profession, the orchestral workplace, the musical identities of players and the purpose and future of orchestras, in order to gain additional insight on the role of the music industry in shaping classical music futures.

Discussion with Adam Szabo

In the months since we had undertaken the surveys and interviews, Manchester Collective had produced their first 'Winter Residency', described as a unique training programme for emerging string players that focused on 'flexibility, freedom, collaboration and musicianship'.[40] In doing so, Manchester Collective were positioning themselves as part of the solution to the problems raised in our discussions with players, stemming from a realisation that 'maybe it's completely unrealistic to think that anyone would come out fully-baked when they leave higher education' (all quotes in this section are from Adam Szabo, interviewed by Tom Spurgin). Like the players, Adam was ambivalent about the effectiveness of performance training beyond achieving high levels of instrumental skill, suggesting that what might be called stagecraft or musicianship was rarely taught in sufficient depth: 'I guess there's a difference between having one stage deportment workshop where someone says "sit up straight and engage your audience" and then actually doing it in a really profound way.'

A striking difference in Adam's management perspective, however, was the responsibility he placed on the players to tackle the challenges of the orchestral role themselves, rather than expecting those to be made easier at an organisational level:

> I'm here for the musicians but I generally don't have much sympathy for people feeling uncomfortable about things: life is a big succession of feeling uncomfortable about things that we all have to do. That's literally the nature of every single job. In a way, this is one of the problems is that there is a sense, even in younger musicians – I don't know whether it's a kind of entitlement or something, but there's a sense that work should be comfortable and should be predictable and you should know exactly what the parameters of that job are.

Adam talked about 'the job' in a way that was generally resisted, or self-corrected, in the musicians' interviews, and he suggested that this view

---

40 The Strad, 'Building my confidence and developing as a well-rounded musician': Manchester Collective's Winter Residency for string players (2022), https://www.thestrad.com/education-hub/building-my-confidence-and-developing-as-a-well-rounded-musician-manchester-collectives-winter-residency-for-string-players/14440.article

of the orchestral player as pursuing 'a passion' rather than 'doing it to pick up a pay cheque' is unique to the orchestral profession (though viewed from the similarly emotionally invested workplace of academia, we might disagree on that point[41]). He sympathised with players who find themselves thrust into education work for which they do not feel fully equipped, likening this to a sushi chef who ends up working in a vegan canteen: 'it's a different thing [and] I do actually take some issue with the conflating of the orchestral profession and [learning and participation] stuff as if it was a natural progression.'

There are tensions between Adam's understanding of the musicians' practical and emotional challenges, which are similar to those reflected in our wider data collection, and the need to find a solution that fuels Manchester Collective's mission to bring classical music in new formats to new audiences. We reflected at the outset of our research that changes in the classical music profession generally have the audience at their heart, and the impact on players can be overlooked, with the risk of entrenching the attitudes of it being 'all about the instrument' as change is experienced as a threat to musical identity. Like some of our respondents, Adam felt that emotional resilience and support might be at the heart of including players in the transformation of the profession:

> In a way, I guess that is the whole project of the Collective in a sentence: trying to create an environment where it's okay for everyone to be uncomfortable together.

Conclusions and Implications

Our participants provided rich and passionate accounts of their motivations and experiences as professional musicians. They described strong musical identities and a calling to music, recognising the wider value of their work for audiences and communities, and aligning their own values with the organisational aims. This helped to sustain motivation to work, despite frustrations and negative experiences, and made many respondents optimistic and invested in the future of the classical music profession.

---

41 See for example Emmanuel Ogbonna and Lloyd C. Harris, 'Work Intensification and Emotional Labour Among UK University Lecturers: An Exploratory Study', *Organization Studies* 25:7 (2004), 1185–1203.

There is a sense of acceptance woven into the stories presented above; acceptance that the role is associated with frustration, challenge, exhaustion, too much travel and long or antisocial hours. Daykin discusses the powerful influence of traditional narratives of hegemony and heroism in the development of creative practice, which can 'naturalize sacrifice' such that individuals do not feel empowered to pursue alternative approaches.[42] There are hints of this in the accounts above: feelings of not being heard, of poor management and relationships, and a lack of control in a workplace that has high demands and financial precarity. Such experiences have implications for the wellbeing of musicians, particularly because strong identification with music can mean they persist in their musical pursuits even when that may become unhealthy or negative. This in turn, can also affect their capacity to respond and adapt to new challenges.

The pandemic provided a space for our participants to reflect on their working lives, and it is interesting to note that many found new hobbies or interests that they were keen to retain. The managing of musical self-identity is also demonstrated by Burland, who discusses the ways in which musicians at the start of their professional careers seek out non-musical activities to offer balance and perspective to their lives.[43] Fostering healthy and positive behaviours towards physical and psychological health is crucial to ensure a sustainable and adaptable workforce,[44] and should be a part of musicians' ongoing training and an important feature of transitional support into working life.[45] Likewise, it needs to be part of the management of players in the orchestral workplace, since our research has confirmed that the focus on audiences in classical music innovation comes at a psychological cost to the players.

One of our interviewees highlighted a perceived shift in the skills and mindsets of younger generations of performers,[46] recognising the impact that this is having on cultural norms and expectations within organisations. This perhaps suggests that training programmes are

---

[42] Daykin, 'Disruption, Dissonance and Embodiment', p. 85.
[43] Burland, 'Becoming a Musician'.
[44] Pecen and others, '"It's Your Problem. Deal with It."'
[45] Adele Teague and Gareth Dylan Smith, 'Portfolio Careers and Work-Life Balance Among Musicians: An Initial Study into Implications for Higher Music Education' in *British Journal of Music Education* 32:2 (2015), 177–93.
[46] C.f. Albinsson, 'Musicians as Entrepreneurs or Entrepreneurs as Musicians?'.

broadening, but if organisations simply wait for the next generation to lead a change, this will be a very slow process. The alternative, already in evidence, of relying on individuals to proactively seek to change and develop new skills without any support or training, risks being maverick and unsustainable. However, if performers have several and diverse multi-genre opportunities to experience different musical practices, then this might reflect the changes already beginning, and afford new opportunities for innovation and creativity.

Adam Szabo suggests that it is unrealistic to expect performers to emerge from their training 'fully baked', and to some extent this is true, particularly in terms of the specific skills that performers may need as part of a portfolio career. However, there is undoubtedly scope for training programmes to adapt to support musicians more fully: to identify their personal and musical values and priorities; to reflect on abilities and skills in order to create plans to address perceived gaps; to develop appropriate psychological tools to manage the fluctuations associated with performance work; and to develop strategies for achieving a healthy work-life balance. Such strategies should empower musical performers to embrace the uncertain future which lies ahead, confident in their abilities to flex, adapt and learn new skills. However, the work involved in adapting to change also needs to be recognised as continuing professional development and supported by classical music organisations, in order to mitigate the class-related barriers of precarity and resilience in the profession.[47]

One of our survey respondents (S15) summarised the perspective of an engaged and reflective orchestral player in a way that offers a poignant end to our chapter:

Listen.

Know what makes you tick.

Know what kind of artist you want to be and boldly chase this ideal.

Take both triumphs and disappointments with a pinch of salt.

---

47   Neil T. Smith and Rachel Thwaites, 'The Composition of Precarity: "emerging" Composers' Experiences of Opportunity Culture in Contemporary Classical Music' in *British Journal of Sociology* 70:2 (2019), 589–609.

If something doesn't feel right: move, change...don't get stuck in an unhappy artistic place.

You didn't become a musician to be rich so try not to be guided too much by money.

Keep practising, your education in some ways BEGINS at graduation.

References

Albinsson, Staffan, 'Musicians as Entrepreneurs or Entrepreneurs as Musicians?', *Creativity and Innovation Management* 27 (2017), 348–357, https://doi.org/10.1111/caim.12254

Bartleet, Brydie-Leigh and others, 'Building Sustainable Portfolio Careers in Music: Insights and Implications for Higher Education', *Music Education Research* 21:3 (2019), 282–94, http://dx.doi.org/10.1080/14613808.2019.1598348

Breakwell, Glynis M. and Rusi Jaspal, 'Identity processes and musicians during the COVID-19 pandemic', *Musicae Scientiae* 26:4 (2022), 777-798, https://doi.org/10.1177/10298649221102526

Bull, Anna, *Class, Control and Classical Music* (New York, NY: Oxford University Press, 2019), https://doi.org/10.1093/oso/9780190844356.001.0001

Burland, Karen, 'Becoming a Musician: A Longitudinal Study Investigating the Career Transitions of Undergraduate Music Students' (Unpublished doctoral thesis, University of Sheffield, 2005).

Burland, Karen, and Dawn Bennett, 'Creating a Sustainable Performance Career', in *The Oxford Handbook of Music Performance: Insights from Education, Psychology, Musicology, Science and Medicine*, ed. by Gary E. McPherson (New York: Oxford University Press, 2022), pp. 135–153, https://doi.org/10.1093/oxfordhb/9780190058869.013.8

Chamberlain, Paul and David Morris, *The economic impact of Covid-19 on the Culture, Arts and Heritage (CAH) sector in South Yorkshire and comparator regions* (University of Sheffield, 2021), https://www.sheffield.ac.uk/city-region/enhancing-cultural-vibrancy/covid-research-0

Cohen, Susanna and Jane Ginsborg, 'The Experiences of Mid-Career and Seasoned Orchestral Musicians in the UK During the First COVID-19 Lockdown', *Frontiers in Psychology* 12 (2021),

645967–645967,
https://doi.org/10.3389/fpsyg.2021.645967

Coulson, Susan, 'Getting "Capital" in the Music World: Musicians' Learning Experiences and Working Lives', *British Journal of Music Education* 27:3 (2010), 255–70, https://doi.org/10.1017/S0265051710000227

Creech, Andrea, Ioulia Papageorgi, Celia Duffy, Frances Morton, Elizabeth Haddon, John Potter, and others, 'From Music Student to Professional: The Process of Transition', *British Journal of Music Education* 25:3 (2008), 315–31, https://doi.org/10.1017/S0265051708008127

Daykin, Norma, 'Disruption, Dissonance and Embodiment: Creativity, Health and Risk in Music Narratives', *Health: An Interdisciplinary Journal for the Social Study of Health, Illness and Medicine* 9:1 (2005), 67–87.

Dobson, Melissa C., 'Insecurity, Professional Sociability, and Alcohol: Young Freelance Musicians' Perspectives on Work and Life in the Music Profession', *Psychology of Music* 39:2 (2011), 240–60, https://doi.org/10.1177/0305735610373562

Dromey, Christopher and Julia Haferkorn, *The Classical Music Industry* (New York; London: Routledge, Taylor & Francis Group, 2018).

Dweck, Carol S., 'Motivational Processes Affecting Learning' in *American Psychologist* 41:10 (1986), 1040–48, https://psycnet.apa.org/doi/10.1037/0003-066X.41.10.1040

Glow, Hilary, Anne Kershaw and Matthew Reason, 'Leading or Avoiding Change: The Problem of Audience Diversification for Arts Organisations', *International Journal of Cultural Policy* 27:1 (2021), 130–148, https://doi.org/10.1080/10286632.2019.1709060

Hadley, Steven, *Audience Development and Cultural Policy* (London: Palgrave Macmillan, 2021), https://doi.org/10.1007/978-3-030-62970-0

Haferkorn, Julia, 'Dancing to Another Tune: Classical Music in Nightclubs and Other Non-traditional Venues', in *The Classical Music Industry*, ed. by Christopher Dromey and Julia Haferkorn (New York; London: Routledge, Taylor & Francis Group, 2018), pp. 148-182.

Hager, Paul and Mary C. Johnsson, 'Learning to Become a Professional Orchestral Musician: Going Beyond Skill and Technique', *Journal of Vocational Education & Training* 61:2 (2009), 103–18, https://doi.org/10.1080/13636820902933221

Juuti, Sini and Karen Littleton, 'Tracing the Transition from Study to a Contemporary Creative Working Life: The Trajectories of

Professional Musicians', *Vocations and Learning* 5:1 (2011), 5–21, http://dx.doi.org/10.1007/s12186-011-9062-9

Middleton, Jerry C. and Jason A Middleton, 'Review of Literature on the Career Transitions of Performing Artists Pursuing Career Development', *International Journal for Educational and Vocational Guidance* 17:2 (2016), 211–32, https://doi.org/10.1007/s10775-016-9326-x

Morgan, George, and Julian Wood, 'Creative Accommodations: The Fractured Transitions and Precarious Lives of Young Musicians', *Journal of Cultural Economy* 7:1 (2014), 64–78, https://doi.org/10.1080/17530350.2013.855646

Oakland, Jane, Raymond MacDonald and Paul Flowers, 'Identity in Crisis: The Role of Work in the Formation and Renegotiation of a Musical Identity', *British Journal of Music Education* 30 (2013), 261–276, https://doi.org/10.1017/S026505171300003X

Ogbonna, Emmanuel, and Lloyd C. Harris, 'Work Intensification and Emotional Labour Among UK University Lecturers: An Exploratory Study', *Organization Studies* 25:7 (2004), 1185–1203, https://doi.org/10.1177/0170840604046315

Pecen, Ellis, David J. Collins and Áine MacNamara, '"It's Your Problem. Deal with It." Performers' Experiences of Psychological Challenges in Music', *Frontiers in Psychology* 8:2374 (2018), https://doi.org/10.3389/fpsyg.2017.02374

Pitts, Stephanie E., 'What Makes an Audience? Investigating the Roles and Experiences of Listeners at a Chamber Music Festival', *Music & Letters* 86:2 (2005), 257–269, https://doi.org/10.1093/ml/gci035.

Pitts, Stephanie E. and Sarah M. Price, *Understanding Audience Engagement in the Contemporary Arts* (Abingdon, Oxon; New York, NY: Routledge, Taylor & Francis Group, 2021).

Russell Hochschild, Arlie, *The Managed Heart: Commercialization of Human Feeling*, 3rd edition (Berkeley: University of California Press, 2012).

Smith, Neil T. and Rachel Thwaites, 'The Composition of Precarity: "emerging" Composers' Experiences of Opportunity Culture in Contemporary Classical Music', *British Journal of Sociology* 70:2 (2019), 589–609, https://doi.org/10.1111/1468-4446.12359

Teague, Adele, and Gareth Dylan Smith, 'Portfolio Careers and Work-Life Balance Among Musicians: An Initial Study into Implications for Higher Music Education', *British Journal of Music Education* 32:2

(2015), 177–93, https://doi.org/10.1017/S0265051715000121

The Strad, 'Building my confidence and developing as a well-rounded musician': Manchester Collective's Winter Residency for string players (2022), https://www.thestrad.com/education-hub/building-my-confidence-and-developing-as-a-well-rounded-musician-manchester-collectives-winter-residency-for-string-players/14440.article

Umney, Charles and Lefteris Kretsos, 'That's the Experience', *Work and Occupations* 42:3 (2015), 313–34, https://doi.org/10.1177/0730888415573634

Vaag, Jonas, Fay Giæver and Ottar Bjerkeset, 'Specific Demands and Resources in the Career of the Norwegian Freelance Musician', *Arts and Health* 6:3 (2014), 205–222, http://dx.doi.org/10.1080/17533015.2013.863789

Walmsley, Ben, Abigail Gilmore, Dave O'Brien and Anne Torreggiani, *Culture in Crisis: Impacts of Covid-19 on the UK cultural sector and where we go from here* (Centre for Cultural Value, 2022), https://www.culturehive.co.uk/CVIresources/culture-in-crisis-impacts-of-covid-19/

7. The Global Conservatoire: Towards an Integrated Approach to Developing Twenty-First-Century Artists

Diana Salazar and Christina Guillaumier

This chapter introduces the 'Global Conservatoire', a new model for online teaching in Higher Music Education. We explore, from a UK perspective, how the future needs of contemporary conservatoires and their students might be met through an integrated approach that combines traditional conservatoire methods of learning and teaching with new online and transnational approaches. We set out the aims and guiding principles of the online Global Conservatoire initiative before examining some of the opportunities, risks and challenges presented by online asynchronous teaching. Throughout this discussion, and in order to fully contextualise our model, we examine the Global Conservatoire model in practice with specific reference to a pilot undergraduate course, *Music and Words*, designed and delivered by the Royal College of Music, London.

Reflections on Today's Environment for Conservatoire Learning and Teaching

Preparing Graduates for an Arts Profession in Recovery

During the global COVID-19 pandemic, musicians around the world experienced a sustained period of significant disruption and uncertainty. For many musicians, this called into question the viability of their career as a performer in traditional 'live' classical music settings, such as the concert hall or opera theatre.[1] The already precarious nature of a career in the performing arts was amplified by the pandemic, prompting deep reflection in conservatoires about the skills, knowledge and experience future graduates will require to be sufficiently agile and resilient in their lifelong careers. Around the world, the professional musicians and music organisations who survived and thrived during the pandemic were those who could adapt their practice in innovative ways, exploit digital technologies and collaborate effectively with others, even when in-person interactions were unavailable to them.[2] As a result, the pandemic shone a light on the vulnerability of those conservatoire graduates who lacked the skills to adapt and, consequently, where there might be gaps in conservatoires' professional preparation.

The arguments for preparing conservatoire graduates to be innovative, entrepreneurial and versatile in their careers are not new.[3] For these graduates it has long been the case that portfolio careers are

---

1   Susanna Cohen and Jane Ginsborg, 'The Experiences of Mid-Career and Seasoned Orchestral Musicians in the UK During the First COVID-19 Lockdown', *Frontiers in Psychology* 12:645967 (9 April 2021), https://doi.org/10.3389/fpsyg.2021.645967; Nicole Canham, 'Background Music: Using Narrative Inquiry to Explore the Hidden Aspects of Musicians' Career Development', *Action, Criticism, and Theory for Music Education* 20:4 (December 2021), 146–70, https://doi.org/10.22176/act20.4.146.

2   Shams Bin Quader, 'How the Central Sydney Independent Musicians Use Pre-Established "Online DIY" to Sustain Their Networking during the COVID-19 Pandemic', *The Journal of International Communication* 28:1 (2 January 2022), 90–109, https://doi.org/10.1080/13216597.2021.1989703; Ties Van De Werff et al., 'Missing the Audience. Online Musicking in Times of COVID-19 / Missing the Audience. Online Musicking in Times of COVID-19', *Journal of Cultural Management and Cultural Policy / Zeitschrift* Für *Kulturmanagement Und Kulturpolitik* 7:1 (1 July 2021), 137–50, https://doi.org/10.14361/zkmm-2021-0107; Josephine Caust, 'Sustainability of Artists in Precarious Times; How Arts Producers and Individual Artists Have Adapted during a Pandemic', *Sustainability* 13:24 (8 December 2021), 13561, https://doi.org/10.3390/su132413561.

3   Peter Renshaw, 'Lifelong Learning for Musicians: Critical Issues Arising from a Case Study of Connect', *Lifelong Learning in Music*, n.d., https://research.hanze.nl/ws/portalfiles/portal/12420030/06_1_.pdf; Dawn Bennett, 'Utopia for Music Performance Graduates. Is It Achievable, and How Should It Be Defined?', *British Journal of Music Education* 24:2 (July 2007), 179–89, https://doi.org/10.1017/S0265051707007383; Helena Gaunt et al., 'Supporting Conservatoire Students towards Professional Integration: One-to-One Tuition and the Potential of Mentoring', *Music Education Research* 14:1 (March 2012), 25–43, https://doi.org/10.1080/14613808.2012.657166; Brydie-Leigh Bartleet et al., 'Preparing for Portfolio Careers in Australian Music: Setting a Research Agenda', *Australian Journal of Music Education* 2012 (2012), 32–41.

the dominant career model.⁴ Such a career today will almost certainly involve some elements of international collaboration or touring and the use of digital technology, whether for promotional activities, artistic production, teaching or communication. With the emergence of AI technologies, and the challenges these bring to concepts of creativity, the importance of digital fluency in classical musicians' lives will grow exponentially in the coming years. Yet conservatoire curricula can be slow to change and entrenched hierarchies, which tend to privilege analogue modes of performance, do not map well to a fast-moving global and digital world. Following the pandemic there is even greater urgency for conservatoires to 'design programmes that offer a more rounded education linked to both developing employability as well as expert skills'.⁵

Music and Words, the online undergraduate module discussed in this chapter, seeks to align with this contemporary professional landscape by expanding students' understanding of audiences for art and culture. This online elective module was created for undergraduate students in response to what we determined was a specific gap in the preparation of the conservatoire student – namely the ability to speak and write about music with conviction and persuasion and act as advocates, especially through digital means. The module supports students to communicate effectively about their musical practice through writing and speaking activities that reflect real-world audience interactions for musicians, for instance writing interactive programme notes, accessible online concert introductions, or engaging scripts for music broadcasts. These 'outward facing' activities encourage students to reach out beyond the practice room, reflecting on the evolving professional world and situating themselves in the dual position of listener/viewer and performer.

In this chapter we unpack the ways in which *Music and Words* supports conservatoire students to rise to the challenge of presenting and framing

---

4   Brydie-Leigh Bartleet et al., 'Building Sustainable Portfolio Careers in Music: Insights and Implications for Higher Education', *Music Education Research* 21:3 (27 May 2019), 282–94, https://doi.org/10.1080/14613808.2019.1598348; Lotte Latukefu and Jane Ginsborg, 'Understanding What We Mean by Portfolio Training in Music', *British Journal of Music Education* 36:1 (March 2019), 87–102, https://doi.org/10.1017/S0265051718000207

5   Kate Gee and Pamela Yeow, 'A Hard Day's Night: Building Sustainable Careers for Musicians', *Cultural Trends* 30:4 (8 August 2021), 338–54, https://doi.org/10.1080/09548963.2021.1941776 (p.351).

their working practice in a world that is in digital flux. In so doing, the module addresses a key element of the future of conservatoire training, that of contextualising practice in emerging digital cultures.

Global Perspectives in the UK Conservatoire

The immense value of intercultural learning experiences for music students is well recognised.[6] International exchange, the exposure to new cultures, divergent ideas or practices and international networking can grow confidence, communication and employability. As Vassiliki Papatsiba notes:

> Mobility involves encounters and confrontation with differences, requiring a broad range of individual adaptive responses, and also encouraging their renewal. Hence, mobility would maintain individuals in a state of awakening akin to the acquisition of new competences and new knowledge.[7]

Moving one step further, such encounters can equip students with the confidence and awareness to navigate increasingly complex social, cultural, and political contexts for performing artists today, as recognised by Bartleet et al.:

> [...] intercultural learning experiences can also bring students new recognition of their own cultural subjectivities; a better awareness of the social, political, economic, cultural environment in which they operate as musicians; heightened recognition of privilege and the concomitant responsibilities it brings, including as a musician; and greater recognition of their identities not only as citizens in their local communities or nations, but as global citizens.[8]

---

[6] Catherine Grant, 'Developing Global Citizenship in Tertiary Performing Arts Students Through Short-Term Mobility Programs', 2018, https://doi.org/10.18113/P8IJEA1915; Brydie-Leigh Bartleet et al., 'Global Mobility in Music Higher Education: Reflections on How Intercultural Music-Making Can Enhance Students' Musical Practices and Identities', *International Journal of Music Education* 38:2 (May 2020), 161–76, https://doi.org/10.1177/0255761419890943.

[7] Vassiliki Papatsiba, 'Making Higher Education More European through Student Mobility? Revisiting EU Initiatives in the Context of the Bologna Process', *Comparative Education* 42:1 (February 2006), 99, https://doi.org/10.1080/03050060500515785

[8] Bartleet et al., 'Global Mobility in Music Higher Education', p. 174.

In a post-Brexit and post-pandemic environment, this type of cross-cultural and socially engaged learning seems more important than ever, but also more fragile. Both Papatsiba and Bartleet focus on the traditional model of international mobility – physical travel – but it is important to acknowledge the growing awareness of carbon emissions and sustainability issues for today's artists, particularly in relation to touring. It is, therefore, unlikely that increased international travel between partner institutions is the answer. Instead, is it possible that UK conservatoires can offer such 'encounters and confrontations' with cultural diversity in a more accessible, sustainable, online environment, harnessing digital technology to enhance students' intercultural awareness and global competencies? While it may seem a radical proposition for conservatoires, increased socio-cultural connectivity in the classical music curriculum is long overdue.

In this global context, the module *Music and Words* offers students an opportunity to navigate and structure intercultural awareness, enabling them to articulately explore and express their individual artistry and find a voice with which they are comfortable communicating their creativity. The module implicitly critiques and contextualises the notion of artistic citizenship, scrutinising the concept of artistry and global culture in ways that require students to understand how to present their work to an international audience.

The Global Conservatoire: A Model for Online Learning

In response to our global and digital world, today's conservatoire students now require expertly designed courses for their professional development, that complement their practical activities while preparing them for an evolving, and potentially volatile, future. To prepare them for this future, students will require access to more inclusive, globally informed and progressive learning experiences that expand their horizons beyond their home institution. As small and specialist institutions, often with fewer than a thousand students, it is logical for conservatoires to pool their resources and technologies to develop such courses.

Launched in 2021, the Global Conservatoire is a consortium built on the digital expertise of four world-leading conservatoires: the Royal Danish Academy of Music; the University of Music and Performing Arts,

Vienna; the Royal College of Music, London; and Manhattan School of Music in New York City. By combining online experience, digital resources and unique subject expertise, the four institutions are building a set of conservatoire-specific online courses to explore best practice in online transnational education in the performing arts. The project sets out to optimise online teaching for a conservatoire environment, enabling it to occupy a significant, credited position in the curriculum while complementing traditional, face-to-face provision.

The overarching aims of the project are:

- To consolidate and develop the online teaching practices that emerged during the COVID-19 pandemic, focussing on the specific needs of today's conservatoire students;
- To pool the expertise of four conservatoires, each with their own teaching and research strengths, with a view to
  - i) sharing best teaching practice in online course design, delivery and assessment;
  - ii) expanding student access to a wider range of subject areas and international perspectives on music-making;
  - iii) developing shared models for conservatoire staff professional development;
- harnessing combined online learning and teaching capabilities to foster global artistic citizenship in our students;[9]
- developing a global online learning community distinguished from other online communities of practice by its core values in artistic innovation, inclusion, collaboration and excellence;
- co-curating a conservatoire-specific online learning and teaching framework, and associated professional development training, informed by these core values. This is designed to disseminate the lessons of the project beyond the four founding institutions.

---

9   David Elliott, 'Artistic Citizenship, Personhood, and Music Education', in *Giving Voice to Diversity in Music Education: Diversity and Social Justice in the Classroom*, ed. by Lisa DeLorenzo (New York: Routledge, 2015), pp. 13–35.

Rather than *replacing* traditional models of conservatoire teaching, such as the one-to-one lesson, masterclass or practical workshop, Global Conservatoire modules complement and enhance these existing models of delivery. This ideal, where online and face-to-face practices co-exist in the conservatoire in a non-hierarchical learning culture, is an ambitious goal, but one that could transform how we conceive of conservatoire education.

Such ambition requires institution-wide input from managers, teachers, learning technologists, administrators and IT staff in all four institutions. The initial phase of this project has been supported by a two-year Erasmus+ Strategic Partnership Grant, which provided essential start-up funding for staff training, course development, technical support and research-led evaluation.

The undergraduate module *Music and Words* was delivered in autumn 2021 as the initial, pilot module of this transnational project. In configuring this course to align with the Global Conservatoire goals set out above, concepts of internationalism and transnationalism informed the materials as well as the teaching. It is inevitable that as we discuss these concepts with our students, who join from different parts of the globe and from contrasting disciplines and cultures, we scrutinise the digital potential that the world around us affords.

Furthermore, one of the underlying curriculum design principles of this course is the concept of generative thinking; we acknowledge that knowledge is not constructed purely by one individual – rather, in a digital world more than ever before, joint thinking and collaborative relationships in virtual spaces can and will influence the development of a project.

Designing Online Transnational Courses for the Conservatoire

Online learning and teaching in conservatoires are not new. Before the pandemic, projects using high-speed network technology such as LoLa and Polycom had facilitated international performance projects at a distance, with the Global Audition Training Programme a particularly innovative example of distributed teaching that provided students with international artistic perspectives.[10] However, such technologies, even today, are highly specialised and require extensive technical preparation and support, while projects may benefit only very small numbers of students. Due to their ad hoc and specialised nature, projects are rarely formal or credited elements of degree programmes.

Historically, there has been some resistance in conservatoires to adopting digital learning technologies, such as virtual learning environments, videoconferencing or distance-learning programmes.[11] This is perhaps understandable due to the traditional emphasis on practical, embodied learning experiences in the conservatoire teaching environment and indeed the music profession more broadly. However, the pandemic created a situation in which the adoption of digital learning was essential in *all* areas, including the performance core, traditionally the domain of 'hands-on' delivery. This digital pivot was helpful in normalising online teaching and learning for conservatoire students and staff alike. It foregrounded unequivocally what was possible using digital technology in the conservatoire precisely because staff and students had no choice but to explore what was possible.

This moment presented an ideal opportunity to integrate online teaching on a permanent basis but now, as we emerge from this emergency era, there is a growing sense that online teaching has been tainted with scepticism about quality, effectiveness and 'value for money'.[12] Online learning offers significant benefits for student learning, not least in accessibility, flexibility and the development of self-regulated learning. We therefore propose that having acquired myriad digital skills at pace, it is time for conservatoires to move beyond the state of 'emergency

---

10 Cleveland Institute of Music, 'Distance Learning Kicks off the 2016-17 Global Audition Training Program', 11 October 2016, https://www.cim.edu/aboutcim/news/distance-learning-kicks-2016-17-global-audition-training-program.

11 Evangelos Himonides and Ross Purves, 'The Role of Technology in Music Education in the 21st Century in the United Kingdom: Achievements, Analysis and Aspirations', in *Music Education in the 21st Century in the United Kingdom: Archievements, Analysis and Aspirations*, ed. by Susan Hallam and Andrea Creech, Bedford Way Paper Series (London: Institute of Education, University of London, 2010), pp. 123–40; Gaunt et al., 'Supporting Conservatoire Students towards Professional Integration'.

12 Charles Hodges et al., 'The Difference Between Emergency Remote Teaching and Online Learning', *Educause Review*, March 2020, https://er.educause.edu/articles/2020/3/the-difference-between-emergency-remote-teaching-and-online-learning

remote teaching' into a more considered and strategic phase for online course design and delivery.[13]

The pandemic highlighted that online teaching can be delivered effectively using more accessible technologies. This too is not new: MOOCs have existed for over a decade, and platforms such as Coursera and FutureLearn are well established. However, with the exception of Berklee College of Music, conservatoires have generally been slow to occupy the online distance learning space. MOOC providers deliver on a large scale, often to many hundreds if not thousands of students. While the Global Conservatoire draws on some of the delivery methods used in MOOCs, such as the use of a VLE platform for asynchronous delivery, the pedagogical aims of the project are quite different. The courses are only available to partner students (i.e. conservatoire learners within the consortium) and the classes are limited to small numbers, which is relatively rare in online delivery.[14] There are still questions about whether the Global Conservatoire initiative is truly 'global' in outlook when access to the modules is so exclusive, and all four partners are Western institutions (albeit with very international student bodies). This reality must be recognised as we seek to develop culturally inclusive courses and communities. Nonetheless this bespoke approach is designed to address conservatoire students' learning needs, and it also goes some way to addressing the concerns about reduced quality and high levels of attrition in large-scale MOOC environments.[15] The challenge however is that these courses are costly to design and deliver, which raises questions about their long-term sustainability.

Each Global Conservatoire course is limited to a small group of students, usually around five students from each of the four partner institutions, and is led by an expert teacher based at one of the institutions. The small cohort size of twenty to twenty-five students means that teachers can get to know their students more quickly, establish rapport

---

13   Ibid.
14   JISC, *Student Digital Experience Insights Survey 2020/21: UK Higher Education Findings*, March 2021, https://repository.jisc.ac.uk/8318/1/DEI-P1-HE-student-briefing-2021-FINAL.pdf
15   Sara Isabella de Freitas, John Morgan, and David Gibson, 'Will MOOCs Transform Learning and Teaching in Higher Education? Engagement and Course Retention in Online Learning Provision: Engagement and Course Retention in Online Learning Provision', *British Journal of Educational Technology* 46:3 (May 2015), 455–71, https://doi.org/10.1111/bjet.12268

and construct a sense of 'presence' or 'being there' in the digital realm.[16] This approach aligns with the traditional conservatoire ethos of nurturing the individual student and their personal needs. The aim is to provide a more personalised approach that mirrors what students would expect in a face-to-face setting. With a small cohort, teachers have the capacity to give students individual feedback, comments and tutorial support. Likewise, students are more likely to establish connections with their peers, a vital ingredient to cultivate students' cultural awareness and global outlook.

Shared Principles for Online Learning

An important starting point of the project was that all four partners shared an international outlook and had prior experience of working together on other projects, including distance learning projects as well as student and staff exchanges. This ensured that we commenced work with a common set of values and shared aims for development. During the planning year 2020-21, the project management group discussed and refined these values, settling on a set of five overarching learning aims for the Global Conservatoire. These are to develop students':

- digital fluency;
- skills in remote collaboration;
- awareness of international arts practices;
- application of an entrepreneurial mindset;
- global citizenship and social inclusion.

The above learning aims build on Bridgstock and Hearn's conceptual model of four 'metacapabilities' for successful careers: disciplinary agility; social networking capability; creative enterprise; and career self-management.[17] However, these themes are repositioned in a contemporary international context where cultural awareness, global

---

16 Rosemary M. Lehman and Simone C. O. Conceição, *Creating a Sense of Presence in Online Teaching: How to 'Be There' for Distance Learners*, 1st ed., Jossey-Bass Guides to Online Teaching and Learning (San Francisco: Jossey-Bass, 2010).

17 Ruth Bridgstock and Greg Hearn, 'A Conceptual Model of Capability Learning for the Twenty-First-Century Knowledge Economy', in *Handbook on the Knowledge Economy. Volume Two*, ed. by David Rooney, Greg Hearn, and Tim Kastelle (Cheltenham, UK; Northampton, MA: Edward Elgar, 2012), pp. 105–19.

citizenship and digital communication are in the foreground. This approach aligns with Carey and Coutts' proposal for a transformative pedagogical approach, characterised by a 'shift in focus from discipline-specific knowledge and skill acquisition only, to developing students' social responsibility, leadership, and entrepreneurial capabilities. [...] students are challenged to expand their understanding of global topics'.[18]

The Global Conservatoire portfolio is curated with these principles in mind, with module subjects (and teachers) selected for their potential to realise this vision. In addition, the structure, content and assessments of each module are designed to maximise these broad learning aims. Rather than bespoke technology or platforms, it is the way in which these shared *values* are embedded into the GC learning and teaching framework and, furthermore, the way in which these values are *realised* online in partnership with students, that distinguish this project from a variety of other online teaching projects. The technology itself is viewed as a facilitating tool rather than a pedagogical driver.

With four different partners, each bringing their own learning culture, it is important to develop a robust pedagogical framework approach that can maximise engagement and active learning, but also do so with some consistency. Practically, the Global Conservatoire must strike the right balance between consistency of experience and the distinctive environment offered by the delivering institution. These include values, inclusion and learning principles as well as platform experience. Moving from 'resources' to 'activities' and ensuring teachers feel confident and equipped to design their courses in this way is also a testing challenge for the teacher.[19] Designing modules that enable a consistent and sustained student experience that resonates with Lourdes Guàrdia and Marcelo Maina's model of online pedagogy as being motivating, agile and situated is yet another of the more complex challenges that teachers face.[20] With *Music and Words*, these challenges are addressed directly

---

18   Gemma Carey and Leah Coutts, 'Fostering Transformative Professionalism through Curriculum Changes within a Bachelor of Music', in *Expanding Professionalism in Music and Higher Music Education: A Changing Game*, ed. by Heidi Westerlund and Helena Gaunt, 2022, pp. 42–58.

19   Chrysi Rapanta et al., 'Online University Teaching During and After the Covid-19 Crisis: Refocusing Teacher Presence and Learning Activity', *Postdigital Science and Education* 2:3 (October 2020), 923–45, https://doi.org/10.1007/s42438-020-00155-y

20   Lourdes Guàrdia and Marcelo Maina, 'FUTURA - Next Generation Pedagogy. IDEAS for Online and Blended Higher Education', *The Envisioning Report for Empowering Universities* (2018), 28–30.

since this module focuses specifically on a deeper understanding of artistic citizenship and its location within individual artistry.

Asynchronous Learning in the Conservatoire

The first set of Global Conservatoire courses are based on a series of asynchronous learning units, supported by three synchronous contact points with learners. Synchronous contact usually takes the form of a ninety-minute 'live' class on Zoom. This blended approach offers some practical benefits, such as overcoming time zones and reducing timetabling challenges between institutions. However other benefits of asynchronous learning include deeper and more meaningful engagement with the subject matter.[21] Effective design of asynchronous learning also facilitates rich peer-learning encounters, which can cultivate an online 'collaborative spirit'.[22] Offering students the flexibility to engage with the course as and when it is convenient is especially important to students in the intensive learning environment of a conservatoire, where students have complex and demanding schedules. Indirectly this flexibility and ownership over the time and place for one's learning may assist with student wellbeing and accessibility.[23]

The role of asynchronous online learning in cultivating diverse artistic communities of practice has been explored by Szram and van Gammeren.[24] Although they focussed on the diversity of musical genres among students, the Global Conservatoire project extends

---

21 Shirley Bach, Philip Haynes, and Jennifer Lewis Smith, *Online Learning and Teaching in Higher Education* (Maidenhead: Open University Press, 2007); Anna McNamara, 'Flipping the Creative Conservatoire Classroom', *Theatre, Dance and Performance Training* (19 February 2021), 1–10, https://doi.org/10.1080/19443927.2 020.1864462.

22 Andrea Schiavio, Michele Biasutti, and Roberta Antonini Philippe, 'Creative Pedagogies in the Time of Pandemic: A Case Study with Conservatory Students', *Music Education Research* (12 February 2021), 1–12, https://doi.org/10.1080/146138 08.2021.1881054

23 Jonathan Bergmann and Aaron Sams, *Flip Your Classroom: Reach Every Student in Every Class Every Day* (Eugene, Or: International Society for Technology in Education, 2012); Schiavio, Biasutti, and Antonini Philippe, 'Creative Pedagogies in the Time of Pandemic'; JISC, *Student Digital Experience Insights Survey 2020/21: UK Higher Education Findings*.

24 Aleksander Szram and Dario van Gammeren, 'Embracing Diversity: The Role of Asynchronous Online Learning in Building Musical Communities', *Spark: UAL Creative Teaching and Learning Journal* 3:2 (n.d.).

this to international cultural perspectives. This includes diversifying course offerings to include musicians and repertoire traditionally under-represented in classical music conservatoire curricula; the study of non-Western musics, interdisciplinary studies and other research specialisms. As two examples, Royal College of Music students now have access to modules in African American Music History and Dance for Musical Theatre, taught by international experts based at Manhattan School of Music.

A fundamental theoretical framework behind the design of *Music and Words* is that of 'affordances' as explored by Bill Cope and Mary Kalantzis in their work on transformative e-learning ecologies.[25] The emergence of a strong digital culture for musicians affords opportunities in developing and enhancing students' artistic voices. *Music and Words* is designed to encourage confidence in students' abilities to move away from their instruments and their comfort zones toward conceptualising themselves as artists in society. The module materials are selected with a view to elevating their articulation of practice and artistry within a supportive environment. Discussion boards, group work, synchronous and asynchronous peer interaction are critical for the creation of a meaningful community of practice.

The synchronous workshops presented an opportunity to participate in a collaborative environment which, though online, nonetheless provides students with a powerful but intimate landscape in which to explore concepts that translate differently across cultures. As Resta and Laferrière have argued, 'Technology-supported collaborative learning in higher education represents a confluence of trends: the development of new tools to support collaboration [...] and the need to create more powerful and engaging learning environments.'[26] Within this context, the approach to module design and content is to enable inclusion of all ideas, diverse as they may be, from our international student body with a view to modelling and articulating ideas that explore internationalism and transnationalism as it is applied to contemporary artistic work.

---

25   Bill Cope and Mary Kalantzis, eds., *E-Learning Ecologies: Principles for New Learning and Assessment* (New York, NY: Routledge, 2017).

26   Paul Resta and Thérèse Laferrière, 'Technology in Support of Collaborative Learning', *Educational Psychology Review* 19:1 (22 February 2007), 65, https://doi.org/10.1007/s10648-007-9042-7

Uncovering Hidden Complexities in the Online Conservatoire

The 'Iceberg' of Administration

Before considering course subjects, online platforms, technical support and teachers, operational challenges have included making decisions on credit transfer, quality assurance, institutional regulations, term dates and establishing clear lines of communication. The shared model of online delivery across four international partners adds a layer of complexity which should not be underestimated, an iceberg beneath the surface of online teaching. As Dewey and Duff note: 'International engagement involves extensive bureaucratic procedures and administrative red tape that is a burden to the faculty member'.[27] Online delivery might appear to provide a streamlined and convenient solution that could strip out much of the bureaucracy required for traditional exchange experiences, but the administrative infrastructure to align registry, quality and regulatory processes for shared credit-bearing courses is significant. Establishing shared protocols that are understood by all partners is vital and continues to be an area of development. We have discovered that true alignment between all institutions is not possible: the Global Conservatoire cannot and should not dictate individual institutional calendars and processes. Instead, flex is built in wherever possible. As an example, modules can be delivered and assessed within a delivery 'window' to accommodate four different academic calendars. In addition, strong communication between dedicated points of contact in management, administrative and technical areas enables focussed decision-making and planning. Robust communication and clearly defined responsibilities will not be limited to the start-up phase of the project; this will be required continuously to maintain the highest quality of student and staff experience.

It is important that this operational infrastructure is as 'invisible' as possible so students can focus on their learning. Providing a seamless experience for the students, both in terms of administration and the

---

27 Patricia Dewey and Stephen Duff, 'Reason before Passion: Faculty Views on Internationalization in Higher Education', *Higher Education* 58:4 (October 2009), 497, https://doi.org/10.1007/s10734-009-9207-z

learning platform, requires significant investment of time and resources, including policy development. This might appear burdensome (and costly), but one reward of this endeavour is that the distributed community of administrators, teachers, technicians and managers connected by email, Zoom and biannual in-person Erasmus meetings is beginning to form a strong community of practice. Through co-curation and collaborative learning, the project is delivering a unique form of cross-cultural staff development.

Dissonance and Hierarchies in the Extended Conservatoire Environment

The focus on asynchronous delivery with limited synchronous contact represents a very different learning experience for students who are accustomed to traditional models of conservatoire teaching. Arguably the 'Covid' academic years of 2019-20 and 2020-21 will have prepared students for online working, but nonetheless adaptation is required to meet the expectations of this mode of learning, especially the emphasis on independent learning and student-led activity. As a result, there is a risk of students experiencing a 'dissonance' between their 'typical' conservatoire experience and the Global Conservatoire experience. The asynchronous environment demands a very different type of engagement to face-to-face practical activities, and this dissonance may be amplified by learning from an unfamiliar teacher, with new classmates and in a learning and teaching culture that is quite different to one's home institution. Here, at the intersection of digital, transnational and conservatoire education we encounter an especially complex environment for learning and teaching. During the design phase, each Global Conservatoire teacher must recognise how unfamiliar the online learning environment will feel to students and equally the range of experiences that students will bring to this environment.

A teacher designing a Global Conservatoire course, therefore, needs to consider multiple layers of student experience and expectations that could impact on student motivation, understanding, contribution, commitment and performance. One must reflect on why students have chosen this course and what their experience of online learning is. It may be that not all content is suitable for effective online pedagogy. Virtual learning environments are critical within this context because this frames the community of practice that students will inhabit. Within this space, the module's identity takes its shape, teachers share knowledge and students build professional relationships that are both challenging and rewarding. Teachers must therefore consider how best to utilise this space to create a tangible and responsive community. Within this space in *Music and Words*, teachers were available to chat during virtual office hours, and this mitigated a sense of isolation that some students, who may struggle with self-regulation, might feel. As much as possible we avoided assigning work that engaged students but with limited pedagogical purpose. Even if the temptation is to replicate the in-person experience online, teachers observed that this kind of assigned work just for the sake of occupying student time was not a solution that would enhance the student experience. Nor would it provide students with a sense of progress or achievement. Indeed, one of the challenges of designing such a course is for the teachers to precisely separate material that is completely new from that which is implicitly known or that which students can acquire from each other. Short videos were created by the teacher to introduce new material, supported by visual aids as appropriate. The teacher's primary aim in this instance was to engage with the students, and to enable them to form a connection with her. Although this connection might not have been made in real-time, it was a relevant connection nonetheless and certainly familiar to students who use social media in similar ways. For this course, the teacher kept the videos short, under seven minutes, and ensured that follow up activities were interactive, either through discussion boards or peer-led tasks.

Another thorny issue is that of assessments and what is already familiar to students. Language has the potential to become a barrier if teachers are not sufficiently reflective and responsive to the levels and needs of students in their online classes. Is English their first, second or third language? What are their accessibility needs? And how equipped are they to follow a module that relies on an independent trajectory of self-regulated study? Careful attention must be paid to these considerations to minimise dissonance and maximise inclusion in the learning environment.

Integrating Design Principles into Content

How we make music today, the way our students are exposed to it, the very paradigm of 'Musicians as Makers in Society'[28] forces us to reimagine our relationship with our audiences, particularly when performances are being livestreamed. Godlovitch has characterised such a broader view of performance in terms whereby the 'performer-listener axis [carries] more weight than the performer-composer pair.'[29] This proves to be a concept that both intrigues and concerns students, partly, it would seem, because they are at times unaware of how the technology is constructing the performances in real time, and partly because they are not getting the feedback or energy from the audience being present. Studies demonstrate that much of the work done in the teaching studio and the practice room at times focusses on the sharing of embodied knowledge that may be taken for granted by the teacher, and eagerly absorbed by the student.[30] Ultimately, the conservatoire tends to rely on the apprenticeship model of learning. Individual tuition is considered the main model for teaching with Gaunt characterizing it as an 'indispensable, intense and intricate' part of instrumental and vocal learning.[31] *Music and Words*, by nature of its content and design, challenges these ideals, and equips students with the tools necessary to be fully engaged as music makers in contemporary society.

In our view, the role of the teacher in this module is firstly to curate the content and support the students' conceptualisation of the artistic and increasingly digital world they inhabit, to enable them to evaluate

---

28 Helena Gaunt et al. explore this new paradigm in 'Musicians as "Makers in Society": A Conceptual Foundation for Contemporary Professional Higher Music Education', *Frontiers in Psychology* 12 (3 August 2021), 713648, https://doi.org/10.3389/fpsyg.2021.713648

29 Stanley Godlovitch, *Musical Performance: A Philosophical Study* (New York: Routledge, 1998), p. 50.

30 Sam Duffy and Patrick G. T. Healey, 'Music, Speech and Interaction in an Instrumental Music Lesson: An Ethnographic Study of One-to-One Music Tuition', in *Language, Music and Interaction*, ed. by M. Orwin, C. Howes, and R. Kempson (College Publications, 2013), pp. 231–80; Lilian Simones, Franziska Schroeder, and Matthew Rodger, 'Categorizations of Physical Gesture in Piano Teaching: A Preliminary Enquiry', *Psychology of Music* 43:1 (January 2015), 103–21, https://doi.org/10.1177/0305735613498918

31 Helena Gaunt, 'One-to-One Tuition in a Conservatoire: The Perceptions of Instrumental and Vocal Teachers', *Psychology of Music* 36:2 (April 2008), 230, https://doi.org/10.1177/0305735607080827

their role within it and then to mediate it through the selected topics covered in the seminars and workshops. McWilliam's model of the teacher as 'meddling-in-the-middle' has been influential for negotiating the balance between encouraging peer learning and creative risk-taking throughout the seminars and workshops, which often draw directly from the students' creative work. Inevitably, the teacher will use their experience to understand not only the relationship between the digital arts and education, in a swiftly shifting pedagogical landscape, but also to look at ways of enabling the students to make connections between the tools they have already encountered in their practice with those they are unfamiliar with. Given the nature of the subject area explored in this module, consideration also needs to be given to the introduction and prior exposure that students may already have had to the tools, devices, technologies and platforms explored on the module. In deconstructing this, teachers have an opportunity to gain a deeper understanding of how peer culture and contemporary society has contributed to their conceptualisation of specific technology.

In keeping with the ethos of the Global Conservatoire project, when designing materials for this module, the teacher harnessed the potential of the digital to provide new opportunities for expression, employment and differentiation in a rapidly evolving sector. Through a series of seminars and hands-on practical workshops, students explore a range of techniques, approaches and technologies to develop and sustain their artistic vision. The module materials explore distinct ways of communicating about music in spoken and written form by familiarising them with the contexts in which this might be experienced. This entails developing an awareness of how musicians approach each of these modes when communicating about music. Utilising modelling and predictive methods, we explore creative writing as a means of self-expression, and critique and analyse the writings of others once we have the tools with which to complete such a task.

Challenging Insularity

While conservatoires are often criticised for their insularity, the Global Conservatoire project is designed to extend our institutional outlooks to global perspectives that are aligned with the needs of twenty-first-century musicians. As such, the project represents a concerted, collaborative effort to embed transformative global citizenship in today's conservatoire curricula.[32] Our reflection on the module *Music and Words* illustrates how the online learning environment can be an ideal vehicle for nurturing global artistic citizenship. Here, teachers worked in partnership with an international cohort of students to explore concepts that are critical to the development of young artists in a conservatoire environment. Furthermore, the teachers had the additional opportunity to be part of a supportive transnational community of practice that fostered the values of inclusion and diversity across global cultures.

Nonetheless, the Global Conservatoire model is at an early stage. Already we have seen significant challenges emerge. These include practical obstacles, such as administration, communication, financial investment and the demands on staff time, through to pedagogical and cultural challenges including inclusive course design for diverse cohorts, aligning different institutional learning cultures and addressing negative perceptions of online teaching in the conservatoires. On this latter point, considering current discourses around online learning being 'poor value' or a temporary 'stopgap' during a time of crisis, it will be important to avoid Global Conservatoire modules being perceived as the poor relation of 'conventional' conservatoire modules. Long term, we hope that a fully-fledged online Global Conservatoire model will become an equally valued part of the learning fabric of conservatoire study. We must avoid unhelpful binaries such as the notion that online learning is for academic study and face-to-face teaching for practice-led study, by ensuring that Global Conservatoire modules recognise artistic practice in their design and delivery and encouraging teaching staff to embrace the model. In order to work through these challenges, the next step will be to understand the student and teacher experience of this online model through robust qualitative research, quantitative data-gathering and critical evaluation.

---

32   Jennifer Mellizo, 'Music Education as Global Education: A Developmental Approach', *TOPICS for Music Education Praxis*, July 2019, http://topics.maydaygroup.org/articles/2019/Mellizo_2019.pdf

References

Bach, Shirley, Philip Haynes, and Jennifer Lewis Smith, *Online Learning and Teaching in Higher Education* (Maidenhead: Open University Press, 2007).

Bartleet, Brydie-Leigh, Dawn Bennett, Ruth Bridgstock, Paul Draper, Scott David Harrison, and Huib Schippers. 'Preparing for Portfolio Careers in Australian Music: Setting a Research Agenda', *Australian Journal of Music Education* 2012 (2012), 32–41.

Bartleet, Brydie-Leigh, Catherine Grant, Charulatha Mani, and Vanessa Tomlinson, 'Global Mobility in Music Higher Education: Reflections on How Intercultural Music-Making Can Enhance Students' Musical Practices and Identities', *International Journal of Music Education* 38:2 (May 2020), 161–76, https://doi.org/10.1177/0255761419890943

Bennett, Dawn, 'Utopia for Music Performance Graduates. Is It Achievable, and How Should It Be Defined?', *British Journal of Music Education* 24:2 (July 2007), 179–89, https://doi.org/10.1017/S0265051707007383

Bergmann, Jonathan, and Aaron Sams, *Flip Your Classroom: Reach Every Student in Every Class Every Day* (Eugene, Or: International Society for Technology in Education, 2012).

Blackstone, Kate, 'How Do Conservatoire Graduates Manage Their Transition into the Music Profession? Exploring the Career-Building Process', University of Leeds, 2019.

Bourdieu, Pierre, and Richard Nice, *Outline of a Theory of Practice*, 2019, https://doi.org/10.1017/CBO9780511812507

Bridgstock, Ruth, and Greg Hearn, 'A Conceptual Model of Capability Learning for the Twenty-First-Century Knowledge Economy', in *Handbook on the Knowledge Economy. Volume Two*, ed. by David Rooney, Greg Hearn, and Tim Kastelle (Cheltenham, UK; Northampton, MA: Edward Elgar, 2012), pp. 105–19.

Buckingham, David, *Beyond Technology Children's Learning in the Age of Digital Culture* (Cambridge, UK: Polity Press, 2013).

Burnard, Pamela, 'Rethinking "Musical Creativity" and the Notion of Multiple Creativities in Music' in *Musical Creativity: Insights from Music Education Research*, ed. by Oscar Odena (London: Routledge, 2016), pp. 5–27.

Canham, Nicole, 'Background Music: Using Narrative Inquiry to Explore the Hidden Aspects of Musicians' Career Development', *Action, Criticism, and Theory for Music Education* 20:4 (December 2021),

146–70,
https://doi.org/10.22176/act20.4.146

Carey, Gemma, and Leah Coutts, 'Fostering Transformative Professionalism through Curriculum Changes within a Bachelor of Music', in *Expanding Professionalism in Music and Higher Music Education: A Changing Game*, ed. by Heidi Westerlund and Helena Gaunt (London: Routledge, 2022), pp. 42–58,
https://www.taylorfrancis.com/books/oa-edit/10.4324/9781003108337/expanding-professionalism-music-higher-music-education-helena-gaunt-heidi-westerlund

Caust, Josephine, 'Sustainability of Artists in Precarious Times; How Arts Producers and Individual Artists Have Adapted during a Pandemic', *Sustainability* 13:24 (8 December 2021), 13561,
https://doi.org/10.3390/su132413561

Cleveland Institute of Music, 'Distance Learning Kicks off the 2016-17 Global Audition Training Program', 11 October 2016,
https://www.cim.edu/aboutcim/news/distance-learning-kicks-2016-17-global-audition-training-program

Cohen, Susanna, and Jane Ginsborg, 'The Experiences of Mid-Career and Seasoned Orchestral Musicians in the UK During the First COVID-19 Lockdown', *Frontiers in Psychology* 12 (9 April 2021), 645967,
https://doi.org/10.3389/fpsyg.2021.645967

Cope, Bill, and Mary Kalantzis (eds.), *E-Learning Ecologies: Principles for New Learning and Assessment* (New York, NY: Routledge, 2017).

Csikszentmihalyi, Mihaly, *Creativity: Flow and the Psychology of Discovery and Invention*, 1st ed. (New York: Harper Collins Publishers, 1996).

Dewey, Patricia, and Stephen Duff, 'Reason before Passion: Faculty Views on Internationalization in Higher Education', *Higher Education* 58: 4 (October 2009), 491–504,
https://doi.org/10.1007/s10734-009-9207-z

Duffy, Sam, and Patrick G. T. Healey, 'Music, Speech and Interaction in an Instrumental Music Lesson: An Ethnographic Study of One-to-One Music Tuition', in *Language, Music and Interaction*, ed. by M. Orwin, C. Howes, and R. Kempson (London: College Publications, 2013), pp. 231–80.

Elliott, David, 'Artistic Citizenship, Personhood, and Music Education', in *Giving Voice to Diversity in Music Education: Diversity and Social Justice in the Classroom*, ed. by Lisa DeLorenzo (New York: Routledge, 2015), pp. 13–35.

Elliott, David, Marissa Silverman, and Wayne Bowman, *Artistic Citizenship: Artistry, Social Responsibility, and Ethical Praxis* (Oxford: Oxford

University Press, 2016), https://doi.org/10.1093/acprof:oso/9780199393749.001.0001

Freitas, Sara Isabella de, John Morgan, and David Gibson, 'Will MOOCs Transform Learning and Teaching in Higher Education? Engagement and Course Retention in Online Learning Provision: Engagement and Course Retention in Online Learning Provision', *British Journal of Educational Technology* 46:3 (May 2015), 455–71, https://doi.org/10.1111/bjet.12268

Gaunt, Helena, Andrea Creech, Marion Long, and Susan Hallam, 'Supporting Conservatoire Students towards Professional Integration: One-to-One Tuition and the Potential of Mentoring', *Music Education Research* 14:1 (March 2012), 25–43, https://doi.org/10.1080/14613808.2012.657166

Gaunt, Helena, Celia Duffy, Ana Coric, Isabel R. González Delgado, Linda Messas, Oleksandr Pryimenko, and Henrik Sveidahl, 'Musicians as "Makers in Society": A Conceptual Foundation for Contemporary Professional Higher Music Education', *Frontiers in Psychology* 12 (3 August 2021), 713648, https://doi.org/10.3389/fpsyg.2021.713648

Gee, Kate, and Pamela Yeow, 'A Hard Day's Night: Building Sustainable Careers for Musicians', *Cultural Trends* 30:4 (8 August 2021), 338–54, https://doi.org/10.1080/09548963.2021.1941776

Godlovitch, Stanley, *Musical Performance: A Philosophical Study* (London ; New York: Routledge, 1998).

Grant, Catherine, 'Developing Global Citizenship in Tertiary Performing Arts Students Through Short-Term Mobility Programs', *International Journal of Education and the Arts* 19:15 (2018), https://doi.org/10.18113/P8IJEA1915

Guàrdia, Lourdes, and Marcelo Maina, 'FUTURA - Next Generation Pedagogy. IDEAS for Online and Blended Higher Education', *The Envisioning Report for Empowering Universities*, 2018, 28–30.

Guillaumier, Christina, 'Reflection as Creative Process: Perspectives, Challenges and Practice', *Arts and Humanities in Higher Education* 15:3–4 (July 2016), 353–63, https://doi.org/10.1177/1474022216647381

Guillaumier, Christina, Ruth Slater, and Peter Argondizza, 'Recontextualised Learning through Embedded Creativity: Developing a Module That Applies Historically Informed Performance Practice to Baroque Music', in *Creative Teaching for Creative Learning in Higher Music Education*, ed. by Elizabeth Haddon and Pamela Burnard (London: Routledge, 2016), pp. 186–97.

Himonides, Evangelos, and Ross Purves, 'The Role of Technology in Music Education in the 21st Century in the United Kingdom: Achievements, Analysis and Aspirations', in *Music Education in the 21st Century in the United Kingdom: Achievements, Analysis and Aspirations*, ed. by Susan Hallam and Andrea Creech, Bedford Way Paper Series (London: Institute of Education, University of London, 2010), pp. 123–40.

Hodges, Charles, Stephanie Moore, Barb Lockee, Torrey Trust, and Aaron Bond, 'The Difference Between Emergency Remote Teaching and Online Learning', *Educause Review*, March 2020, https://er.educause.edu/articles/2020/3/the-difference-between-emergency-remote-teaching-and-online-learning

JISC, *Student Digital Experience Insights Survey 2020/21: UK Higher Education Findings*, March 2021, https://repository.jisc.ac.uk/8318/1/DEI-P1-HE-student-briefing-2021-FINAL.pdf

John-Steiner, Vera, *Creative Collaboration* (Oxford; New York: Oxford University Press, 2006).

Latukefu, Lotte, and Jane Ginsborg, 'Understanding What We Mean by Portfolio Training in Music', *British Journal of Music Education* 36:1 (March 2019), 87–102, https://doi.org/10.1017/S0265051718000207

Lehman, Rosemary M., and Simone C. O. Conceição, *Creating a Sense of Presence in Online Teaching: How to 'Be There' for Distance Learners*, 1st ed, Jossey-Bass Guides to Online Teaching and Learning (San Francisco: Jossey-Bass, 2010).

M. Prior, Helen, 'How Can Music Help Us to Address the Climate Crisis?', *Music & Science* 5 (January 2022), 205920432210757, https://doi.org/10.1177/20592043221075725

McNamara, Anna, 'Flipping the Creative Conservatoire Classroom', *Theatre, Dance and Performance Training* 12:4 (19 February 2021), 1–10, https://doi.org/10.1080/19443927.2020.1864462

McWilliam, Erica, 'Teaching for Creativity: From Sage to Guide to Meddler', *Asia Pacific Journal of Education* 29:3 (September 2009), 281–93, https://doi.org/10.1080/02188790903092787

Mellizo, Jennifer, 'Music Education as Global Education: A Developmental Approach', *TOPICS for Music Education Praxis*, July 2019, http://topics.maydaygroup.org/articles/2019/Mellizo_2019.pdf

Moran, Nikki, 'Music, Bodies and Relationships: An Ethnographic Contribution to Embodied Cognition Studies', *Psychology of*

Music 41:1 (January 2013), 5–17,
https://doi.org/10.1177/0305735611400174

Papatsiba, Vassiliki, 'Making Higher Education More European through Student Mobility? Revisiting EU Initiatives in the Context of the Bologna Process', *Comparative Education* 42:1 (February 2006), 93–111,
https://doi.org/10.1080/03050060500515785

Quader, Shams Bin, 'How the Central Sydney Independent Musicians Use Pre-Established "Online DIY" to Sustain Their Networking during the COVID-19 Pandemic', *The Journal of International Communication* 28:1 (2 January 2022), 90–109,
https://doi.org/10.1080/13216597.2021.1989703

Rapanta, Chrysi, Luca Botturi, Peter Goodyear, Lourdes Guàrdia, and Marguerite Koole, 'Online University Teaching During and After the Covid-19 Crisis: Refocusing Teacher Presence and Learning Activity', *Postdigital Science and Education* 2:3 (October 2020), 923–45,
https://doi.org/10.1007/s42438-020-00155-y

Reid, Anna, and Peter Petocz, *Educating Musicians for Sustainability*, 1st ed. (New York: Routledge, 2021),
https://doi.org/10.4324/9781003044642

Renshaw, Peter, 'Lifelong Learning for Musicians: Critical Issues Arising from a Case Study of Connect', *Lifelong Learning in Music*, n.d.,
https://research.hanze.nl/ws/portalfiles/portal/12420030/06_1_.pdf

Resta, Paul, and Thérèse Laferrière, 'Technology in Support of Collaborative Learning', *Educational Psychology Review* 19:1 (22 February 2007), 65–83,
https://doi.org/10.1007/s10648-007-9042-7

Robinson, Ken, *Out of Our Minds: Learning to Be Creative*. Fully rev. and updated ed. (Chichester: Capstone, 2011).

Rooney, David, Greg Hearn, and Tim Kastelle, eds., *Handbook on the Knowledge Economy. Volume Two* (Cheltenham, UK; Northampton, MA: Edward Elgar, 2012).

Savage, Jonathan, 'The Painting of Sound', in *Routledge Companion to Music, Technology, and Education*, ed. by Andrew King, Evangelos Himonides, and S. Alex Ruthmann (Abingdon, UK; New York, NY: Routledge, 2019).

Schiavio, Andrea, Michele Biasutti, and Roberta Antonini Philippe, 'Creative Pedagogies in the Time of Pandemic: A Case Study with Conservatory Students', *Music Education Research* 23:2 (12

February 2021), 1–12, https://doi.org/10.1080/14613808.2021.1881054

Schön, Donald A., *Educating the Reflective Practitioner: Toward a New Design for Teaching and Learning in the Professions*, 1st ed. [Nachdr.] The Jossey-Bass Higher Education Series (San Francisco: Jossey-Bass, 2000).

Simones, Lilian, Franziska Schroeder, and Matthew Rodger, 'Categorizations of Physical Gesture in Piano Teaching: A Preliminary Enquiry', *Psychology of Music* 43:1 (January 2015), 103–21, https://doi.org/10.1177/0305735613498918

Szram, Aleksander, and Dario van Gammeren, 'Embracing Diversity: The Role of Asynchronous Online Learning in Building Musical Communities', *Spark: UAL Creative Teaching and Learning Journal* 3:2 (2018), 142-149.

Van de Werff, Ties, Neil Thomas Smith, Stefan Rosu, and Peter Peters, 'Missing the Audience. Online Musicking in Times of COVID-19, *Journal of Cultural Management and Cultural Policy / Zeitschrift* Für *Kulturmanagement Und Kulturpolitik* 7:1 (1 July 2021), 137–50, https://doi.org/10.14361/zkmm-2021-0107

Westerlund, Heidi, and Helena Gaunt, *Expanding Professionalism in Music and Higher Music Education: A Changing Game* (London: Routledge, 2022).

8. Meaningful Music in Healthcare: Professional Development and Discovered Identities of Classical Musicians Working in Hospital Wards

Krista de Wit and Beste Sevindik

Introduction: Musicians as 'Makers in Society' in Participatory Socially Engaged Practices

As is widely known, due to the changes in the musicians' professional landscape, it is increasingly less typical for professional musicians to hold only one position. Instead, they develop so-called *portfolio careers*, where they flexibly seek opportunities to build professional practices in various contexts.[1] Simultaneously, musicians are increasingly encouraged to respond to societal needs as *makers in society*.[2] These developments require adaptation skills and a flexible and proactive outlook to connect meaningfully in different societal contexts.[3]

Recently, more and more musicians have created participatory practices, where the emphasis of music-making lies on the reciprocal

---

[1] See Rineke Smilde, *The Music Profession and the Professional Musician: A Reflection* (paper presented at the European Association of Conservatoires, Strasbourg, 2017). See also, Rineke Smilde, *Musicians Working in Community Contexts: Perspectives of Learning* (Learning and teaching conference, the Royal College of Music in Stockholm, 2019).

[2] See Helena Gaunt, Celia Duffy, Ana Coric, Isabel R. González Delgado, Linda Messas, Oleksandr Pryimenko and Henrik Sveidahl, *Musicians as "Makers in Society": A Conceptual Foundation for Contemporary Professional Higher Music Education* (Front. Psychol, 2021).

[3] Ibid.

processes between musicians and their audiences. Participatory music refers to practices where the focus lies on the co-creative, social processes of music-making rather than performance, in which the division between the audience and performer is accentuated.[4] Participatory music focuses on facilitating musical engagement, creative processes and social participation through musicking. It means that the forms of the music-making are often loosely threaded rather than pre-composed, responsive to change and diverse impulses in the moment, and actively searching to answer the participants' musical needs as the musical interactions unfold.[5] Participatory music-making is, thus, highly sensitive to the *ethics of care* underpinning the musicians' work: having an attentive, caring, responsive and receptive disposition towards the participants without assuming to know their needs or interests in advance.[6]

One of the quickly evolving contexts of musicians' participatory professional practices as makers in society is the emergence of professional musicians in various healthcare contexts. Increasingly, since the turn of the millennium professional musicians have started to build their practices in the healthcare sector, particularly in elderly care contexts, as a response to the rapid ageing of populations. As a result, various music practices in healthcare have formed alliances, such as the National Alliance of Musicians in Healthcare (UK), and cultural policies have been put into place to support arts in healthcare, such as the French National Policy for Culture and Health.[7] At the same time, the number of conferences and symposia on music and healthcare, as well as educational programmes for musicians and music students, such as Care Music in Finland, have increased. Yet, the professional landscape of, as well as the educational programmes for, musicians in healthcare remains fragmented and largely undocumented, increasing

---

[4] See François Matarasso, *A Restless Art: How Participation Won, and Why It Matters* (London: Calouste Gulbenkian Foundation, UK Branch, 2019).

[5] See Thomas Turino, *Music as Social Life: The Politics of Participation*. (Chicago: The University of Chicago Press, 2018).

[6] See David Lines, 'The Ethics of Community Music', in *The Oxford Handbook of Community Music*, ed. by Brydie-Leigh Bartleet and Lee Higgins (Oxford: Oxford University Press, 2018), 385-402.

[7] See Eve-Laure Gay, The French National Policy Culture and Health – A Transferable Model?, in *Arts – Health – Entrepreneurship? A Conference on Arts and Health Projects and Practices on 22-23 October 2013 in Helsinki*, ed. by Pia Strandman (Helsinki: Helsinki Metropolia University of Applied Sciences, 2012), 17-19.

the vulnerability of musicians' work in the healthcare sector. Koivisto and Tähti write:

> At the moment, the work of healthcare musicians mostly occurs in projects or small-scale interventions and is temporary in nature. It seems that, although their work is appreciated by the healthcare system(s) and healthcare personnel, and many times they work in collaboration with music therapists, the overall picture of healthcare musicians' work is one of being non-systematized, unsustainable, and economically vulnerable in nature.[8]

Similarly, Daykin points out: 'There is as yet no consensus about the prerequisites for this work in terms of education, training, and professional development.'[9] For example, there is currently no agreement on what to call professional conservatoire-trained musicians who work in healthcare. Suggestions include various terms, e.g. 'health musicians'[10], 'healthcare musicians',[11] 'care musicians' and 'hospital musicians',[12] 'visiting musicians', 'extra-clinical musicians',[13] 'participatory musicians'[14] and 'professional facilitators'[15] or more broadly as community musicians.

This chapter aims to provide new perspectives on musicians' professional development and learning in a participatory music practice

---

8 See Taru-Anneli Koivisto and Taru Tähti, 'Professional entanglements: A qualitative systematic review of healthcare musicians' work in somatic hospital wards', *Nordic Journal of Music Therapy* 29:5 (2020), 416-436 (p. 423).
9 See Norma Daykin, 'Developing Social Models for Research and Practice in Music, Arts, and Health: A Case Study of Research in a Mental Health Setting', in *Music, Health, and Wellbeing*, ed. by Raymond MacDonald, Gunter Kreutz, and Laura Mitchell (Oxford: Oxford University Press, 2012), 65-75.
10 See Even Ruud, 'The New Health Musicians', in *Music, Health, and Wellbeing*, ed. by Raymond MacDonald, Gunter Kreutz, and Laura Mitchell (Oxford: Oxford University Press, 2012), 88-96.
11 See Koivisto & Tähti, *Professional Entanglements*.
12 See Liisa-Maria Lilija-Viherlampi, *Care music - sairaala- ja hoivamusiikkityö ammattina*. (Turku: Turku University of Applied Sciences, 2013).
13 See Lea Wolf, Thomas Wolf, *Music and Health Care. A Paper Commissioned by the Musical Connections Program of Carnegie Hall's Weill Music Institute* (New York: Carnegie Hall and Wolf Brown, 2011).
14 See De Wit, *Legacy: Participatory Music Practices with Elderly People as a Resource for the Well-being of Healthcare Professionals.* (Doctoral dissertation, the University of Music and Performing Arts Vienna, 2020).
15 See Laura Huhtinen-Hildén, 'Perspectives on Professional Use of Arts and Arts-Based Methods in Elderly Care', *Arts & Health, An International Journal for Research, Policy and Practice* (2014).

in the Dutch hospital care context, Meaningful Music in Healthcare (MiMiC), and to discuss the implications of the growing field of music and healthcare for higher music education in conservatoires.

Meaningful Music in Healthcare (MiMiC): Person-Centred Music-Making Supporting Hospital Care

In a single-person hospital room there is a woman who had said 'no' to having music the day before but she is now open to hearing it. She seems very vulnerable, so the mediator who is guiding the musicians on the ward tells the musicians to take a very soft approach when playing for her. The musician team consists of a viola player, a cellist and a violinist who is a student at a Dutch conservatoire taking part as an intern in the project.

Inside the room, the woman tells the musicians that she enjoys classical music, as long as it is not too complex and polyphonic. So, taking this preference as a point of departure, the musicians propose to play an arrangement of the Flower Duet from the opera *Lakmé* by Delibes. The woman agrees and so, the music fills the room. After the piece ends, the woman seems satisfied and tells that the music was not too 'full'.

There are red tulips in a vase on her window sill and so, the musicians make a remark on the flowers fitting the theme of the Flower Duet. The woman answers playfully: 'Tulips from Amsterdam' as a reference to a well-known old Dutch song. By now, the music-making and conversation have opened the interaction more, and the woman looks out of the window and tells the musicians that last night there was a full moon. Inspired by the image of a full moon, the musicians propose an improvisation about the full moon and the tulips. The woman agrees to the idea but asks for confirmation: 'a piece especially made for me?' The musicians confirm.

So, the improvisation begins. The piece is calming, meditative, and colourful, yet keeping the energy contained to avoid the 'fullness' that the woman wishes not to hear. At the end of it, the woman tells the musicians that the piece relaxed her. She says that she had had some back pain and tension in her body and that she could now feel the tension escaping her body during the piece. The musicians are happy to hear this and wish her a good day. Tomorrow they will come back again to ask if she might need another musical visit.

(Reconstructed from observation notes,
ProMiMiC research, January 2022)

This vignette is a reconstruction of an observed moment in a participatory MiMiC project, where professional classically trained musicians play diverse genres of live music, both improvised and arranged, inside hospital wards for patients and healthcare professionals.[16] The practice of MiMiC has been developed by the research group Lifelong Learning in Music in collaboration with the University Medical Center Groningen (UMCG) (2015-2017). The practice was further researched in an international research project Professional Excellence in Meaningful Music in Healthcare (ProMiMiC) (2019-2023) focusing on the interprofessional learning and collaboration of musicians and nurses. Additionally, a training module 'Music and Healthcare' was developed in the masters' programme at the Prince Claus Conservatoire in Groningen in 2017. The module includes a semester-long training period focusing on the development of necessary preparatory contextual, musical and facilitation skills, followed by an onsite MiMiC internship project led by professional a MiMiC musician.

The practice of MiMiC focuses on providing live music sessions on hospital wards in four- to six-day projects, with a focus on safeguarding the quality of musical experiences from three intertwined perspectives: the patient's well-being and *flourishing*[17] through tailor-made music-making; supporting the occupational well-being of nurses and their compassionate contact with their patients; and finally, the ongoing professional development of MiMiC musicians and the educational opportunities of conservatoire students and working musicians. In a daily MiMiC music session, the musicians play for nurses in their coffee room to connect to them informally without the presence of the patients, after which they make visits to the patients' rooms when invited. A typical visit to one patient's room lasts around ten to fifteen minutes. Visiting the same patients daily during the project allows the social processes of music-making to deepen between the musicians, patients and nurses.

---

16 See Smilde et al., *If Music Be the Food of Love, Play On*.
17 Martin E. P. Seligman, *Flourish: A Visionary New Understanding of Happiness and Well-Being* (New York: Free Press, 2011).

Person-Centred Music-Making as a Cultural Counterpart for Person-Centred Care

As their main musical approach, the MiMiC musicians use *person-centred music-making* to connect with patients and nurses. Person-centred music-making is an approach in which contact with audiences is central to any musical choice.[18] The participants' unique musical wishes, preferences and needs are at the core of the musical approaches, as described in the vignette above. A team of MiMiC musicians consists of three players in different instrumental combinations out of a group of professional musicians working in the Foundation MiMiC Muziek.[19] At the time of writing, these instrumentalists include cellists, viola players, violinists, clarinettists, a guitarist and a flautist, and all of them are classically trained musicians holding Masters' degrees in the performing arts.

To meet the demands of person-centredness in music-making, the musicians must be flexible improvisers (see also the vignette above) making music based on the participants' verbal and non-verbal cues, such as improvisations connecting to the patients' biographies, e.g. favourite holiday destinations or landscapes near home, which can be portrayed musically. In pre-pandemic conditions, the musicians would also ask the participants to conduct them with a conductor's baton as a means to respect and promote the participants' autonomy and control over the musical creative process. Additionally, the musicians write trio arrangements of music of various genres and styles, from Bach to contemporary pop, and from classic rock by Queen to Debussy. The catalogue of music accumulates over time, as more pieces are, where possible, arranged based on the nurses' and patients' particular wishes, though without the musicians becoming 'living jukeboxes'. Some arrangements are made without writing a score at all, and, instead, created directly based on a recording of the original piece (as was done in preparation for a live performance together with a doctor-in-training, who was also an experienced musical singer, at the University Medical Center Groningen).[20] On some occasions, patients may be present

---

18 See Smilde et al., *While the Music Lasts – On Music and Dementia*; Smilde et al., *If Music Be the Food of Love, Play On.*
19 www.mimicmuziek.nl
20 See video recording: https://fb.watch/bNptGurBMg/

during the process of arranging ad-hoc versions of pieces that have special significance to them.

As Gaunt et al. propose, underpinning musicians' work as makers in society are so-called 'partnering artistic and social values',[21] through which musicians can respond to societal needs with professional integrity and vision. In the context of the MiMiC, these partnering values are particularly pronounced. The musical approaches to person-centred music-making, which build upon respect for the participants' musical needs, wishes and preferences, can be directly connected with the values and aims of person-centred care. As such, person-centred music-making requires constant awareness of the previously mentioned *ethics of care,* combined with the general ethical protocols of the hospital context regarding privacy, confidentiality and safety. De Wit reports that, given the ethical sensitivity of the musical approach, nurses taking part in the MiMiC sessions tend to recognise person-centred music-making as a cultural counterpart to providing person-centred care that respects patients' unique situations and needs.[22]

Learning Pathways and 'Gates' of Development

When it comes to the musicians' learning processes in the context of work, Smilde et al. found that musicians taking part in MiMiC share a typical learning pathway, beginning from a place of 'disconnectedness' from their new context and 'apprehension' about how to go about bringing live music into it.[23] Through connecting with the patients in 'sharing their grief' about their hospitalisation through musical interactions, as well as through displaying 'compassion' towards the patients and themselves, the musicians begin to find ways into this new context and start to 'share leadership' of the musical facilitation.[24] A sense of increased inclusion helps to inspire the confidence to engage in interprofessional collaboration with nurses and for the social and artistic connections between nurses, musicians, and patients to take

---

21 Gaunt et al., *Musicians as 'Makers in Society'*, p. 8.
22 De Wit, *Legacy*, p. 202.
23 Smilde et al., *If Music Be the Food of Love, Play On*, p. 77.
24 Ibid.

form.²⁵ 'Being in the moment' is a crucial element of the musicians' work in MiMiC: responding to participants' verbal and physical cues about the music-making, most prominently in improvised pieces, and flexibly adjusting to every new situation as it unfolds.²⁶ The musicians then reflect on the 'quality of the artistic response' both from patients and the nurses to further adjust their 'tailor-made approaches'.²⁷ This learning pathway and reflection on its processes leads to an increased 'awareness of (professional) development' connected to the musicians' evolving artistic identities in the practice.²⁸

This description of a learning pathway resonates with another exploration of musicians' processual development working in hospitals: that of Björkman, which is published in a Finnish *Care Music* report.²⁹ Björkman explains that musicians in hospitals work by feeling and exploring the needs of each situation they encounter. This requires them to move through various 'gates'. At first, the musicians will pass the gate of the hospital as an environment to their practice, meaning they have to learn to cope with unpredictable situations, noise and bustle. Secondly, Björkman explains that musicians need to cope with and look past patients' vulnerability brought upon by illness and pain. Thirdly, the musicians need to find ways to enable consensual musical interactions, meaning sensitively observing, feeling and listening to the patient in the moment. Finally, the musicians make musical and artistic choices to facilitate meaningful musical interaction, using their professional knowhow in initiating musical participation.

The similarities of the descriptions of musicians' learning and the development of professional performance in Smilde et al. and Björkman give a strong basis to the assertion that musicians' adjustment to a new context of work in the hospital environment is above all a processual, socially and contextually sensitive journey.³⁰

---

25 Ibid.
26 Ibid.
27 Ibid.
28 Ibid.
29 See Pia-Maria Björkman, 'Musiikkipedagogina lasten klinikalla — musiikillisia kohtaamisia', in *Care music - sairaala- ja hoivamusiikkityö ammattina*, ed. by Lilja-Viherlampi, L-M. (Turku: Turku University of Applied Sciences, 2013), pp. 58-80.
30 Smilde et al., *If Music Be the Food of Love, Play On*; Björkman, *Musiikkipedagogina lasten klinikalla*.

Methodological Approach

The qualitative research data used for this chapter have been collected by the research group Lifelong Learning in Music (now Music in Context) in collaboration with the surgical department of the University Medical Center Groningen (UMCG) during two research projects into the practice of MiMiC. The data collection employed an ethnographic research approach, combining participant observation, group discussion both among musicians and in mixed groups of musicians and nurses, interviews with individual musicians and nurses, and reflective journals written by musicians. Firstly, a research project into the development of the MiMiC practice (2015-2017) aimed to answer the research question: 'What does music actually move in the hospital?'[31] Secondly, a follow-up research project, Professional Excellence in Meaningful Music in Healthcare (ProMiMiC, 2019-2023),[32] focused on the interprofessional learning and collaboration of musicians and nurses in MiMiC practice, as well as on the cultivation of nurses' compassionate care through the participatory music sessions.

The qualitative data has been processed with a grounded theory approach to data analysis, meaning theorising categories of data, which emerge from the coding of empirical data and interpretations thereof.[33] This chapter has an autoethnographic thread underpinning the knowledge construction, as both authors are classically trained violinists and experienced MiMiC musicians working in various hospital wards, as well as in other elderly care contexts in The Netherlands.

---

31 See Smilde et al., *If Music Be the Food of Love, Play On*.
32 ProMiMiC was led by the Research group Lifelong Learning in Music of Hanze University Groningen. Partners in the project are University Medical Center Groningen, Research group Nursing Diagnostics of Hanze University, Royal Conservatoire in The Hague, Haaglanden Medical Centre The Hague, University of Music Performing Arts Vienna, Allgemeines Krankenhaus Vienna, Royal College of Music / Centre of Performance Science London, Chelsea and Westminster Hospital London, and Foundation Mimic Muziek. The project was co-financed through the RAAK-Pro programme of Regieorgaan SIA, part of the Dutch Research Council (NWO), https://www.hanze.nl/nl/onderzoeken/centers/kenniscentrum-kunst-en-samenleving/projecten/promimic
33 See Kathy Charmaz, *Constructing Grounded Theory. A Practical Guide Through Qualitative Analysis* (London: SAGE, 2006).

Findings

Interprofessional Communities of Practice Nurturing Professional Development

As previously suggested, musicians' apprehension and initial experiences of contextual disconnectedness in MiMiC practice can be eased by a sense of inclusion through the development of interprofessional collaboration with nurses. Here, Lave and Wenger's concept of *communities of practice* is helpful to explain the emergence of membership in the joint practice between nurses and musicians, and its meaningfulness for the musicians and nurses' professional development.[34] As discovered by Smilde et al. and De Wit,[35] in MiMiC, communities of practice can emerge between musicians and care professionals, meaning that through coming together and getting to know each other, the musicians and nurses alike may begin to find ways to share the practice as equal partners. A viola player reflects upon the processes of learning to know the 'other' (from a musicians' group discussion after a ProMiMiC research lab):

> I thought, 'okay, [...] great that we are aware of these professional differences within the teams because it helps us, you know... when you have medical nurse[s], [...] they give a different kind of point of contact [to the patients] for us. So, that kind of an ecosystem, knowing it, being aware of it I think is hugely important when you come to a new ward.

A cellist reflects on the emerging interprofessional collaboration and the combining of the different expertise for providing positive care for patients (from a mixed group discussion during a ProMiMiC research lab):

> [...] we complement each other very nicely, in facilitating the music for the patient. We both use our expertise in this to make the best possible assessment about the situation and to make it run as smoothly as possible.

The data suggest that through the growing mutual engagement and collaboration, the musicians begin to learn how to navigate professionally

---

34   See Jean Lave and Etienne Wenger, *Situated Learning. Legitimate Peripheral Participation* (New York: Cambridge University Press, 1991).
35   See Smilde et. al., *If Music Be the Food of Love, Play On*; and De Wit, *Legacy*.

in the new context and how to engage with their new audiences. When it comes to higher music education, however, current music students rarely have an opportunity to enter collaborative learning together with healthcare students or professionals during their studies. This lack of interprofessional training hinders musicians' early familiarisation of working together with healthcare professionals in the new context. Therefore, one of the aims of the ProMiMiC research project was to strengthen the interprofessional collaboration and learning of musicians and nurses, and additionally, to develop concrete training opportunities for music students together with nursing students in the Netherlands.

With regards to MiMiC musicians' professional development, mutual trust in the nurses is crucial for the musicians' performance in particularly vulnerable or challenging situations of engaging with a patient. A violinist reflects (in a musicians' group discussion during a ProMiMiC research lab):

> You just try to deliver a beautiful piece, [while] you are checking with the nurses: 'it seems appropriate, okay, [the patient] is responding to [the music].'

Being in the moment remains an important element of the interactions in the emerging community of practice, which means responding to each moment without any kinds of pre-decided or planned 'formulas' of music-making. One concrete example is to avoid habitually asking nurses to engage in the music sessions and gift improvised pieces to their patients, without truly considering the unique circumstances of each encounter. A cellist explains in an interview after a ProMiMiC research lab:

> [...] giving a piece [of music as a gift to a patient] is the most meaningful, I think, when we have a nurse and a patient, just sitting together, you know? And when you really sense that they have this sort of a bond. [...] You see it in their looks in the way that [the nurses] look at their patient or talk with a patient or the patient look[s] at them, you sense that there is a bond or less of a bond. You sort of sense that, yeah. [...] The circumstances have to be right. So there has to be a felt bond at least [rather than] trying to repeat something that was successful in the past, but then the circumstances are completely different now.

Here, the cellist is describing the need for social sensitivity to feel the needs of the situation, which can catalyse change in interpersonal dynamics: 'the nurse stops being an observer and starts being a participant', the cellist concludes. The social sensitivity required to facilitate musical participation reflects Björkman's notion of the gate of consensual musical interaction,[36] namely sensitively observing and feeling the musical needs of the participants before initiating music-making. Relatedly, Smilde et al. make a case for the musicians' 'situational excellence' in MiMiC practice,[37] meaning the developed ability to exercise one's artistic excellence in the most appropriate way possible, while taking into account various contextual variables, and qualities like modesty, integrity and having antennae for the social environment. As such, situational excellence goes far beyond the musicians' artistic skills as 'makers'[38] in the societal context. Increasing students' opportunities in higher music education to engage with different audiences in various social contexts beyond pre-designed performance conventions could develop their situational excellence further, not least for working in the hospital environment.

An important place for professional development in the emergence of a community of practice is a so-called 'backstage region' of the MiMiC practice. According to Erwin Goffman (1959), a 'backstage' is a space of social interaction, to which people can retreat from the 'frontstage', on which they actively 'perform' the assumed characteristics of their profession, e.g. nurses perform the expected role of caregiving and musicians perform the expected qualities of artists.[39] In the backstage region, however, professionals can behave 'out of character', relax their professional front and interact informally.[40] They may joke, give each other advice or even argue, which they would not do on the frontstage of the professional performance. In the MiMiC practice, the frontstage can be understood as the presence of patients, to whom both nurses and musicians aim to convey the best qualities of their respective professions. A violinist reflects on the importance of having backstage contact with the nurses (in a musicians' group discussion after a ProMiMiC research lab):

---

36 See Björkman, *Musiikkipedagogina lasten klinikalla*.
37 Smilde et. al., *If Music Be the Food of Love, Play On*.
38 See Gaunt et al., *Musicians as 'Makers in Society'*.
39 See Goffman, *The Presentation of Self in Everyday Life*.
40 Ibid., p. 70.

I felt that it is so refreshing, [that] the nurses said [in the coffee room], 'You know what, [the music] is not always good for me' or 'It is not always handy for me.' I appreciate that honesty so much because then, it can open us doors on how can we do it better. Or 'how can we make it better for [them], what could be a better option?' So, I like that.

The data on musicians' and nurses' interprofessional collaboration in MiMiC practice suggests that, in the backstage region of the nurses' private break room, the musicians learn more closely how to adapt to the new context of their work as artistic collaborators. In particular, musicians reflect on the honesty and informality between them and nurses, which is fostered backstage, and how it feeds into their professional development, as described in the reflection above. On the other hand, as proposed by De Wit,[41] nurses accepting musicians as collaborators and contributors to care requires a bottom-up process of experiential learning, where nurses – through gaining first-hand experience of MiMiC sessions – begin to reflect on the value of musical interactions for care. Such learning processes are significantly facilitated by collegial encouragement among nurses, and management support from the team leaders of hospital wards.

Re-Defining Classical Music Identities

As explained above, the MiMiC musicians operate with formal classical music training behind them. This classical training gives them rich tools to express various moods, colours and impressions, particularly in the person-centred improvisational landscapes they create, as well as to play to classical repertoire securely by heart with professionally written arrangements and a high level of ensemble playing. Smilde et al. and De Wit found that nurses tend to notice the qualities of the musicians' communicational ensemble and teamwork skills, in particular their non-verbal communication and cues to each other, which likely have been developed partly through extended chamber music studies and practices.[42]

41　See De Wit, 2020, pp. 200-201.
42　See Smilde et. al., *If Music Be the Food of Love, Play On*; De Wit, *Legacy*.

Yet, the fact that the musicians play instruments (mainly strings and woodwinds) that are directly associated with classical music performance can also limit how patients and nurses relate to the musicians as a professional group. Some musicians speak about how their identity as a classical musician seems to dominate in the eyes of the nurses, and how they seek to break away from being identified that way. A cellist talks in an interview about how musical genre divisions are not relevant for tailor-made person-centred music-making and so, instead of being assumed to be a classical musician, he could instead be seen as 'exploring different personas that work the best in different cases.' The cellist explains:

> Maybe there was one remark [made by nurses] about pop music [wrapped] in a 'classical jacket'. That just feels like, 'Oh, come on, we're really trying, we're really doing our best here,' you know? I don't think we played that classically, like some of this pop stuff or folk stuff, but that's apparently how [the nurse], I guess, perceived it. That's something I really would like to turn around and make other people see differently, like that we're really more versatile than that, more versatile than doing classical covers of pop songs, which is not what we're doing, but maybe what we were perceived to be doing.

Similarly, another cellist reflects in an interview on breaking through the labels attached to classical musicianship and being recognised as a musician in more holistic terms:

> Yeah, this is also something as a classical musician, I've constantly dealt with my whole life. That people make assumptions about what sort of a person you are, I think, [...] and that's totally understandable. Because of pop culture, and because of how classic musicians are depicted in the media: always these very strait-laced, strict people, very disciplined. And you do have to have certain character traits like that, in a way to do it. But at the same time, I think most musicians are pretty relaxed people.

It appears that the MiMiC musicians seek to be recognised as versatile musicians across the borders of classical music rather than identifying as classical music ambassadors. Genre fluidity seems to be a central element of person-centred music-making. Yet, as discovered by De Wit,[43] being brought into contact with classical music through MiMiC sessions

---

43   De Wit, *Legacy*.

can also be a meaningful experience for nurses, who otherwise may not choose to listen to classical music. A nurse reflects in an interview:[44]

> The first time [...] I said: 'I do not like classical music', but since [the musicians] have visited, I sometimes put on some classical music on the radio. [...] So, I have started to listen more [to classical music].

With regards to the value of classical music for the care of patients, a coordinating nurse explains:[45]

> I think that classical music touches a lot of emotions. It loosens people up. Perhaps it can be a tool to help people who have a difficulty expressing themselves verbally. They feel that music makes it a little easier for them. So, something can be released. We notice that now. Afterwards, [the patients] talk about it.

It appears that although classical music has an important place in MiMiC in supporting patients' positive musical experiences and well-being in the hospital, the MiMiC musicians are actively working to re-define their classical musicianship in it.

Developing New Relationships with Audiences and Recognising One's Impact as a Social Change-Maker

What stands out in the musicians' reflections on MiMiC and their interprofessional collaboration in healthcare is the closeness and intimacy of their relationship with their audiences compared to traditional podium performance. This closeness leads to a sense of urgency to create similar bonds in the stage performance contexts. A cellist reflects on the connectedness within the process of creating person-centred improvisations in the hospital:[46]

> You feel the kinetic energy of your fellow musicians or the person for whom you are playing in the room. This is a direct, engaged way of playing and listening, you are physically close and in fact, that is ideal for good musical communication. I would want to strive for this communication in any concert I am playing.

---

44 Ibid., p. 178.
45 Ibid,. p. 178.
46 Smilde et al., *If Music Be the Food of Love, Play On,* p. 74.

The understanding of the directness, connectedness and collectiveness of person-centred music-making as an *ideal* form of musical communication with new audiences challenges the conventional approaches to musicians' professional training and performance practices. The cellist explains:[47]

> It is difficult to create the same urgency which you feel at a visit in the rooms of UMCG in a concert situation. In UMCG, music is not a luxury product, but something extremely important. I would love to find other contexts in which this can take shape and find ways in which a normal concert can get more urgency.

Similarly, in a Master's thesis on transferable learning from person-centred music-making in healthcare contexts to classical podium performance, Gonzáles Pastor discovered that the closeness in her relationship with the audiences in the hospital made her feel less intimidated when performing to audiences on stage, as the division between audience and performer suddenly felt unnecessary, and thus, the need to connect with the audiences on a more personal level exceeded the initial performance anxiety.[48] Gonzáles Pastor writes:[49]

> [Based on the] person-centred approach, I have developed my self-confidence and self-esteem as a classical player through new understandings of what I can reach with my music. This is visible in [the] classical music-making in the way I now present myself on the stage and the way I introduce the music to the audience trying to connect and create links.

On the other hand, during the COVID-19 pandemic, when the musicians' professional opportunities to work in their conventional performance settings almost entirely disappeared, having the opportunity to carry out MiMiC projects virtually to patients served as a crucial platform to connect meaningfully with audiences again and to feel a sense of purpose in society. A viola player reflects in a musicians group discussion after a ProMiMiC research lab:

---

47 Ibid.
48 Sara Gonzáles Pastor, 'Developing Classical Musicianship: Transferable musical skills development through person-centred music-making in healthcare settings' (Unpublished Master's thesis, Prince Claus Conservatoire of Hanze University of Applied Sciences Groningen, 2020).
49 Ibid., p. 64.

Also this kind of trust [the nurses] give us to really feel like we are part of the team, so we are kind of like 'musician-nurses', in that sense, and they really [consider] us as a tool to get closer to the patients. Also, for them to kind of relax or help them with their daily work. That is why it was so nice and special.

The growing sense of being able to contribute to daily hospital care through music and recognising oneself as a social change-maker in this new context is significant for the musicians' sense of belonging as cultural collaborators in person-centred hospital care. It appears that person-centred improvisations in particular present artistic possibilities for creating positive change in the hospital environment. A flautist reflects upon a moment when a female patient, originally from Suriname, asked to hear a landscape from her home country evoked musically by an improvisation, while her nurse was sharing this musical interaction (from a musicians' group discussion after a ProMiMiC research lab):

> What stood out for me, in terms of somebody taking part in the co-creation of an improvisation, was [when] one nurse said that when you are visualising this landscape, for example the Suriname moment, you are asking for this input, you start to create it together, and it becomes this kind of a place that the person can kind of visit. The nurse [said that she] can professionally also use this technique, sans music, but just do it. I thought, 'wow, okay, so there is a lot of potential to learn or to get some new tools in their professional toolkit [influenced by person-centred music-making].'

A violinist agrees with what the flautist is proposing in the musicians' group discussion:

> What [the nurse] said made a lot of sense: using the creative mental images as a way of connecting socially and creating calmness for the patients and in her work. This made me realise how much power there is in the improvisations [...].

The consistent findings about the transformative potential of person-centred improvisations to create connectedness and support a sense of well-being in the moment, which is also described by Smilde et al. and De Wit, emphasise the need for improvisation to be recognised as a central approach to socially engaged music-making by institutes of higher music education.[50]

Shared Values of Integrity and Compassion Underpinning the Practice

The data from the ProMiMiC research into the interprofessional collaboration of musicians and nurses suggest that the cornerstones of the practice are the shared ethical values of person-centredness both in music and healthcare: integrity, compassion and respect towards the patients' personhood and preferences in the moment. The mutual recognition of these shared values is important for the interprofessional community of practice between musicians and nurses to grow. Musicians often reflect on these deeper social processes emerging through music-making, and how they are tied to their developing professional identities as musicians. A flautist reflects on moments of music-making for an older woman who was receiving palliative end-of-life care (from a reflective journal after a ProMiMiC research lab):

> We played every day for her, something classical and calm. It was very beautiful, especially when we got to play for her and her family. I really felt emotional (in a good way) seeing how the music moved the family being in the middle of saying goodbye to [the patient] and being there with her in her last days here. The family also expressed how much it meant to them. Encounters like this always make me aware of the power of music and how deep and multi-faced it is. That what we do is not just about 'music as a medicine', it is also about dignity and somehow [connecting with] people's lives and relationships in a meaningful way.

Not only does the practice of MiMiC enable the musicians to display compassion and dignity in their professional practice, as described in the reflection above, it also seems to open possibilities for healthcare professionals to display compassion to their patients through the socially shared musical processes.[51] A flautist reflects in her reflective journal (after a ProMiMiC research lab):

---

50 See Smilde et. al., *If Music Be the Food of Love, Play On*; De Wit, *Legacy*.
51 See also as corroborated by Krista De Wit, 'Person-centred Music-making as a Cultural Change Agent for Compassionate Healthcare: through the Lens of Experiential Workplace Learning', in *Critical Artistic Research and Arts Practices*

I was observing the way the nurses were touching and caring for the patients during the music-making. I was convinced that in those moments, their care was intertwined with the musical situation: it was not either care or music, it was both at the same time. Very special to witness.

These findings on music supporting nurses' compassionate care by blending with it are corroborated by De Wit.[52] The findings suggest a strong foundation of shared understanding and the display of ethics of care in the interprofessional collaboration of musicians and nurses.

Concluding Thoughts

Given the ongoing developments in the emerging professional profile of classically trained musicians working in hospitals, or more widely in the healthcare sector, it is worthwhile discussing these in the framework of classical music futures. As described, working in the hospital ecosystem is not only personally significant for classically trained musicians but it enables a strong professional sense of being able to contribute meaningfully to society as recognised allies for compassionate person-centred healthcare. MiMiC also enables musicians to develop versatile professionalism and build a completely different kind of closeness with their audiences than conventional podium performance does. The feeling of urgency to connect deeper with one's audiences in concert settings implies that more dialogical means of re-thinking classical music performance could result in more meaningful shared musical experiences for both performing musicians and their audiences.

The high contextual sensitivity of MiMiC helps musicians to develop their situational excellence beyond artistic excellence,[53] which is especially significant when working with vulnerable audiences. Situational excellence is a transferable concept to any social context of music-making, but it requires a real commitment to taking the

---

as Forms of (Radical) Care, ed. by Marie-Andrée Godin, Mira Kallio-Tavin and Abdullah Qureshi (= *Research in Arts and Education*, 2021:4 (2021)), 326-354, https://doi.org/10.54916/rae.119540

52 See De Wit, *Legacy*; De Wit, 'Person-centred Music-making as a Cultural Change Agent for Compassionate Healthcare: through the Lens of Experiential Workplace Learning'.

53 See Smilde et al., *If Music Be the Food of Love, Play On*.

situational needs of the participants as a point of departure for the music-making instead of the artistic approach itself. This is where curricular reconsiderations of higher music education are necessary. The development of situational excellence in music-making cannot be fostered separately from a global vision of what socially engaged music-making means for the education of professional musicians. Moreover, discussion about the ethics of socially engaged music-making is needed in conservatoires in order to understand the aspects of safety, responsibility and dialogue when working with particularly vulnerable people. Entering new healthcare spaces as ethically well-informed professional musicians requires sufficient understanding of person-centredness both in music-making and care, as well as knowledge of and respect towards contextual protocols.

Through the developments in musicians' professional performance in the practice of MiMiC, as well as in their interprofessional collaboration with nurses, the musicians' professional identities are shaped. The data suggest that there is a need to re-imagine the role of classical music and classically trained musicians working in person-centred participatory music practices in healthcare from a more genre-fluid perspective. Instead of labelling themselves as classical musicians, the MiMiC musicians begin to identify more holistically as musicians working to create tailor-made music to fit participants' unique musical and artistic needs, no matter the musical style. Finally, the MiMiC musicians' professional identities may extend past the lines of music and healthcare, meaning that they may feel a strong connectedness and belonging to the new field of practice and see themselves as legitimate cultural change agents supporting person-centred care.[54]

These findings have educational consequences for institutes of higher music education. Firstly, classical music education needs to hold a more genre-neutral view when educating future musicians. Person-centred music-making in healthcare asks for musicians' flexibility to play music of various styles, both improvised and arranged. Secondly, we must better educate classical musicians as improvisers in conservatoires. Rather than simply introducing classical musicians to improvisation as a form of music-making, improvisation training should be connected to

---

54   See also Smilde et al., *If Music Be the Food of Love, Play On*.

ensemble skills development and contextual awareness: for whom are we creating a piece of music, how do we go about it and why?

Thirdly, the questions above require structurally created opportunities for novice musicians to take part in socially engaged arts practices as part of their studies, to explore and reflect upon their relationships with their audiences, as well as their artistic voices in society at large. Such opportunities should also take place in cross-sectoral settings to support early familiarisation with interprofessional collaboration. Fourthly, there is a need to educate classical musicians to recognise their capacity to make music beyond their main instrument: using one's voice to connect with vulnerable audiences, arranging music for specific audiences or contexts, as well as learning various musical roles in an ensemble, such as keeping rhythm and bass, melody-making, harmonising and soloing, which are all musical skills needed for person-centred music-making. These more horizontal skills can be learned from dedicated training programmes in conservatoires. However, they also require cultivating a conservatoire culture that appreciates generalist skills development parallel to fostering specialism in podium performance.

Finally, given the currently fragmented professional landscape of musicians in healthcare, it is important to prepare novice musicians with robust competences in cultural entrepreneurship to help them to successfully enter this new sector of work, as well as to form national and international networks and alliances both in practice and in education to help musicians access and navigate various healthcare contexts. Conservatoires offering music students local training opportunities for socially engaged music-making in healthcare contexts have a role in the process of co-defining the emerging professional profile of musicians in healthcare. Therefore, higher music education also needs to recognise musicians in healthcare as a growing professional group of 'makers in society' in classical music futures. Simultaneously, explicit medical guidelines supporting the legitimacy of live music in healthcare, as well as further research on the impact of live music on the well-being of patients and healthcare professionals, remain necessary for the wider implementation and sustainability of participatory live music practices in hospitals and other healthcare contexts.

References

Björkman, Pia-Maria, 'Musiikkipedagogina lasten klinikalla — musiikillisia kohtaamisia', in *Care music – sairaala- ja hoivamusiikkityö ammattina*, ed. by Lilja-Viherlampi, L-M. (Turku: Turku University of Applied Sciences, 2013), 58-80.

Charmaz, Kathy, *Constructing Grounded Theory. A Practical Guide Through Qualitative Analysis* (London: SAGE, 2006).

Daykin, Norma, 'Developing Social Models for Research and Practice in Music, Arts, and Health: A Case Study of Research in a Mental Health Setting', in *Music, Health, and Wellbeing*, ed. by Raymond MacDonald, Gunter Kreutz, and Laura Mitchell (Oxford: Oxford University Press, 2012), pp. 65-75, https://doi.org/10.1093/acprof:oso/9780199586974.003.0005

Gaunt, Helena, Celia Duffy, Ana Coric, Isabel R. González Delgado, Linda Messas, Oleksandr Pryimenko and Henrik Sveidahl, *Musicians as "Makers in Society": A Conceptual Foundation for Contemporary Professional Higher Music Education* (Front. Psychol, 2021), https://doi.org/10.3389/fpsyg.2021.713648

Gay, Eve-Laure, The French National Policy Culture and Health – A Transferable Model?, in *Arts – Health – Entrepreneurship? A conference on Arts and Health Projects and Practices on 22-23 October 2013 in Helsinki*, ed. by Pia Strandman (Helsinki: Helsinki Metropolia University of Applied Sciences, 2012), 17-19.

Goffman, Erving, *The Presentation of Self in Everyday Life*. (London: Penguin Books, 1959/1990).

Gonzáles Pastor, Sara, 'Developing Classical Musicianship: Transferable Musical Skills Development Through Person-Centred Music-Making in Healthcare Settings' (Unpublished Master's thesis, Prince Claus Conservatoire of Hanze University of Applied Sciences, Groningen, 2020).

Huhtinen-Hildén, Laura, 'Perspectives on Professional Use of Arts and Arts-Based Methods in Elderly Care', *Arts & Health, An International Journal for Research, Policy and Practice* 6:3 (2014), 223-234, https://doi.org/10.1080/17533015.2014.880726

Koivisto, Taru-Anneli, and Taru Tähti, 'Professional entanglements: A qualitative systematic review of healthcare musicians' work in somatic hospital wards', *Nordic Journal of Music Therapy* 29:5, (2020), 416-436, https://doi.org/10.1080/08098131.2020.1768580

Lave, Jean, and Etienne Wenger, *Situated Learning. Legitimate Peripheral Participation* (New York: Cambridge University Press, 1991).

Lilija-Viherlampi, Liisa-Maria, *Care music - sairaala- ja hoivamusiikkityö ammattina* (Turku: Turku University of Applied Sciences, 2013).

Lines, David, 'The Ethics of Community Music', in *The Oxford Handbook of Community Music*, ed. by Brydie-Leigh Bartleet and Lee Higgins (Oxford: Oxford University Press, 2018), pp. 385-402, https://doi.org/10.1093/oxfordhb/9780190219505.001.0001

Matarasso, François, *A Restless Art: How Participation Won, and Why It Matters* (London: Calouste Gulbenkian Foundation, UK Branch, 2019).

Ruud, Even, The New Health Musicians', in *Music, Health, and Wellbeing*, ed by Raymond MacDonald, Gunter Kreutz, and Laura Mitchell (Oxford: Oxford University Press, 2012), pp. 88-96, https://doi.org/10.1386/ijcm.11.1.7_1

Seligman, Martin E. P., *Flourish: A Visionary New Understanding of Happiness and Well-Being* (New York: Free Press, 2011).

Smilde, Rineke, Kate Page and Peter Alheit, *While the Music Lasts – On Music and Dementia* (Delft: Eburon, 2014).

Smilde, Rineke, 'The Music Profession and the Professional Musician: A Reflection' (Paper presented at the European Association of Conservatoires, Strasbourg, 2017).

Smilde, Rineke, *Musicians Working in Community Contexts: Perspectives of Learning* (Learning and teaching conference, The Royal College of Music in Stockholm, 2019).

Smilde, Rineke, Erik Heineman, Krista de Wit, Karolien Dons and Peter Alheit, *If Music Be the Food of Love, Play On: Meaningful Music in Healthcare* (Utrecht: Eburon, 2019).

Turino, Thomas, *Music as Social Life: The Politics of Participation* (Chicago: The University of Chicago Press, 2018).

Wit, Krista de, *Legacy: Participatory Music Practices with Elderly People as a Resource for the Well-being of Healthcare Professionals* (Ede, The Netherlands: GVO drukkers & vormgevers B.V., 2020), https://research.hanze.nl/ws/portalfiles/portal/34894647/Krista_de_Wit_dissertation..pdf

Wit, Krista de, 'Person-centred Music-making as a Cultural Change Agent for Compassionate Healthcare: through the Lens of Experiential Workplace Learning', *Critical Artistic Research and Arts Practices as Forms of (Radical) Care*, ed. by Marie-Andrée Godin, Mira Kallio-Tavin and Abdullah Qureshi (= *Research in Arts and Education*, 2021:4 (2021)), 326-354, https://doi.org/10.54916/rae.119540

Wolf, Lea, Thomas Wolf, *Music and Health Care. A Paper Commissioned by the Musical Connections Program of Carnegie Hall's Weill Music Institute* (New York: Carnegie Hall and Wolf Brown, 2011).

9. Roundtable 3: Orchestras in a Changing Climate

Neil Thomas Smith and Peter Peters with contributions from Teemu Kirjonen, Detlef Grooß, Georgina MacDonell Finlayson, and Jan Jaap Knoll

Classical music is often seen as a practice that struggles to react to contemporary events. Yet, it does register societal changes, with perhaps the most important being climate change. There is a sense of urgency, as well as a need for concrete action on this topic within the field. Climate change and the measures and policies to address it will affect us all in myriad ways. This chapter discusses how the classical music sector might respond. For instance, orchestras today depend on travel and mobility as a global art form: conductors, soloists, musicians and, of course, the audience rely on emission-heavy travel. What would it mean for the practice if we were to travel less? How would it change?

There is also of course the question of how to respond artistically and creatively, not just organisationally. Attempts are being made for music to help counter, for instance, the imagination gap with regard to climate change, with artists trying to give audiences a real sense of how the actions of humans can have catastrophic effects on the natural world. The emotional power of music to reach and inspire people is being used to counteract the difficulties in imagining what the future will look like. An example is composers and musicians who use climate change data to make music compositions so that people can engage and experience these data in different ways.

There are also the very concrete and practical questions of where to start and the steps we can take as individuals, or students or employees, with regards to this issue. Is creating meaningful change within the classical sector nearly as worthwhile as fighting politically for change in industrial, energy and agricultural policy? And how can you guarantee that changes are not 'skin-deep'? The spectre of greenwashing – i.e. giving activities a veneer of climate action without making meaningful change – is always present.

The following roundtable began as a part of the online Maastricht Centre for the Innovation of Classical Music's 2021 Corona Conversations series, which engaged with major issues in classical music. Centre director, Peter Peters, was joined by four panellists with a stake in the issue: Teemu Kirjonen, general manager of the Finnish Lahti Symphony Orchestra, an orchestra that decided to go carbon neutral; Detlef Grooß from Germany, a violist and also chairperson of the Orchester des Wandels (the orchestra of change), which is a group of musicians from various orchestras around Germany who want to address climate issues; Georgina MacDonell Finlayson who is sustainability manager at the Scottish Nevis Ensemble, Scotland's 'street orchestra', who play in unusual locations and tour extensively around their home country;[1] and finally, Jan Jaap Knol who is the director of the Boekman Foundation, which is the institute for arts culture and related policy in the Netherlands, known for their research in the cultural sector. The Boekman Foundation published a report on sustainability in the cultural sector in 2019, as described in the first contribution.[2]

---

1   As mentioned in the Introduction, the Nevis Ensemble folded in 2023 due to financial pressures. Many arts organisations are tackling these issues, as well as those posed by the *demographic problem*, despite their own perilous funding position.
2   Christine Skovbon from the Erasmus University Rotterdam also took part in the original discussion but is represented in the volume by her own chapter.

Culture and Climate

Jan Jaap Knol

Today we will reflect, in different ways, on the three aspects in which culture, including music, can contribute to the big theme of sustainability and climate change. Firstly, we must do our utmost to make our own practices more sustainable. Secondly, there is the question of how we as a cultural sector can contribute to the public awareness of sustainability by telling the story of climate change using the power of imagination. This can range from the most dystopian scenarios to more optimistic ones. The third and final aspect is the design potential of culture: how can the creativity and innovation of artists contribute to designing more sustainable ways of living? As Georgina formulates below, we need to redefine success after all those years when it was about growth: growth of people attending performances, growth of economic resources, growth of touring etc. But if we find ways to redefine our success, we can also stimulate others to rethink patterns in a way that can contribute to a more sustainable and greener world. At the Boekman Foundation, research on culture and sustainability is one of our core themes and I'd like to very briefly discuss some of our work.

In 2019 we surveyed around 250 cultural organisations in the Netherlands, whom we questioned about their attitude and actions when it comes to sustainability.[3] From that report, on the positive side, I can say that many cultural organisations are increasingly aware of the need to become more sustainable and there is concrete action, mainly concerning waste and electricity consumption. Honestly, there were not that many activities, at least in 2019, when it comes to the area of public awareness-raising, while we also found that most respondents did not have structural policies regarding sustainability, nor did they monitor their progress in this area. There were three barriers often mentioned here: there was too little money, too little knowledge, and that there was too little time to become more active.

---

3   Bjorn Schrijen, 'Duurzaamheid in de culturele sector. Steppingstones voor toekomstig duurzaamheidsbeleid', *Boekmanstichting*, 2019, https://www.boekman.nl/verdieping/publicaties/duurzaamheid-in-de-culturele-sector/

Given the urgency of climate change, however, these are barriers that we should overcome together. In 2020 we undertook a second research project in which we analysed cultural policy documents of municipalities who are responsible for a large part of cultural funding in the Netherlands.[4] There again we saw a positive trend in that more and more municipalities pay attention to the subject in their policy plans. Yet, they do it in many different ways and it is often about plans to make buildings more sustainable, as well as involving cultural organisations in the sustainable development of cities, but again with a big variety in ambition and in the concreteness of the proposals.

Now, for 2021, we are working on a new publication on the relationship between the cultural sector and sustainability. We are undertaking this in partnership with organisations from seven European countries, including Finland, Germany and Scotland.[5] Three points are relevant here. Firstly, it is clear that there are a great many artists engaged in this subject at the moment. To mention a few composers that are well known in the Netherlands, for example: Merlijn van Twaalfhoven is one and also Tim Kliphuis, whose composition *Phoenix Reborn* premiered in the Concertgebouw in Amsterdam in 2021. So there is this engagement on the artistic side.

Secondly, although increasing attention is paid to the subject of climate change in public and in policy plans, there is too little institutional attention for it at a national level. Government could address the theme much more explicitly and stimulate targeted energy initiatives in the cultural sector. For example, the creative climate action that is a programme of the Irish Ministry of Culture, together with the Ministry of Environment, is a funding programme for specific cultural activities when it comes to this theme. Creative Carbon, a networking community in the cultural sector in Scotland, is another example. We in the Netherlands miss such a networking community.

---

4 Bjorn Schrijen, 'Duurzaamheid in de culturele sector. Inspiratie voor toekomstig Beleid', *Boekmanstichting*, 2020, https://www.boekman.nl/verdieping/publicaties/duurzaamheid-in-de-culturele-sector-2020/

5 Meanwhile the research is published. Boekman Foundation (2022), 'Towards sustainable arts: European best practices and policies', 14 February 2022, https://www.boekman.nl/en/in-depth/publications/towards-sustainable-arts-european-best-practices-and-policies/

This brings me to my third observation: that there is a lot to gain by sharing knowledge, not only nationally but also internationally. So it is important to learn about symphony orchestras from Finland, the Nevis Ensemble, and Das Orchester des Wandels. I hope we can exchange more in the future and we do not need to tour for that.

Towards Net Zero with the Lahti Symphony Orchestra

Teemu Kirjonen

Lahti in Finland is a traditional winter sports city; there is even a ski jumper in our logo, reaching towards a better future. It is a town of some 120,000 inhabitants in the south of the country, roughly one hundred kilometres north of Helsinki. The symphony orchestra is a group of around sixty-seven musicians, plus the administrators, located in the wooden Sibelius Hall.

We launched the project, Carbon Neutral Lahti Symphony Orchestra, in 2015, which happened to be the 150th anniversary of the birth of our national composer, Jean Sibelius. The aim of the project is to try and become the first carbon neutral symphony orchestra in the world by 2025. Although it's only six years since 2015, the world is already a quite different place when it comes to these discussions. Then, it was very exotic that a Finnish symphony orchestra was starting to work on these issues, but of course things are progressing and new projects are starting all the time.

At the very beginning, a Master's thesis was done at the local university by Pilvi Virolainen in which the carbon footprint of the orchestra was calculated and examined. It was not only the orchestra's activities but also the activities around us: the audience, the concert hall, the recording company etc. The idea is that carbon neutrality is achieved by 'first identifying the greenhouse gas emissions resulting from the functions. After this, the identified functions are changed to low emission operations and finally the remaining greenhouse gas emissions are compensated.'[6] So, first examine, second reduce, third compensate. The five principal burdens are transport, energy, recording,

---

6   Pilvi Virolainen, 'Sinfoniaorkesterin hiilijalanjälki. Case: Sinfonia Lahti', 2015, https://lutpub.lut.fi/handle/10024/117794

acquisitions and spin-offs. On the first, our input has been quite limited lately as an orchestra, as we have not been touring during the Covid era, but we can encourage our own people and those in the audience to use greener solutions when coming to the concerts and to the workplace.

For me as the manager of the orchestra it was very important that, from the very beginning, the whole organisation was committed to this. This can't be the kind of project that management just imposes. The whole thing started by having a workshop for the whole orchestra and we discussed these themes and brainstormed ideas. By the end of the day, we had the idea that we could become the first carbon neutral orchestra in the world. Are we in or are we out? We had a vote, and the result was unanimously 'yes, we are in'. We want to be an active part of society, not just a kind of isolated artistic palace, appearing once a week with great symphonic programmes. One thing that has been a real delight is that, when we have had less active periods, the musicians themselves have been asking 'what more can we do?' and that is a really good sign of their commitment.

I'll give a couple of brief examples of our work. Firstly, we had a 'green button' initiative so when people were buying tickets from the web there was a button with which you could donate money to certified projects in order to compensate for travelling to the concert. Secondly, we worked with Sibelius Hall, our wooden hall. There this year the heating became carbon neutral and hopefully the electricity of the whole place will be carbon neutral next year. The waste management has been carbon neutral for some time and food outlets are also taking action. Thirdly, the orchestra has a longstanding relationship with the Swedish record label BIS and they started their BIS eco pack (cardboard packaging) in 2019. In 2019 for the annual day for the orchestra we planted 6,000 spruce trees and this is a good example of the way organisations can have events that are fun but also beneficial. It was one of the best recreational days the orchestra has ever had.

I think the most important area of work at the moment is the reduction of paper usage. So, this has come down enormously now the rehearsal copies of the sheet music are distributed digitally and of course we are examining, for example, reducing handouts and trying to figure out the best way to do brochures digitally. Concerning transport, which is the biggest category of emissions, we are trying to be involved in the discussions externally to make it easier for the audience to come to the concerts. At the moment, if we encouraged our audience to come to our concerts by bicycle, and say 400 of them did so, we would be in great trouble because we don't have any places here at the Sibelius Hall to park the bicycles!

When we started in 2015 of course we wanted to be a reference hopefully locally, maybe nationally or even internationally. What happened in Lahti surprised us however, as the local ice hockey team, the Pelicans, decided to become the first carbon neutral ice hockey team in the world. They did a similar kind of survey and had our project as a reference. Internationally, it has brought attention to the orchestra, winning the Classical:NEXT Innovation Award in 2018.

So, of course, we need to examine our daily operations so that they become more carbon neutral but one very important issue in this whole project is to raise awareness of climate issues. In 2021 Lahti was the EU green capital and a good example of how the EU green capital organisation has utilised the orchestra can be found in their commission for a new work from Finnish composer Cecilia Darmström called *ICE* (which also stands for 'In Case of Emergency'). The piece was premiered in a square in central Helsinki via video from the Sibelius Hall, and there were a number of large ice cubes brought to the square which melted as an installation. There was also a possibility to hear the work in situ as a recorded loop. The names of the cities that are most urgently in danger when the sea levels rise were written on the ground so that the water from the ice cubes flushes these names away. It was impressive, although the ice melted quicker than expected, though that of course only highlights the emergency. If and when we become carbon neutral, it does not make as much difference as a factory or other huge polluter. It is because of this that I want to point to the importance of raising awareness. At the same time, we have to take care of our own field as well and we have tried to examine our daily operations that have an environmental impact.

Orchester des Wandels

Detlef Grooß

Orchester des Wandels means Orchestras of Change. Society is changing, the climate is changing and we have to go with and shape the change. We started in Berlin ten years ago. The Staatskapelle Berlin first did something very similar to what the Lahti Symphony Orchestra did with ice cubes, as well as putting on climate concerts to raise money for environmental projects, such as planting trees. We are now an organisation with members from thirty-three different orchestras in Germany who come together and put on events. It is not the official orchestras but only the members as private individuals who take part: it is a grassroots movement.

A few years later, in 2020, we gathered many more members and orchestras to build a really Germany-wide organisation. We asked ourselves what the role of culture is and what the role of theatres and orchestras can be in this situation, as well as considering how we can make the strongest impact on this theme in society. As cultural institutions we have a very different role to factories or companies, as Teemu states. We are so much more visible in society. For example, in my theatre we sell 350,000 tickets a year, so that has a huge potential impact and if we do things differently and if we communicate our message, it can influence the whole of society.

Our first thought was that this really had to be a positive approach. When talking about culture and environmental impact we get into a corner where it seems that we are the problem, but I deeply believe that culture is not the problem, rather the solution, because culture itself does not destroy the environment. It gives fulfilment without having to go shopping or engaging in consumerist culture. Culture can work against consumption, and over-consumption, which is one of the most pressing problems of our time. We thought about how we can approach this and we said that, rather than wallowing in how bad everything is, we must go out and act.

When we thought about what an orchestra could do and what we could do together, we isolated four main issues, four columns for our work. The first thing was to put the protection of climate and the environment at the centre of what we do. Everything was considered in relation to our cultural mandate. Secondly, we wanted to use our formats to push this issue in society, then we could collect – and we do collect – a lot of money for environmental projects. The third thing is caring for our own carbon footprint and the last, and probably the most important thing, is what we are doing now: networking and communication. If we act as a whole scene together then we have a chance to shape the change and not to react to what comes from politicians.

Our biggest environmental project at the moment is reforesting a 700-hectare rainforest in Madagascar. Why Madagascar you may ask: it is because the wood that makes the black pieces on violins and cellos is made of ebony, which grows there. Ninety-five percent of the surface of Madagascar has been deforested. This has occurred for many reasons but partly because of the hunger for ebony for instruments, so we wanted to send a signal and heal this wound a little bit. We are doing a development project in north-east Madagascar and we are working together with the people there and giving them the ability to establish sustainable agriculture, for example by buying cacao plants and vanilla plants so they don't have to eradicate the forest. We also show them how to reforest the original wood, not only the ebony but the original wood ecosystem. We also do regional environmental projects here in Germany. We're just planting flowers in the garden of the theatre to be used by insects and bees. It is a very small thing, and only costs about €200, but it's going to have a huge impact and be very visible. Through this, it has a big influence on the city and society.

We also care, of course, for the CO_2 footprints of our orchestras. We do a lot of studies and workshops with all our member orchestras and theatres. We have a green manual for how you can create an environmental strategy; we have a green touring guide that came out in 2021.[7] How can you, if you're touring with the orchestra, limit your emissions? One recent example is the Munich Philharmonic: they just rebuilt their instrument cases and they are saving €100,000 a year in transport costs because they are more efficient. Even when you are flying, there is a lot you can do. We also plan on establishing a carbon offsetting platform.

---

7   Orchester des Wandels, https://www.orchester-des-wandels.de/erste-schritte/

We are collecting data on the use of paper. We are trying to develop a sustainable digital music stand. Using an iPad for reading music is not sustainable for many reasons but especially because an iPad is not made for this purpose, so it is capable of doing thousands of other things you don't need. It's also just not big enough, it's just not stable enough for everyday work. They will break and so we are working on a music desk with a big simple screen, where you can exchange every part and do not have to throw the whole thing away after three years. It would only be capable of showing music.

One further campaign that we are now undertaking is asking our audience if they come by bicycle or public transport and, if they do, they will get the programme as a podcast for free. This is called 11.5 minutes and we state that if you use public transport, you need 11.5 minutes more to travel, and we donate this podcast to you to make up that time. Perhaps the most important thing, though, is networking. We have to overcome this basic attitude of competition in orchestras and work together. It's very honourable to want to be the first green orchestra but it's even better if you share your experience with all orchestras. This means cultural, environmental and sustainability issues require teamwork. So we find partners, we partner together with the thirty-three orchestras and we are really working together and sharing our knowledge. We liaise with politicians and scientists and, because we are so big now, we really get the best scientists in Germany.

At present, Orchester des Wandels is just eight people contributing their free time, though we are looking for a foundation to create one support position. But what this means is this organisation is indeed central, so we just organise, we connect the people, we suggest the ideas and once in the year we put on a concert with all our members. Our systems are strong now and we get people conducting and playing solo with us who are at an amazing level. It's really crazy who's asking us to play but it only works if we have an organisation committed to putting these issues front and centre.

Green Travelling with the Nevis Ensemble

Georgina MacDonell Finlayson

Nevis Ensemble is Scotland's Street Orchestra. We are a forty-piece orchestra that goes on tour four or five times a year, giving concerts everywhere from airports and train stations to care homes and refugee groups. We also do pop-up performances on the streets, in supermarkets, libraries, and we've even performed in places like the top of Ben Nevis, Scotland's highest mountain, as well as way out on the islands of St Kilda on the west coast of the country. Our mission is to remove the barriers that classical music sometimes has in being truly accessible to everyone, everywhere. So that means that we take orchestral music to people wherever they are. In parallel with our orchestral work, we run a number of community-based projects, working with different groups of people, including looked-after children, older people living with dementia, those experiencing homelessness and adults with learning disabilities. We have partnerships with voluntary and third-sector organisations which are nurtured to ensure that the most vulnerable and marginalised in society do not miss out. Recently, we've had projects working with survivors of domestic violence and young carers, where they worked with composers and songwriters to write new music reflecting their experiences.

At the core of our work is a desire to contribute to a more equal and sustainable society and environmental sustainability is a key component of that, and in practical terms, we aim to run the ensemble in the most sustainable way that we can. We're lucky in that we're a young organisation, established in 2018, so sustainability has been on our minds from the word go. The main challenge is in our touring. We take music to people all over Scotland, so the orchestra is travelling on one coach. However, for instance, we plan our tours in a circular route so that we're not doubling any miles and really reaching as many people as possible.

We are currently exploring other ways of being able to tour that are completely zero carbon. So, for example, we've done a tour on bicycles in Glasgow. Obviously that doesn't take us quite as far as travelling to some of the more remote parts of Scotland but we are still able to reach a lot of the communities in Glasgow, to whom we previously took the coach. That is something that we'll explore more, especially in urban areas, as well as touring using public transport, even using public transport not just as a journey to get to a place but also as a location for performance in itself. In team meetings we've discussed the idea that transport itself, if we're going on public transport, or stops on the way, can also be a location for performance, for making music and engaging an audience, whether they expect it or not.

When we're out on tour we have established protocols and practices to make sure that we are being sustainable in what we're eating and how we're doing things on the bus: we recycle our waste, for example, and in this – and much else – our musicians are really engaged with these protocols. We have actually run two public-facing campaigns over the last two years to try and highlight for our musicians and our audiences what it is we can do to be more sustainable. In 2019 we toured the Outer Hebrides, which are the islands in the north-west of Scotland, and for this we ran a campaign called 'Green Nevis'. This was an online social media campaign in which we wanted to highlight and embed awareness of what arts organisations, musicians and individuals can do to be more sustainable. We partnered with a number of green-leaning organisations such as Scottish Water, Save Some Green and Nevis Sport. These companies helped us through sponsorship and we were able to highlight the work they're doing, but also provide our musicians with some resources to use on tour, as well as in their own lives away from the orchestra. We were very public about this on our social media and it led to some interesting discussions with audience members. It highlighted some of the small things we can be doing but it also set up a premise for our musicians being really engaged in everything that we're doing on tour: each little action amounts to us reducing our waste and being as environmentally conscious as we can be.

At the beginning of 2021 we ran another campaign,'#100DaysOfGreenNevis', which was essentially inspired by the musicians' practice trend called '100 Days of Practice' where you practise a little bit every single day, reflecting on the process and how it becomes habitual. As musicians, we're really good at doing things every day. We had a group of about thirty to forty musicians – as well as board members and trustees – picking an action for one hundred days. These ranged from going vegan, reducing plastic, to walking or cycling five hundred miles to raise money for charity. We had people doing more creative things like writing little songs on environmental issues that were really accessible and which we put out online. We had a number of people performing daily improvisations on endangered species and sharing these online with short videos and there was quite a lot of feedback from that with people saying: 'Gosh, I just didn't realise quite the scale of it'. On our website you can see the history of everybody posting about what they're doing.

That's us as an organisation: what we've been doing and how we've been engaging our musicians and our audiences. But we also recently set up the Scottish Classical Sustainability Group. We felt like it was time for classical music organisations in Scotland to come together to discuss the climate crisis on a regular basis. So, this group now contains about forty organisations, including large orchestras, festivals, individuals, smaller ensembles, duos and we also have representatives from the Association of British Orchestras, Creative Scotland (the Scottish arts funding distribution body), Creative Carbon Scotland, and the Musicians Union. We're making sure that our discussions are really tied into a more global and national discussion. We have met regularly for about a year and within that year we produced our Scottish Classical Music Green Guide, which came out in July 2021.[8] This is an in-depth document in which we try to cover as much ground as possible: everything from buildings, touring and digital emissions, to programming and accessibility. It will be a living document that will change with the times. As we know, the world is changing very quickly.

What has been a recurring theme in our discussions with Scottish organisations is how we deal with international touring because it is such a big part of what we do as orchestras and what we do in classical music. I think one of the key takeaways is reimagining how we define success as classical music organisations. At the moment, a lot of success is judged by the scope of our international outreach and there's a certain glamour associated with international touring as, for many, there is a huge amount of economic benefit and revenue that comes from that. But in the times that we're in, and the crisis that we face, I think international

---

8   Creative Carbon Scotland, Scottish Green Classical Music Guide, https://www.creativecarbonscotland.com/wp-content/uploads/2021/07/SCSGG-2021-FINAL.pdf

touring really has to become a thing of the past: not entirely, but it has to be on a level that is sustainable. This presents a really exciting opportunity to reimagine our business models so that we're not putting economic gain and growth first. We shouldn't think that we measure our success by the tickets, the audiences, the places we visit and that it all comes down, in the end, to economic gain.

How does this square with our budget and financial projections? I think what we need to be doing is reimagining these so we're thinking with a de-growth mindset. There's definitely a movement in the UK and Scotland that we emphasise success not in terms of GDP but rather in terms of people and planet and on social and environmental qualities. This is a really exciting opportunity to focus on the people in our local area. I'm talking about Scotland here but similarly across the world we can put people and their local communities first. From there we collaborate internationally in interesting ways that aren't just another international tour.

References

Boekman Foundation, 'Towards sustainable arts: European best practices and policies', 14 February 2022, https://www.boekman.nl/en/in-depth/publications/towards-sustainable-arts-european-best-practices-and-policies/

Creative Carbon Scotland, 'Scottish Green Classical Music Guide', 2021, https://www.creativecarbonscotland.com/wp-content/uploads/2021/07/SCSGG-2021-FINAL.pdf

Orchester des Wandels, https://www.orchester-des-wandels.de/erste-schritte/

Pilvi Virolainen, 'Sinfoniaorkesterin hiilijalanjälki. Case: Sinfonia Lahti', 2015, https://lutpub.lut.fi/handle/10024/117794

Schrijen, Bjorn, 'Duurzaamheid in de culturele sector. Steppingstones voor toekomstig duurzaamheidsbeleid', *Boekmanstichting*, 2019, https://www.boekman.nl/verdieping/publicaties/duurzaamheid-in-de-culturele-sector/

Schrijen, Bjorn, 'Duurzaamheid in de culturele sector. Inspiratie voor toekomstig Beleid', *Boekmanstichting*, 2020, https://www.boekman.nl/verdieping/publicaties/duurzaamheid-in-de-culturele-sector-2020/

10. Is It Time for Brahms, Again? The Many Roles of Classical Music in the German-Speaking Lands in 2023

Jutta Toelle

'It felt like a niche music that wasn't presenting itself to a wider audience. So, I started putting on classical music in these alternative venues and straight away it did reach new audiences.'[1] Gabriel Prokofiev, founder and artistic director of London-based *nonclassical*,[2] makes it all seem quite easy: change location and people start coming to classical music concerts. The circumstances under which Prokofiev says this are noteworthy: in the *nonclassical* YouTube video, a contribution to the PanelPicker website which the South by Southwest (SXSW) festival in Austin, Texas, uses as an 'official user-generated session proposal platform' for the coming festival edition in 2023.[3] In the video, Prokofiev and his colleagues stress the alternative approach of their performances and claim that they 'completely believe[s] in the future of classical music outside the concert hall, of classical music as a living art form.'[4] The SXSW festival, presenting itself as 'an essential destination for global professionals' with conference sessions, film screenings, music festival showcases and exhibitions, promises: 'unparalleled discovery, learning, professional development, and networking with creatives from around

---

1   SXSW festival, *A New Era for Classical Music in a Post-Genre World*, online video recording, https://panelpicker.sxsw.com/vote/126769
2   Nonclassical, *A music promoter, record label and events producer presenting the best new classical, experimental and electronic music*, https://www.nonclassical.co.uk/about-us
3   SXSW festival, *A New Era for Classical Music in a Post-Genre World*, online video recording, https://panelpicker.sxsw.com/vote/126769
4   Ibid.

the world.' It is amazing that even at this venue there seems to be a place for classical music!

Of course, no music practitioner would deny any of *nonclassical*'s claims. In the continental European context of heavily subsidised classical music institutions, however, the situation appears a little more complicated. Practitioners, music lovers and other stakeholders perceive a crisis and an immense pressure to innovate. In 2023 – with a war raging in Europe, a resulting gas crisis, high inflation in many countries and the perception that climate catastrophe has taken hold of the world – classical music, its survival and its futuring may not seem to be one of the most pressing topics, but the question of continuing heavily subsidised cultural traditions is becoming ever more relevant. This essay will present some pressing issues and challenges in classical music practices and trace changes; it focuses on the challenging situation in Germany, and on the different roles classical music and its practices play.

I.

The 'big questions' in the classical music realm concern audiences and repertoires: the perception that classical music mainly caters and appeals to white, well-off, elderly audiences, and the 'museum problem' (as stated in the introduction of this volume) with its strong canonical practices and so many performances of music written by dead, white, male composers. Is classical music really 'a practice trapped in the past, unable to respond to contemporary currents in society and increasingly irrelevant to what is happening around it'?[5]

Some big societal challenges have meanwhile arrived in the seemingly old-fashioned classical music world: ensembles and musicians are starting to talk about the carbon dioxide output of their continuous travelling (also due to the lockdowns and the forced periods of rest during the COVID-19 pandemic).[6] The #MeToo movement has taken hold,

---

5   See Introduction, p. 2.
6   This trend was pioneered by Helsingborg Konserthus and symphony orchestra in Sweden who pledged a no-fly policy in 2018, see this article in VAN Magazin, https://van-magazin.de/mag/helsingborg-ausgeflogen/ and https://van-magazin.de/mag/klima-deutschland/. In 2019, musicians of several German orchestras started the initiative Orchester des Wandels, focusing on the effects of climate

driving people to observe the behaviour of conductors, stage directors and performers more carefully instead of excusing inappropriate or violent behaviour with a nod to somebody's genius.[7] As a result, some well-known men in the classical music world were stripped of their jobs, status and reputation. However, below this societal level and a multitude of ongoing discussions about gender representation, diversity and postcolonial issues in classical music (which will not be discussed here), the closely connected issues of audiences and repertoires constitute the pillars of a massive problem.[8] Both are inherent to classical music – and only to classical music – for a third reason.

Classical music is very expensive to produce. It relies on musicians and other practitioners, often many of them, all of whom need years of specialised training. Due to historical developments,[9] in continental Europe (the German-speaking lands, France and Eastern Europe) classical music is heavily subsidised and mainly produced in big, expensive and cumbersome institutions like radio stations, theatres and orchestras.[10]

Lately, these subsidies have come under some pressure. Some German theatres, orchestras and opera houses, especially in less wealthy towns, have been forced to cut spending, leading to fewer performances

---

change, https://www.orchester-des-wandels.de. The post-COVID-19 situation of 2022 might have changed things for the worse again, in that many orchestras have not travelled for two or three years and feel obliged to catch up.

7   Christina Scharff and Anna Bull, 'Classical Music after #MeToo: Tackling Sexual Harassment and Misconduct in Higher Music Education', in *Higher Music Education and Employability in a Neoliberal World*, ed. by Rainer Prokop and Rosa Reitsamer (London, New York: Bloomsbury, forthcoming), also: Christina Scharff, *Gender, Subjectivity, and Cultural Work. The Classical Music Profession* (London: Routledge, 2018).

8   See Introduction to this volume, also, Kira Thurman, *Singing like Germans. Black Musicians in the Land of Bach, Beethoven, and Brahms* (Ithaca: Cornell University Press, 2021); Jennifer Lynn Stoever, *The Sonic Color Line. Race and the Cultural Politics of Listening* (New York: NYU Press, 2016).

9   Martin Rempe, *Kunst, Spiel, Arbeit. Musikerleben in Deutschland (1850–1960)* (Göttingen: Vandenhoeck & Ruprecht, 2019), p. 332.

10 The available statistics by Musikinformationszentrum are confusing. They show public subsidies on municipal, federal and national levels but combine subsidies for music (including music schools, music festivals etc) with those for theatre (for theatres and opera houses, i.e. opera orchestras). In any case, a total of 4.5 billion euros in public subsidies were paid for music and theatre in 2020; 51.4 percent by municipalities, 44.1 percent by the federal states, 4.5 percent by the national state, www.miz.org.de

because up to eighty-five percent of funds are spent on wages. At most of these institutions, however, there is a limit to the amount one can save,[11] and ultimately the only option is to cut one 'Sparte' (a division of the theatre, like children's theatre or ballet) or to close down the orchestra or opera house. In November 2022, the director of the WDR (Westdeutscher Rundfunk) asked a rhetorical question that hinted at the ensembles maintained by his employer (the largest German broadcaster, and the second largest in Europe after the BBC): 'Do the contributors want the total of sixteen ensembles: orchestras, big bands, choirs that ARD currently maintains?' He alluded to the fact that all radio stations (and their music ensembles) are maintained by monthly contributions by every German household, but didn't mention that of the monthly eighteen euros and thirty-six cents, only forty-two cents are used for the music ensembles.[12] Until now, the big broadcasters and German municipalities have mostly refrained from extreme measures. At least from an outside perspective, the 129 German professional orchestras with their nearly 10,000 musicians still thrive[13], thanks to a very strong trade union and strict contracts – to the point that one gets the impression that musical life in Germany happens in order to give the orchestras something to do, and not in order to perform music or make the music heard.[14] Another issue is that several big concert halls, theatres and opera houses in Germany are awaiting overdue renovation works,

---

11 In 2004, the Deutscher Bühnenverein protested against the decision of the Saarland to decrease the subsidies for the Staatstheater in the capital Saarbrücken by twenty-five percent; however, in 2022 there seemed to be a moment of pause and reassessment by German politicians. There are still lots of open letters by the GDBA (trade union of German theatre workers) protesting plans to cut subsidies from the 2010s to be found online.

12 Hartmut Welscher, Rundfunkorchester ohne Rundfunk, april 26, 2023, <https://van-magazin.de/mag/rundfunkorchester-ohne-rundfunk/>

13 In January 2022, there were 110 publicly subsidized (municipal or regional) orchestras, 8 publicly subsidized chamber orchestras and 11 radio orchestras in Germany, DOV Statistik Planstellen und Einstufung der Berufsorchester, <https://www.dov.org/klassikland-deutschland/dov-statistik-planstellen-und-einstufung-der-berufsorchester>; also see the map by Deutscher Musikrat, Öffentlich finanzierte Orchester, <https://www.dov.org/wp-content/uploads/2022/06/2018-03-Orchesterkarte-MIZ.pdf>; Andreas Heinen, *Wer will das noch hören? Besucherstrukturen bei niedersächsischen Sinfonieorchestern* (Wiesbaden: Springer VS, 2013), p. 165.

14 Andreas Heinen wants to 'fill the big halls with broader parts of the population in order to guarantee the survival of small orchestras' ('So gilt es, breitere Bevölkerungsschichten für das klassische Konzert zu begeistern, um so die großen

involving extremely high sums. So, while there are very few options for savings in this field, and a lot of money is being spent continuously (and uncoupled from the number of performances taking place), the ambivalence is growing; an ambivalence about the public financing of art forms that only a third of the population is slightly or really interested in, while an even smaller percentage of the German population actually attends classical music concerts.[15] This makes German concert life vulnerable. Also, the majority of classical music concerts still take the form of a symphony concert (in a concert hall, with a fixed, classical concert programme, starting between seven and eight pm) and they are attended by audiences incorporating the above-mentioned categories of class, race, wealth and age.

This 'standard classical music concert' is the default option and starting point for all discussions about the future of classical music,[16] at least in countries with a tradition of subsidised institutions for classical music. Even if Igor Toronyi Lalic, director of the London Contemporary Music Festival, claims that 'we're beyond that, [beyond the idea] of a town going to a concert hall',[17] these concerts do provide a basic service for the population, like a pharmacy or a bakery. The 'experience economy', however, cherishes unique experiences, and not these basic services; and

---

Säle zu füllen und den kleinen Orchestern das Überleben zu sichern.', Heinen, *Wer will das noch hören*, p. 12.

15   There are few statistics to rely on. In 2016, 31.5% of the German population over 14 said 'I like to listen to this music/ a lot.' [‚Diese Musikrichtung höre ich sehr gern/ auch noch gern.'] The category was called ‚classical music, piano concerts, symphonies'. 22% of the German population said the same thing about 'opera operetta, singing', see the statistics and the article by Karlheinz Reuband, *Musikpräferenzen und Musikpublika* (2019/22), <https://www.miz.org/de/beitraege/musikpraeferenzen-und-musikpublika.de>. Also, see Mina Yang, *Planet Beethoven. Classical Music at the Turn of the Millennium* (Middletown, CT: Wesleyan University Press, 2014).

16   Again, it is impossible to pin down statistically what percentage of classical music concerts happens inside or outside the major institutions. The available statistics only enlist those inside the institutions, see Deutscher Musikrat, <https://www.miz.org> and Deutsche Orchestervereinigung, <https://www.dov.org>; see also Heinen, *Wer will das noch hören*, p. 168.

17   *Nonclassical*, a new music scene is emerging in London', online video recording, <https://www.youtube.com/watch?v=rKVm1AGMpXY&t=83s>, minute 2.15-2.20.

the mere perpetuation of a long-held and highly subsidised tradition is probably not the answer to the challenge of 'futuring' classical music.[18]

In other countries, the situation differs. Practitioners from the German-speaking lands, France and Eastern Europe tend to envy and admire many outreach activities at classical music institutions in the UK. These are often organised by lean and flexible ensembles, obviously due to the (historically) different conditions under which classical music practitioners operate: underfinancing through a lack of long-term subsidies, project-related work with low sustainability and the need to stress the social impact of artistic projects. Neoliberal working conditions and an emphasis on entrepreneurship hardly allow the musicians to make a living out of their art, which is in turn unusual and seen critically in the German-speaking realm of classical music.[19]

II.

The 'audience issue' and the 'repertoire question' are closely interconnected and are being discussed continuously: in the German-speaking lands, nearly all the classical music institutions – radio stations, theatres, concert halls and orchestras – began in the 1990s and early 2000s to hire people to cater for new kinds of audiences. A first wave resulted in new (generally young, female, underpaid and precarious)[20] staff responsible for *Musikvermittlung*,[21] trying to attract predominantly

---

18 The term was coined by Joseph Pine and James H. Gilmore in 1998 (Joseph Pine and James H. Gilmore, *The Experience Economy* (Boston: Harvard Business School Press, 1999), here quoted after Karen Burland and Stephanie Pitts, *Coughing and Clapping: Investigating Audience Experience* (Farnham: Ashgate, 2014), p. 31.
19 John Pippen, 'Hope, Labour and Privilege in American New Music', in *Music as Labour: Inequalities and Activism in the Past and Present*, ed. by Dagmar Abfalter and Rosa Reitsamer (London: Routledge, 2022).
20 See the following evaluation of a 2018 survey amongst employees in Musikvermittlung: Educult, Netzwerk Junge Ohren (eds.), *Arbeitsbedingungen für Musikvermittler*innen im deutschsprachigen Raum. Hochmotiviert, exzellent ausgebildet, prekär bezahlt. Auswertung der gleichnamigen Umfrage im April 2018*, https://educult.at/wp-content/uploads/2018/03/NJO_MV_Umfrage2020-1.pdf
21 See the discussion around the usage of the German term in English in *Tuning up! The Innovative Potential of Musikvermittlung*, ed. by Sarah Chaker and Axel Petri-Preis (Bielefeld: transcript, 2022), pp. 16. The authors argue that no English term possesses all of the connotations of the term in German.

children and young adults to specially tailored projects.[22] The German Music Information Centre lists a threefold increase in educational performances by German orchestras between 2003/04 (2,000 plus) and 2017/18 (about 6,400).[23]

Another, much more recent wave – responding to the finding that the roughly twenty-five percent of people living in Germany without German-born parents are less likely to attend performing arts events – resulted in agents for diversity being hired by opera houses and orchestras, such as in Ludwigshafen, Berlin, Bielefeld and at the Staatsoper Hannover.[24] This is all the more topical because there is the perception that the (up to now loyal) white, well-off, elderly audiences are dwindling, especially after COVID-19, and considering that some German subscription audiences[25] for standard classical music concerts have a very high average age of sixty-nine years.[26] Karlheinz Reuband sees the classical music audience threatened by an erosion process, due to a decreasing appreciation of classical music in the younger generations (and generally a shrinking population).[27] Some fear that members of the 'Baby-Boomer' generation, born between 1945 and 1960 and by now mostly in the typical subscriber age bracket, are not as interested in classical music as their predecessors, because they were the

---

22   Claire Nicholls, 'Listening and Audience Education in the Orchestral Concert Hall' (unpublished doctoral thesis, Monash University, 2019), https://bridges.monash.edu
23   Deutsches Musikinformationszentrum, Veranstaltungen der öffentlich finanzierten Orchester und Rundfunkensembles 2019, https://www.miz.org/de/statistiken/veranstaltungen-der-oeffentlich-finanzierten-orchester-und-rundfunkensembles
24   For a list of agents for diversity at German institutions of classical music see Aufbrechen! Ran an die Strukturen, https://www.aufbrechen.net/360-agent-innen; for the thematic discussion see Christiane Griese and Helga Marburger, *Interkulturelle Öffnung. Ein Lehrbuch* (Munich: Oldenbourg Wissenschaftsverlag, 2012), https://www.degruyter.com/document/doi/10.1524/9783486716900/html
25   Subscription audiences pay a regular subscription fee for admittance to a series of events in a concert season, rather than buying a ticket for a particular event.
26   There are not many reliable statistics, but Andreas Heinen, in his study about concert subscribers of seven symphony orchestras in the state of Niedersachsen, identifies an average age of sixty-nine years amongst his questionnaire respondents; Heinen, *Wer will das noch hören?* (Wiesbaden: Springer VS Wiesbaden, 2012), p. 51, https://doi.org/10.1007/978-3-658-00303-6
27   See above, Karlheinz Reuband, *Musikpräferenzen und Musikpublika* (2019/22), www.miz.org/de/beitraege/musikpraeferenzen-und-musikpublika.de, www.miz.org/de/beitraege/musikpraeferenzen-und-musikpublika.de

first generation raised with rock music and the Beatles.[28] Other statistics indicate that the numbers of potential audience members in this age group will start to decrease around 2035, when the Baby-Boomers slowly become too old to lead an active concert-going life.[29]

In any case, all practitioners in the field of classical music are aiming to strengthen their ties with existing audiences and attract new audiences – younger, more diverse or just different. In the last decades, not only children, young adults, seniors or people with a disability have become the focus of specialised music projects, but also refugees, poor people, parents with babies, amateur musicians, the rural population or the homeless. When music practitioners (or organisers) decide to reach out to audiences beyond their 'regulars', it influences all aesthetic decisions as well. Many of these often short-lived projects are not merely performance-orientated but also focus on the process leading up to a performance.[30] The pressure to communicate with audiences, to make them become interested, to connect with them is immense, everywhere – even for the big classical music institutions in the German-speaking lands.

Terms that keep coming up in all discussions about audiences are closeness, resonance, contact, participation, engagement, accessibility, relationship, meaningfulness, immersion and of course relevance. This term does not only refer to the possibility that classical music is important to certain people, or that one can relate to a performance (as the audience researcher Martin Barker asks, 'How might what this performance is trying to do relate to you?').[31] What the term relevance could mean, and how it could work, and to whom the performance should be or become relevant, is unclear. It is a cliché, and also an argument that kills any further discussion: that because classical music in many countries is heavily subsidised, it has a duty to make an effort to appeal to all kinds of people.[32] Maybe this is also asking too much of

---

28 Ibid.
29 Heinen, *Wer will das noch hören?*, pp. 22–23, https://doi.org/10.1007/978-3-658-00303-6
30 Astrid Breel, 'Audience agency in participatory performance: a methodology for examining aesthetic experience', *Participations* 12:1 (2015), 368–87 (p. 12).
31 Martin Barker, 'I Have Seen the Future and It Is Not Here Yet …; or, On Being Ambitious for Audience Research', *The Communication Review* 9:2 (2006), 123–41.
32 See e.g., the Heidelberg Music Conference 2020, https://www.heidelberger-fruehling.de/heidelberger-fruehling/ueber-uns/festivals-projekte/

an art form whose practices were formed in the nineteenth century, with performance traditions firmly rooted in Central European upper-class style and behaviour.[33]

III.

Of the three issues mentioned above, it can be argued that the 'repertoire question' – or the 'museum problem'[34]– is the only intrinsically aesthetic one. It is also the most accessible and most easily changeable one. Here, in the daily practice of classical music, a lot of experimenting has been happening for a long time; however, merely changing the programming of a concert does not necessarily result in less pressure to innovate. The probability that any standard classical music concert presents a piece by Mozart, Beethoven, Brahms, or Tchaikovsky is still quite high, but the canon has definitely been enlarged in the last few decades. Statistical overviews are hard to come by,[35] and it is difficult to prove the perception that more unknown or unusual works and more pieces by twentieth-century or living composers are being played than twenty or forty years ago. This refreshing of the canon attempts to counter the 'museum' allegations – the perception that classical music practices are merely about representing the past – but structurally it does not change much.

Alternatives are offered by non-institutionalised performers, who are free from the burden of the big institutions but also responsible for providing their own income. They do not perform standard classical music concerts but focus on more concept-orientated performances. In Germany, these mostly take place in major cities (with diverse audiences) or in places out of reach of the big institutions, in the countryside. Not all concept-orientated performances focus on a certain topic, but they all have some 'spark' to set off this particular concert from others: the

---

heidelberg-music-conference/ and its topic 'What's next? Auf der Suche nach der Relevanz von morgen' ['What's next? Searching for the relevance of tomorrow'].
33 Walter Salmen, *Das Konzert. Eine Kulturgeschichte* (Munich: Verlag C. H. Beck, 1988); James H. Johnson, *Listening in Paris. A Cultural History* (Oakland: University of California Press, 1996).
34 See the Introduction and Chapter 2 of this volume.
35 The website https://www.operabase.com publishes statistics about the most performed operas, while https://www.dov.org/klassikland-deutschland/dov-konzertstatistik/ has statistics on the number of classical music concerts, not on the pieces performed.

musicians are specialists in new/old/contemporary/electronic music, play without a conductor, in unusual locations, late at night; they actively engage the audience, create immersive performances, play by heart, collaborate with artists from other fields, target very special audiences (visually impaired people, mothers with babies), or do other things to make themselves stand out. The German website, www.betterconcerts.org, aimed at practitioners, collects best-practice examples: categories focus either on hard facts (actors/location, space, technical facilities), on requirements for aesthetic decisions (cast, concert format, genre, epoch, composer, intersection to other arts, etc.) or on audience issues (target audience, activity grade of the audience etc). The subcategory *topic*, though, includes the most entries (such as identity, future, loneliness, love, liberation, longing, isolation, pain, mourning, darkness) and thus tries to be attractive to the kind of audiences the organisers are imagining.[36] This 'spark' feature, setting off one concert from another one, is thus concept- and repertoire-driven. It spills over, however, into all other aesthetic decisions, and of course influences the question of audiences – so instead of playing a standard classical music concert with an overture, a concerto and a symphony for a random or undefined audience, a concept-orientated performance will start with an idea for the programme and (hopefully) also for a target audience.

In this way, such a performance has tackled two of the three 'big questions' inherent to classical music in the German-speaking lands: repertoire and audiences. The third big question, the financing, does not even apply because if non-institutionalised performers receive subsidies (and in Germany, most do), they will be almost negligible to the public eye: a subsidy of 10,000 or even 50,000 euros for a performance series seems nothing in comparison to the annual subsidy of a municipal theatre.

At the same time, all concept-orientated performances also achieve something extra-musical: they generate attention and sell their avant-garde feel, show politicians and stakeholders that musicians are making an effort and that they work innovatively on many levels. But while these kinds of concert by non-institutionalised performers appear fashionable and different, they often only supplement the big classical

---

36 Georgina Born, 'The Audience and Radical Democracy', *Darmstädter Beiträge zur Neuen Musik* 25 (2020), 51–59 (p. 53).

music institutions and depend on them in an almost parasitical way: orchestral musicians find more liberating work in concept-orientated performances, concert halls trade rehearsal spaces for some of the cachet and the 'spark' of the free ensembles.[37] 'The wealth of novelty is fuelled by tradition',[38] as the *nonclassical* musicians from London also claim: all freelance classical musicians are standing on the shoulders of giants—of cumbersome, subsidised, classical music giants (not only in the German-speaking world); their novel approaches, however, challenge the classical music giants, in more ways than both sides are probably aware of. By moving away from the safe and subsidised shores of the (German-speaking) classical music lands, non-institutionalised performers innovate and rethink classical music practices.

It is probably time for the subsidised classical music giants to catch up – institutions have to prove that they also do important work, and at a grassroots level. They are thus called upon to make themselves heard and to show that they are indispensable, not only for the cultural, but also for the social and political life of a community, city or region, rather than dangerously perpetuating the status quo. They are obliged to reach out to everybody beyond barriers of age, income, race or education; they have to let their intrinsic hierarchies be challenged by audience projects and develop wise strategies for the 'futuring' of institutionalised classical music. They need to not only provide basic services to a community, but also facilitate excellent music performances at the same time, which is probably the biggest challenge. There might still be room for standard classical music concerts, but their 'near-natural occurrence' is severely challenged: do concerts really have to take place just to keep the (employed and paid) musicians active? Should it not be the other way round: that musicians perform at a concert because they want to, and have something to say? Even wines have to tell stories nowadays[39]

---

37 There is also an in-between space inhabited by several independent German orchestras, who are subsidised from time to time but not structurally: Ensemble Resonanz, Ensemble Modern, Deutsche Kammerphilharmonie Bremen and others.

38 Marta Peris-Ortiz, Mayer Rainiero Cabrera-Flores and Arturo Serrano-Santoyo (eds.), *Cultural and Creative Industries: A Path to Entrepreneurship and Innovation* (Cham: Springer, 2019).

39 See the wine blog Just Taste, www.just-taste.com

– should classical music concerts just take place because the subscription series[40] says it is time for Brahms (again)?

Music, and classical music, can play many roles. It can provide basic services for learning, entertaining, socialising, meeting others, forgetting the everyday world. It can foster one-of-a-kind experiences, create networks and connect communities – and that is why classical music practitioners discuss the boundaries, challenges and futures inherent to their art form not only at a German municipal theatre, but also at the South by Southwest festival 2023 in Austin, Texas.

References

Aufbrechen!, *360 Agent*innen*,
https://www.aufbrechen.net/360-agent-innen

Barker, Martin, 'I Have Seen the Future and It Is Not Here Yet …; or, On Being Ambitious for Audience Research', *The Communication Review* 9:2 (2006), 123–41,
https://doi.org/10.1080/10714420600663310

Born, Georgina, 'The Audience and Radical Democracy', *Darmstädter Beiträge zur Neuen Musik* 25 (2020), 51–59.

Breel, Astrid, 'Audience Agency in Participatory Performance: a Methodology for Examining Aesthetic Experience', *Participations* (2019), 368–87,
https://www.participations.org/Volume%2012/Issue%201/23.pdf

Brown, Jeff, '19 Covid-Thesen', *Van Magazin*, 8 April 2020,
https://van-magazin.de/mag/19-thesen/

Burland, Karen and Stephanie Pitts, *Coughing and Clapping: Investigating Audience Experience* (Farnham: Ashgate, 2014),
https://doi.org/10.4324/9781315574455

Chaker, Sarah and Axel Petri-Preis, *Tuning up! The Innovative Potential of Musikvermittlung* (Bielefeld: transcript, 2022),
https://doi.org/10.14361/9783839456811

Deutsches Musikinformations Zentrum, *Homepage*,
https://miz.org/de

---

40   Subscription series are selected events within a concert season that audiences can buy a subscription for.

Deutsche Musik-und Orchestevereinigung, *Homepage*,
https://uni-sono.org/

Genossenschaft Deutscher Bühnen-Angehöriger, *Homepage*,
https://www.buehnengenossenschaft.de/

Griese, Christiane and Helga Marburger, *Interkulturelle Öffnung. Ein Lehrbuch* (Munich: Oldenbourg Wissenschaftsverlag, 2012),
https://www.degruyter.com/document/
doi/10.1524/9783486716900/html

Heidelberg Music Conference 2020, *What's next? Auf der Suche nach der Relevanz von morgen* (2020),
https://www.heidelberger-fruehling.de/heidelberger-fruehling/ueber-uns/festivals-projekte/heidelberg-music-conference/

Heinen, Andreas, *Wer will das noch hören? Besucherstrukturen bei niedersächsischen Sinfonieorchestern* (Wiesbaden: Springer VS, 2013),
https://doi.org/10.1007/978-3-658-00303-6

Johnson, James H., *Listening in Paris. A Cultural History* (Oakland: University of California Press, 1996),
https://doi.org/10.1525/9780520918238

Krafeld, Merle, 'Ausgeflogen', *Van Magazin*, 7 February 2019,
https://van-magazin.de/mag/helsingborg-ausgeflogen/

Krafeld, Merle, 'Content vs. Klima?' *Van Magazin*, (7 March 2019),
https://van-magazin.de/mag/klima-deutschland/.

Nicholls, Claire, 'Listening and Audience Education in the Orchestral Concert Hall' (Unpublished doctoral thesis, Monash University, 2019),
https://bridges.monash.edu

Nonclassical, About us,
https://www.nonclassical.co.uk/about-us

Orchester des Wandels,
https://www.orchester-des-wandels.de/

Pine, Joseph and James H. Gilmore, *The Experience Economy* (Boston: Harvard Business School Press, 1999).

Pippen, John, 'Hope, Labour and Privilege in American New Music', in *Music as Labour: Inequalities and Activism in the Past and Present*, ed. by Dagmar Abfalter and Rosa Reitsamer (London: Routledge, 2022), pp. 81–96,
https://doi.org/10.4324/9781003150480-6

Rempe, Martin, *Kunst, Spiel, Arbeit. Musikerleben in Deutschland (1850–1960)* (Göttingen: Vandenhoeck & Ruprecht, 2019),
https://dx.*doi*.org/10.13109/9783666352508

Reuband, Karlheinz, *Musikpräferenzen und Musikpublika* (2019/22), https://miz.org/de/beitraege/musikpraeferenzen-und-musikpublika?term=reuband&position=0

Salmen, Walter, *Das Konzert. Eine Kulturgeschichte* (Munich: Verlag C. H. Beck, 1988).

Scharff, Christina and Anna Bull, 'Classical music after #MeToo: Tackling sexual harassment and misconduct in higher music education', in *Higher Music Education and Employability in a Neoliberal World*, ed. by R. Prokop and R. Reitsamer (London, New York: Bloomsbury, forthcoming).

Scharff, Christina, *Gender, Subjectivity, and Cultural Work. The Classical Music Profession* (London: Routledge, 2017), https://doi.org/10.4324/9781315673080

Stoever, Jennifer Lynn, *The Sonic Color Line. Race and the Cultural Politics of Listening* (New York: NYU Press, 2016), https://doi.org/10.2307/j.ctt1bj4s55

SXSW festival, *A New Era for Classical Music in a Post-Genre World*, online video recording, https://panelpicker.sxsw.com/vote/126769

Thurman, Kira, *Singing like Germans. Black Musicians in the Land of Bach, Beethoven, and Brahms* (Ithaca: Cornell University Press, 2021), https://doi.org/10.1515/9781501759864-008

Unisono Deutsche Musik- und Orchestervereinigung, *unisono-Statistik Planstellen und Einstufung der Beufsorchester*, https://uni-sono.org/klassikland-deutschland/statistik-planstellen-einstufung-berufsorchester/

Unisono Deutsche Musik- und Orchestervereinigung, Öffentlich finanziete Orchester: Strukturlle Entwicklungen seit 1990, https://uni-sono.org/wp-content/uploads/2022/06/2018-03-Orchesterkarte-MIZ.pdf

Yang, Mina, *Planet Beethoven. Classical Music at the Turn of the Millennium* (Middletown, CT: Wesleyan University Press, 2014), https://doi.org/10.1007/9780819574879

11. The Environmental Sustainability of Symphony Orchestras: Challenges and Potential Solutions

Stine Skovbon

Defining Sustainability

Sustainability has become a much-debated topic, both within academic research, where the number of papers on the issue keeps growing, and in society at large. Nations and organisations worldwide are making efforts to become more sustainable and there is a general willingness to act in line with the UN Sustainable Development Goals (SDGs). The SDGs are a part of the 2030 Agenda for Sustainable Development and serve as guidelines for the UN member states, setting out seventeen priority areas for a more sustainable future.

The implementation of this widely recognised paradigm, consisting of financial, social and environmental sustainability respectively,[1] has tended to focus on a limited range of goals.[2] In the classical music sector, for instance, attention has focused on financial and social sustainability. The former is frequently addressed in discussions of orchestra's dependence on subsidies,[3] while social sustainability is often concerned

---

1 Ben Purvis, Yong Mao, and Darren Robinson, 'Three pillars of sustainability: in search of conceptual origins', *Sustainability Science* 14:3 (2019), 681-95.
2 Joshua Long, 'Constructing the narrative of the sustainability fix: sustainability, social justice and representation in Austin, TX', *Urban Studies* 53:1 (2016), 149-172. Kate Power, 'Sustainability and the performing arts: discourse analytic evidence from Australia', *Poetics* 89 (2021), https://doi.org/10.1016/j.poetic.2021.101580
3 Robert J. Flanagan, *The Perilous Life of Symphony Orchestras* (Yale: Yale University Press, 2012).

with audience development,[4] as well as various aspects of pursuing a career as a professional classical musician.[5] In contrast to these relatively well-documented topics, the environmental sustainability of orchestras as organisations is an under-researched domain, with few exceptions such as the roundtable focusing on the impact of climate change on symphonic practices facilitated by Maastricht Centre for Innovation of Classical Music in 2021, and recent pioneering work conducted by Prado-Guerra et al.[6]

Indeed, symphony orchestras have a role to play in the ongoing transition to more sustainable development and in the endeavours to reduce the environmental footprint of nations. They can do this by supporting, for example, the twelfth and thirteenth SDGs: to 'Ensure sustainable consumption and production patterns' and to 'Take urgent action to combat climate change and its impact' respectively. Factors such as CO_2 emissions due to travel, inefficient use of electricity, or use of materials such as paper for the printing of scores, are being recognised as environmental challenges faced by the music industry more widely. In spite of this fact, environmental considerations have not yet been mainstreamed in the sector. Studies on the environmental impact of popular music indicate that various activities are creating negative impacts. To date, the study by Prado-Guerra et al. is seemingly the only existing work conducted on the environmental impact of orchestral activities; nonetheless, many findings related to popular music are relevant to classical orchestras.

The aim of this chapter, therefore, is firstly to draw attention to some of the main areas of interest when considering the environmental sustainability of symphony orchestras and, secondly, to explore whether prioritising sustainability has the potential to positively influence the future of these orchestras. Hence, one result of this focus is that limited

---

4   Claire D. Nicholls, Clare Hall and Rachel Forgasz, 'Charting the past to understand the cultural inheritance of concert hall listening and audience development practices', *Paedagogica Historica* 54:4 (2018), 502-516.
5   Warren Brodsky, 'In the wings of British orchestras: a multi-episode interview study among symphony players', *Journal of Occupational and Organizational Psychology* 79:4 (2006), 673-690.
6   Alba Prado-Guerra, Sergio Paniague Bermejo, Luis Fernando Calvo Prieto, and Monica Santamarta Llorente, 'Environmental impact study of symphony orchestras and preparation of a classification guide', *The International Journal of Environmental Studies* 77:6 (2020), 1044-1059.

attention is given to the intersection of the various artistic goals of orchestras and environmental, financial and social sustainability. Consequently, it is beyond the scope of this chapter to thoroughly discuss the dilemmas orchestras face when prioritising sustainability, such as that increasing sustainability within one area can cause decreased sustainability within another.

To examine the above-mentioned aims, the following questions will be addressed:

- What are the main environmental sustainability challenges symphony orchestras face, as identified in existing academic research?
- Which opportunities exist for symphony orchestras to reduce their environmental impact?

In order to answer these questions, this chapter provides a review of existing literature on some of the activities related to classical orchestras that cause adverse environmental impacts, followed by some recommendations on how to reduce this impact drawn from organisations such as the culture and climate non-profit Julie's Bicycle. The chapter concludes with examples of how The Royal Liverpool Philharmonic Orchestra and The Flanders Symphony Orchestra are implementing strategies to become more sustainable.

Exploring the Causes of the Environmental Impact of Symphony Orchestras

CO_2 (carbon dioxide) is a type of greenhouse gas, increasing concentrations of which in the atmosphere – for instance through industrial activities or energy combustion – are viewed as one of the main causes of climate change. Reducing greenhouse gas emissions is a key cornerstone of efforts to address climate risk.[7] As a result, CO_2 emissions have been given a lot of attention, and an effort to reduce them is essential in the endeavour to limit global warming and work towards

---

[7] *Climate Change 2022. Impacts, Adaptation and Vulnerability. Summary for Policymakers*, IPCC Working Group II contribution to the Sixth Assessment Report of the Intergovernmental Panel on Climate Change (2022), WMO and UNEP.

the SDGs. So, in the case of symphony orchestras, what type of activities pose CO_2 emission challenges? Touring and audience travel, printing of scores, music dissemination methods, and electricity use in venues are activities that result in varying degrees of environmental impact in the form of CO_2 emissions. The following is an elaboration on the impact of these activities, as well as the different factors that might exacerbate or mitigate it.

CO_2 Emissions, Touring, and Audience Travel

Reducing the amount of CO_2 emissions resulting from the travel activities of musicians and audiences has a significant role to play in mitigating the environmental impact of the music industry[8], with symphony orchestras being no exception. Of the various activities orchestras are involved in, touring-related travelling has the largest environmental impact. Comparing different types of impact (not including audience travel), Prado-Guerra et al. draw this conclusion on the basis of their analysis of the travelling activities of five orchestras. By calculating the amount of CO_2 emissions caused by each of the musician's travel on a tour, and by knowing the distance the orchestras travelled for touring each year, the authors were able to measure the overall emissions caused by the orchestras annually. Aside from the large number of people involved, one reason for the high amount of CO_2 emissions is that it is not always possible for orchestras to make use of the most efficient route when touring. This is the case when agreements on exclusion zones have been made to ensure that the venues where the orchestras are performing are located far enough from each other in order to optimise audience attendance.[9] Such agreements are usually made between orchestras and venues, and there are seemingly no fixed standards for where the lines for these exclusion zones are drawn. This would suggest that if financial considerations are given more weight than the environmental

---

8   Catherine Bottrill, Diana Liverman, and Max Boykoff, 'Carbon soundings: greenhouse gas emissions of the UK music industry', *Environmental Research Letters* 5:1 (2010), 014019; F. Berry, L. E. Wynne, and C. Riedy, *Changing Our Tune: Scoping the Potential of the Australian Music Industry to Address Climate Change* (Ultimo: Institute for Sustainable Futures, Report 2014), pp. 1-57.

9   *Julie's Bicycle Practical Guide: Touring* (2015), https://juliesbicycle.com/wp-content/uploads/2019/10/Touring_guide_2015.pdf

impact when the tours are planned, it could lead to increased travelling activities and higher amounts of CO_2 emissions.

The amount of travelling orchestras engage in can depend on many factors. Prado-Guerra et al. (2020) found a significant difference in the distance travelled during a season by the five orchestras included in the study. For example, while the Euskadi Symphony orchestra travelled 6,084 kilometres, the Symphony Orchestra of Madrid travelled only 144.6 kilometres. While some of the examined orchestras are serving a city, others are serving regions, resulting in more travelling activities for those serving the largest areas. Prado-Guerra et al. were able to estimate the sustainability of the travel activity of the orchestras by having access to information on the means of transport used by the musicians throughout a season (including train, bus and car), the distance travelled, and by drawing on calculations of the amount of CO_2 emissions per passenger from various means of transport. Contrary to Hill and colleagues,[10] who calculated the emission of a car containing only one person, Prado-Guerra et al. concluded that there is a significantly lower environmental impact when more people share a car compared to other forms of transport. This means that cars should not be entirely dismissed as an unsustainable type of transport for orchestras if the sharing of vehicles is prioritised.

Shifting the focus from musicians to audiences, research on Polish concertgoers shows that even in cases where concert venues were located close to public transport and the majority of the audience members were living in the city where the concerts took place, more than seventy-five percent of the concertgoers came by car.[11] However, the implications of this finding are contradicted by studies showing that there is a willingness amongst audiences to make use of public transport to go to one-day events when connections are good.[12] Nevertheless, such

---

10 N. Hill, H. Venfield, C. Dun, and K. James, *Government GHG Conversion Factors for Company Reporting: Methodology Paper for Emission Factors*, (London: Department of Energy and Climate Change (DECC) and Department for Environment, Food and Rural Affairs (Defra), 2013).

11 Lukasz Wróblewski, and Zdzislawa Dacko-Bikiewicz, 'Sustainable consumer behavior in the market of cultural services in Central European countries: the example of Poland', *Sustainability* 10:11 (2018), 38-56.

12 Francesca Pagliara, Luigi Biggiero, and Ilaria Henke, 'The Environmental Impacts Connected with to events: The Case Study of the City of Naples in Italy', *2019 IEEE International Conference on Environment and Electrical Engineering and 2019 IEEE*

conditions are not always present, as venues potentially can be difficult to access by public transport.[13] Significant factors influencing the choice of means of transport by arts audiences are age-related constraints in physical health and mobility, which can be a reason for travelling by car instead of public transport, as well as routine and habit.[14] Since classical music audiences often are older than popular music audiences,[15] it seems likely that both routine and habit – which potentially become more fixed the older people get – and age-related constraints in physical health have a role to play in their choice of transport.

Thus, more factors influence the degree of the environmental impact of both the touring of orchestras and audience travel. The location of the orchestras and the community the orchestras have to serve seem to be crucial for the distances travelled, and hence also for the amount of CO_2 emissions linked to touring. Regional orchestras have travelling built into their concert practices in order to serve their region. Therefore, orchestras serving a city will most likely be involved in a lower degree of touring than the regional ones, and will thus also have lower CO_2 emissions. Orchestras fixed in one place might, however, not contribute as much to equal access for audiences as the regional orchestras, and hence a dilemma of environmental sustainability in the form of fewer emissions comes into play. Avoiding exclusion zones to make touring routes more efficient would further contribute to reducing emissions of touring orchestras, unless it results in performances in even more venues and thus increases rather than decreases travelling activities. Lastly, and most obviously, using the means of transport with the lowest CO_2

Industrial and Commercial Power Systems Europe (EEEIC/I&CPS Europe, 2019), 1-66. C. Bottrill, and S. Papageorgiou, *Jam Packed Part 1: Audience Travel to UK Festivals* (2009), Julie's Bicycle and Environmental Change Institute (2009).

13   Betty Farrell, 'Changing Culture and Practices Inside Organizations', in *Entering Cultural Communities: Diversity and Change in the Nonprofit Arts*, ed. by Diane Grams and Betty Farrell (New Brunswick: Rutgers University Press, 2008), pp. 38-63.

14   Andrea Collins, and Dimitris Potoglou, 'Factors influencing visitor travel to festivals: challenges in encouraging sustainable travel', *Journal of Sustainable Tourism* 27:5 (2019), 668-688.

15   Victor Fernandez-Blanco, Maria J. Perez-Villadoniga, and Juan Prieto-Rodriguez, 'Looking into the profile of music audiences', in *Enhancing Participation in the Arts in the EU*, ed. by Victoria M. Ateca-Amestoy, Victor Ginsburgh, Isidoro Mazza, John O'Hagan, and Juan Prieto-Rodriguez (Springer, Cham. 2017), pp. 141-154. Semi Purhonen, Jukka Gronow, and Keijo Rahkonen, 'Highbrow culture in Finland: knowledge, taste and participation', *Acta Sociologica*, 54:4, (2011), 385-402.

emissions is a way of minimising adverse impacts. The main conclusion that can be drawn about audience travel is that access to good public transport connections within a short distance from the venue seems essential to increase sustainability. Easily accessible transport options would not only benefit those who already indicate a willingness to use public transport, but also, to a considerable degree, audiences with mobility issues. Thus, orchestras must work together with local partners and transport providers to learn to meet the individual needs of their audiences and break the habits that are driving up emissions.

CO_2 Emissions and Sheet Music

Travel is not the only activity with emission implications. During performances, musicians have traditionally used paper sheet music. Paper manufacturing is an energy-consuming process in terms of both electricity use and CO_2 emissions. Therefore, it is a domain in which efforts to reduce energy consumption are viewed as necessary. Having access to a programme covering the works performed by an orchestra within a year, enables Prado-Guerra et al. to determine the paper used for the printing of scores by each of the musicians. Subsequently, the annual impact was found by comparing the weight of the printed scores to known data on the energy consumed when manufacturing one ton of paper. It was found that the consumption of paper varies depending on the different instrument groups, and that string players used the highest number of scores, 631 per player yearly, while brass used the lowest with 299 scores. Moreover, the energy consumption varies depending on whether new or recycled paper is used, and on the printing methods, with eco-print being mentioned as energy efficient. While this example provides a useful way of measuring an orchestra's paper consumption when it comes to sheets that have not been printed before, it would appear that Prado-Guerra et al. do not account for the fact that existing sheets might be available from orchestral libraries, which means that printing often is not necessary.[16] Prado-Guerra et al. conclude that printing of scores is an activity that constitutes a significant environmental impact.

---

16   Matthew Naughtin, 'It's all online: Creating digital study resources for orchestral musicians', in *Future Directions in Digital Information*, ed. by David Baker and Lucy Ellis (Cambridge, MA: Chandos Publishing, 2021), pp. 209-216.

Yet the question is: what are the alternatives and how do they fare in terms of emissions?

An alternative to printed scores is digital scores. In 2012, the Brussels Philharmonic performed a concert solely using this format as an experiment, finding that the performance was not negatively impacted by this change.[17] This proved that using digital sheet music is an option for orchestras, and different digital sheet music readers and formats have been developed to facilitate such a digitalization and make it as convenient as possible for the musicians.[18] However, more factors influence the choice of paper versus digital parts. Musicians might have reasons for preferring paper sheet music, such as the cost of devices and notation-reading software, the possible lack of software compatibility with file formats, the amount of time needed to learn to use the software, and the fact that screens are more tiring to look at for longer periods than paper. Furthermore, an electronic device can constitute an 'extra cognitive step' compared to paper when musicians are annotating the scores, which can have a negative influence on creative processes.[19]

Prado-Guerra and colleagues have compared the annual orchestral energy consumption of printing scores and accessing them on electronic devices respectively, and concluded that due to the low energy usage, the most environmentally friendly way of reading scores is on an eBook device. However, objections can be raised about the sustainability of the digital format. Indeed, digital scores are accessible through libraries, professional organisations, or via either commercial or private individuals' websites.[20] This means that the energy usage of the centres storing the data that constitutes the scores needs to be accounted for, as well as the energy use and waste resulting from the production, the

---

17 Anneleen van Boxstael, 'The dawn of digital sheet music: a look at neoscores', *Fontes Artis Musicae* 61:3 (2014), 284-289.

18 Javier Merchán Sánchez-Jara, 'Digital schola: music readers as learning/teaching tools', in *Proceedings of the Second International Conference on Technological Ecosystems for Enhancing Multiculturality*, ed. by Francisco José Garcia-Penalvo (New York: Association for Computing Machinery, 2014), pp. 547-553.
Van Boxsteal, 2014. P. Bellini, I. Bruno, and P. Nesi, 'Automatic formatting of music sheets through MILLA rule-based language and engine', *Journal of New Music Research* 34:3 (2005), 237-257.

19 Karen Lin and Tim Bell, 'Integrating paper and digital music information systems', ISMIR 1 (2000), 23-25.

20 Ana Dubnjakovic, 'Navigating digital sheet music on the web: challenges and opportunities', *Music Reference Services Quarterly* 12:1-2 (2009), 3-15.

usage and the afterlife of the electronic devices necessary for reading them. When comparing the sustainability of printed and digital scores, additional factors also play a role, such as whether recycled paper is used for the printing, and whether the printed scores are being used multiple times. As yet, no comparative studies exist within this specific area, and future research measuring the relative impact of data storage and electronic waste is thus necessary in order to establish the potential positive impact of digital scores compared to the various types of printed scores.

While it might be difficult to draw conclusions on whether digital or printed scores are the most sustainable, it is safe to say that environmental impacts are linked to both formats, and that the individual choices within the orchestras regarding this matter can have an influence on the degree of this impact at an organisational level.

CO_2 Emissions and Music Dissemination

In addition to live performances, music can be enjoyed either as physical albums on vinyl records, and CDs, or digitalized as mp3 files or via streaming services. Research indicates that classical music listeners to some degree have been hesitant to include streaming services in their listening practices. A survey conducted by Alessandri and colleagues amongst 1,200 listeners of the genre from multiple countries showed that music very frequently or frequently was accessed by more than half of the respondents on YouTube (fifty-six percent), as digital files (fifty-six percent), on CD (fifty-four percent), via Spotify (twenty-eight percent), and via iTunes (twenty-two percent). Even though the usage of the two latter options is relatively limited, this does not mean that these listeners are not acquainted with various ways of accessing music, as more than fifty percent indicate that they rarely use six to seven different formats or platforms on average.[21] As mentioned above, classical music listeners are often relatively old,[22] and age seems to

---

21 Elena Alessandri, Dawn Rose, Olivier Senn, Katrin Szamatulski, Antionio Baldasarre, and Victoria J. Williamson, 'Consumers on critique: a survey of classical music listeners' engagement with professional music reviews', *Music & Science* 3 (2020) 1-19.

22 Henk Roose, Koen van Eijck & John Lievens, 'Culture of distinction or culture of openness? Using a social space approach to analyze the social structuring

have a determining influence on choices of formats for music listening. Regardless of genre preferences, Lepa and Hoklas (2015) find that older cohorts are inclined to use CDs, while younger ones rely more on digital media and streaming services.[23] Classical music listeners mention familiarity, usability and selection of music as reasons for their choice of media format.[24] The importance of familiarity might explain the high preference for CDs amongst these older listeners, since this format is older than the digital media formats. Another reason for the limited use of different streaming services mentioned above might relate to the varied quality of selection and visibility of classical music tracks provided by these services.[25] However, streaming platforms dedicated solely to classical music have recently started to emerge. Classical music listeners, like everybody else, have been forced to temporarily 'attend' performances online via live streaming due to the COVID-19 pandemic that began in 2020,[26] and many orchestras have broadcasted concerts via websites and streaming. While audiences are certainly eager to return to the concert halls for live performances, it will be interesting to see whether the usage of streaming services during the pandemic will make classical music listeners more inclined to use such services in the future.

Though there are complexities around the consumption of the genre, it is clear that streaming and CDs still play a major role. Thus, it is relevant to look at the environmental impact connected to both CDs and digital formats.

Music dissemination methods refer to the various ways music is made accessible to consumers and, in the case of both physical formats and

---

of lifestyles', *Poetics* 40:6 (2012), 491-513. Gerbert Kraaykamp and Koen van Eijck, 'Personality, media preferences, and cultural participation', *Personality and Individual Differences* 38:7 (2005), 1675-1688.

[23] Steffen Lepa and Anne-Kathrin Hoklas, 'How do people really listen to music today? Conventionalities and major turnovers in German audio repertoires', *Information, Communication & Society* 18:10 (2015), 1253-1268.

[24] Alessandri et al., 2020.

[25] Godefroy Dang Nguyen, Sylvain Dejean, and François Moreau, 'On the complementarity between online and offline music consumption: the case of free streaming', *Journal of Cultural Economics* 38:4 (2014), 315-330.
Clayton E. Crenshaw, 'Availability of New Releases in Streaming Audio Databases', in *Music Library Association, 2018 Annual Meeting*.

[26] Åsa Bergman, "Wherever you are whenever you want': captivating and encouraging music experiences when symphony orchestra performances are provided online', *Open Library of Humanities* 7(2):6 (2021), 1-23.

streaming, these methods are another energy-consuming activity. When it became clear that the digital consumption of music was becoming a fundamental part of music consumption, it was debated how this change would influence the environmental impact of the record industry as a whole. It is a question that is still discussed today.

Different activities causing CO_2 emissions are linked to the various means of dissemination: activities we as consumers seldom are aware of. In the case of CDs, emissions are caused by packaging as well as transportation to distribution centres, record stores and customers. When music is downloaded as digital albums, the energy usage of the data centres where the data is stored creates CO_2 emissions.[27] Additionally, the energy used by streaming devices also needs to be accounted for. When it comes to CDs, Weber et al. compare the amount of CO_2 emissions in these different methods, concluding that buying a CD in a record store involves the largest amount of emissions. Fewer emissions are caused by buying CDs online since many customers need transport to get to their nearest record store. Downloading and privately burning digital music on a CD creates an even smaller amount of emissions as transportation is completely avoided, while the authors find that downloading and solely consuming music digitally creates the least emissions. Moreover, other studies show that the environmental impact of CD packaging is substantial and should not be underestimated.[28] Weber et al. (2010) suggest that the digitalization of music has the potential to significantly reduce the CO_2 emissions caused by music delivery methods, a conclusion shared by Cameron, who found that: 'Digital distribution has tremendous environmental benefits'.[29]

However, this conclusion is contested. Firstly, in the era of transportable mp3 players, it was argued that the production and waste

---

27   Christopher L. Weber, Jonathan G. Koomey, and H. Scott Matthews, 'The energy and climate change implications of different music delivery methods', *Journal of Industrial Ecology* 14:5 (2010), 754-769.

28   Samuel Cameron, 'Past, present and future: music economics at the crossroads', *Journal of Cultural Economics* 40:1 (2016), 1-12. F. Berry, L.E. Wynne, and C. Riedy, Changing Our Tune: Scoping the Potential of the Australian Music Industry to Address Climate Change (Ultimo: Institute for Sustainable Futures, Report 2014), pp. 1-57. Arup, Environmental Change Institute and Purchasing for Profit, *Impacts and Opportunities: Reducing Emissions of CD Packaging* (London: Julie's Bicycle and Environmental Change Institute, 2009).

29   Weber et al, , 'The energy and climate change implications of different music delivery methods', p. 9.

related to that kind of hardware potentially could result in a considerable material impact that would be a counterweight to the digitalization and dematerialization of music.[30] Later, when live streaming became possible, the conclusion drawn by Weber et al. that the amount of energy use related to the packaging and transportation of CDs was higher than the energy usage of data centres was questioned. Bach suggests that streaming an album twenty-seven times potentially leads to a higher amount of energy consumption than manufacturing a CD.[31] Comparing the amount of greenhouse gas emissions involved in the process of making vinyl records, cassettes, CDs, and using streaming services, Brennan and Devine similarly suggest that streaming is an activity with considerable adverse environmental impacts due to its greenhouse gas emissions.[32] Thus, music dissemination methods are a contested domain, and – as Brennan and Devine state – even though streaming apparently is not as environmentally friendly as earlier research suggested, it is not possible to go back to the old CD and vinyl formats; formats of which the manufacturing and afterlife as waste entail other problematic aspects, such as bad working conditions for those involved in the production.

The above indicates that both CDs and streaming create an adverse environmental impact, but following the suggestions by Weber et al (2010), a way of minimising impacts would be to refrain from buying new CDs to avoid the impact of transportation. Similarly, the findings by the authors suggest that using digital files (that are not stored in data centres) is the most environmentally friendly option. However, while these ways of consumption might be the most sustainable in terms of environmental impact, the decreased revenues for musicians might impede the already perilous financial sustainability of the classical music sector. This is a prime example of the complexities of balancing the various types of sustainability.

---

30 Nick Hogg and Tim Jackson, 'Digital media and dematerialization: an exploration of the potential for reduced material intensity in music delivery', *Journal of Industrial Ecology* 13:1 (2009), 127-146.

31 Dagfinn Bach, *The Dark Side of the Tune: The Hidden Energy Cost of Digital Music Consumption* (London: Music Tank, University of Westminster, 2012).

32 Matt Brennan and Kyle Devine, 'The cost of music', *Popular Music* 39:1, (2020), 43-65.

CO_2 Emission, Electricity Use, and Venues

Symphony orchestras perform and rehearse in large concert venues, and these buildings, like other similar venues, have an environmental impact in the form of both CO_2 emissions and energy use. The necessity of making efforts to reduce this impact is widely recognised. For example, the Event Industry Council, a global organisation with over thirty member organisations, is working on enabling the event industry worldwide to implement sustainable practices. The negative environmental impact of such events is well documented in academic literature, which provides recommendations on how to improve event management and the sustainability of venues.[33] Kellison and McCullough identify four indicators promoting sustainable practices within venues for the entertainment and sport industries, including concert venues: growing public concern for the environment; a more comprehensive understanding of costs and benefits; the formation of cross-functional and cross-sector teams; and greater emphasis on developing specialists and research agendas.[34] Despite such recommendations, reducing the impact of events is rarely given a lot of attention by associations of event managers, and this pattern is often replicated within the organisations hosting the events.[35] The indicators can be viewed as a sign of the great importance for organisations of prioritising sustainability in order to continuously receive support from consumers and the wider society. Since symphony orchestras usually perform in the same concert hall season after season, opportunities exist for orchestra managers to have an impact on the daily management of the venues and to support the prioritising of sustainability.

---

33   Andrea Collins, Calvin Jones, and Max Munday, 'Assessing the environmental impacts of mega sporting events: two options?', *Tourism Management* 30:6 (2009), 828-837. Walker J. Ross & Haylee Uecker Mercado, 'Barriers to managing environmental sustainability in public assembly venues', *Sustainability* 12:24 (2020), 10477.

34   Timothy Kellison and Brian McCullough, 'A forecast for the mainstreaming of environmental sustainability', *Sport and Entertainment Review* 2:1 (2016), 11–18.

35   Chantal Dickson and Charles Arcodia, 'Promoting sustainable event practice: the role of professional associations', *International Journal of Hospitality Management* 29:2 (2010), 236-244. Myrsini Koukiasa , 'Sustainable facilities management within event venues', *Worldwide Hospitality and Tourism Themes* 3:3 (2011), https://doi.org/10.1108/17554211111142185

Professional classical musicians employed in symphony orchestras rehearse many hours weekly, both individually and in group rehearsals.[36] Prado-Guerra et al. find that the light source used during these rehearsals and performances is an important type of environmental impact related to orchestral activities. Additionally, there is the overall electricity use linked to concert venues, as temperature regulating systems and IT equipment used in office spaces need to be as energy efficient as possible.[37] Indeed, prioritising sustainability related to light sources and air conditioning systems is relevant for all types of big buildings. For instance, Algarvio and colleagues found that efforts to reduce energy consumption in a big public library led to a significant reduction in electricity usage, with a corresponding decrease in the annual costs of energy.[38] Temperature regulating systems were regulated more efficiently during peak hours and advantageous renegotiations were made with the energy retailer of the library, leading to annual savings.[39] The above indicates no relevant differences between the ways to improve the sustainability of concert venues and other types of big buildings. Such case studies, therefore, contain findings that can provide valuable knowledge in order to reduce the energy consumption of existing concert halls, as well as to potentially minimise the adverse impact of new venues. Although implementing sustainability measures in venues can lead to energy savings, doing so requires resources in the form of time and expertise and is another illustration of the recurring challenge of prioritising environmental sustainability over the cost of other assets. Moreover, Smith exemplifies the complexity of decision-making

---

36 Jesper Hvass Schmid, Ellen Raben Pedersen, Peter Moller Juhl, Jakob Christensen-Dalsgaard, Ture Dammann Andersen, Torben Poulsen, and Jesper Bælum, 'Sound exposure of symphony orchestra musicians', *Annals of Occupational Hygiene* 55:8 (2011), 893-905. Heli M. Laitinen, Esko M. Toppila, Pekka S. Olkinuora, and Kaarina Kuisma, 'Sound exposure among the Finnish National Opera personnel', *Applied Occupational and Environmental Hygiene* 18:3 (2003), 177-182.
37 Julie's Bicycle, *Green Orchestras Guide: A Simple Guide to Sustainable Practices* (2011), https://juliesbicycle.com/wp-ontent/uploads/2019/11/Green_Orchestras_Guide_2011.pdf
38 Hugo Algarvio, Joaquim Viegas, Fernando Lopes, Diogo Amaro, Anabela Pronto, and Susana M. Vieira, 'Electricity usage efficiency in large buildings: DSM measures and preliminary simulations of DR programs in a public library', in *International Conference on Practical Applications of Agents and Multi-Agent Systems* (Cham: Springer, Cham, 2015), pp. 249-259.
39 Algarvio et al., 2015.

concerning the building of new venues dedicated to fine arts, which are venues that are often seen as assets for the cities where they are located, and that can be viewed as symbols of 'highbrow' culture.[40] By analysing the opposing viewpoints expressed by those present during a planning hearing for the construction of a new concert hall, Smith suggests that, in the explicit debate on the types of building materials, a more implicit and value-laden discussion on elitism and valuation of culture takes place.[41] Hence, decisions regarding arts venues can be particularly complex with many factors in play alongside their environmental impact.

Where Do We Go From Here?

Various organisations are working on ways to develop and strengthen sustainable musical practices, and their projects are providing knowledge that can also be of use in classical orchestras. Organisations such as Julie's Bicycle (UK), Green Track Ghent (Belgium), Green Events (the Netherlands), Green Music Initiative (Germany), and Greener Events (Norway) are leading the way on these issues. The former in particular is one of the leading and most influential among these organisations.[42] Julie's Bicycle was founded in 2007, and even though the organisation was originally established to provide advice on how to strengthen environmentally friendly practices within the music sector, it has now expanded its consultancy to include the arts sector as a whole. It offers a wide range of reports, practical guides, webinars and case studies, and some of the material, such as the 'Green Orchestras Guide', is targeted specifically at classical orchestras. In order to examine the opportunities for orchestras to incorporate more environmentally friendly practices, some of the recommendations provided by Julie's Bicycle which are related to the topics discussed above will be reviewed, followed by two examples of how symphony orchestras are taking concrete action to become more sustainable.

---

40 Neil T. Smith, 'Concrete Culture: The Planning Hearing as a Stage for Cultural Debates', *Cultural Sociology* 16:2, (2021), 147-164.
41 Smith, 2021.
42 Matt Brennan, 'The infrastructure and environmental consequences of live music', in *Audible Infrastructures: Music, Sound, Media*, ed. by Kyle Devine and Alexandrine Boudreault-Fournier (Oxford University Press 2020), pp. 117-134.

The recommendations can be divided into three overarching categories: information and communication; reducing environmental impact; and monitoring of results. Information and communication have to do with the planning of actions to reduce impact, as well as communicating these intentions and actions both internally within organisations and externally, e.g. via an explicit organisational environmental policy.[43] A way of reducing the environmental impact is to encourage musicians and audiences to use the most environmentally friendly means of transport. Furthermore, the consumption of energy of concert venues as well as the usage of paper can be limited as much as possible.[44] Finally, monitoring in the form of knowing the current level of impact, setting goals for reduction and keeping track of the progress enables organisations to evaluate the outcome of their actions.[45]

The above does not offer an exhaustive overview but only an extract of the available material provided by Julie's Bicycle. Nevertheless, it can serve as a basis for investigating whether orchestras are focusing on the same areas when dealing with environmental issues.

Examples of Environmentally Sustainable Practices of Orchestras

More and more symphony orchestras are aware of how their activities might result in environmental impacts, and they are actively taking steps to reduce these. Two of these orchestras are The Royal Liverpool Philharmonic Orchestra and The Flanders Symphony Orchestra, which in various ways are engaged in pro-environmental practices.

The Royal Liverpool Philharmonic Orchestra provide an elaborated overview of their environmental sustainability policy on their website.[46] The aims of the orchestra's environmental policy are explained, as well as how they are going to be achieved, a strategy which includes, among other things, cross-organisational collaboration and involvement of, for example, the orchestra's executive and leadership team. Moreover,

---

43 Julie's Bicycle, 2011.
44 Julie's Bicycle, 2011 and 2015.
45 Julie's Bicycle, 2011.
46 Royal Liverpool Philharmonice, *Environmental Sustainability Policy* (2023), https://www.liverpoolphil.com/about-us/environmental-sustainability-policy/

an action plan shows the current areas the orchestra is working on to engage and train staff to improve sustainable behaviour. Concrete steps the orchestra is taking to reduce its environmental impact include a travel policy to reduce CO_2 emissions; reducing energy by measuring consumption and making efficient use of heaters, lighting and electrical equipment; reducing waste related to the catering and printed materials; making a procurement policy that includes taking environmental conditions into consideration when dealing with suppliers; and regularly communicating the progress related to the above both to relevant stakeholders and to audiences.

The Flanders Symphony orchestra also provide a list on their website of the domains they are focusing on in order to become more sustainable.[47] The orchestra encourages more environmentally friendly travel by offering incentives to staff members who travel by bike, while discouraging driving by removing all on-site parking facilities. Moreover, they engage in a number of other practices: for instance, monitoring energy and water consumption in order to make it more efficient; limiting the use of printed materials and taking care to reuse paper where possible; limiting waste and taking care of sustainable waste management; using local catering options; and making optimal use of building spaces. Lastly, the orchestra is a member of Green Track Ghent, a non-profit organisation the members of which include various cultural organisations, and which focuses on enhancing both environmental and social sustainability.

The above examples illustrate that the two orchestras are making efforts to improve their practices within more domains in compliance with the recommendations from Julie's Bicycle, for example the implementation of travelling policies and monitoring of energy consumption. Engaging in such improvements obviously requires information and planning, and these endeavours are communicated publicly via the orchestra's websites. All three recommended elements—the information and communication, the reduction of impact and the monitoring—are present in these examples. Nevertheless, concrete information on the orchestras' websites about the achieved results would make the communication about their efforts even more impressive.

---

47   Symfonie orkest Vlaanderen, *The Orchestra & Greeentrack*, https://www.symfonieorkest.be/en/pQ0j4CM/greentrack

Sustainability and the Future of Classical Music

This chapter has provided an overview of the current insights about the environmental impact of symphony orchestras, recommendations on how this impact can be reduced, and examples of environmentally friendly initiatives implemented by orchestras.

Reviewing research on the various activities performed by symphony orchestras with a negative environmental impact has led to more insights. Firstly, the finding by Prado-Guerra et al. that these activities vary in terms of the degree of their impact is discussed. The authors find that touring is the activity with the biggest impact, followed by printing of scores, noise profusion and usage of light within the venues. Thus, travelling is found to be significant; a conclusion repeated in this chapter. I have chosen to also include audience travel, and I ague that this, as well as touring, has the biggest impact. Hence, examining how to reduce the impact of these activities is more urgent than, for example, finding the most environmentally friendly format for sheet music. Secondly, it is apparent that the solutions to the problem of how this impact can be reduced are not always unambiguous. While making efforts to change the travelling patterns of both musicians and audiences to more sustainable means of transport is seemingly an obvious way of reducing CO_2 emissions, dealing with music dissemination and sheet music in the most environmentally friendly way is more complex. In both cases, there is research suggesting that digitalization provides more sustainable solutions than before, yet this viewpoint is challenged by others. Thirdly, it has become clear that the environmental sustainability of orchestras is a domain of great importance. Not only can reduction in energy use result in savings for orchestras on an organisational level, but making efforts to increase negative environmental impact is essential to the future of classical orchestras in general. Drawing on the research by Kellison and McCullough,[48] the societal demand for organisations to demonstrate awareness of environmental issues and a willingness to engage in reducing them is crucial for symphony orchestras to take into consideration. According to the authors, refraining from acting in line with the public concern related to the environment can cause a decrease

---

48   Kellison and McCullough, (2016).

in the support from the general public, for example their potential audience. For symphony orchestras, this would be unfortunate due to '[…] an ongoing debate on the relevance of the institution itself'.[49]

Thus, much can be gained for orchestras by investigating their environmental impact more thoroughly, actively engaging in sustainable practices to reduce this impact, and communicating this as a priority and part of their organisational profile in the future. Prioritising sustainable practices within symphony orchestras can serve as a means to safeguard the future of classical music by making sure the values and endeavours of the sector regarding sustainability are in line with the goals set to address the ecological challenges for society as a whole.

References

Alessandri, Elena, Dawn, Rose, Senn, Olivier, zamatulski, Katrin, Baldassarre, Antonio Baldassarre, & Williamson, Victoria Jane, 'Consumers on Critique: A Survey of Classical Music Listeners' Engagement with Professional Music Reviews', *Music & Science* 3 (2020), 1-19, https://doi.org/10.1177/2059204320931337

Agarvio, Hugo, Viegas, Joaquim, Lopes, Fernando, Amaro, Diogo, Pronto, Anabela, & Vieira, Susana M., 'Electricity usage efficiency in large buildings: DSM measures and preliminary simulations of DR programs in a public library', in *Highlights of Practical Applications of Agents, Multi-Agent Systems, and Sustainability - The PAAMS Collection*, ed. by Bajo, J., et al., PAAMS 2015, Communications in Computer and Information Science 524 (2015), pp. 249-259, https://doi.org/10.1007/978-3-319-19033-4_21

Arup, Environmental Change Institute and Purchasing for Profit, *Impacts and Opportunities: Reducing Emissions of CD Packaging* (London: Julie's Bicycle and Environmental Change Institute, 2009).

Bach, Dagfinn, *The Dark Side of the Tune: The Hidden Energy Cost of Digital Music Consumption* (Music Tank, 2012).

Bellini, Pierfrancesco, Bruno, Ivan, & Nesi, Paolo, 'Automatic formatting of music sheets through MILLA rule-based language and engine',

---

49   Arne Herman, 'Pragmatized aesthetics: the impact of legitimacy pressures in symphony orchestras', *The Journal of Arts Management, Law, and Society* 49:2 (2019), 136-150.

Journal of New Music Research 34:3 (2005), 237-257, https://doi.org/10.1080/09298210500236051

Bergman, Åsa, 'Wherever You Are Whenever You Want': Captivating and Encouraging Music Experiences when Symphony Orchestra Performances are Provided Online', *Open Library of Humanities* 7:2 (2021), 1-23, https://doi.org/10.16995/olh.4679

Berry, Feona, Wynne, Laura E., & Riedy, Chris, *Changing our Tune: Scoping the Potential of the Australian Music Industry to Address Climate Change* (Institute for Sustainable Futures Report, 2014).

Bottrill, Catherine and Papageorgiou, Stavros, *Jam Packed Part 1: Audience Travel to UK Festivals* (Julie's Bicycle and Environmental Change Institute, 2009), https://juliesbicycle.com/wp-content/uploads/2022/01/Jam_Packed_Festival_Audience_Report_2009.pdf

Bottrill, Catherine, Liverman, Diana, and Boykoff, Max, 'Carbon soundings: greenhouse gas emissions of the UK music industry', *Environmental Research Letters* 5:1 (2010), https://doi.org/10.1088/1748-9326/5/1/014019

Brennan, Matt, 'The infrastructure and environmental consequences of live music', in *Audible Infrastructures: Music, Sound, Media*, ed. by Kyle Devine and Alexandrine Boudreault-Fournier (Oxford: Oxford University Press, 2020), pp. 117-134, https://doi.org/10.1093/oso/9780190932633.003.0006

Brennan, Matt, & Devine, Kyle, 'The cost of music', *Popular Music* 39:1 (2020), 43-65, https://doi.org/10.1017/S0261143019000552

Brodsky, Warren, 'In the wings of British orchestras: A multi-episode interview study among symphony players', *Journal of Occupational and Organizational Psychology* 79:4 (2006), 673-690, https://doi.org/10.1348/096317905X68213

Cameron, Samuel, 'Past, present and future: music economics at the crossroads', *Journal of Cultural Economics* 40:1 (2016), 1-12, https://doi.org/10.1007/s10824-015-9263-4

Collins, Andrea, Jones, Calvin, & Munday, Max, 'Assessing the environmental impacts of mega sporting events: Two options?', *Tourism Management* 30:6 (2009), 828-837, https://doi.org/10.1016/j.tourman.2008.12.006

Collins, Andrea, & Potoglou, Dimitris, 'Factors influencing visitor travel to festivals: Challenges in encouraging sustainable travel', *Journal of Sustainable Tourism* 27:5 (2019), 668-688, https://doi.org/10.1080/09669582.2019.1604718

Crenshaw, Clayton E, 'Availability of New Releases in Streaming Audio Databases', *Music Library Association, 2018 Annual Meeting* (March 2018).

Dickson, Chantal, & Arcodia, Charles, 'Promoting sustainable event practice: The role of professional associations', *International Journal of Hospitality Management* 29:2 (2010), 236-244, https://doi.org/10.1016/j.ijhm.2009.10.013

Dubnjakovic, Ana, 'Navigating digital sheet music on the web: challenges and opportunities', *Music Reference Services Quarterly* 12:1-2 (2009), 3-15, https://doi.org/10.1080/10588160902894972

Farrell, Betty, 'Changing Culture and Practices Inside Organizations', in *Entering Cultural Communities: Diversity and Change in the Nonprofit Arts*, ed. by Farrell B. & Grams D (New Brunswick, NJ: Rutgers University Press, 2008), pp. 38-63.

Fernandez-Blanco, Victor, Perez-Villadoniga, Maria J., & Prieto-Rodriguez, Juan, 'Looking into the profile of music audiences', in *Enhancing Participation in the Arts in the EU* (Cham: Springer, 2017), pp. 141-154.

Flanagan, Robert J., *The Perilous Life of Symphony Orchestras* (New Haven, CT: Yale University Press, 2012).

Herman, Arne, 'Pragmatized aesthetics: The impact of legitimacy pressures in symphony orchestras', *The Journal of Arts Management, Law, and Society* 49:2 (2019), 136-150, https://doi.org/10.1080/10632921.2018.1473311

Hill, Nikolas, Venfield, Helen, Dun, Craig, & James, Keith, *Government GHG Conversion Factors for Company Reporting: Methodology Paper for Emission Factors* (London: Department of Energy and Climate Change (DECC) and Department for Environment. Food and Rural Affairs (Defra), 2013).

Hogg, Nick, & Jackson, Tim, 'Digital media and dematerialization: An exploration of the potential for reduced material intensity in music delivery', *Journal of Industrial Ecology* 13:1 (2009), 127-146, https://doi.org/10.1111/j.1530-9290.2008.00079.x

IPCC Working Group II, *Climate Change 2022. Impacts, Adaptation and Vulnerability. Summary for Policymakers*. Working Group II contribution to the Sixth Assessment Report of the Intergovernmental Panel on Climate Change (WMO and UNEP, 2022).

Julie's Bicycle, *Green Orchestras Guide: A Simple Guide to Sustainable Practices* (2011), https://juliesbicycle.com/wp-ontent/uploads/2019/11/Green_Orchestras_Guide_2011.pdf

Julie's Bicycle, *Julie's Bicycle Practical Guide: Touring* (2015), https://juliesbicycle.com/wp-content/uploads/2019/10/Touring_guide_2015.pdf

Kellison, Timothy & McCullough, Brian. P., 'A forecast for the mainstreaming of environmental sustainability', *Sport and Entertainment Review* 2:1 (2016), 11–18.

Koukiasa, Myrsini, 'Sustainable facilities management within event venues', *Worldwide Hospitality and Tourism Themes* 3:3 (2011), https://doi.org/10.1108/17554211111142185

Kraaykamp, Gerbert, & Van Eijck, Koen, 'Personality, media preferences, and cultural participation', *Personality and Individual Differences* 38:7 (2005), 1675-1688, https://doi.org/10.1016/j.paid.2004.11.002

Laitinen, Heli M., Toppila, Esko M., Olkinuora, Pekka S., & Kuisma, Kaarina, 'Sound exposure among the Finnish National Opera personnel', *Applied Occupational and Environmental Hygiene* 18:3 (2003), 177-182, https://doi.org/10.1080/10473220301356

Lepa, Steffen & Hoklas, Anne-Kathrin, 'How do people really listen to music today? Conventionalities and major turnovers in German audio repertoires', *Information, Communication & Society* 18:10 (2015), 1253-1268, https://doi.org/10.1080/1369118X.2015.1037327

Lin, Karen, & Bell, Tim, 'Integrating Paper and Digital Music Information Systems', *ISMIR* 6:1 (2000), 23-25.

Long, Joshua, 'Constructing the narrative of the sustainability fix: Sustainability, social justice and representation in Austin, TX', *Urban Studies* 53:1 (2016), 149-172, https://doi.org/10.1177/0042098014560501

Nguyen, Godefroy. Dang, Dejean, Sylvain, & Moreau, François, 'On the complementarity between online and offline music consumption: the case of free streaming', *Journal of Cultural Economics* 38:4 (2014), 315-330.

Nicholls, Claire D., Hall, Clare, & Forgasz, Rachel, 'Charting the past to understand the cultural inheritance of concert hall listening and audience development practices', *Paedagogica Historica* 54:4 (2018), 502-516, https://doi.org/10.1080/00309230.2017.1397718

Naughtin, Matthew, 'It's all online: Creating digital study resources for orchestral musicians', in *Future Directions in Digital Information*, ed. by David Baker and Lucy Ellis (Hull: Chandos Publishing, 2021), pp. 209-216, https://doi.org/10.1016/B978-0-12-822144-0.00034-3

Pagliara, Francesca, Biggiero, Luigi, & Henke, Ilaria, 'The Environmental Impacts Connected with Travelling to events: The Case Study of the City of Naples in Italy', *2019 IEEE International Conference on Environment and Electrical Engineering and 2019 IEEE Industrial and Commercial Power Systems Europe* (EEEIC/I&CPS Europe, 1-6 June 2019), http://dx.doi.org/10.1109/EEEIC.2019.8783594

Power, Kate, 'Sustainability and the performing arts: Discourse analytic evidence from Australia', *Poetics* 89 (2021), 101580, https://doi.org/10.1016/j.poetic.2021.101580

Prado-Guerra, Alba, Bermejo, Sergio Paniagua, Prieto, Luis Fernando Calvo, & Llorente, Monica Santamarta, 'Environmental impact study of symphony orchestras and preparation of a classification guide', *The International Journal of Environmental Studies* 77:6 (2020), 1044-1059, https://doi.org/10.1080/00207233.2020.1746546

Purhonen, Semi, Gronow, Jukka, & Rahkonen, Keijo, 'Highbrow culture in Finland: Knowledge, taste and participation', *Acta Sociologica* 54:4 (2011), 385-402.

Purvis, Ben, Mao, Yong, & Robinson, Darren, 'Three pillars of sustainability: in search of conceptual origins', *Sustainability Science* 14:3 (2019), 681-95, https://doi.org/10.1007/s11625-018-0627-5

Roose, Henk, Van Eijck, Koen, & Lievens, John, 'Culture of distinction or culture of openness? Using a social space approach to analyze the social structuring of lifestyles' in *Poetics*, 40:6 (2012), 491-513, https://doi.org/10.1016/j.poetic.2012.08.001

Ross, Walker J., & Mercado, Haylee Uecker, 'Barriers to managing environmental sustainability in public assembly venues', in *Sustainability* 12:24 (2020), https://doi.org/10.3390/su122410477

Sánchez-Jara, Javier Merchán, 'Digital schola: music readers as learning/ teaching tools', *Proceedings of the Second International Conference on Technological Ecosystems for Enhancing Multiculturality* (October 2014), 547-553, https://doi.org/10.1145/2669711.2669954

Schmidt, Jesper Hvass, Pedersen, Ellen Raben, Juhl, Peter Møller, Christensen-Dalsgaard, Jakob, Andersen, Ture Dammann, Poulsen, Torben, & Bælum, Jesper, 'Sound exposure of symphony orchestra musicians', *Annals of Occupational Hygiene* 55:8 (2011), 893-905, https://doi.org/10.1093/annhyg/mer055

Smith, Neil T., 'Concrete Culture: The Planning Hearing as a Stage for Cultural Debates', *Cultural Sociology* 16:2 (2021), 147-164, https://doi.org/10.1177/17499755211040959

Van Boxstael, Anneleen, 'The dawn of digital sheet music: a look at neoscores', *Fontes Artis Musicae* (2014), 284-289.

Weber, Christopher L., Koomey, Jonathan G., & Matthews, H. Scoot, 'The energy and climate change implications of different music delivery methods', *Journal of Industrial Ecology* 14:5 (2010), 754-769, https://doi.org/10.1111/j.1530-9290.2010.00269.x

Wroblewski, Lukasz and Dacko-Bikiewicz, Zdzisława, 'Sustainable consumer behaviour in the market of cultural services in Central European countries: The example of Poland', *Sustainability* 10:11 (2018), 38-56, https://doi.org/10.3390/su10113856

12. The 'Museum Problem' Revisited: Learning from Contemporary Art Conservation

Denise Petzold

Classical music is supposed to have a 'museum problem'. In the introduction to this book, Neil Thomas Smith and Peter Peters describe this problem as 'a practice trapped in the past, unable to respond to contemporary currents in society and increasingly irrelevant to what is happening around it.' The future of classical music – and the current drive for innovation that seeks to secure this music and its relevance in society – is often seen to be complicated by the 'rigidity' of this music's past, meaning the traditions and routines engrained in its production, performance and experience. Particularly in Western symphonic and orchestral music, these traditions have remained very stable, relying on well-established rituals that aim to deliver profoundly aesthetic encounters with artworks for whose performance musicians have undergone years of education and training.[1]

In her seminal book *The Imaginary Museum of Musical Works*, philosopher Lydia Goehr demonstrates that classical music and the museum are indeed no strangers to each other.[2] She identifies the emergence of the musical work in the late eighteenth century, when the establishment of art museums was in full swing. As visual art became

---

1   James H. Johnson, *Listening in Paris: A Cultural History* (Berkeley, CA: University of California Press, 1996).

2   Lydia Goehr, *The Imaginary Museum of Musical Works: An Essay in the Philosophy of Music* (Oxford: Oxford University Press, 2007).

collectible and thus conservable for future display, it enjoyed a new autonomy enabled and safeguarded by the museum. Connected to this,

> music had to find a plastic or equivalent commodity, a valuable and permanently existing product, that could be treated in the same way as the objects of the already respectable fine arts. Music would have to find an object that could be divorced from everyday contexts, form part of a collection of works of art, and be contemplated purely aesthetically. [...] The object was called 'the work.'[3]

This development is commonly understood as the objectification of music. It led to the formation of canons, repertoires and collections, which Goehr has famously called the 'imaginary museum of musical works'.[4] This (supposedly intangible) collection might be argued, however, to be far from imaginary: as the author herself shows, the 'musical work' has become regulative of the institutions, organisations, and everyday practices of classical music. It has become a crucial part of the traditions of Western classical music. While Goehr's insights are still relevant and helpful to understand the persistence and solidity of musical works in classical music practice, they do not necessarily solve the challenges that classical music faces in relation to the future, and which Smith and Peters outline at the beginning of this book.

In this chapter, I revisit the museum in order to re-articulate classical music's 'museum problem'. I propose that this comparison is in urgent need of correction; a correction that might give rise to new insights, potential and lessons for classical music. The museum is an important institution to investigate when asking how classical music and its works can be brought into the future. This has also been recognised by scholars of classical music. In their book *Classical Concert Studies: A Companion to Contemporary Research and Performance*, Martin Tröndle and Esther Bishop emphasise recent developments in the museum, and in museum studies, as exemplary for classical concert studies. The authors suggest that museum studies' increasingly interdisciplinary approaches, as well as their forward-looking discourse, have contributed positively to the institution's development and relevance in society.[5] It is no coincidence

---

3   Goehr, *The Imaginary Museum of Musical Works*, pp. 172–73.
4   Goehr, *The Imaginary Museum of Musical Works*, p. 8.
5   Martin Tröndle and Esther Bishop, 'Concert Studies', in *Classical Concert Studies: A Companion to Contemporary Research and Performance*, ed. by Martin Tröndle (London: Routledge), pp. 1-8.

that these authors turn their glance towards the museum: after all, both art museums and classical music institutions (such as orchestras or conservatoires) are in the business of transmitting artworks and artistic heritage.[6] Both also look back on long-standing organisational systems, historical traditions and professionalised practices that are now considered to be in crisis and require a response.

Yet, in contrast to Tröndle and Bishop's rather general outlook, I propose that it is in two intertwined, concrete aspects that the contemporary art museum is particularly relevant to classical music: firstly, to gain new understandings of the ontology – the existence – of artworks over time; and secondly, to explore how new understandings of this ontology may transform the institution and its practices. Both of these points are anchored in a particular branch of the art museum and its studies: contemporary art conservation. New understandings of how artworks exist, after all, fundamentally relate to the task of conserving artworks for the future, and the role that the museum plays in this process. This question of conservation is relevant for classical music. The future of classical music cannot only be one of changed concert formats on the one hand, and a decolonised and diversified canon on the other. The future of classical music also needs to address how we, as classical music practitioners, can and want to take care of those extant works that have become so beloved and iconic, and for which we have built our concert halls and conservatoires. What role can these works play in the future of the practice and how can we transport them there in meaningful ways, especially in the light of recent economic, political and social developments and movements? An answer to this question, I propose, can be found in a specific theoretical approach from contemporary art conservation studies, which I will introduce shortly: conservator and media art researcher Hanna Barbara Hölling's take on the artwork's archive, which includes the notions of archival potentiality

---

6   The orchestra as a conserving apparatus is for example highlighted by James P. Burkholder, 'The Twentieth Century and the Orchestra as Museum', in *The Orchestra: A Collection of 23 Essays on its Origins and Transformations*, ed. by Joan Peyser (Milwaukee, WI: Hal Leonard, 2006), pp. 452–479, and Veerle Spronck, 'Listen Closely: Innovating Audience Participation in Symphonic Music' (unpublished doctoral thesis, Maastricht: Maastricht University, 2022).

and actualisation.⁷ This approach highlights the heterogeneous and shifting relations between actors and materials that are involved in an artwork's identity, history and 'realisations' over time and which posit that change, transformation and process are at the heart of an artwork's meaningful existence.

Connected to this, it is the fluidity and process-based nature of contemporary artworks that have caused transformations in the museum as a conserving, 'fixating' institution. In their book *Museum of the Future*, Christina Bechtler and Dora Imhof describe the tension that results from the coming-together of the 'liquidity' of the contemporary arts and the 'solidity' of the museum, and how this tension has enabled changes in the institution.⁸ For many art museums and their professionals, the question of how contemporary artworks can be 'kept' is not merely a rhetorical or philosophical one but an urgent, practical concern. How to keep, for example, artworks that are unstable or unruly in terms of their materials, that change or unfold over time, that are ephemeral and even immaterial, such as performance art, conceptual art or time-based media art?⁹ This problem has forced museum professionals to actively rethink and transform well-established ideas and practices of conservation, thereby critically interrogating the potential futures of such works, as well as their own and the museum's role in them. The result is a radical expansion of the understanding and practices of conservation, which moves away from attempting to 'fixate' artworks and towards caring for changing artworks on an institutional level. This shifts the emphasis from the artwork as a transcendent and universal object to a complex

---

7   Hanna B. Hölling, 'The Archival Turn: Toward New Ways of Conceptualising Changeable Artworks', in *Data Drift: Archiving Media and Data Art in the 21ˢᵗ Century*, ed. by Rasa Smite, Raitis Smiths and Lev Manovich (Riga: RIXC / Liepaja University Art Research Lab, 2015), pp. 73–89; Hanna B. Hölling, *Paik's Virtual Archive: Time, Change, and Materiality in Media Art* (Oakland, CA: University of California Press, 2017).

8   *Museum of the Future*, ed. by Christina Bechtler and Dora Imhof (Zurich: JPR Ringier, 2014), pp. 5–6.

9   As time-based media art conservator Pip Laurenson explains, 'the term time-based media refers to works that incorporate a video, slide, film, audio or computer-based element. Time-based media installations involve a media element that is rendered within a defined space and in a way that has been specified by the artist. Part of what it means to experience these works is to experience their unfolding over time according to the temporal logic of the medium as it is played back.' See Pip Laurenson, 'Authenticity, Change and Loss in the Conservation of Time-Based Media Installations', *Tate Papers* 6 (2006), n. p.

entity situated in concrete, localised practices. This understanding, I believe, is of utmost importance for the future of classical music practice and how we understand musical pieces within it. It concerns not only how to continue or change the performance of musical works, but also addresses how these works are introduced, taught and learned at musical education institutions such as conservatoires in the first place.

In what follows, I will first provide insight into the challenges raised by contemporary artworks for museums and the changed notion of conservation that went hand in hand with these challenges. This is important for classical music, as it sheds new light on both the theoretical and practical implications of 'conserving' artistic heritage – and the potential role of institutions and organisations in this process. I will then continue to examine Hölling's theoretical understanding of the artwork's archive, archival potentiality and actualisation in more detail. This chapter will then introduce two practical examples in relation to the archive – the MCICM's experimental concert *People's Salon* and my own ethnographic research at the Conservatorium Maastricht – before ending with some concluding remarks.

Transformed and Transforming Museums

Since roughly the late 1950s, contemporary artworks have challenged the logics and workings of museums in many domains of practice, above all conservation. They do so through their materialities, which have become increasingly processual, fluid and ephemeral. There are countless examples that vividly illustrate the problems these works cause for conservation: performance artworks like the sung works of Tino Sehgal are supposed to leave no trace or documentation behind; the installations of Nam June Paik incorporate already obsolete technologies; works featuring organic matter such as those by Anya Gallaccio slowly decay in the midst of the museum's exhibition space.[10] The dematerialisation and changeability of contemporary artworks

---

10 Artworks that consist of actual music and sounding elements also played an increasingly important role in galleries and museums, as can be seen with help of the avant-garde Fluxus movement of the 1960s.

marked a point of departure for museum conservators.[11] So far, studies and practices of conservation built on a scientific paradigm at whose heart lay physical preservation, including the prevention of damage or decay, minimal intervention, reversibility and the authenticity of the object.[12] With the advent of contemporary art and the introduction of ever more materially complex artworks in the museum, conservators were forced to seek out complementary understandings and approaches to account for those works that exceeded the limits of this scientific paradigm.[13]

This led to the emergence of contemporary art conservation as a field that is – just like music – very much positioned at the intersection of practice and theory. As conservator and researcher Hélia Marçal explains, contemporary art conservation experienced a significant boom in the mid-1990s, roughly ten years after its establishment as a field.[14] It consists of an active network of museum professionals who address and examine the new and manifold challenges of contemporary art conservation.[15] The result is an extensive, ever-emerging body of theoretical and practical work that interrogates how artworks exist, as well as the museum's tasks and responsibilities in these existences.[16]

---

11 Lucy Lippard and John Chandler, 'The Dematerialization of Art', *Art International* 12 (1986), 31–36; Lucy Lippard, *Six Years: The Dematerialization of the Art Object from 1966 to 1972* (Berkeley, CA: University of California Press, 1973).

12 Miriam Clavir, 'The Social and Historic Construction of Professional Values in Conservation', *Studies in Conservation* 43 (1998), 1–8. For earlier histories of art conservation in Europe see also Alessandro Conti, *History of the Restoration and Conservation of Works of Art* (London: Routledge, 2007); as well as *Histories of Conservation and Art History in Modern Europe*, ed. by Sven Dupré and Jenny Boulboullé (London: Routledge, 2022).

13 Importantly, even today, many discussions in conservation studies are informed by the non-interventionist ethics implied in the scientific paradigm.

14 Hélia Marçal, *Contemporary Art Conservation* (Tate.org.uk, 2019), https://www.tate.org.uk/research/reshaping-the-collectible/research-approach-conservation

15 For an in-depth look into these developments and histories, as well as specific projects and events, see Marçal, *Contemporary Art Conservation*, n. p. It is also important to note that many of the old networks still exist today, yet new cross-institutional collaborations and projects are being continuously founded and added, making the field a particularly active and dynamic one.

16 Famous examples include *Modern Art: Who Cares? An Interdisciplinary Project and an International Symposium on the Conservation of Modern and Contemporary Art*, ed. by IJsbrand Hummelen and Dionne Sillé (London: Archetype Publications, 2005); Pip Laurenson, 'Emerging Institutional Models and Notions of Expertise for the Conservation of Time-Based Media Works of Art', *Techné* 37 (2013), 36–42; Salvador Muñoz Viñas, *Contemporary Theory of Conservation* (London: Routledge,

Often, such artworks have also stimulated museum professionals to come up with new ways of working and organising, for example when it comes to documenting, seeking collaborations with external stakeholders, and considering new institutional models for such external and interdisciplinary collaborations.[17] Contemporary artworks thus have fundamentally challenged and changed the logics and workings of the museum. Importantly, conservators have described them as similar to music due to their fleeting nature, and sought out different kinds of music in order to better understand the existence and performance of such artworks – going so far as to introduce musical practices like the writing of scores or notations into conservation practice.[18]

While the performative nature of artworks is nothing new to classic music practitioners, this point is important insofar as it shows that an institution – which is made for preserving artistic heritage, and which rests on long-standing ideas and practices – can calibrate, change and expand its ways of working based on new theoretical understandings of what an artwork is and how it exists.[19] One of these new

---

2005); *Preserving and Exhibiting Media Art: Challenges and Perspectives*, ed. by Julia Nordegraaf, Cosetta G. Saba, Barbara Le Maître and Vinzenz Heidiger (Amsterdam: Amsterdam University Press / Eye Film Institute Netherlands, 2013); Vivian van Saaze, *Installation Art and the Museum: Presentation and Conservation of Changing Artworks* (Amsterdam: Amsterdam University Press, 2013); *Conservation: Principles, Dilemmas and Uncomfortable Truths*, ed. by Alison Richmond and Alison Bracker (London: Routledge, 2009); *Inside Installations: Theory and Practice of Contemporary Artworks*, ed. by Tatja Scholte and Glenn Wharton (Amsterdam: Amsterdam University Press, 2011); Renée van de Vall, Hanna B. Hölling, Tatja Scholte and Sanneke Stigter, 'Reflections on a Biographical Approach to Contemporary Art Conservation' in *ICOM Committee for Conservation 16th Triennial Meeting Lisbon 19–23 September 2011* (São Paulo: Critério Artes Gráficas / ICOM, 2011), pp. 1–8; Renée van de Vall, 'The Devil and the Details: The Ontology of Contemporary Art in Conservation Theory and Practice', *British Journal of Aesthetics* 55 (2015), 285–302.

17 Laurenson, *Emerging Institutional Models and Notions of Expertise for the Conservation of Time-Based Media Works of Art*, p. 42.

18 Laurenson, *Authenticity, Change and Loss in the Conservation of Time-Based Media Installations*, n. p.; Hölling, *Paik's Virtual Archive*, p. 42.

19 For example, conservators and museum studies scholars have addressed the potential death or complete loss of the artwork in the realm of the thinkable, raising the question of what that would mean for the museum and its relevance to culture and society. See: Alison Bracker and Rachel Barker, 'Relic or Release: Defining and Documenting the Physical and Aesthetic Death of Contemporary Works of Art' in *ICOM Committee for Conservation 14th Triennial Meeting The Hague 12–16 September 2005*, Preprints Volume II (London: James & James / Earthscan, 2005), pp. 1009–1015; Katrina Crear, 'The Material Lives and

understandings has changed the notion of conservation fundamentally: the acknowledgement that change is an inherent part of the identity of artworks, and that the institution's task is to take care of these changing works rather than attempting to 'fixate' them. Thus, focus has very much shifted from a dichotomous understanding of a work's transcendent or unchanging identity and how to perform or 'execute' this identity, towards tracing the complex, heterogeneous entanglements in which a work's identity is embedded in specific contexts and environments including various actors and materials. Connected to this, Marçal highlights the question of how to conserve the social and participatory dimensions of performative works, a question relevant also to classical music practitioners, for example when considering the role of different concert formats and how they may connect to the artwork.[20]

The insight that artworks are embedded in changing networks and relations – and that these have a fundamental effect on the work – is also valid for institutions such as the orchestra and the conservatoire, in which practice is still very much directed at faithfully executing a musical work. While constructivist insights like the above have been extensively discussed in new musicology and music (and art) sociology, it is remarkable how separated these theoretical insights have remained from the practical organisations and workings of most classical music institutions and organisations.[21] Coming back to the beginning of this

---

Deaths of Contemporary Artworks' (unpublished doctoral thesis, London: Goldsmiths University of London, 2012); Rosario Llamas-Pacheco, 'Some Theory for the Conservation of Contemporary Art', *Studies in Conservation* 65 (2020), 487–498. Moreover, insights from contemporary art conservation do not stop at contemporary works; they are now also used to question how museums deal with seemingly 'fixed' objects such as paintings and sculptures. See: Fernando Domínguez Rubio, *Still Life: Ecologies of the Modern Imagination at the Art Museum* (Chicago, IL: University of Chicago Press, 2020).

20 Hélia Marçal, 'Conservation in an Era of Participation', *Journal of the Institute of Conservation* 40 (2017), 97–104.

21 Relevant art and music sociological work includes for example: Howard S. Becker, *Art Worlds*, 25th Anniversary Edition (Berkeley, CA: University of California Press, 2008); *Art from Start to Finish: Jazz, Painting, Writing, and Other Improvisations*, ed. by H. S. Becker, R. R. Faulkner and B. Kirshenblatt-Gimblett (Chicago, IL: University of Chicago Press, 2006); Nicholas Cook, *Beyond the Score: Music as Performance* (Oxford: Oxford University Press, 2013); Tia DeNora, *Music in Everyday Life* (Cambridge: Cambridge University Press, 2000); Antoine Hennion, 'From Valuation to Instauration: On the Double Pluralism of Values', *Valuation Studies* 5 (2017), 69–81; Antoine Hennion, 'Objects, Belief, and the Sociologist: The

chapter, the reason for this lies partially in what is considered the 'museum problem', which hampers change and innovation. Luckily, contemporary art conservation might provide one understanding of the ontology of artworks that is particularly interesting in that regard: Hölling's take on the archive, archival potentiality and actualisation.[22] Together these notions prompt an alternative understanding of the artwork 'itself', while at the same time allowing for the history, surrounding practices and traditions of a work or practice to exist (and change) in meaningful ways. Achieving this balance seems an important task for classical music institutions, which rely on a long-standing practice on the one hand, but desire to experiment and innovate on the other.

Into the Archive!

An archive is, usually, a physical place for storing, preserving, organising and cataloguing information, such as (historical) documents, materials or public records. Yet, as the philosophers Michel Foucault and Jacques Derrida have famously pointed out, the archive is by no means a neutral space – rather it is one that presents specific cultural, political and systemic conditions for knowledge production.[23] In the archive, information is not only kept and preserved but also discarded, eradicated and (actively) forgotten. This insight has resulted in the archive existing in a state between physical repository and theoretical concept, the latter of which has gained increasing popularity in recent decades in the humanities and social sciences. This development is described as the 'archival turn'.[24] While the concept draws on a long and complex history, which I do not intend to trace here, it is important to note that recently

---

Sociology of Art as a Work-to-be-Done', in *Roads to Music Sociology*, ed. by Alfred Smudits (Wiesbaden: Springer, 2019), pp. 41–60.
22 Hölling, *The Archival Turn: Toward New Ways of Conceptualising Changeable Artworks*, p. 87; Hölling, *Paik's Virtual Archive*, p. 154.
23 Michel Foucault, *The Archaeology of Knowledge and The Discourse on Language* (New York, NY: Pantheon Books, 1972); Jacques Derrida, 'Archive Fever: A Freudian Impression', *Diacritics* 25 (1995), 9–63.
24 Sara Callahan, *Art – Archive: Understanding the Archival Turn in Contemporary Art* (Manchester: Manchester University Press, 2022); Gabriella Giannachi, *Archive Everything: Mapping the Everyday* (Cambridge, MA: MIT Press, 2016).

the archive has become subject to discussions on postcolonial thought and decolonisation, as well as the performance of cultural memory.[25]

In this archival turn, the concept has, inevitably, also entered the arts.[26] Contemporary artworks have increasingly been understood as archives themselves, consisting of and presenting complex material, with often fragmentary pieces of information and histories that need to be navigated and negotiated by curators, conservators and collectors. In contemporary art conservation studies, the concept of the archive gives rise to new understandings of the continuing existence of artworks. Hölling, for example, has used this concept to grasp how the artworks by video and media artist Nam June Paik relate to issues of change and variability. She argues that

> Conceiving of an artwork apart from its archive is unthinkable because the artwork is irreversibly bound to its archive, which shapes its identity, and because its actualization is dependent on the archival realm. The archive is, in fact, an active part of the artwork, rather than some distinct and static repository of documents.[27]

An artwork is thus inherently attached to an archive. This archive, according to Hölling, includes those elements that the artwork needs to exist or to be brought to existence, that give it form.[28] These are physical and 'virtual'. The physical sphere of the archive contains the materials that are part of the artwork, such as objects and materials, historical documents or physical settings. The virtual sphere entails intangible elements such as knowledges and embodied skills, like being able to perform certain artistic techniques.[29] These two archival spheres cannot exist without each other: both of them are needed to 'actualise'

---

[25] For a more in-depth look into history of the archive as a concept, see Marlene Manoff, 'Theories of the Archive from Across the Disciplines', *Portal: Libraries and the Academy* 4 (2004), 9–23. For a reflection on postcolonialism, decolonisation and cultural memory see: Ann Laura Stoler, 'Colonial Archives and the Arts of Governance: On the Content in the Form', *Archival Science* 2 (2002), 87–109; Diana Taylor, *The Archive and the Repertoire: Performing Cultural Memory in the Americas* (Durham, NC: Duke University Press, 2003).

[26] *Art + Archive: Understanding the Archival Turn in Contemporary Art; Cinema and Art as Archive, Form, Medium, Memory*, ed. by Francesco Federici and Cosetta G. Saba (Milan: Memesis International, 2014).

[27] Hölling, *Paik's Virtual Archive*, p. 160.

[28] Hölling, *Paik's Virtual Archive*, pp. 9–10.

[29] Hölling, *Paik's Virtual Archive*, pp. 142–53.

the artwork. Actualisation is the process of bringing the artwork into existence. Crucially, what this actualisation ultimately looks like is dependent on what Hölling calls 'archival potentiality'. Archival potentiality describes a state of possibility and openness in regard to the elements from the two archival spheres that are activated for this actualisation.[30] So, what the artwork will be is not obvious or fixed to begin with: rather, this is a creative and largely unpredictable process, in which conservators and other involved (human and nonhuman) actors negotiate the available (and unavailable) contents of the physical and virtual sphere to bring the artwork into existence. Crucially, this process is also not completely open but contingent: the artwork cannot be simply 'anything' but draws on what is in the archive's two spheres. In addition, 'not only does each new actualization emerge on the basis of the archive, but every new actualization of a work enriches its archival potentiality and generates subsequent realizations.'[31] This means that every actualisation again enters the artwork's archive, expanding and adding to possibilities of future existences. Actualisation, then, is an accumulative – rather than repetitive – process of realisation brought about by the various entangled actors, who navigate the artwork's archive and its potentiality.

Importantly, this reading of the archive also entertains certain ideas of the past and history. As the formation of the archive is recursive and ongoing, it does not present a static domain that only refers to or draws from the past. Instead, it hosts a myriad of potential present and future paths of action. As a 'dynamic entity directed to the future', changeability and transformation is an inherent part of this archive.[32] Hölling notes that in the context of conservation, this means 'not to return to a past "original state" or to yield to a preoccupation with a distant past, but to effect an active and creative "presencing" of artworks.'[33] The archive, therefore, allows for a future-orientated understanding of the changing existence of artworks. As the archive is dynamic, so are the artworks and their identities: they exist as shifting entities in which past, present and future co-exist.

---

30 Hölling, *Paik's Virtual Archive*, p. 154.
31 Ibid.
32 Hölling, *Paik's Virtual Archive*, p. 164.
33 Ibid.

Looking at Hölling's theory from the perspective of classical music, the archive might be argued to enable both a more constructivist or performative reading, as well as a more essentialist music philosophical one. Particularly the distinction between archival potentiality and actualisation seems, at first glance, to echo the dichotomy between the 'transcendent' musical work (embodied in the score) and its performance proclaimed in so many Platonist literatures.[34] After all, how is actualisation ontologically different from the music philosophical idea of performing or transmitting a fixed work? In other words: what new lessons can classical music draw from the archive's understanding of artistic ontology? In the next section, I will dive deeper into the implications of the archive for classical music and offer two examples of how this concept might be understood to work in practice.

Archives of Classical Music: *The People's Salon* and Violoncellos

Instead of suggesting an iterative understanding of performing 'the work itself', Hölling's archival theory underlines the heterogeneous actors and materials that are involved in a work's continuing existence. Thereby, the archive, archival potentiality and the process of actualisation emphasise this existence as one that is constantly changing and future-directed. Through its attention to the archive's situated contents, Hölling's approach can help us to understand and attend to how an artwork is in a continuous process of becoming.[35] The possibility to make this process

---

[34] Stephen Davies, *Musical Works & Performances: A Philosophical Exploration* (Oxford: Oxford University Press, 2001); Peter Kivy, *Authenticities: Philosophical Reflections on Musical Performance* (Ithaca, NY: Cornell University Press, 1995).

[35] From this perspective, the archive is much more akin to recent approaches in relational musicology, music sociology and music mediation theory, which focus on how music is mediated in and through the relations between human and nonhuman actors. See for example: Georgina Born, 'On Musical Mediation: Ontology, Technology and Creativity', *Twentieth-Century Music* 2 (2005), 7–36; Georgina Born, 'For a Relational Musicology: Music and Interdisciplinarity, Beyond the Practice Turn', *Journal of the Royal Musical Association* 135 (2010), 205–243; Antoine Hennion, *The Passion for Music: A Sociology of Mediation* (Farnham: Ashgate, 2015); Floris Schuiling, 'The Instant Composers Pool: Music Notation and the Mediation of Improvising Agency', *Cadernos de Arte e Antropologia* 5 (2016), 39–58; Floris Schuiling, 'Notation Cultures: Towards an Ethnomusicology of Notation', *Journal of the Royal Musical Association* 144 (2019), 429–458.

explicit with help of this theory is also what makes it so important for classical music: acknowledging and working with a musical work's archive and its potentialities may foster innovation, help us understand what *meaningful* innovation in classical music can concretely look like, and enable new or alternative existences of these musical works in the future.

A crucial benefit of this approach for classical music consists in the idea that the change a work goes through is neither arbitrary, nor does it happen simply for the sake of changing. Instead, it proposes that change is rooted, anchored. This means that although change is constantly happening, not everything is possible, because the archive draws from past actualisations and histories. For classical music, this is a particularly helpful aspect: it means that what is already there does not need to be radically overturned or broken away from in order for the practice to change or open up in meaningful ways. An example of this is the recent rise of innovative or experimental concert formats. Instead of introducing new ways of performing or participating in a classical music concert for the sake of innovation, attending to a work's archive could enable ways of experimenting and engaging with the histories, practices, contexts, and experiences that it is connected to. In short, the archive teaches us that the past and history are something to be worked *with*, instead of *from*. And not only that: having to negotiate a work's archival potentialities means that this past, its histories and resources, need to be addressed explicitly rather than implicitly.

One example of this is a concert organised by the Artful Participation team of the Maastricht Centre for the Innovation of Classical Music (MCICM) in January 2020, called the *People's Salon*.[36] The programme of the *People's Salon* was built on and inspired by the personal memories and (hi)stories of the friends of Philzuid (South Netherlands Philharmonic), a community of loyal audience members and supporters of the orchestra, in a collective effort between the friends, the orchestra and the team of researchers. Their memories and stories, often connected to

---

36 For more information on the concert, as well as the MCICM's Artful Participation project, please see: https://artfulparticipation.nl/experiments. Notably, the *People's Salon* has been received so positively by the audience that the format has been repeated again in April 2023 at the Parkstad Limburg Theaters in Heerlen, this time under the title 'De Verhalententoonstelling'.

particular pieces of classical music, became the baseline for composing the evening's programme. In the concert, a handful of friends shared these personal memories and experiences with the help of touching personal introductions before having the orchestra play the pieces of music in question. The performance space (AINSI in Maastricht) as well as the programme notes played an important part in contributing to this evening. The space invited participants to exchange their own stories about the music in the breaks with its cosy and open atmosphere and card prompts distributed across tables; the programme booklet became a tangible materialisation of the histories and memories shared, which people could take home and re-read later.

Although the *People's Salon* addressed the question of meaningful participation and not archives, in hindsight it might be argued to have also done the latter: activating and exploring these musical works' archives and potentialities in ways that drew from the situatedness of these pieces in the specific orchestra and its community. It also questioned who may be involved in the actualisation of those musical works and how so. This arguably changed not only the concert format and audience experience. It also affected the archives of these musical pieces, which expanded and became filled with new and hitherto unknown stories, creating new understandings, meanings, and (hi) stories of these works and their contexts; not only for the audience but also for the musicians, other involved orchestra staff, and the organising team. At the heart of the *People's Salon* was not a faithful execution of preconceived ideas of what these artworks should sound like, but the creation of a musical experience that would do justice to and acknowledge the relation between these pieces and the people who listen to them. With the help of the *People's Salon*, it also becomes clear that the actualisation of a work can never be a complete representation of its archive. Rather, actualisation – as seen with help of the specific focus of the concert – is fragmentary and dependent, both in terms of the contents of the archive, as well as the decisions and judgments made by who- or whatever is involved. It is an exploration into the hidden and the possible, without undoing the concert event as such. In fact, it was exactly because it simultaneously built on well-established concert conventions that it was so well received by the participants. The *People's Salon* struck a balance between employing an innovative approach while acknowledging the routines of the orchestra staff and audience that were needed to enable and enjoy this concert format in the first place.

While the *People's Salon* created new shared meanings that entered the musical works' archives in the context of the concert event, in her theory, Hölling elaborates that the archive of an artwork is decentralised.[37] For classical music, this means that resources for actualisation may also be found outside the concert event or the very moment of performance. Therefore, the theory also provides the opportunity to investigate other connected materials and practices that are involved in these musical archives, but have remained largely neglected or invisible.

In my own doctoral research project, also part of the MCICM, I used the concepts of the archive, archival potentiality and actualisation to investigate how different musical artefacts continue to bring classical music into existence practically.[38] One of my case studies revolved around the violoncello, a string instrument that is – also from a historical perspective – deeply embedded in the practices and traditions of classical music. Through ethnographic research – meaning observations of cello lessons over the course of one academic year at the Conservatorium Maastricht, as well as semi-structured, qualitative interviews with cello students and teachers – I found out that not only artworks have archives but that actors such as musicians and artefacts (here: instruments) are attached to archives, too. For example, how students learn to play a musical work – and what they learn – is fundamentally shaped by how they experience their concrete physical and affective relationship to their own instrument, meaning how they navigate its specificities and characteristics and the stories that they connect with it. During my research, students illustrated that aspects such as corpus form, fingerboard (in what distance the notes are arranged), positioning of the bridge (which dictates the distance between strings and fingerboard), the strings, and capabilities for projection and sound affect the decisions they would make regarding playing, technique and performance of a work. For one student, this meant that he avoided playing certain notes on the A string, as he perceived the sound as too sharp; for another, this

---

37 Hölling, *Paik's Virtual Archive*, p. 146.
38 Denise Petzold, 'Archives of Change: An Art Conservation Studies Approach to Innovating Classical Music' (unpublished doctoral thesis, Maastricht: Maastricht University, 2023).

entailed being able to flexibly react to the occasional 'moods' of her cello, expressing that she saw her instrument more like a significant other than a tool, which, at some points, seemed to actively contradict her ways of playing and ideas for a piece. The cellos thus afforded certain manners of handling and playing a given piece, which were intimately connected to the students' understandings of this human-instrument relationship as an archive. But not only the physical aspects of playing or performing technique played a role. During their studies, musical works merged with the students' biographies, their relationship with their instrument, including their musical but also personal development. Therefore, it can be argued that the relationship between a musician and their instrument is an integral part of the archives and thus actualisations of musical works. These relationships are, however, often silenced in practice: students are expected to demonstrate excellent technical skill on any given instrument, while the affective connection to their instrument is at best ignored.

Insights like these reveal new archival potentialities to act(ualise) on, new options for exploring how musical works exist. For example, giving students room to attend to the physical and affective relationship with their own instrument in music education institutions (such as the conservatoire) might enable a better understanding into how this relationship concretely affects the understandings, performance and experience of musical works. Connected to this, asking students to research or write a biography of their instrument could be insightful in grasping how its particularities and characteristics could add to a work's archive. This might give students a tool to address and engage also with the affective aspects of this long-lasting relationship, a relationship in which they then could also start to interrogate what these works and this tradition mean to them. Especially at the conservatoire, activities like this can shift focus from the aesthetic idea of transcendence of the musical work – which still very much revolves around the idea of the performer as mere executioner controlling and mastering an inanimate instrument – toward understanding the learning of this tradition as being part of a situated dialogue or engagement between various humans and materials. This would also consider the changes that these actors and materials go through over time, again shifting the archives of the musical works. More importantly, it might help us to attend to the exclusionary systems within which classical music still operates: for example, the so-far dismissed role of disabled bodies in the performance of this artistic heritage.

Past as Prologue

In this chapter, I have sought to demonstrate how the museum, and particularly contemporary art conservation, can help us to address the future of classical music, its works, tradition and practice. The contemporary art museum illustrates that change and innovation within an art institution – which is meant to preserve artworks – is intimately tied to new understandings of how artworks exist through time. Contemporary art conservators have recognised that change plays an important role in the works' identities and their continued meaningful existence. The idea to take care of this change (instead of trying to 'freeze' artworks) thereby also draws attention to the heterogeneous networks and relations in which these works are embedded, all of which are subject to transformation over time. Connected to this, I proceeded to illuminate one of these new theoretical understandings on the artwork's ontology: conservator Hölling's take on the archive, archival potentiality and actualisation. In what followed, I described the implications of this approach and explored how it could be used practically, accompanied by the examples of the MCICM's experimental concert *People's Salon* and a case study on a classical music instrument – the violoncello – taken from my own research.

Drawing on this theoretical approach, two main arguments can be made for the case of classical music. Firstly, it highlights the existence and importance of the archival potentiality of musical works, meaning the manifold available and unavailable resources in these works' archives on whose basis they will be actualised. This means that by examining these works' archival potentialities further, we can expand and add to the ideas, materials, actors and sites used for actualisation. This is what happened at the *People's Salon*, which opened up and added to these works' archives from a perspective of the audience members, potentially shifting the works' performances, understandings, as well as how they are experienced.

This is connected to the fact that secondly, not only might works might be seen as attached to archives; but they are part of archives of other actors and artefacts, too – such as instruments and the people who play them. This has become visible when for example wanting to understand how the relationship between musicians and their instruments shapes musical tradition. This opens up further potentials for exploring how and where musical works 'reside', indicating that understanding musical works merely as archives of particular musical tradition(s) is a narrow and limiting conception. Moreover, and connected to this, the theory helps us to become aware of the exclusionary systems, logics and workings within which classical music operates as a practice, such as ableism, racism, sexism, classicism and the like.

Yet, and this is a crucial point when thinking about the future of classical music, the archive does necessarily enable a complete disconnect from or letting go of its contents, meaning the histories, pasts and traditions of this practice. Rather, both archival potentiality and actualisation *start* from what is present in the archive. That way, the archive – and specifically archival potentiality – presents these past practices, conventions and traditions as something that exists alongside present and future ways of actualisation. The recursive logic of the archive can engage materials and practices from different times in a dialogue, to let them affect each other in a dynamic fashion directed toward actualisation. This way, classical music's heritage might step into a fruitful engagement with contemporary life: history becomes a prologue, so to say, for a book that is still to be written.

This approach not only shakes the idea of a 'fixed' or transcendent work but raises the question of how to care for the musical works and the actors connected to them for the future in new ways, a question that has so far remained largely unarticulated. With its focus on existing artworks, the archive is particularly good at helping to forge new histories, articulations, re-contextualisations, and connections. This is what the 'imaginary museum of musical works' will need: a re-attending to these work's potentials and openings, because it is only through change that these works can stay relevant and meaningful in the future – especially a future that will, hopefully, be further characterised by decolonisation, diversification and equality.[39]

As seen in contemporary art conservation on both a practical and scholarly level, this acknowledgment or engagement will require a new kind of work from the institutions in which these works are so firmly embedded, meaning orchestras, ensembles, collectives, conservatoires, music schools, art schools, festivals, concert halls. It might thus be helpful to critically interrogate what understandings of musical works these organisations currently employ or imply, and what kind of understandings are necessary for these works to remain meaningful. After all, archives do not just exist: they are made. If these works ought to stay not only artistically and culturally, but societally relevant, we need to better understand our own normative frameworks, which have long been compliant with the idea of transmitting transcendent artworks, finding a universal language, and fixing the music. In contrast, archives are scattered, localised, incomplete; this is what makes their contents so colourful, so diverse, and worth attending to.

To conclude, the 'museum problem' is not a problem about the keeping of the past, and how this past supposedly exists in tension with contemporary culture and society. Contemporary art conservation has demonstrated that the 'museum problem' of today is a radically different one from before: it is the question of how to manage change and forge new (hi)stories, of how to appropriately care for works that are by nature transforming and transformable, leading us to question the very institutions that have a duty to keep, to maintain and to preserve. And why should it be any different for classical music?

---

39 I am not suggesting, of course, that there is no acknowledgement or agreement on the idea that change is inherent part of this music – particularly movements like Historically Informed Performance (HIP) are very aware of acknowledging the changes that musical works may undergo, including the impossibility of returning to an 'authentic' or 'original' state. The works we play today are not played, experienced, or listened to in the same way than even years or decades ago. Rather, the archive brings different questions to the surface, such as how we can take care of this change, and what kind of change we envision for these works.

References

Bechtler, Christina and Dora Imhof, eds., *Museum of the Future* (Zurich: JRP Ringier, 2014).

Becker, Howard S., *Art Worlds*, 25th Anniversary Edition (Berkeley, CA: University of California Press, 2008).

Becker, Howard S., Faulkner, Robert R. and Barbara Kirshenblatt-Gimblett, eds., *Art from Start to Finish: Jazz, Painting, Writing, and Other Improvisations* (Chicago, IL: University of Chicago Press, 2006).

Born, Georgina, 'On Musical Mediation: Ontology, Technology and Creativity', *Twentieth-Century Music* 2 (2005), 7–36, https://doi.org/10.1017/S147857220500023X

Born, Georgina, 'For a Relational Musicology: Music and Interdisciplinarity, Beyond the Practice Turn', *Journal of the Royal Musical Association* 135 (2010), 205–243, https://doi.org/10.1080/02690403.2010.506265

Bracker, Alison and Rachel Barker, 'Relic or Release: Defining and Documenting the Physical and Aesthetic Death of Contemporary Works of Art' in *ICOM Committee for Conservation 14th Triennial Meeting The Hague 12–16 September 2005*, Preprints Volume II (London: James & James / Earthscan, 2005), pp. 1009–1015.

Burkholder, James P., 'The Twentieth Century and the Orchestra as Museum', in *The Orchestra: A Collection of 23 Essays on its Origins and Transformations*, ed. by Joan Peyser (Milwaukee, WI: Hal Leonard, 2006), pp. 452–479.

Callahan, Sara, *Art + Archive: Understanding the Archival Turn in Contemporary Art* (Manchester: Manchester University Press, 2022).

Clavir, Miriam, 'The Social and Historic Construction of Professional Values in Conservation', *Studies in Conservation* 43 (1998), 1–8, https://doi.org/10.2307/1506631

Conti, Alessandro, *History of the Restoration and Conservation of Works of Art* (London: Routledge, 2007).

Cook, Nicholas, *Beyond the Score: Music as Performance* (Oxford: Oxford University Press, 2013).

Crear, Katrina, 'The Material Lives and Deaths of Contemporary Artworks' (unpublished doctoral thesis, London: Goldsmiths University of London, 2012), https://research.gold.ac.uk/id/eprint/7199/

Davies, Stephen, *Musical Works & Performances: A Philosophical Exploration* (Oxford: Oxford University Press, 2001).

DeNora, Tia, *Music in Everyday Life* (Cambridge: Cambridge University Press, 2000), https://doi.org/10.1017/CBO9780511489433

Derrida, Jacques, 'Archive Fever: A Freudian Impression', *Diacritics* 25 (1995), 9–63, https://doi.org/10.2307/465144

Domínguez Rubio, Fernando, *Still Life: Ecologies of the Modern Imagination at the Art Museum* (Chicago, IL: University of Chicago Press, 2020).

Dupré, Sven and Jenny Boulboullé, eds., *Histories of Conservation and Art History in Modern Europe* (London: Routledge, 2022).

Federici, Francesco and Cosetta G. Saba, eds., *Cinema and Art as Archive, Form, Medium, Memory* (Milan: Memesis International, 2014).

Foucault, Michel, *The Archaeology of Knowledge and The Discourse on Language* (New York, NY: Pantheon Books, 1972).

Giannachi, Gabriella, *Archive Everything: Mapping the Everyday* (Cambridge, MA: MIT Press, 2016), https://doi.org/10.7551/mitpress/9780262035293.001.0001

Goehr, Lydia, *The Imaginary Museum of Musical Works: An Essay in the Philosophy of Music*, Revised Edition (Oxford: Oxford University Press, 2007).

Hennion, Antoine, *The Passion for Music: A Sociology of Mediation* (Farnham: Ashgate, 2015).

Hennion, Antoine, 'From Valuation to Instauration: On the Double Pluralism of Values', *Valuation Studies* 5 (2017), 69–81, https://doi.org/10.3384/VS.2001-5992.175169

Hennion, Antoine, 'Objects, Belief, and the Sociologist: The Sociology of Art as a Work-to-be-Done', in *Roads to Music Sociology*, ed. by Alfred Smudits (Wiesbaden: Springer, 2019), pp. 41–60, https://doi.org/10.1007/978-3-658-22279-6_4

Hölling, Hanna B., 'The Archival Turn: Toward New Ways of Conceptualising Changeable Artworks', in *Data Drift: Archiving Media and Data Art In the 21st Century*, ed. by Rasa Smite, Raitis Smits and Lev Manovich (Riga: RIXC / Liepaja University Art Research Lab, 2015), pp. 73–89.

Hölling, Hanna B., *Paik's Virtual Archive: Time, Change, and Materiality in Media Art* (Oakland, CA: University of California Press, 2017), https://doi.org/10.1080/01971360.2019.1676902

Hummelen, Ijsbrand and Dionne Sillé, eds., *Modern Art: Who Cares? An Interdisciplinary Project and an International Symposium on the Conservation of Modern and Contemporary Art* (London: Archetype Publications, 2005).

Johnson, James H., *Listening in Paris: A Cultural History* (Berkeley: University of California Press, 1996).

Kivy, Peter, *Authenticities: Philosophical Reflections on Musical Performance* (Ithaca, NY: Cornell University Press, 1995).

Laurenson, Pip, 'Authenticity, Change and Loss in the Conservation of Time-Based Media Installations', *Tate Papers* 6 (2006), https://www.tate.org.uk/research/tate-papers/06/authenticity-change-and-loss-conservation-of-time-based-media-installations

Laurenson, Pip, 'Emerging Institutional Models and Notions of Expertise for the Conservation of Time-Based Media Works of Art', *Techné* 37 (2013), 36–42.

Lippard, Lucy, *Six Years: The Dematerialization of the Art Object from 1966 to 1972* (Berkeley, CA: University of California Press, 1973).

Lippard, Lucy and John Chandler, 'The Dematerialization of Art', *Art International* 12 (1968), 31–36.

Llamas-Pacheco, Rosario, 'Some Theory for the Conservation of Contemporary Art', *Studies in Conservation* 65 (2020), 487–498, https://doi.org/10.1080/00393630.2020.1733790

Manoff, Marlene, 'Theories of the Archive from Across the Disciplines', *Portal: Libraries and the Academy* 4 (2004), 9–23.

Marçal, Hélia, 'Conservation in an Era of Participation', *Journal of the Institute of Conservation* 40 (2017), 97–104, https://doi.org/10.1080/19455224.2017.1319872

Marçal, Hélia, *Contemporary Art Conservation* (Tate.org.uk, 2019), https://www.tate.org.uk/research/reshaping-the-collectible/research-approach-conservation

Muñoz Viñas, Salvador, *Contemporary Theory of Conservation* (London: Routledge, 2005).

Noordegraaf, Julia, Cosetta G. Saba, Barbara Le Maître and Vinzenz Hediger, eds., *Preserving and Exhibiting Media Art: Challenges and Perspectives* (Amsterdam: Amsterdam University Press / Eye Film Institute Netherlands, 2013).

Petzold, Denise, 'Archives of Change: An Art Conservation Studies Approach to Innovating Classical Music' (unpublished doctoral thesis, Maastricht: Maastricht University, 2023).

Richmond, Alison and Alison Bracker, eds., *Conservation: Principles, Dilemmas and Uncomfortable Truths* (London: Routledge, 2009).

van Saaze, Vivian, *Installation Art and the Museum: Presentation and Conservation of Changing Artworks* (Amsterdam: Amsterdam University Press, 2013).

Scholte, Tatja and Glenn Wharton, eds., *Inside Installations: Theory and Practice of Contemporary Artworks* (Amsterdam: Amsterdam University Press, 2011).

Schuiling, Floris, 'The Instant Composers Pool: Music Notation and the Mediation of Improvising Agency', *Cadernos de Arte e Antropologia* 5 (2016), 39–58, https://doi.org/10.4000/cadernosaa.1028

Schuiling, Floris, 'Notation Cultures: Towards an Ethnomusicology of Notation', *Journal of the Royal Musical Association* 144 (2019), 429–458, https://doi.org/10.1080/02690403.2019.1651508

Spronck, Veerle, 'Listen Closely: Innovating Audience Participation in Symphonic Music' (unpublished doctoral thesis, Maastricht: Maastricht University, 2022).

Stoler, Ann Laura, 'Colonial Archives and the Arts of Governance: On the Content in the Form', *Archival Science* 2 (2002), 87–109, http://dx.doi.org/10.1023/A:1020821416870

Taylor, Diana, *The Archive and the Repertoire: Performing Cultural Memory in the Americas* (Durham, NC: Duke University Press, 2003).

Tröndle, Martin and Esther Bishop, 'Concert Studies', in *Classical Concert Studies: A Companion to Contemporary Research and Performance*, ed. by Martin Tröndle (London: Routledge), pp. 1-8.

van de Vall, Renée, Hanna B. Hölling, Tatja Scholte and Sanneke Stigter, 'Reflections on a Biographical Approach to Contemporary Art Conservation' in *ICOM Committee for Conservation 16th Triennial Meeting Lisbon 19–23 September 2011* (São Paulo: Critério Artes Gráficas / ICOM, 2011), pp. 1–8.

van de Vall, Renée, 'The Devil and the Details: The Ontology of Contemporary Art in Conservation Theory and Practice', *British Journal of Aesthetics* 55 (2015), 285–302, https://doi.org/10.1093/aesthj/ayv036

13. Futuring Classical Music through Contemporary Visual Art: Innovative Performance and Listening in the Works of the Artist Anri Sala

Noga Rachel Chelouche

In the introduction to this volume, the 'problems' of classical music in the present were introduced. One of them is the *museum problem*, according to which the musical performance 'is trapped in the past,' completely detached from contemporary issues. While this problem is addressed by musicians through different approaches and innovative projects, a fruitful discussion may emerge if we explore musical performances created within the field of visual art.

Since the twentieth century, sound and music have entered the world of visual art in various ways, through different genres such as sound art, video art and performance art, and through collaborations between artists and musicians. These encounters between music and visual art led to the creation of fascinating multimedia works that include sound and music from different styles and genres. In such hybrid works by several contemporary artists, classical compositions that belong to the category of 'concert music' are used and recontextualised.[1] The music in

---

1 Examples of such hybrid works by well-known artists are The Forty Part Motet (2001) a sound installation by Janet Cardiff, based on a composition by Thomas Tallis, and 7 Deaths of Maria Callas (2020) a performance by Marina Abramovich which portrays the singer through arias from famous operatic scenes. Another fascinating artist who frequently incorporates classical music into her work is Annika Kahrs. Through works such as Strings (2010), Our Solo (2021) and Playing to the Birds (2013) she demonstrates a unique approach to classical compositions and to the concert event.

these cases is modified through various practices, suggesting innovative forms of performance and listening.

This chapter focuses on the alternative performance of classical compositions created in the works of the Albanian artist Anri Sala (b. 1974). Sala studied art in Tirana and then moved to Paris where he studied film and video. In 2005 he moved to Berlin where he lives and works today. Sala works with various media including painting, video, installation art and performance. In his time-based works he investigates relationships between image, sound and architecture. Though a visual artist, Sala uses music as a central element in his works. He manipulates the music according to different contexts and artistic ideas, thus creating unconventional performances as well as a unique listening experience.[2] This chapter argues that through his works, Sala enables different perspectives that lead classical music along unpredictable and innovative paths.

Throughout the chapter, I discuss three seminal works created by Sala from the past decade: *The Last Resort* (2017), *The Present Moment* (2014), and *If and Only If* (2018). In each of these, a classical Western composition is the point of departure. In my analysis, I compare the experience created in Sala's artworks to conventional performances in the concert hall by focusing on elements such as space and architecture, extra-musical contexts, fidelity to the musical score, and the use of visual means and technology. My argument is that these artworks, in which the music is very dominant, may be experienced as unique musical performances. Moreover, I claim that these works allow the spectator/listener to rethink customary concert hall conventions, which are associated with the classical Western repertoire.

These conventions, related to different parameters such as the performance practices, the dress code, the expected behaviour of the audience, the architecture and seating arrangement, did not come about by chance. They frame the concert as a unique musical event, and

---

2   One of Sala's major works Ravel, Ravel Unravel (2013) which was made for the French pavilion at the 55th Venice Biennale is analysed by Xenia Hanusiak in her article 'The New Sound of Music: Marina Abramovic's Goldberg + Anri Sala's Ravel Ravel'. Hanusiak relates to the new listening experience created in the works of visual artists: Xenia Hanusiak, 'The New Sound of Music: Marina Abramovic's Goldberg + Anri Sala's Ravel Ravel', *Music and Literature* (2016), 1-8.

increase the aesthetic experience.³ However, in the present, they often preserve norms that do not always coincide with artistic, technological and social changes. Steven Walter points out that throughout history, concerts were more dynamic and evolved according to changing audiences. Nevertheless, the classical musical landscape nowadays (which preserves nineteenth century conventions and approaches) offers 'art that, apart from a few interpretative moments of glory, has become a form of historical preservation'.⁴ I claim that artworks from different fields, such as the works discussed in this chapter, allow a dynamic character, and create enhanced musical experiences. Classical compositions that are strongly associated with the traditional concert event are heard through these works in new and exciting interpretations.

The Last Resort

The first example I will examine is an installation titled *The Last Resort* (2017). This site-specific work was commissioned from Sala by the Kaldor Public Art Projects, an Australian organisation that collaborates with international artists and supports artistic projects in public spaces.⁵ The location chosen for this project was the Observatory Hill Rotunda in Sydney. The geographical site of the installation, as in many of Sala's works, embodies political and cultural references manifested through visual and musical means. In this case, the pastoral Observatory Hill, overlooking the bay and the Harbor Bridge, is a place strongly associated with the colonial history of Sydney. It was where the colonists went to gaze at the stars and chart the weather, and as it was the highest point in the new settlement, it became a lookout point to monitor any ships that might be entering Sydney Harbour.

---

3   In his thorough essay 'A Concert Theory', in which Martin Tröndle relates to the concert as a subject for musicological investigation, these conventions are discussed as part of the evolution of the concert: Martin Tröndle, 'A Concert Theory', in *Classical Concert Studies: A Companion to Contemporary Research and Performance*, ed. by Martin Tröndle (New York: Routledge, 2021), pp. 11–28.

4   Steven Walter, 'A Manifesto of Concert Culture', in *Classical Concert Studies: A Companion to Contemporary Research and Performance*, ed. by Martin Tröndle (New York: Routledge, 2021), pp. 329-335 (p. 329).

5   The organisation was established in 1969 by John Kaldor, an art collector and philanthropist. It supports artistic projects that take place in different locations in Australia. The Last Resort was their 33rd project.

The Last Resort is a sound installation that centres on the Adagio movement from Mozart's Clarinet Concerto in A major, K.622, composed in 1791. Sala's idea regarding the music was to choose a musical piece associated with the Age of Enlightenment and to give it a different historical context.[6] As in other of his works, instead of using a traditional recording 'true to the work,' Sala decided to make changes in the music that will convey his ideas. In his words, he aims to use the music as a 'matter that you take by the hand and accompany towards its own future.'[7] This approach to music as a 'matter' enables the artist to reshape the chosen compositions and make changes, at times quite extreme, in the original score, which in conventional concert practice is perceived as an 'ideal object', realised through repeated performances.[8]

In *The Last Resort*, the changes in the Adagio movement were made according to a literary text chosen by the artist: a private journal by James Bell, a British sailor who made his voyage to the colony of Adelaide, Australia, in the first half of the nineteenth century.[9] Through the new arrangement of Mozart's music according to this text (as detailed below), Sala intended to bring up the complexity of the period, which involved the ideals of liberation along with the devastation of imperialism.[10] In an interview with the philosopher and musicologist Peter Szendy, Sala mentioned the 'contradiction within the departure point and the receiving end.'[11] The departure point in this work is the European Enlightenment represented by the original music by Mozart, and the receiving end is the New World with the rearranged music.

---

6   Anri Sala, interview with the author, Berlin, October 10, 2018. Mozart was highly recognized with ideals of the Enlightenment. He was a member of the Freemasons (and has several Masonic compositions) and a few of his operas convey notions of the Enlightenment. On this topic see: 'Mozart and the Enlightenment' in Richard Ned Lebow, *The Politics and Ethics of Identity: In Search of Ourselves*, (Cambridge: Cambridge University Press, 2012), pp. 110-150.
7   Anri Sala, interview with the author, Berlin, 10 October 2018.
8   Lawrence Kramer, *Why Classical Music Still Matters* (California: University of California Press, 2007), pp. 23.
9   The new interpretation of Mozart with the changes determined by Bell's journal was recorded by the Munich Chamber Orchestra. The recording is repeated throughout the installation.
10 Sala mentions that the Clarinet Concerto was composed a short time after the journey of the first fleet to Australia, which arrived in Sydney in 1788 in order to establish the new British colony in the New World. Anri Sala, 'The Last Resort,' in *Anri Sala: The Last Resort*, Kaldor Public Art Project 33, Exhibition Catalogue, 8.
11 Anri Sala in conversation with Peter Szendy, online video recording, Vimeo, 9 March 2018.

Sala's basic idea for this installation was to imagine a fictional journey of the masterpiece by Mozart on its way to the other side of the world.[12]

Rearrangement of the Music According to the Text

In Bell's journal, each day of the voyage is described first with a comment regarding the weather and the winds.[13] Sala picked different weather descriptions from the text and used them to make rhythmic changes in the score. Each description from the text was summarised to create a basic weather condition such as 'calm,' 'breeze,' 'strong wind,' etc., which was then translated into a rhythmic pattern (see Figure 13.1).

	Wind unfavourable or stiff	Off counter and syncopated, different rhythms, in general quarter pulse
	Hurricane	Syncopated /accentuated + irregular metric
	Calm	Tremolo double tongue staccato pulse – triggering the drumsticks
	Breeze (Mozart)	Eighth pulse
	Strong wind	Triolic
	Breeze +	Sixteenth pulse
	Thunder	Combination of different layers
	Gale	Fast kangaroo

#	Bars	Wind Description	Symbol
1		25 November 1838. Sunday *As our Pilot dreads a squall (...).*	
2	1–8	26 November 1838. Monday *It blows fresh and straight in our face so we cannot stir.*	
3		27 November 1838. Tuesday *Still blows a stiff breeze (...).*	
4	9–15 TUTTI	28 November 1838. Wednesday *After last nights hurricane we have calmer wind and more favourable.*	
5		29 November 1838. Thursday *Dreadful hurricane.*	

Fig. 13.1 Anri Sala, table of wind descriptions: quotes from James Bell's journal and their translation into rhythmic patterns used in *The Last Resort* (2017).
© Anri Sala VG Bild-Kunst, Bonn c/o Pictoright Amsterdam 2023.

In some parts of the rearranged score, if the text indicates calm weather, the music will sound very similar to the original Mozart in triple metre. In different parts, where a chosen quote indicates the instability of the weather, the music will sound unstable and dynamic, with changing

---

12 Sala, 'Anri Sala: The Last Resort', p. 8.
13 The importance of the wind for the journey is one of the reasons Sala chose a concerto for a woodwind instrument.

rhythms and alternating time signatures. The rhythmic alterations in the Adagio movement have influence on other musical parameters of the piece, which now sounds 'relocated' after its journey: the changing rhythms as well as moments of silence that do not exist in the original piece directly affect the symmetry and fluency of Mozart's balanced phrases. The melodic lines are now disrupted by stops and time signature changes, which create frequent accelerations and decelerations. The image of a journey through the ocean becomes very clear in the revised concerto, which sounds as if it is 'carried' by the winds and unpredictable waves. Unlike any traditional performance or recording of Mozart's music, the well-known masterpiece sounds alternately familiar and unpredictable, as intended by Sala:

> My intention was to subvert Mozart's Clarinet Concerto, its flow as a whole, its gravity and its pace, in order to produce the perception of a concert that has travelled a long distance, endured the high seas of journey, making it to another shore, although not necessarily in the original form intended by its creator.[14]

Although the fragmentation in the revised movement derives from ideas related to this specific installation, it is a repeated theme in Sala's art. Fragmentation, or rupture, as Sala refers to it, is an essential part of the rearranged music in different works. For example, in his film *1395 Days Without Red*, it is the first movement of Tchaikovsky's Sixth Symphony that is played non-continuously, and in the video *If and Only If*, it is Stravinsky's Elegy for Solo Viola that undergoes time manipulations. Sala mentions that, to him, 'continuity is not a given [...] in the west there is less disruption in the narrative, fewer earthquakes in the system of values.'[15] According to curator Natalie Bell, and as expressed in different texts and conversations with the artist, the discontinuity and the feeling of rupture goes back to Sala's life in Albania, where he experienced many rapid political and cultural changes. The rupture created by artistic means (and through the music, in Sala's case) is thus related to historical and political complexities.[16] Regarding *The Last Resort*, these complexities are beautifully described by Ross Gibson:

---

14   Sala, 'Anri Sala: The Last Resort', p. 8.
15   Anri Sala in conversation with Peter Szendy.
16   Natalie Bell, 'Eluding Language, Escaping Time', in *Anri Sala: Answer Me*, ed. by Margot Norton and Massimiliano Gioni (New York and London: Phaidon Press, 2016), pp. 52-65 (p. 52).

> Upside down in the Observatory Hill Rotunda, under the wheeling stars that have witnessed every persisting moment of Sydney's time – pre-colonial, colonial and post-colonial – Sala offers not a perfect jewel of leavened rationale but rather a warped disturbance of Mozart's crystalline sonic intricacies. He has troubled the predominantly melodic settings that normally govern the serene and symmetrical piece, transposing its soothing rectitude into a percussive tempo-tattoo so that we hear and see instead a stutter utterer that never settles into a stable pattern and that sounds more bellicose and intemperate than regular and melodious.[17]

It is important to mention that the historical and political contexts which Sala brings forth do not exist in his works as 'fixed ideas', as mentioned by critic John McDonald.[18]

Colonialism in this case, becomes a part of the narrative of the work through its contradiction with the Enlightenment - represented by Mozart's original concerto. Sala combines the different elements – the space, the music, the text and the visual means – in a way that does not emphasise these notions as clear categories. Instead, it portrays them by moving between order and disorder, noise and silence, synchronization and asynchronization.

Other than the duality of Enlightenment and colonialism presented in this work, an implicit duality is created through the juxtaposition of natural forces and human rationality represented by a masterpiece from the Age of Enlightenment. In a review of the *The Last Resort*, McDonald writes about the wind as a natural element that contrasts with the Enlightenment: 'Letting the wind dictate the tempi [...] enacts a struggle between nature and culture, between the Enlightenment dream of perfect control and understanding, and the unruly interruptions of the weather.'[19]

In the interview with Szendy, Sala refers to the notion of natural elements, such as the winds in this work, and points out that he is interested in 'the journey that accompanies the music to its becoming. And very often its becoming could coincide [...] with an element of nature.'[20] Regarding the natural elements that affect the music, he

---

17 Ross Gibson, 'Bumpkin Calculus', in 'Anri Sala: The Last Resort', pp. 26-35 (p. 32).
18 John McDonald, 'Review: Anri Sala's The Last Resort, an Exemplary Work of Public Art', *Sydney Morning Herald*, 17 October 2017, https://www.smh.com.au/entertainment/art-and-design/review-anri-salas-the-last-resort-20171017-gz28qw.html
19 Ibid.
20 Anri Sala in conversation with Peter Szendy.

proposes an aleatoric approach, applied to a pre-existing classical composition: 'I wanted to include another will besides the will of the composer, a *force majeure*, something that overtakes the will of the creator.'[21] Szendy also describes the original presence of nature in *The Last Resort*: 'The breezes and trade winds are omnipresent, but implicitly; they manifest themselves through the traces that they leave on what they have transported, carried, damaged or worn out.'[22]

Rearranged Music: Examples

Let us briefly examine some examples of the actual changes Sala made in the new score according to Bell's text. As well as the addition of time signatures, the relation between the Solo and the Tutti parts is also altered. This can be demonstrated with the opening bars of the second theme of the movement (see Figure 13.2), in which the theme played by the clarinet originally starts, together with the orchestra, on the first beat:

Fig. 13.2 Wolfgang Amadeus Mozart, Clarinet Concerto in A major (1791), Adagio, beginning of 2nd theme, mm. 17-20, CC BY-SA 4.0.

---

21 Richard Jinman, 'Anri Sala's The Last Resort Transforms Sydney's Observatory Hill Rotunda', *Sydney Morning Herald*, 3 October 2017, https://www.smh.com.au/entertainment/art-and-design/anri-salas-the-last-resort-transforms-sydneys-observatory-hill-rotunda-20171002-gysqht.html

22 Peter Szendy, 'Aeolian Reflections (Mozart Exposed to the Winds)', in 'Anri Sala: The Last Resort', pp. 14-25 (p. 14).

What we see next in Figure 13.3 (the same bars as they appear in Sala's revised score) is a quote that, according to the table of weather descriptions, follows the instruction: 'Off counter and syncopated, different rhythms, in general quarter pulse.' The clarinet part, which originally starts on the first beat, is now shifted and delayed. This shift is heard clearly in the installation.

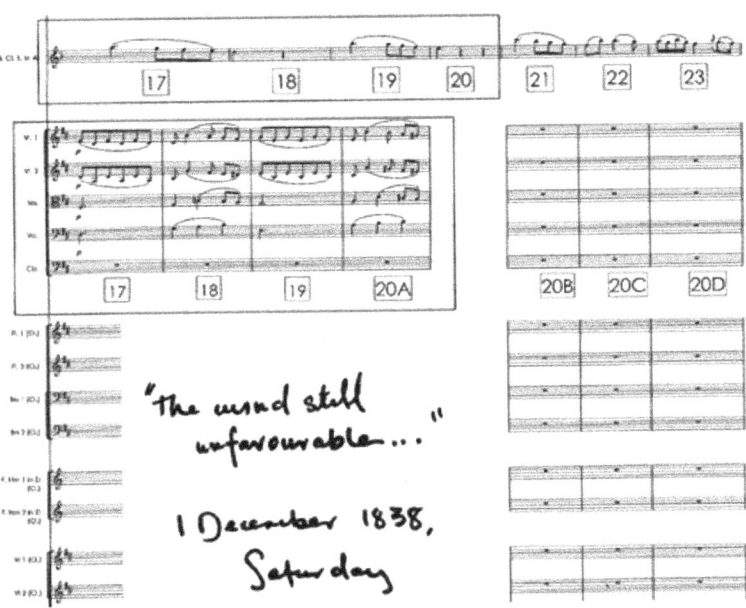

Fig. 13.3 Anri Sala, excerpt from the score of *The Last Resort*: Based on Mozart's Clarinet Concerto in A major, Adagio, mm. 17-23 © Anri Sala VG Bild-Kunst, Bonn c/o Pictoright Amsterdam 2023.

After a few bars, a new quote appears: '6 December 1838. Thursday. The fine breeze yesterday, which gradually veered round to northwest.' Following the table, this quote indicates calm weather, which returns the music to Mozart's order. The clarinet is not playing in this passage, but the theme played by the first violin section and the flutes returns in its 'right' place, starting on the first beat.

This imperfect version, suggested by Sala, creates an unusual way of listening to the original parts of the music, which become far less predictable. This innovative reworking of Mozart's well-known music is not heard in its original flow, but rather as a collage in which unbalanced, and less harmonious parts appear alternately with moments where the original order returns.

Visual Means in *The Last Resort*

In addition to the rearranged score, the visual means in *The Last Resort* create another significant change in the music, specifically regarding the orchestration. The recorded music is heard through loudspeakers concealed inside thirty-eight snare drums that are hung from the ceiling of the rotunda. Instead of the passive sitting in the concert hall, aimed at focussing the audience's attention on the performers,[23] the spectator/listener hears the music while walking around underneath the source of the sound. Each snare drum has a pair of drumsticks attached. Inside each drum, there are two loudspeakers: one propagates inaudible infrasounds that vibrate the drumheads and move the sticks, and from the other one, the rearranged music is heard.[24] Sala enlarges the orchestra by using a whole section playing in correspondence with the recorded music, reacting to its vibrations.[25] This new percussion section suggests an interesting juxtaposition between the classical orchestra and the snare drum, which is Sala's modern addition to Mozart.

Two kinds of dialogues are created in the installation. The first is between two sources of sound: the recorded music heard from the speakers and the live drumming, which is a reaction to it. The second dialogue is between a typical classical ensemble of the eighteenth century and the snare drum, which was considered both a folk and military instrument, but was less common in compositions for the classical orchestra.[26]

---

23 On the gradual process of focusing the audience's attention in concert halls see Christian Thorau, 'From Program Leaflets to Listening Apps', in *Classical Concert Studies: A Companion to Contemporary Research and Performance*, ed. by Martin Tröndle (New York: Routledge, 2021), pp. 61-80.
24 Peter Szendy, 'Aeolian Reflections (Mozart Exposed to the Winds)', p. 16.
25 Another example for the juxtaposition of live and recorded music is Sala's work 3-2-1 (Serpentine Gallery, 2011), where the saxophonist Andre Vida reacts with live improvisations to the video work Long Sorrow, which focuses on the free-jazz playing of saxophonist Jemeel Moondoc.
26 Rey M. Longyear, 'The Domestication of the Snare Drum' in *Percussionist* 3 (1965), 1–2.

Another important parameter that dramatically changes the work, compared to a standard performance of classical music, is the active and immersive listening experience created by the unique design of the installation. The modern concert hall enables an attentive listening by creating a passive and silenced audience. As described by Lewis Kaye, 'traditional musical performance, and the practice of architectural acoustics, tends toward privileging a single, well-defined source transmitted to an undifferentiated mass of passive, silenced consumers'.[27] In *The Last Resort*, as in other installations by Sala, the sound design enables unconventional listening which involves movement and changes the conventional separation between listener and performer.

Other Versions of *The Last Resort*

Although this work is the result of a site-specific project exhibited first in Sydney, it has also been exhibited in New York (at the Marian Goodman Gallery), in Moscow (at the Garage Museum of Contemporary Art), in Luxemburg (at the MUDAM Museum), and in Houston (at the Moody Center for the Arts at Rice University). As opposed to the generic concert hall, the different spaces and locations of Sala's installations enable modifications to his original work. Each space has a different architecture and acoustic conditions, which affect the construction of the installation as well as the listening experience created in each specific exhibition. For example, in Sydney, the installation was located outdoors, next to Sydney's harbour.[28] In Moscow, by contrast, it was located indoors, in a 9.5-metre-high atrium. Another important variation in the version of the work exhibited in Moscow was the inclusion of a live ensemble (the Studio for New Music ensemble) that joined and played next to the installation at the opening of the exhibition (see Figures 13.4 and 13.5). The ensemble surrounded the audience and played Sala's version of the Adagio. The same music that was recorded for the installation

---

27   Lewis Kaye, 'The Silenced Listener: Architectural Acoustics, the Concert Hall and the Conditions of Audience' in *Leonardo Music Journal* 22 (2012), pp. 63-65 (p. 64-65).

28   An excerpt from the installation in its first version in Sydney is available on YouTube: Anri Sala: The Last Resort/Kaldor Public Art Projects, Sydney online video recording, YouTube, 30 October 2017, https://www.youtube.com/watch?v=yeFNzhQ_n7I

was performed live this time and heard alternately or in parallel with the drums.

Fig. 13.4 Anri Sala, *The Last Resort* (2017), installation and live performance, Garage Museum for Contemporary Art, Moscow. © Ivan Erofeev, Anton Donikov.

Fig.13.5 The soloist, located above the orchestra. Anri Sala, *The Last Resort* (2017), installation and live performance, Garage Museum for Contemporary Art, Moscow. © Ivan Erofeev, Anton Donikov.

In any version of The Last Resort, the installation may be experienced as an innovative musical event. The traditional concerts, as described by Lydia Goher, are 'transitory sound events intended to present a work by complying as closely as possible with the given notational specification'.[29] In this case, as in other works by Sala, the multiple versions suggest

---

29   Lydia Goehr, 'Being true to the work' in *The Journal of Aesthetics and Art Criticism* 47:1 (1989), 55-67 (p. 55).

versatile performances of the music, which keeps going through modifications according to the changing venues and the given context of each event or exhibition.

The Present Moment

A work that deals with similar themes in a different way is Sala's 2014 work *The Present Moment*.[30] This work is charged with historical tension created by the chosen composition and the space where the work was first exhibited. It is a video and sound installation commissioned by the German project 'Der Öffentlichkeit—Von den Freunden Haus der Kunst' (To the Public—From the Friends of Haus der Kunst) that explores the relationship between art and the museum as a space of public culture.[31]

I will focus on its first exhibition, which took place at the museum Haus der Kunst in Munich. Nowadays, this is a museum for contemporary art, but originally it was built by the Nazis in order to display what the party considered 'Great German Art.'[32] The building remains in its original design, which features the neoclassicist German architecture that characterised Nazi buildings. The work was installed in the central hall, formerly known as the Hall of Honour (Ehrenhalle). This hall was used for speeches at openings of the Große Deutsche Kunstausstellung (Great German Art Exhibition) held in the building between 1937 and 1944.[33] In contrast to the monumental architecture of the space, Sala chose a chamber music composition for this project. The choice of this genre, which is associated with the act of conversation and social activity among musicians, creates a contradiction with the

---

30 There are two versions of this work: The Present Moment in D and The Present Moment in Bb. They are independent versions; each one focuses on the D notes and the Bb notes, respectively. The two versions were also exhibited simultaneously as a single installation at the New Museum in New York and at the Instituto Moreira Salles in Rio de Janeiro.

31 Okwui Enwezor, 'Foreword', in *Anri Sala: The Present Moment*, Exhibition Catalogue ed. by Patrizia Dander (Cologne: Walther Konig, 2015), pp. 11-15 (p. 11).

32 Anri Sala and Massimiliano Gioni, 'Guided by Voices, Lured by Sounds: An Interview', in *Anri Sala: Answer Me*, ed. by Margot Norton and Massimiliano Gioni (New York and London: Phaidon Press, 2016), pp. 80-96 (p. 96).

33 Patrizia Dander, 'Notes on The Present Moment', in *Anri Sala: The Present Moment*, Exhibition Catalogue ed. by Patrizia Dander (Cologne: Walther Konig, 2015), pp. 44-54 (p. 44). For more information about the Ehrenhalle, see Sabine Brantl's article 'On the History of the Former "Ehrenhalle,"' Ibid., pp. 83-85.

hierarchical arrangement of the space, which was originally used for propaganda.[34]

The musical piece chosen as a point of departure for this work is the string sextet *Verklärte Nacht* (*Transfigured Night*, 1899) by Arnold Schoenberg, whose work was considered 'degenerate' by the Nazis. This is a post-romantic piece to which, as detailed below, Sala applies changes that allude to the later Schoenberg and his twelve-tone system. This composition is an instrumentalisation of a poem of the same title by the German poet Richard Dehmel. It was composed as a single movement by the young Schoenberg, who was then pushing the bounds of tonality without fully over-reaching them, with the piece starting in D minor which transforms to D major.

Installation Structure

The music in the installation is heard through nineteen loudspeakers grouped in different locations in the hall.[35] In two spots, at the entrance and at the end of the hall (marked by letters A and D in the layout of the installation on the right side of Figure 13.6), the loudspeakers are hung in a semi-circular shape (see installation view on the left side of Figure 13.6). This arrangement refers to the seating of the ensemble members in the video projected at the last part of the installation.[36] The work consists of four parts that lead the listeners through the hall and through different soundtracks, each one exploring a transformation of the original sextet. The music gradually wanders through the loudspeakers, creating a path of sounds that ends with a video projection. At each phase of the work, one or two sections of loudspeakers are active. Sala describes the general progression of the work as

> a journey of sounds that saunter through the hall before they eventually end up in a film hidden at the very end of the space [...] the focus of *The Present Moment* is a chamber-sized composition and the journey of its ensuing sounds across a large public space.[37]

---

34 Ibid., p. 45.
35 In this part, I give a description of the D version of the installation, based on the catalogue from the exhibition at Haus der Kunst.
36 'The Present Moment, ANRI SALA,' in EstherSchipper.com, https://www.estherschipper.com/exhibitions/156/
37 Sala and Gioni, 'Guided by Voices, Lured by Sounds,' p. 96.

A fundamental element of this work is the space, along with the sound that travels through it. Curator and art critic Okwui Enwezor described it as a 'choreography of sounds' that leads the listener through the journey of the composition.[38] Music's temporal dimension, which is explored in different works by Sala, is especially emphasised in this installation: Schoenberg's composition travels through the hall with its original development determined by the composer and with constant transformations suggested by Sala. Thus, as the music travels through the space, the inherent quality of music as an art that unfolds through time is physically perceived.

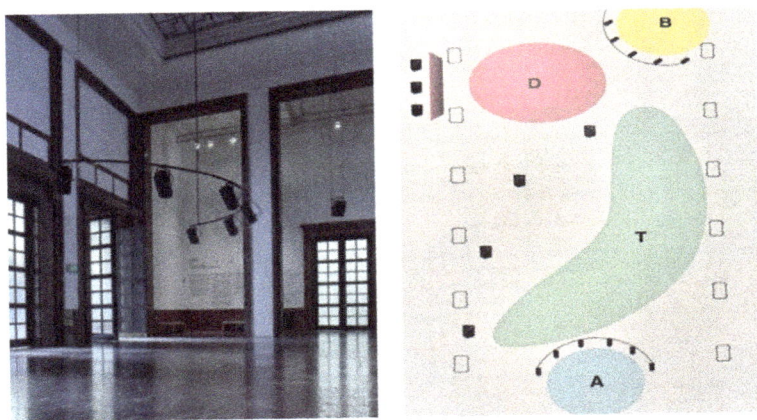

Fig. 13.6 Left: Anri Sala, *The Present Moment (In D)* (2014), Haus der Kunst, Munich. © *Jens Weber*. Right: Physical layout of speakers and projection of *The Present Moment (in D)* at Haus der Kunst.

Musical Transformation

The progression of the installation, which dictates the spectator/listener's movement in the space, is based on Sala's idea of leading the musical piece on a fictional journey to its nonconventional future. In this case, the point of departure is the post-romantic original, and the destination is an imagined dodecaphonic version of it. Sala's idea regarding Schoenberg's music was to gradually isolate specific tones from the piece in a process that refers to dodecaphonic rules: at the

---

38   Enwazor, 'Foreword,' p. 12.

first point (A), the original sextet is heard. Then, Sala applies the basic rule of the twelve-tone series. He does this by filtering notes that repeat themselves before the eleven other tones are played. In the T part, with its four loudspeakers, the music is heard with its revised serial version.[39] Then, in the B part, another metamorphosis occurs as each tone that made it through the elimination now repeats itself with the same rhythmic values until the next tone of the series appears. Finally, in the D part, in which the film is projected, the music goes through one last transformation: the series is reduced only to repeated D notes. These Ds are gradually isolated from the original piece, and eventually they are repeated according to the rhythmic patterns of *Verklärte Nacht*.[40] The process is perhaps easier to comprehend with Sala's description of the musical journey:

> Upon entering the hallway where *Verklärte Nacht* is played, solitary notes from the appearance of each new tone in Schoenberg's score and brief musical gestures are released and drift across the space, as if expelled from the main body of the music. As these reach the far end of the hall, they accumulate and play repetitively, seemingly trapped in a dead end, a space where acoustic memory is condensed.[41]

As mentioned above, at each phase of the work, one or two groups of loudspeakers are active. This means that the different stages described here do not occur exactly one after the other but in different combinations and in a nonlinear process of four phases, carefully planned. The process ends with the D repetitions played by the sextet, which the spectator/listener can now see in the projected video. At the same time, the original composition is heard from afar as it is played in the A section (located at the starting point of the installation).[42]

---

39 In this part, each tone is heard four times, once through each speaker. In the recording of this soundtrack, the notes are actually played quickly one after the other, without digital intervention.
40 Peter Szendy, 'The Bent Ear', in *Anri Sala: The Present Moment*, Exhibition Catalogue ed. by Patrizia Dander (Cologne: Walther Konig, 2015), pp. 69-80 (p. 70-71).
41 Anri Sala, 'The Present Moment (in D)', in *Anri Sala: The Present Moment*, Exhibition Catalogue ed. by Patrizia Dander (Cologne: Walther Konig, 2015), p. 17.
42 Szendy, 'The Bent Ear', p. 72.

Visual Means in *The Present Moment*

This work, in its first version exhibited at the Haus der Kunst, is a video and sound installation but it takes a while before the music is joined by the main visual element (the film). In the first phases of *The Present Moment*, sound dominates. Another visual dimension that exists throughout the whole work as it was exhibited in Haus der Kunst is the lighting: the different phases of the installation are characterized by different levels of light that are gradually dimmed. Eventually the video becomes the source of illumination, with the other lights switched off.[43]

The video projected at the end of the installation focuses on the physical gestures involved in playing the music. It appears in parallel with the last transformation of the composition, where only the D notes are repeated (see stills from the video in Figures 13.7 and 13.8). This repetitive texture is overlaid with images of bow movements, hands and elbows. As in other works by Sala in which he focuses on the physical act of sound production, here too the physical gestures involved in the act of playing the music are visually emphasised.

Fig. 13.7 Anri Sala, installation view of *The Present Moment (In D)* (2014), video projection added in the last phase of the revised music. Haus der Kunst, Munich. © Jens Weber.

---

43   Dander, 'Notes on The Present Moment', p. 48.

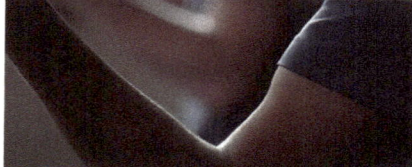 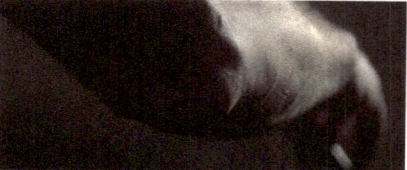

Fig. 13.8 Anri Sala, *The Present Moment (In D)* (2014), Haus der Kunst, Munich
© Anri Sala.

The sextet by Schoenberg is heard through Sala's work in a new version that consists of multiple soundtracks, starting with the original composition, which is gradually transformed. This transformation suggests an unconventional execution of the post-romantic piece in a dodecaphonic version. Whereas in many of Sala's works the musical changes are determined by what can be categorised as extramusical ideas, in this case the musical changes lie in the music itself: a modern composition technique is applied to an earlier piece composed in a different style. As in *The Last Resort*, here too the progression of the composition and the sound design of the installation enable an alternative listening experience, which consists of movement as the spectator/listener walks through the hall and follows the travelling sounds.

If and Only If

The last work I will briefly discuss is *If and Only If* (2018), a video work based on Stravinsky's Elegy for Solo Viola (1944). The Elegy, which is composed mostly in a two-voice texture, is played by the soloist Gérard Caussé, who is filmed with a second protagonist: a garden snail that makes its journey from the lower end of the violist's bow to the tip. The film is nine minutes forty-seven seconds in duration, approximately twice as long as the original musical piece. Sala aimed to synchronise the music with the journey of the snail. Thus, in order to gain time, he made some modifications to the original score: the first consists of splitting the two voices in specific parts and playing each voice separately, and the second consists of repetitions of notes, which the soloist plays when the snail does not move.[44]

---

44 Anri Sala, interview with the author, Berlin, 10 October 2018.

Figure 13.9 is extracted from the score used by Sala. It is Stravinsky's original score, notated in red and blue according to the division of the two voices. This part, as it is played in the film, demonstrates both the manipulation of voice splitting and the repetition (these manipulations are heard but not written in the score). Bar 11 starts with the two voices played simultaneously. The notes B-flat and D are still played together as a harmonic interval, and from that point, only the upper voice (starting from the B-flat half note) continues independently until the end of bar 14. Then, the music goes back to where the voices split in bar 11, and the lower voice is played, starting with the coupled eighth notes of D-flat and E-flat (end of bar 11), which are repeated twice before moving on to the next bar. Eventually, the two voices are played together again in bar 15:

Fig. 13.9 Igor Stravinsky, mm. 11-15 from the Elegy for Solo Viola, score used by Anri Sala for the film *If and Only If* (2018) © Anri Sala VG Bild-Kunst, Bonn c/o Pictoright Amsterdam 2023.

As a result of the two voices being played separately, we clearly hear each one as if it is part of an independent melody. Although all the notes are played, the two-voice texture sometimes disappears throughout the work. In this way, and also by means of repetition, the soloist gains time and adjusts himself to the movement of the snail.

In Sala's film, Stravinsky's solo piece becomes a speechless 'dialogue' between Caussé and the silent snail that determines the progression of the Elegy. The two are making the journey together, the snail to the end of the bow and the musician to the end of the piece. The result is a unique performance of the Elegy, created by adding another participant that is mute yet very dominant.[45]

---

45 The performance of a soloist in the context of a dialogue also occurs in Sala's work Ravel Ravel Unravel (2013), first exhibited at the 55th Venice Biennale. The composition in the centre of this installation is Ravel's Piano Concerto for the Left Hand, which is performed by two soloists instead of one. The two pianists go

Fig. 13.10 Anri Sala, *If and Only If* (2017) the exhibition AS YOU GO (2019), Castello di Rivoli Museum of Contemporary Art, Turin © The author, 23 April, 2019.

Different Exhibitions

If and Only If is another example of how Sala's works may be experienced in various ways through different performances. The film has been shown in several exhibitions so far. One took place in Galerie Chantal Crousel in Paris in 2018 and had the same title as the film. In this exhibition, Sala used works from different media (paintings, sculptures, films), where 'each work explores in its own way and with the means of its medium, the impact of a singular action – i.e. a manipulation – on an existing situation, composition or object.'[46] In this exhibition, another film was projected in a different space. This film, entitled *Slip of the Line* (2018), has the same duration as *If and Only If*. During the exhibition, the two films were projected in parallel, and the result was that the Elegy (heard

---

in and out of synchronisation, creating another layer of interaction added to the traditional soloist-orchestra relation.

46 'Anri Sala: If and Only If' in GalleriesNow, https://www.galleriesnow.net/shows/anri-sala-2/#

in one space) functioned both as the central element of *If and Only If* and as a sort of a soundtrack of the second film, *Slip of the Line* (screened in another space).⁴⁷

Another solo exhibition where the work was exhibited was AS YOU GO, at the Castello di Rivoli Museum for Contemporary Art. In this exhibition, *If and Only If* was part of a film made of three video works: *Ravel Ravel* (2013), *Take Over* (2017), and *If and Only If* (2018). The film was projected in parts of the exhibition on two screens, which created a corridor where the spectator/listener could walk (see Figure 13.11).

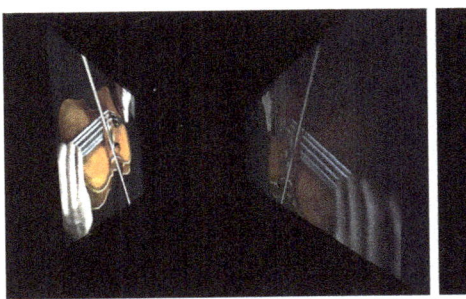

Fig. 13.11 Anri Sala, *If and Only If* (2018) the exhibition AS YOU GO (2019), Castello di Rivoli Museum of Contemporary Art, Turin © The author, 23 April, 2019.

The projected film consisted only of music-based works, so the result in my experience as a visitor was an alternative concert: I could remain in the same place and watch/listen, and I could also move in the corridor and feel totally immersed in sound and image. In addition, the video moved forward not only in time but also in space. As it moved from one room to the other, I could decide whether to follow it or not.

The consistent movement of the films may 'walk' the spectators through the exhibition, but they may also remain in one space while the films move – an option that allows interesting moments of music that are unsynchronised with the image. The fact that the films are screened repeatedly enables exploration of all options: the audience may experience this 'concert' once from a certain distance while facing the screen, and again by walking in-between the two screens. They may

---

47 Anri Sala, interview with the author, Berlin, 30 October 2018.

also walk with the moving image or remain still and wait for the film to come into view again.

Conclusion

Throughout this chapter, I have addressed the 'museum problem' by exploring artworks from the field of visual art in which a classical composition is a central element. I argue that different artworks, as the three cases discussed here, have the potential to create new possibilities and enable an extended musical experience that does not conform to the concert hall conventions.

Each work discussed in this chapter demonstrates a classical Western composition which is heard and performed in a unique and untraditional manner. I described the original contexts added by Sala to the musical works and showed how historical, political, social and artistic contexts led him to the uncommon practice of changing the original musical scores. I demonstrated how the revised compositions are heard in Sala's works (usually recorded, and sometimes also performed live) in combination with the visual means that enhances the musical experience.

Sala's works are displayed in spaces such as museums and galleries (or outside in locations chosen for site-specific works such as *The Last Resort*). The architecture of each space, as well as the sound design (an essential element in Sala's works), create an immersive and more active listening experience, different from the standard concert-hall experience. Heard as a part of an installation and in the context of a visual art exhibition, the music surrounds the listeners, who may explore different possibilities of movement or stillness. The traditional listening experience is also modified as a result of the nonlinear course of the exhibition: unlike the traditional concert, the music in each work is heard repeatedly, and visitors may walk in and out at any time. In addition, the juxtaposition of different music-based works at the same exhibition creates moments in which the different compositions are heard simultaneously, suggesting a fascinating auditory experience.

In the three works I examined, the music does not function as a soundtrack to an artwork or an exhibition, but rather, as part of a hybrid work in which it is combined with different media such as video, installation, and performance. Sala's approach to classical music, as a dynamic creation that enables transformations, brings forth interesting perspectives regarding the future of classical music. I find his works inspiring for both musicians and musicologists, as well as for the listener, who might discover new ways to appreciate and interact with classical music today.

References

Bell, Natalie, 'Eluding Language, Escaping Time', in *Anri Sala: Answer Me*, ed. by Margot Norton and Massimiliano Gioni (New York and London: Phaidon Press, 2016), pp. 52-65.

Dander, Patrizia, 'Notes on *The Present Moment*', in *Anri Sala: The Present Moment*, Exhibition Catalogue, ed. by Patrizia Dander (Cologne: Walther Konig, 2015), pp. 44-54.

Enwezor, Okwui, 'Foreword', in *Anri Sala: The Present Moment*, ed. by Dander, pp. 11-15.

GalleriesNow, *Anri Sala: If and Only If at Galerie Chantal Crousel*, https://www.galleriesnow.net/shows/anri-sala-2

Gibson, Ross, 'Bumpkin Calculus', in *Anri Sala: The Last Resort*, Exhibition Catalogue, ed. by Genevieve O'Callaghan, (Sydney: Kaldor Public Art Projects 2017), pp. 26-35.

Goehr, Lydia, 'Being True to the Work', *The Journal of Aesthetics and Art Criticism* 47:1 (1989), 55-67, https://doi.org/10.2307/431993

Jinman, Richard, 'Anri Sala's The Last Resort Transforms Sydney's Observatory Hill Rotunda', *The Sydney Morning Herald*, 3 October 2017, https://www.smh.com.au/entertainment/art-and-design/anri-salas-the-last-resort-transforms-sydneys-observatory-hill-rotunda-20171002-gysqht.html

Kaye, Lewis, 'The Silenced Listener: Architectural Acoustics, the Concert Hall and the Conditions of Audience', *Leonardo Music Journal* 22 (2012), 63-65, https://doi.org/10.1162/lmj_a_00100

Kramer, Lawrence, *Why Classical Music Still Matters* (California: University of California Press, 2007), https://doi.org/10.1525/9780520933644

Longyear, Rey M, 'The Domestication of the Snare Drum', *Percussionist* 3 (1965), 1–2.

McDonald, John, 'Review: Anri Sala's The Last Resort: an Exemplary Work of Public Art', *The Sydney Morning Herald*, 17 October 2017, https://www.smh.com.au/entertainment/art-and-design/review-anri-salas-the-last-resort-20171017-gz28qw.html

Sala, Anri, 'The Last Resort', in *Anri Sala: The Last Resort*, ed. by O'Callaghan, p. 8.

—— 'The Present Moment (in D)', in *Anri Sala: The Present Moment*, ed. by Dander, p. 17.

Sala, Anri and Massimiliano Gioni, 'Guided by Voices, Lured by Sounds: An Interview', in *Anri Sala: Answer Me*, ed. by Norton and Gioni, pp. 80-96.

Schipper, Esther, *The Present Moment | Anri Sala*, https://www.estherschipper.com/exhibitions/156/

Szendy, Peter, 'Aeolian Reflections (Mozart Exposed to the Winds)', in *Anri Sala: The Last Resort*, ed. by O'Callaghan, pp. 14-25.

—— 'The Bent Ear', in *Anri Sala: The Present Moment*, ed. by Dander, pp. 69-80.

Tröndle, Martin, 'A Concert Theory', in *Classical Concert Studies: A Companion to Contemporary Research and Performance*, ed. by Martin Tröndle (New York: Routledge, 2021), pp. 11–28, https://doi.org/10.4324/9781003013839-3

Vimeo, 'Anri Sala in Conversation in Peter Szendy,' 2018.

Walter, Steven, 'A Manifesto of Concert Culture', in *Classical Concert Studies*, ed. by Tröndle, pp. 329-335, https://doi.org/10.4324/9781003013839-40

14. Changing Rooms: A Diary of Spatial Innovation

Neil Thomas Smith

This is an exploration of attempts to innovate concert spaces. The aim is to contribute to efforts in appraising, and sensitising ourselves to, their musical possibilities. Already a hot topic in attempts to innovate the classical music concert, the pandemic has seen an unprecedented (if enforced) explosion of experimentation in this area, whether online, outdoors, or in unusual buildings. What we have learnt from these experiences is far from clear. Indeed, vacating the concert hall may simply make people desperate to return. This chapter presents a diary of unconventional concert spaces, two pre- and four post-pandemic. It explores the effects of spatial innovation, providing insights for the future of performances outside the concert hall.

Evaluating space in concert settings poses distinct challenges, in particular the difficulties of isolating the space itself from other elements of performance. In a chapter that attempts to get closer to what space can mean to the concert experience, it is important to realise that there can be no direct comparison between particular spaces. All the elements that go into concert experience – occasion, time, individual performance, audience; not to mention the vagaries of listeners' moods and the complexities of their trajectories – mean that even the same piece in a different space (the most seemingly direct means of comparison) cannot give an incontrovertible sense of how space acts on performance, though such circumstances may well be informative. Performers, after all, are in constant dialogue with the space in a feedback loop that can have radical effects on their interpretation. No violinist would play Bach Sonatas in a deadly dry 'black box' auditorium as they would in a boomy cathedral.

Many scholars of sound and space are also keen to stress the two-way relationship between space and sound. It is not a pre-existing container for sound to fill.[1] Rather, as Georgina Born argues, space '[a]s an artefact of musical or artistic practice' is 'both *produced* and *transformed*.'[2] This poses challenges when choosing an analytical approach that is open to such subtleties, yet it also makes clear how important is the connection between space and musical experience as an object of study.[3]

Some of the performances explored below are themselves set up as concert formats with an explicitly spatial theme: outdoor performance, for example, or performance in two locations in the same evening. The traditional Western concert experience is fractured in these events, which makes them more revealing as regards the influence of spatial dynamics. Part of the power of the traditional Western concert as a ritual is the way its parts mutually support one another: for example, the canon as a collection of works worthy of complete attention is enforced by separation between audience and musicians, the prohibition of bodily movement, busts of great composers and artists (and patrons), and the hermeticism of the hall. Hennion describes the 'immediacy' of the concert as the 'paradoxical result of a lengthy sequence of mediations', which are not only spatial but also temporal, in that the audience must put themselves 'in the right frame of mind' via a 'series of different stages, none of which can be ignored'.[4] Tampering with this well-established sequence can have unexpected consequences for the concert as a social, as well as musical, event.

---

1 C.f. Nigel Thrift, 'Re-animating the place of thought: Transformations of spatial and temporal description in the twenty-first century' in *Community, Economic Creativity, and Organization*, ed. by A. Amin and S. Roberts (Oxford: Oxford University Press, 2009), pp. 90-119; 'Understanding the Affective Spaces of Political Performance' in Emotion, Place and Culture, ed. by L. Bondi, L. Cameron, J. Davidson, M. Smith (Aldershot: Ashgate, 2016), pp. 79-96.
2 Georgina Born, 'Introduction – music, sound and space: transformations of public and private experience' in *Music, Sound, and Space: Transformations of Public and Private Experience*, ed. by Georgina Born (Oxford: Oxford University Press, 2013), pp. 1–69 (p. 20).
3 This can be seen in the various disciplinary angles from which the question of music and space can be approached. For example, by historians, architects, acousticians, geographers, anthropologists and musicians.
4 Antoine Hennion, 'Music Lovers: Taste as Performance' in *Theory, Culture & Society* 18:5 (2001), 1–22 (p. 13).

From a spatial perspective, it is hard to penetrate the important questions of changing spaces for musical performance when presented with the smooth exterior of such traditional concerts. Thinking about how the sound intersects with the concert hall begins to stray too easily into criticism of performance, or the well-worn descriptions of their acoustics as 'warm', 'dry', 'uneven', or 'lively'. Acoustic criticism of this nature already assumes an acoustic ideal, based on nineteenth-century models.[5] It does not leave much room for different acoustic characters that are in themselves unique or unusual. Gieryn states that buildings 'do as much to structure social relations by *concealing* as by revealing, and therein lies their distinctive force for structuring social relations and practices.'[6] Concert halls are superb examples of this concealment, while events that break the mould provide more purchase for probing the music-space relationship.

The questions of space in performance are not just of theoretical importance. This is an area that is being explored by a huge number of arts organisations. The concert hall is an 'institutional' arts space and, as such, carries with it certain baggage: high art, disciplined silence, little participation. The majority of classical institutions are aware of this and have used space as an explicit means of trying to open up the concert experience. These attempts often link alternative spaces with a sense of *informality*: a more relaxed attitude that is open to different people. This is a significant reason behind orchestras in parks, contemporary music in nightclubs, and pop-up performances in train stations and shopping centres.[7] In fact, space is often one of the first resources that organisations draw on in order to give a sense of excitement and innovation to their projects. While this can be effective, and the intentions are admirable, it might also be too easy a fix: changing space alone is unlikely to achieve the goals of improving classical music's reach and demographic appeal. Concert-hall discipline is not just in the concert hall but in the habits and practices

---

5   See Darryl Cressman, *Building Culture in Nineteenth-Century Amsterdam: The Concertgebouw* (Amsterdam: Amsterdam University Press, 2016).

6   Thomas F. Gieryn, 'What Buildings Do' in *Theory and Society* 31:1 (2002), 25–74 (p. 38). Emphasis in original.

7   Julia Haferkorn, 'Dancing to another tune: classical music in nightclubs and other non-traditional venues', in *The Classical Music Industry*, ed. by Christopher Dromey and Julia Haferkorn (Abingdon: Routledge, 2018), pp. 148–171.

of the people raised within its traditions. Moving space, therefore, but with a majority of the same audience, may displace these practices rather than radically challenge them.

The Diary Approach

The effects of classical music's spatial innovations will be explored in relation to three themes that emerge from a concert diary kept by me between 2019-2021. For this diary I at first sought out concerts that were exploring space in an unusual manner, visiting two of these before the pandemic and its subsequent lockdowns in the UK forced the majority of concerts to innovate spatially in some way. The diary entries were then analysed inductively and three themes isolated. The first theme, *audience and engagement*, isolates passages from the diary that explore whether and in what way unusual performance spaces involve new publics. The second looks at *acoustic*, which becomes particularly important in outdoor performance, or performance in larger buildings, such as railway stations. Finally, the third section explores passages that are relevant to the relationship between interior musical experience and the classical tradition, here labelled *listening and place*. The ability of music to take the listener 'out' of their immediate environment is discussed and, in particular, its intersection with the 'placed' listening that site-specific events encourage.

The following reflections are designed to raise these issues while discussing real live concert events in cities in Scotland (Edinburgh, Glasgow and Aberdeen) and in London. What follows is no quasi-scientific exploration of music in different spaces, but a series of reflections on – mostly unusual – classical performance spaces, which I approached with the explicit aim of thinking about how the space affects the performance. As a composer of, and researcher on, new music, space has always been a fascinating resource to me, though one that it is difficult to make work as well in reality as it does in the imagination.[8]

---

[8] In a similar vein, Blesser and Salter critique spatialised musical performance: 'Placing performers below, above, behind, or to the side of listeners is not intrinsically interesting... Spatial music is interesting precisely because, and only because, it allows combinations of musical elements that would otherwise be artistically weak without using spatial distribution.' Barry Blesser and Linda-Ruth

This study is part of a wider project looking at spatial innovation within the classical sector, which was part of the Maastricht Centre for the Innovation of Classical Music's (MCICM's) research line that explored the societal relevance of classical music. In particular, the project looked at attempts to create new concert halls.[9] The diary material is presented here as a series of scenes that relate to the three themes. These are followed by commentaries that further tease out the challenges and implications of the observations, relating them to relevant literature on space and musical performance.

Clearly, this is a personal story: people have personal reactions to space just as they do to sound. Jonathan Sterne argues that there is 'no "mere" or innocent description of interior auditory experience,'[10] rather our own histories shape our inner auditory worlds: 'what we hear is influenced by how we are allowed, and have been taught, to hear' as Leyshon et al. put it. As a regular attendee not only of traditional concerts but of new music events and festivals, I have a keen interest in the craft of composition and in novel musical experiences. Through education and experience I am a listener at ease in the concert environment, which gives me a large bank of concerts to which I can compare the events described below, but does very much make me a concert 'insider'. This is significant considering that space is often called upon to make the art form more accessible. I cannot judge such attempts in terms of my own feelings of being welcomed or feeling involved, but I can observe my musical reactions and the behaviour of the audience at large.

Ethnography, therefore, is the chosen tool for this chapter as it is well placed to engage with complex questions of spatial dynamics. It can approach the complexity of spatial-sonic experience, with Born stating that there is a 'multiplicity of any human's subject's experience of

---

Salter, *Spaces Speak, Are You Listening?: Experiencing Aural Architecture* (Cambridge, Mass: MIT Press, 2007), p. 169.

9   Neil Thomas Smith and Peter Peters, 'Music for Buildings; Building for Music' in *The Routledge Companion to Applied Musicology*, ed. by Chris Dromey, forthcoming; Neil Thomas Smith, 'Concrete Culture: The Planning Hearing as a Stage for Cultural Debates' in *Cultural Sociology* 16:2 (2022), 147–164; Neil Thomas Smith, 'Constructing the Public Concert Hall' in *Journal of the Royal Musical Association* 146:2 (2021), 255–281.

10 Jonathan Sterne, *The Audible Past: Cultural Origins in Sound Reproduction* (Durham, N.C.: Duke University Press, 2003), p. 19.

music and sound as s/he inhabits a particular physical or virtual space, performance venue or site', something that is complicated further by the 'social multiplicities' of these same spaces, as well as the nuances that emerge from subtle changes in spatial arrangements.[11] Hirschauer argues that 'ethnographic writing puts something into words that, prior to this writing, did not exist in language' and sonic-spatial experience is a good example of experience that escapes everyday expression.[12] Low goes further, contending that 'ethnographic approaches to spatial analysis are crucial for any adequate analysis of the contestation of values and meanings in complex societies.'[13] In aiming to understand some of the effects of space in performance and some of the issues that innovating in this area raises, ethnography is a valuable tool.

There is no attempt here to comprehensively evaluate any of the individual events in question, rather they are used to raise wider issues. Some background to the events considered here will be of help to the reader, however. The first event was a concert given by the Scottish Ensemble (a small string orchestra) in Edinburgh. This event was split between two locations on the same evening, the large expanse of St. Giles Cathedral and the smaller (yet still rather grand) interior of the Georgian Signet Library. This meant the first 'small' half was repeated twice, either side of a single performance in the larger venue, so that the larger audience that fitted in St. Giles could be split between two performances in the Library. Tickets gave the audience access either to the Signet Library *then* the cathedral, or the cathedral *then* the library. The second set of concerts was part of the contemporary concert series The Night With..., organised by composer Matthew Whiteside. In this instance, the young UK-based Hermes Ensemble was heard in concert in Glasgow and in Edinburgh on subsequent evenings. Both the Scottish Ensemble and Hermes Ensemble concerts took place prior to any pandemic restrictions.

---

11   Georgina Born, 'Introduction' in *Music, Sound and Space*, p. 19
12   Stefan Hirschauer, 'Putting things into words: Ethnographic description and the silence of the social' in *Human Studies* 29 (2007), 413–441, p. 414. Blesser and Salter state that for both 'cultural and biological reasons, the language for describing sound is weak and inadequate.' Blesser and Salter, *Spaces Speak, Are You Listening?*, p. 6.
13   Setha Low, 'Spatializing Culture: The Social Production and Social Construction of Public Space in Costa Rica' in *American Ethnologist* 23:4 (1996), 861–879, (p. 862).

Four events were attended after the initial COVID-19 lockdowns, each with special measures in place. *Call* by composer Pete Stollery was a new piece performed in the fishing village of Footdee (Aberdeen, pronounced 'Fittie'), which sits where the river Dee meets the sea, as part of new music incubator Sound Scotland's 'Unbound Sound' festival. This piece was for massed French horns – some of which were placed over 200 metres away on the other side of the river – and, at its conclusion, it made use of the horns of the ships in Aberdeen harbour. The Edinburgh International Festival adapted to COVID-19 restrictions by placing huge tent-like structures in different locations in the city. Pianist Steven Osborne played a concert that included Beethoven, Michael Tippett and George Crumb in the Old College Quad, part of the University of Edinburgh. Also in Edinburgh, Music for Bridges was a series of outdoor performance events around the cycle paths in the north of the city, initiated by myself and organised in collaboration with local arts charity Tinderbox. This is the only I event in which I was involved as a performer and composer. It made use of several pieces of Victorian railway infrastructure, including the eponymous bridges and a large tunnel, which was where the performance described took place. Finally, Lost and Found was a Royal Opera House project that resulted in a series of mini operas composed by different writer-composer combinations for performance in St. Pancras Railway Station, London.

The discussion begins with reflections on audience engagement in three of the events attended.

Audience

The Cycle Path, Edinburgh, 12 September 2021. Music for Bridges

I stand at one end of Trinity Tunnel, almost 120 metres of dark and rather dank former railway tunnel, which (with surprising subtlety) lies under the plush houses and gardens of East Trinity Road above. At the other end, my clarinettist companion stands waiting. The sound had been great in the rehearsal, drifting back and forth between the two instruments. All was set for the performance, about which there were a number of mysteries: was anyone going to be there? Would they stop to listen or move on?

What had not been predicted was an audience of around fifty people, including ten children and several dogs, all standing in between the instruments in the middle of the tunnel. A surprising success, it might be thought, yet with this audience the performance situation changed entirely. The enclosed space meant that no sound dispersed. The most audible thing became the audience rather than the music. What had before been a fragile, meditative piece, became a group of people standing in a tunnel listening, in the main, to sounds they were themselves creating. The very thing that had attracted me to the tunnel in the first place – its ability to transmit sound – became the downfall of the pieces I had written for it. A fellow composer and sound artist described the situation as 'Cageian', which I found a touchingly sympathetic summary.

St. Pancras Station, London, 8 March, 2022. Lost and Found, Royal Opera House

When I arrive at the station I am greeted by an usher in a hi-vis jacket. There are many such volunteers, letting people know where in the large building the action is occurring. The situation needs to be managed and people need to be told. Walking down the concourse, I hear trained, operatic voices before I see anything, eventually joining a circle of people around two singers and some instrumentalists.

An older couple become interested in proceedings. 'It's hard to see' says the woman. They watch for a moment before moving on. Another man in jogging bottoms and his own hi-vis is attracted by the sound. He moves to the front to record a moment on his phone before saying 'I'm not going to miss my train' and moving on. It is as if an invisible cord delays the people walking past for a moment: they slow down, offer a glance, sometimes a smile, but the vast majority pass by without stopping to listen.

Footdee, Aberdeen, 13 June. *Call* by Pete Stollery. Unbound Sound, Sound Festival

The quiet conversations of the people who stop to listen during the rehearsal do not disturb the situation as they would have done in a hall. The dispersion applies to the sound of the audience as much as the sound of the players.

More attentive listening is present in the concert performance. People do say a few words to their companions, but this seems in keeping with the event and not much of a disturbance. During the rehearsal, people walk past with various reactions, indifference, curiosity. None stop for long, as if maybe it is not their business.

Commentary

A key point from literatures on space and sound is that space is not a vessel that is filled with sonic material, rather the two are co-constitutive. For example, Lehtovuori states that 'events not only take place in public urban space, but *partake in its production.*'[14] At the same time, music can create unique coalitions of people and communities, providing good material for answering DiSalvo's question 'How are publics made with things?'.[15] Music, therefore, can define spaces and create publics to a significant degree. 'Can', however, requires a certain emphasis here: there is an idealism that emerges from literal application of literatures on space, or at least it is very easy to overestimate the effects of musico-spatial relations.

The potential to define space and create publics does not guarantee that musical events in public space will achieve these goals. Reviewing my notes, one comment states that outdoor performance is 'Not an immediate means of engaging people' and that the '"Problems" of audience are displaced rather than solved.' Different places obviously come with different publics. The railway station is a good example of very directed presence: few people hang around St. Pancras Station without

---

14 Panu Lehtovuori, 'Towards Experiential Urbanism' in *Critical Sociology* 38:1 (2012), 71–87 (p. 4). Emphases in original.
15 Carl DiSalvo, 'Design and the Construction of Publics' in *Design Issues* 25:1 (2009), 48–63 (p. 49).

a specific aim, or train, in mind. Many of the people who followed the event had come – like me – specifically for the music. Photographs and videos also made their way onto social media and television news programmes, creating a mediatised event: from the point of view of the Opera House the audience was, perhaps, as much online as in the flesh.

There is, however, an undeniable openness to outdoor performance that is arresting; the challenge is making people welcome to stay if they wish. The event in Aberdeen does point to the informality that outdoor performance can achieve from an acoustic point of view. The rigidly policed silence of the concert hall cannot be broken without disturbing other people. The outdoors does give more scope for different levels of attention to sit side-by-side.

Space, however, is not an innocent construction that is just waiting for music to enter it. Massey argues that '[a]ll spaces are socially regulated in some way, if not by explicit rules (no ball games, no loitering) then by potentially more competitive (more market-like?) regulation.'[16] To encourage what Iris Marion Young sees as fundamental to city life – 'The being together of strangers'[17] – such restrictions must be taken into account: adding music does not immediately resolve the tensions around who is comfortable occupying spaces. Yet, it can subtly alter the use of spaces, creating different points of focus.

The word 'can' again emerges. Music, space and audience is full of revitalising potential but without guaranteed results.

Acoustic

The Cycle Path, Edinburgh, 12 September 2021. Music for Bridges

Before the event begins, I take my flute out below the first bridge I come across. The feeling is immediate once I start playing. The enclosure, even

---

16   Doreen Massey, *For Space* (London: Sage, 2005), p. 152. Or, as Lefebvre puts it, 'there is a politics of space because space is political.' Henri Lefebvre, *Espace et politique: La droit à la ville* (Paris: Anthropos, 2000 [1972]), p. 59. See also Stuart Elden, *Understanding Henri Lefebvre: Theory and the Possible* (London: Continuum, 2004), p. 183.
17   Iris Marion Young, *Justice and the Politics of Difference* (Princeton, Princeton University Press, 1990), p. 237.

though partial, is enough to return the sound back, to reinforce and give me confidence. It feels like an acoustic embrace.

Footdee, Aberdeen, 13 June. *Call* by Pete Stollery. Unbound Sound, Sound Festival

The Horn players: 'I hate playing outside' – 'Really? I don't mind it'

Even with ten horn players, the sound immediately reminded me of how 'flat' outdoor playing can be. This, coupled with the instruments' brassy tones, puts me in mind of the bugle playing the 'Last Post' [which is played by the British military on occasions of remembrance]. Sound disperses, immediately. There is no comforting and encouraging room reverberation to spur players on, the transmission of sound seems to only go in one direction: away from you into endless space. As an audience member I am never in the sound, enveloped by it, resonating with it.

Two horns are positioned over 200 metres away at the other side of the Dee. It is a set-up that points to a narrative at which the listener can only guess: why are they over there, so far from their fellow players? What are they trying to communicate to us? The two distant horns are heard surprisingly well, particularly over the closer players' material. Only a little of the sound is lost on the breeze, while the varying dynamics of close and distant players give the sound from over the river a certain clarity: the timbre of horns playing loud from a distance is quite distinct from those playing quieter close by.

While I am surprised by the effectiveness of this constellation, I am – as always with spatial exploration – perhaps slightly disappointed. Perhaps no sound can match the epic sonic experience that I imagine when players are divided up amongst geography on the largest scale.[18] My mind is full of mountains resonating and two horns are a little underpowered for that. Sound cannot conquer landscape with these tools.

That being said, the eventual performance is (unsurprisingly) louder and fuller than the rehearsal, with the spectacular addition of the ships' horns. These are something else. As if the piece is a building

---

18   Claire Bishop, *Artificial Hells: Participatory Art and the Politics of Spectatorship* (London: Verso, 2012).

and the horns are a shattering force that rips off the roof to suddenly reveal the sky. Whereas the sounds of the French horn existed gently in this context, the ships obliterated the space.

Edinburgh, 16 October 2019. Scottish Ensemble: Take Two

'One half of the audience I'd like to welcome, the other half I'd like to welcome back' states the music director. The seats in St. Giles Cathedral are not so comfy, and some of the musicians wear scarves and shawls to keep warm, reminding me of my own experiences performing in chilly British churches. The sound of chairs and stands scraping the stone billows out from the ensemble's position in the crossing. During the music, details of intimate moments are lost in the generous acoustic, but the *maestoso*, slow material sounds great. At times the bass is a little woofy, making for a bad blend, while the higher instruments sound a little far away. The church bells ring at one point, but come to an end just as the piece is also concluding, as if it were planned.

I often find myself thinking how the acoustic is deficient in various ways, though the musicians still pull the pieces off with aplomb. It appears easier to think about what you lack, at least to a listener with significant experience of listening in concert halls. I am taken out of myself entirely by a *slow* [Pietro] Locatelli opening. The bold contrasts of fast and slow offered by the Baroque repertoire allow for easy comparison between the space's reactions to the two speeds. At the end of the half, for some audience members, it is the end of the concert while for the other half, including me, it is only halfway. I realise that there is a particular character to the final applause of a normal concert, one that cannot be fully realised in this configuration.

In the interval, there is less natural opportunity for a drink. We inhabit spaces less as we have to move from one to the other, even though sensitivity to the space is part of the intention of the format. I wonder whether any of the pieces we heard had any particular religious significance. A church is naturally not just an empty box with an acoustic and the relationship between its religious function and the programme was not made explicitly.

The Signet Library part of the performance is a little like having the Scottish Ensemble play in your (very large) front room. I can hear *interaction* between bass/inner and melody and it adds a whole new, human level to the music-making: more social, less ritualistic. Here, big chords do seem to die a little soon. Again the acoustics seem defined by their, to my ear, deficiencies (which are shown up, almost expertly, by the concert format). In the first intimate passage, I immediately think 'Wow, these guys are great [players]', which I never quite did in the church, even though the music was just as virtuosic. The final *tierce de Picardie* [a major chord at the end of a minor piece] must feel rather different depending on whether you heard it in the middle or at the end of the evening.

Commentary

There is a reason why the concert hall was created. Acoustic, as a performer, is usually a positive. The continual feedback and support it offers provides great encouragement, whereas a complete dispersal of sound in the outdoors can be problematic. There is a logic to the covered bandstand in the open park, for example.

It is unsurprising that performers and composers explore spaces and places outside of concert halls, which – as Blesser and Salter state – are a 'very narrow application of aural architecture in a very specific context.'[19] Yet, the material above raises the issue that, although there are innumerable places on earth that can function as locations for musical performance, the *acoustic* differentiation will be artistically significant in a minority. Gieryn describes three defining features of place, namely 'location, material form, and meaningfulness'.[20] Acoustically, changing the first can make little difference, while the second usually falls into broad acoustic types: outdoor performance sounds like outdoor performance in a great many locations. Blesser and Salter use the concept of 'metainstruments' to describe how instruments are tied to the imagination of a particular acoustic and it is this connection that is troubled by alternative performance venues. The temptation is to infer that the outdoors provides a whole panoply of acoustic opportunities for the performer, yet in practice there are certain archetypal spaces

---

19   Blesser and Salter, *Spaces Speak, Are You Listening?*, p. 127.
20   Gieryn, 'What Buildings Do', p. 466.

that cover most locations: large open spaces, valleys, woods, etc. The benefit of placing music in particular locations is usually to be found in other facets, such as the profile of the background noise, the visual panorama, the social function of the space (Gieryn's 'meaningfulness'), the physical sense of being in it, or the affectual impact. Other scholars may well describe this as the difference between 'place' and 'space'.[21]

The dispersion of sound applies to the audience as much as the sound of the players, however, which, as discussed above, is an important reason why outdoor performance does offer a certain kind of informality. Technology is the key to dominate such outdoor space. Think of the racks of speakers at a festival gig, the ships' horns firing sound in all directions.

Listening and Place

Glasgow/Edinburgh, 25/26 November 2019. The Night With... The Hermes Ensemble

This was a typical pub back room: black walls, posters and low lighting with some purple highlights. A disco ball rotates slowly on the ceiling. A fan hums gently in the background, but it is one you can ignore, like a work computer. The group are set up at the far end of the low-ceilinged room, the voice of the singer amplified through some speakers.

Here, we are sheltered from the world outside, by the space but also by the music. The weird, affecting, simple, expressive can all find a place here, but not too lengthy. The gig is a kind of secret despite significant individual efforts at advertising. What is played here is not presented as 'great art'; it is something to momentarily move, amuse, disorientate us. People still listen attentively, with just the occasional sound of ice moving in plastic glasses. After his piece, *Daily Rituals*, composer

---

21 See, for example, Tim Cresswell *Space: A Short Introduction* (Oxford: Blackwell, 2004). For the purposes of this chapter (and following Massey, *For Space*, p. 6) the distinction is not made here as it is taken for granted that all spaces have 'meaning'. Though the concert hall is seen as a space that in some ways tries to underplay its nature as a specific 'place', all concert halls are different and the generalised 'space' of musical performance is an ideal towards which they aspire rather than a reality.

Matthew Grouse stands to take his bow from the middle of the room. In the space there is an effortless shift of perspective from the stage to the composer. The piece's references to selfies, Tinder and other dating software landed with the audience. In this way it feels 'connected' to outside world.

In Edinburgh, the Scottish Storytelling has a vibe I would describe as 'concert in rural arts centre'. The audience dress code is less trendy than Glasgow, the group a little older. The rows of seats also create a feeling of formality that was not present the night before. I draw a diagram of the 'parameters of formality' in terms of seating and audience-performer relations: the smaller the space between audience and performer, the more informality; the more rigid the seating, the more formality.

There were so many more laughs in Glasgow! The older audience perhaps struggled a little with the references, but it was not just a matter of content but of situation. There was still warm applause.

The sound of dishes being moved from behind the screen to my rear irritates me and takes me out of the music. A voice is raised in an easy-going discussion, and later the café staff whistle while working. A noisy tap gushes occasionally. None of this noise contributes to my musical experience, though it does keep me in the real world. But perhaps tied to this kind of real world is not where I want to be.

The Old College Quad, Edinburgh, 12 August 2021. Steven Osborne, Edinburgh International Festival

I notice a curious tension between the 'placeness' of the venue and how I wanted to listen. The moments that I feel most 'inside' the music, struck me as those that were most 'successful'. I close my eyes at times. I prized those moments at which there is a complete interiorisation of experience and the outside world is blocked out. Music transforms space in various ways and part of its great magic is its ability to take your imagination elsewhere, out of the moment in which you find yourself.

Commentary

The 'place' of musical experience is seen to be somewhere between here and elsewhere, the advantage of music in a traditional listening configuration is its ability to transcend its space, or to define it. The space of performance and the space-defining abilities of the music interact in complex ways: this is no one-way street. Most concert halls aspire towards invisibility, focusing attention on the musicians so that the ear is given full rein, the body a comfortable (if restrictive) chair.[22] Music in place presents more to the other senses. Where music takes us is in dialogue with a stronger sense of where we are.

I prized those moments when the outside world – and my own body – was blocked out, i.e. what I have been trained into seeing as the ideal Western (classical) music experience. My training as a musician and many hours spent sitting in concert halls will certainly have a bearing on this. I take this ideal listening experience around with me, whether I am sat in a concert hall or a university quad. Why, then, bother with performing in unusual venues at all? Just because listeners have the ability to close off from their surroundings and join with a musical experience, does not mean the space they inhabit has no bearing. On the contrary, it is the site and context for these musical experiences and can help or hinder them.

The tensions that arise here are partly due to the presentation of what is essentially concert music within a more 'placed' context. The presuppositions of the concert – primarily silence – are not only within me as a listener but within the pieces themselves. Pieces can, to a degree, define their listening expectations. Interaction with the sounds and spaces of the place, as occurs in creative directions inspired by sound art, would immediately create a kind of listening that includes and appreciates the sonic environment outside the work: indeed it questions this divide between the sounds 'inside' and those 'outside'. There is another echo here of the theoretical distinction that can be made between 'place' and 'space'.

The aim of all the spatial explorations discussed here was never to make the musical experience incidental and in this a cornerstone of the Western classical tradition is maintained: contemplative listening. Richard Leppert argues that such listening is 'not philosophically removed from the world, as later aesthetic would have it; it is instead the sign of one's control and domination of the world.' He continues that

---

22 There is a link between this 'invisibility' and the purported universalism of the bourgeois culture from which the concert hall arose.

'[a]s such, it *is* an exercise of power.'[23] Leppert comes to this conclusion through the study of various pieces of visual art, which in part show the nobility enjoying immersive musical experience while peasants toil: his material 'establishes an opposition between contemplation (thought) and physical labour (in essence, nonthought).'[24] While the situation is far from identical, there is an echo of this in the diary material above, in the contrast between the hi-vis jackets of the staff and volunteers of the Royal Opera House and the hi-vis-jacketed man who must catch his train. James Johnson also plots how attentive listening arose in Paris (and spread from the capital) with a similar focus on its potential for distinguishing class credentials.[25] Finally, Richard Sennett considers silence as a matter of privilege, not least in relation to the gentlemen's clubs of Victorian England, where men could sit in silence, undisturbed.[26]

These perspectives cast a different light on what are described above as the most positive musical experiences, which were in the main attentive and undisturbed by noise around, albeit not within a context of pure silence. There is a connection in these concert experiences between attentive listening and deep, musical experience. Are all such experiences an 'exercise of power' or does a new location give them new meaning? Musical immersion is by no means purely an aim of concert music; just think of audiences losing themselves at festivals throughout the world. The experiences described above 'felt' silent to me, in a way, because they spoke of a quality of connection between me and the music.

For the authors above, the supposedly stifling silence of the concert hall is the primary target but is the experience so very different in such 'placed' concerts? Perhaps the more critical question, for myself as much as for anyone else, is why 'successful' musical experience requires some kind of disavowal of the present space and moment. This is a deeply embedded part of Western musical experience. Whether it can be expanded, or even replaced, is still a rather open question and

---

23 Richard Leppert, 'Desire, Power and the Sonoric Landscape: Early Modernism and the Politics of Musical Privacy', in *The Place of Music*, ed. by Andrew Leyshon, David Matless and George Revill (New York: Guilford Press, 1998), pp. 291–321 (p. 302).
24 Leppert, 'Desire, Power and the Sonoric Landscape', p. 301.
25 James H. Johnson, *Listening in Paris: A Cultural History* (Berkeley: University of California Press, 1995), p. 302.
26 Richard Sennett, *The Fall of Public Man* (London: Penguin, 2002 [first published 1978]), pp. 215–216.

is a reason that experimental pieces that puncture this hermetic bubble of experience can still be powerful. Furthermore, there is room for a narrative of musical immersion that is entirely of this world, one that is a precious experience cradled by the context in which listeners find themselves.

For those attempting to innovate concerts in terms of their spatial dynamics, these questions are important because such innovations are often attempts to rid the concert of the formality of Western classical music. There is the issue, however, of the formality of the Western listening experience that is much deeper and is often left untroubled.

Concluding Thoughts

The aim of this chapter is not to discourage musicians from spatial exploration. On the contrary, the great potential of spatial exploration has been noted and should be further exploited. Yet, it is also a corrective to an approach that would imbue space with the ability to transform musical and social relations without the complicating factors of music's previous socialisations and the pre-existing complexities of the new spaces that are used.

The literatures on space provide a good deal of material to consider its potential and complexities, yet the individual nature of particular spaces means that continued, practical experimentation is vital to find solutions that discover that magical moment in which public, space and music fit together, or indeed rub against each other in an arresting manner.[27] The latter point is important, as Born is right to point out that considering music and space can uncover 'a universe not of consensual social relations, but of sometimes agonistic and dissensual relations – pointing to music and sound as the terrain on which not only aesthetic differences but also social, cultural, religious and political differences, inequalities and oppressions may be played out.'[28] Music does not necessarily need to 'fit' its space (which is the aim of most site-specific musical performances) but can be a daring juxtaposition or musico-spatial provocation. This is reminiscent of Chantal Mouffe's description of democratic politics, which '[i]nstead of trying to erase the traces

---

27 C.f. 'utopian' versus 'critical' public art in W. J. Thomas Mitchell, *Art and the Public Sphere* (Chicago: University of Chicago Press, 1992), p. 3.
28 Born, 'Introduction', p. 33.

of power and exclusion... requires that they be brought to the fore, making them visible so that they can enter the terrain of contestation'.[29] Furthermore, shaping the spatial context of musical performance does not guarantee that the responses of individual listeners will 'fit' with the intention.

Concert-hall performance has been in full flow for 200 years and it may take time for other traditions of performance to emerge. In exploring this further, it is important to remain responsive to the new spaces that are used. Transplanting concert music into the outdoors, for example, while potentially novel for some, does not exploit how sound and space can interact, nor does it necessarily encourage ways of listening that are radically new. Consideration of what exactly a new space will add to a performance is all too rarely exhibited. Maximising engagement with space's 'meaningfulness' holds much potential, as does searching out spaces with true acoustic character and playing music that exploits it.

This is where another challenge in truly reacting to spatial dynamics is found. New works written for particular spaces are, by strict definition, not transportable. The concert hall, along with widely used notational practices, was important in establishing composers' reputations as music could be heard across vast distances and, eventually, over many centuries. There is a connection here with the 'white cube' in the world of visual art, which acted as a seemingly 'neutral' space for the presentation of modern works.[30] Composing for one specific space is challenging for current economies in new music, both financial and in terms of 'prestige'.[31] In reality, however, it is likely alternative spaces could be found for most 'placed' pieces and in this there is a sense of continual adaptation and transformation to new spaces that may well be beneficial for each iteration.

Finally, it is worth saying that the affectual experience of a space is very much tied to the behaviour of people within it, and one's previous exposure to it. A welcoming concert-hall environment could well be more effective than a cold or austere outdoor performance. Just as music produces spaces, so can words, actions and conversation.

---

29 Chantal Mouffe, *The Return of the Political*, (London: Verso, 1993), p. 149.
30 See, for example, Brian O'Doherty, *Inside the White Cube: The Ideology of the Gallery Space* (Los Angeles: University of California Press, 1999).
31 Hettie Malcomson, 'Composing Individuals: Ethnographic Reflections on Success and Prestige in the British New Music Network' in *Twentieth-Century Music* 10:1 (2013), 115–136.

References

Bishop, Claire, *Artificial Hells: Participatory Art and the Politics of Spectatorship* (London: Verso, 2012).

Blesser, Barry and Linda-Ruth Salter, *Spaces speak, are you listening?: Experiencing Aural Architecture* (Cambridge, Mass: MIT Press, 2007).

Born, Georgina, 'Introduction – music, sound and space: transformations of public and private experience', in *Music, Sound, and Space: Transformations of Public and Private Experience,* ed. by Georgina Born (Oxford: Oxford University Press, 2013), pp. 1–69, https://doi.org/10.1017/CBO9780511675850

Cressman, Darryl, *Building Culture in Nineteenth-Century Amsterdam: The Concertgebouw* (Amsterdam: Amsterdam University Press, 2016), https://doi.org/10.1017/9789048528462

Cresswell, Tim. *Place: A Short Introduction* (Oxford: Blackwell, 2004).

DiSalvo, Carl, 'Design and the Construction of Publics', *Design Issues* 25:1 (2009), 48–63, https://doi.org/10.1162/desi.2009.25.1.48

Elden, Stuart, *Understanding Henri Lefebvre: Theory and the Possible* (London: Continuum, 2004).

Gieryn, Thomas F., 'What Buildings Do', *Theory and Society* 31:1 (2002), 25–74, https://doi.org/10.1023/A:1014404201290

Haferkorn, Julia, 'Dancing to another tune: classical music in nightclubs and other non-traditional venues', in *The Classical Music Industry*, ed. by Christopher Dromey and Julia Haferkorn (Abingdon: Routledge, 2018), pp. 148–171, https://doi.org/10.4324/9781315471099

Hennion, Antoine, 'Music Lovers: Taste as Performance', *Theory, Culture & Society* 18:5 (2001), 1–22, https://doi.org/10.1177/02632760122051940

Hirschauer, Stefan, 'Putting things into words: Ethnographic description and the silence of the social', *Human Studies* 29 (2007), 413–441, https://doi.org/10.1007/s10746-007-9041-1

Johnson, James H., *Listening in Paris: A Cultural History* (Berkeley: University of California Press, 1995).

Lefebvre, Henri, *Espace et politique: La droit à la ville* (Paris: Anthropos, 2000 [1972]).

Lehtovuori, Panu, 'Towards Experiential Urbanism', *Critical Sociology* 38:1 (2012), 71–87, https://doi.org/10.1177/0896920511407222

Leppert, Richard, 'Desire, Power and the Sonoric Landscape: Early Modernism and the Politics of Musical Privacy', in *The Place of Music*, ed. by Andrew Leyshon, David Matless and George Revill (New York: Guilford Press, 1998), pp. 291–321.

Low, Setha, 'Spatializing Culture: The Social Production and Social Construction of Public Space in Costa Rica', *American Ethnologist* 23:4 (1996), 861–879.

Malcomson, Hettie, 'Composing Individuals: Ethnographic Reflections on Success and Prestige in the British New Music Network', *Twentieth-Century Music* 10:1 (2013), 115–136, http://dx.doi.org/10.1017/S1478572212000436

Massey, Doreen, *For Space* (London: Sage, 2005).

Mitchell, W.J. Thomas, *Art and the Public Sphere* (Chicago: University of Chicago Press, 1992).

Mouffe, Chantal, *The Return of the Political* (London: Verso, 1993).

Smith, Neil Thomas and Peter Peters, 'Music for Buildings; Building for Music', in *The Routledge Companion to Applied Musicology*, ed. by Chris Dromey, forthcoming.

Smith, Neil Thomas, 'Concrete Culture: The Planning Hearing as a Stage for Cultural Debates', *Cultural Sociology* 16:2 (2022), 147–164, https://doi.org/10.1177/17499755211040959

Smith, Neil Thomas, 'Constructing the Public Concert Hall', *Journal of the Royal Musical Association* 146:2 (2021), 255–281, https://doi.org/10.1017/rma.2021.17

Jonathan Sterne, *The Audible Past: Cultural Origins in Sound Reproduction* (Durham, N.C.: Duke University Press, 2003).

Sennett, Richard, *The Fall of Public Man* (London: Penguin, 2002 [first published 1978]).

Thrift, Nigel, 'Re-animating the place of thought: Transformations of spatial and temporal description in the twenty-first century', in *Community, Economic Creativity, and Organization*, ed. by Amin, A., Roberts, S. (Oxford: Oxford University Press, 2009), pp. 90-119.

Thrift, Nigel, 'Understanding the Affective Spaces of Political Performance', in *Emotion, Place and Culture*, ed. by Bondi, L., Cameron, L., Davidson, J., Smith, M. (Aldershot: Ashgate, 2009), pp. 79-96.

Young, Iris Marion, *Justice and the Politics of Difference* (Princeton: Princeton University Press, 1990).

15. *Monsieur Croche* – Concerts at Eye Level

Tal Walker

Introduction

> I dared to tell him that some men had sought, some in poetry, others in painting (with great difficulty, I added a few musicians), to shake off the old dust of tradition [...] Mr Croche continued without flinching, "it doesn't matter. A beautiful idea, in formation, contains something ridiculous for fools" [...] "Remain unique... without blemish" [...] "Discipline must be sought in freedom, not in the formulas of a philosophy that has become obsolete and is good only for the weak. Listen to no one's advice, except the wind as it passes and tells us the story of the world.[1]

Claude Debussy expressed his views on artistic traditions through his alter ego *Monsieur Croche* (Mister Quaver) in his concert reviews written for *La Revue Blanche* and *Gil Blas* journals in Paris. This criticism challenges artistic conventions of France in 1901. Despite the risk of being ridiculed by the media, Debussy calls for innovation and creativity in music inspired by the freedom of art and nature. He is featured here as

---

[1] 'J'osai lui dire que des hommes avaient cherché, les uns dans la poésie, les autres dans la peinture (à grand-peine j'y ajoutai quelques musiciens) à secouer la vieille poussière des traditions [...] continuait M. Croche sans broncher, ça n'a aucune importance. Une idée très belle, en formation, contient du ridicule pour les imbéciles [...] « Rester unique... sans tare [...] « Il faut chercher la discipline dans la liberté et non dans les formules d'une philosophie devenue caduque et bonne pour les faibles. N'écouter les conseils de personne, sinon du vent qui passe et nous raconte l'histoire du monde.' Claude Debussy, 'L'Entretien avec M. Croche', in *La Revue blanche* (Paris: 1 July 1901) as appears in Claude Debussy, *Monsieur Croche et autres écrits* (Paris: Éditions Gallimard, 1971), pp. 51–52.

an intellectual, almost a poet, in his own way. He, and other musicians, mingled with painters, writers, dancers and other artists. Gabriel Fauré, Marcel Proust and Paul Verlaine were no strangers. Maurice Ravel and his group of *Société des Apaches* were composers, writers and visual artists who would gather to perform music, read poetry and discuss art.

Nowadays, a small interdisciplinary fringe society such as the *Apaches* might have been overshadowed by big concert halls and museums. Conservatoires and art academies are playing a big role in this specialisation, which has its advantages and disadvantages. We owe so much to music conservatoires in bringing together international students and faculty members, and inspiring young musicians to aspire towards high achievements, as well as helping to collect knowledge through research and archival work. Many musicians like me, who went through the traditional route of conservatoires, might end up performing in an orchestra, as soloists, as chamber musicians or teaching music. However, despite growing encouragement for interdisciplinarity today, they might rarely be expected to work directly with other artists from theatre, dance, visual art or literature.[2]

This chapter presents a Belgian concert series, *Monsieur Croche*, as a possible future of classical music. It is a concert series which brings French classical music into non-conventional 'concert halls' in an interdisciplinary way. The series' performances take place in less conventional concert venues such as art galleries, museums and cathedrals. Once a unique space is transformed into a concert venue, the audience witnesses a one-of-a-kind experience. *Monsieur Croche* believes in a real 'connection with its audience through emotionally immersing, and intellectually intriguing experiences'.[3] The concert series looks to bring classical music to the audience in an approachable, engaging and interdisciplinary way.

Firstly, this chapter addresses some of today's challenges in the classical music world. It examines salon societies in Paris of the nineteenth and twentieth centuries as a model for *Monsieur Croche*'s

---

2   There is a resurgence in interdisciplinarity and multi-media intersection today. A collection that demonstrates an impressive number of projects as such is Adrian Curtin and Adam Whittaker 'Introduction: Representation in/of Classical Music', in *Open Library of Humanities* 8:1 (2022), https://doi.org/10.16995/olh.8252
3   Monsieur Croche's website, http://www.monsieurcorche.be

concert series. It then investigates challenges such as the specialisation of the arts; alienation and estrangement of the audience; and the challenge of inclusivity and representation of a broad population in classical music. The concert series *Monsieur Croche* is then presented as a case study for a small initiative that addresses the various challenges through interdisciplinarity, approachability, accessibility and inclusion. Additionally, an example of an interdisciplinary project, where music and fashion were brought together, and other examples of outreach initiatives (such as master classes and concerts for children) will be shared, as well as *Monsieur Croche*'s obstacles and successes. The chapter concludes by reflecting on the goals and ideas of *Monsieur Croche*, and where it is heading in the future.

Challenges in Today's Live Classical Music Concerts

A century ago, cultural centres like Paris attracted artists from all disciplines. Composers, visual artists and poets would gather in cafés and salons where their ideas and work inspired each other. Even at the end of the nineteenth and beginning of the twentieth centuries, salon concerts were important venues in the musical scene. Salons such as those of Pauline Viardot and Winnaretta Singer would host musicians such as Fauré and Saint-Saëns as well as writers such as George Sand and Marcel Proust. Other societies such as the *Société national de musique* and the *Société musical indépandante* were important for the development of French music and took place in a salon setting. *Le XX* was a particular salon movement where concerts and lectures were performed alongside symbolist and impressionist art in galleries and museums. Performers such as pianist Cortot and violinist Ysaÿe featured French and Belgian music alongside visual artworks.[4] This particular salon movement, in its juxtaposition of music and visual art, inspired the initiative of the *Monsieur Croche* concert series a century later.

Through my personal experience, as a piano student in Maastricht and Antwerp, I observed that often the conservatoires, big concert halls, museums and art galleries would specialise in their own field. It was

---

4 James Ross, 'Music in the French Salon', in *French Music since Berlioz*, ed. by Richard Langham Smith and Caroline Potter (Aldershot: Ashgate, 2006), pp. 91–96.

relatively rare for me to find interdisciplinary events in these venues. We musicians experience a similar tendency of specialisation. In times of 'inflation' in university degrees, my fellow musicians, me included, tend to specialise in music and perfect their art. It has become the norm for many classical musicians to obtain more university degrees; these correspondingly slowly lose their value, as musicians need more and more degrees to get noticed or find a job. As a classical pianist, I observed my peers pursue not only a bachelor's degree, but often continue for a master's, and even sometimes an artist's diploma, an education diploma or a doctorate. Our focus revolves around playing recitals, participating in music competitions, forming ensembles, recording and teaching, but opportunities to work together with, for example, visual artists or actors very rarely present themselves. The disconnect between classical music and other arts represents a threat to its future as a vibrant art form.

Apart from specialisation, another challenge I observed is classical music's estrangement from a broad public. Attending concert halls and opera houses might be perceived as a statement of status or prestige. People unfamiliar with the conventions of the concert hall may feel intimidated by these venues. What to wear? How to behave? When to applaud? According to Julian Johnson, classical music was and remains accessible to the elite, to those with economic means who are also more likely to access music education.[5] In these prestigious events, the audience might feel alienated, as the artists perform on a distant stage often without any interaction with the listeners. Some might even find it difficult to enjoy the music of the past if it is completely unfamiliar to them.[6] Even though classical music is growing more popular via digital platforms, film soundtracks and mass distribution, live classical music is not necessarily becoming more approachable.[7] Jargon-filled programme notes or complex programming could also contribute to scaring away listeners.[8]

---

5   Julian Johnson, *Who Needs Classical Music?: Cultural Choice and Musical Values* (Oxford: Oxford University Press, 2002), pp. 21–22.
6   Sarah M. Price, 'In Defence of the Familiar: Understanding Conservatism in Concert Selection Amongst Classical Music Audiences', *Musicae Scientiae* 26 (2022), 243–258, https://journals.sagepub.com/doi/full/10.1177/1029864920940034
7   James Parakilas, 'Classical Music as Popular Music', *The Journal of Musicology* 3 (1984), 1–18.
8   Bennet and Ginsborg conclude that programme notes have a small positive impact on a minority of the listeners. Dawn Bennett and Jane Ginsborg, 'Audience

Lastly, a major challenge for classical music lies not only in addressing a broader audience from different socio-economical groups, but also allowing within its circles of performers and leading figures an equal representation of the population. Although the world of classical music of the twenty-first century tries to diversify with respect to gender, race and class, it remains a rather conservative field.[9] Initiatives such as the *La Maestra* competition of the *Philharmonie de Paris*, which promotes women conductors; or *Chineke! Foundation* created by Chi-Chi Nwanoku, which supports the career development of black and ethnically diverse classical musicians, are relatively new in the field.[10] For many years, the majority of leading classical musicians were white men. According to Ewell, despite the call for diversity, a large majority of composers and music theorists are white.[11]

As mentioned above, *Monsieur Croche* took inspiration from salons like *Le XX*, where interdisciplinary artists mingled and collaborated. However, it's it is worth remembering that these salon societies were a remnant of bourgeois and aristocratic cultures. Exclusivity and a particular social circle were strongly associated with the old salon model. Nowadays, in times when awareness of diversity and inclusion is on the rise, it is important for us to draw inspiration from the positive aspects of such events (such as the intimate setting and interdisciplinarity) and create something new which embodies contemporary values (such as diversity and inclusion).

Monsieur Croche – A Project with Missions and Purposes

These issues have led me as a musician to often ask myself how we could produce interdisciplinary classical music concerts of high quality, which at the same time would be approachable to the wider public and inclusive in their programming. And so, together with a cultural producer (and close friend), I initiated a small project, hoping it could bring together different art forms and bring classical music down to

---

reactions to the program notes of unfamiliar music', *Psychology of Music* 46:4 (2018), 588–605.
9   Philip Ewell, 'Music Theory's White Racial Frame', *Music Theory Spectrum* 26 (2021), 324–329.
10 *La Maestra: Concours et académie de cheffes d'orchestre*, http://www.lamaestra-paris.com; *Chineke! Foundation*, https://www.chineke.org
11 Ewell, 'Music Theory's White Racial Frame', pp. 324–327.

'eye level'.[12] As suggested by Devlin and Ackrill, innovation in classical music together with educational outreach could help breathe new life into classical music and attract younger audiences.[13] Founded in 2017, *Monsieur Croche* produces interdisciplinary events in non-conventional venues, while trying to programme diverse artists. In order to pick our artists for the concerts, we combine those who specialise in the repertoire with people who share our enthusiasm for an intimate and innovative concept.

The first iteration of *Monsieur Croche* looked to reflect its values, mission, purpose, ecosystem and offering. During an interactive workshop, *Monsieur Croche*'s team of volunteers co-created its strategy and implementation plan.[14] The latter outlined roles and responsibilities in the team and has been translated into a *Strategy and Playbook* document, which includes a blueprint that outlines key activities of future seasons. Our overall mission and purpose were articulated as the following:

> Monsieur Croche's reason for existence is to make French music from the 19th and 20th centuries, in combination with other forms of arts (such as literature and visual art), accessible to a large audience and to support young talent in their musical development.[15]

We divided these aims into three different topics: experience of French music; accessibility and approachability; and lastly, opportunities for young talent. The organisation creates events with an artistically thought-through programme focusing each time on one composer or theme while inviting international artists, including intriguing narrations and finding special venues. We create events that attempt to be approachable, thanks to narration, the link with the location and other (interdisciplinary) arts (e.g. poetry, fashion). Lastly, the organisation engages the audience in

---

12 Here I use the term 'at eye level' both literally and figuratively. Literally, getting off the high stage and performing in a smaller venue at the height of the audience. Figuratively, in Hebrew 'at eye level' could mean 'as an equal' or 'without condescension', a performance is presented in a 'down-to-earth' manner without pretentiousness.

13 Graham Devlin and Judith Ackrill, *A Review of Orchestral Provision for Yorkshire* (London: Arts Council of England, 2005), https://webarchive.nationalarchives.gov.uk/ukgwa/20150205143656/http://www.artscouncil.org.uk/advice-and-guidance/browse-advice-and-guidance/a-review-of-orchestral-provision-for-yorkshire

14 I elaborate on *Monsieur Croche*'s ecosystem and team below.

15 *Monsieur Croche's Strategy and Playbook* (version 1.0, April 2020).

a dialogue, which gives an intimate yet educational character to the events. Additionally, *Monsieur Croche* creates opportunities for young talent to connect with more experienced artists through performances and masterclasses. The organisation invites emerging artists to perform at their main events and brings classical music to a younger audience through masterclasses, children's concerts and affordable tickets, while always paying the performing artists.

A compact ecosystem with trusted partners enables *Monsieur Croche* to organise its events and explore its future activities. Firstly, a team of volunteers contributes to the success of the non-profit organisation. These are mostly professionals in the cultural sector who work in fields such as cultural management, production and communication. They offered to help *Monsieur Croche* and eventually became an integral part of its team. Some of these volunteers worked regularly in theatre and dance companies or have a background in music or art. They use their talents, energy and experience to contribute to artistic, administrative, legal, communicative or production activities. Furthermore, our ecosystem includes our (returning) audience and growing circles of visitors; a group of well-respected regular, international artists that are connected to our network or who specialise in French repertoire; a selection of trusted partners and venues with whom *Monsieur Croche* collaborates (e.g. art galleries, museums, piano shops etc.); and lastly, *Monsieur Croche*'s hive, an intimate circle that brings its knowledge, experience, inspiration and networks, while contributing ideas for the future and funding opportunities.

Monsieur Croche has a clear understanding of its offer. Firstly, the organisation creates unique musical experiences in which we aim to take the audience on a journey through narrative and different forms of art in an unconventional setting. Secondly, the organisation's public masterclasses are accessible with a voluntary contribution from the public and are free for selected students. Additionally, off-the-shelf concerts (e.g. *Mini Croche* and lecture-recitals) can be presented in schools and other institutions. And finally, carefully considered solo piano or chamber music programmes, based on individual requests, can be presented in private settings. All of these offers are executed by our team through various routes: artistic direction; production; administration and legal; communication and promotion.

Our Activities – Five Seasons of Unique Events

Since our first concert in 2018, *Monsieur Croche* has produced more than eighteen events, including ten main events, three *Mini Croche* children's concerts and five benefit concerts in private venues. Each main event concert is one-of-a-kind, as it tells the story of one specific French composer. A narrator presents the stories behind the composers and their pieces in a creative way through poetry, literature, letters and biographical information in three languages: Flemish (Antwerp's official language), English (to make the narration accessible for our international audiences and artists) and French (which is an official language in Belgium and the original language of some of our source materials). The first composer to be programmed was none other than Claude Debussy, as the festival was initiated as a homage to the centenary of his death. The title, *Monsieur Croche*, as mentioned above, was his pseudonym and the concerts therefore aim to take the audience on a journey through French music of the end of the nineteenth and beginning of the twentieth centuries. Together with Debussy, the first season featured the music of Gabriel Fauré, Maurice Ravel and Francis Poulenc. Since then, we have featured Olivier Messiaen, Camille Saint-Saëns and César Franck. So far – we must admit – no women composers have been programmed, as we have not done sufficient research in finding the artists who play their repertoire. However, it is our highest priority to commission artists in performing the music of Cécile Chaminade, Lili Boulanger, Mélanie Bonis, Germaine Tailleferre, Louise Farrenc and many other important French women composers.[16]

'The audience's journey is not only metaphorical, but also literally a journey through the old city of Antwerp'.[17] The venues include art museums, art galleries, churches, and even private salons. The small venue and the proximity to the artists both make our concerts intimate and exclusive – at eye level with our audience. 'The idea was to give

---

[16] Since writing this chapter, Monsieur Croche has organised a concert around Lili Boulanger, telling her life story and presenting her solo piano pieces, violin pieces and *mélodies* for voice and piano. This concert took place on 7 May 2023 at the art gallery 'Valerie Traan' in Antwerp and on 28 June 2023 at St Mary le Strand church in London in collaboration with the 'Hidden Gems' concert series.

[17] Tal Walker, 'Alumni Stories: Tal Walker' in *Royal Conservatoire Antwerp's Website* (Antwerp: 2018), https://www.ap-arts.be/en/news/alumni-stories-tal-walker

the concert[s] an interdisciplinary feeling by placing them in special artistic locations throughout the city'.[18] Normally, fewer than a hundred people can attend each event except for those in large cathedrals. The venues themselves are mostly rich with art, and so provide a creative environment and interdisciplinary feel. So far, *Monsieur Croche* has collaborated with important art galleries and museums in Antwerp such as *De Zwarte Panter*, *Valerie Traan*, *Museum De Reede* and *Maagdenhuis*. Churches include the *Sint Joriskerk* and the *Sint Walburgiskerk*. Other benefit and promotional concerts included private houses, piano shops (such as *Piano-Atelier Chaerle*) and even a promotion recital during the *Cultuurmarkt van Vlaanderen* at the Royal Flemish Opera.

Diversity and inclusivity are key factors in the choice of artists we work with. Celebrated performers perform side by side with emerging artists. Until now, *Monsieur Croche* has always managed to include both male and female artists from various cultural backgrounds, nationalities, age groups, religious beliefs and those who identify as LGBTQ+. We invite artists according to their performed repertoire, and album releases, and find new ones through networks that surround French music, and through scouting. *Monsieur Croche* currently operates only in Antwerp, but we are intending to expand to other cities and countries.[19]

Social impact is important for us, and therefore besides concerts, we organise outreach events such as masterclasses, narrated concerts for children, digital concerts (which were distributed throughout the COVID-19 lockdowns), and other benefit chamber music concerts. Our masterclasses are given by select artists who perform during our concerts (e.g. the first four of those mentioned above). The young students (or those who are young in spirit) who participate in the masterclass are given the opportunity to play in front of a live audience and receive live feedback from these renowned artists. Some of our masters are professors in leading music schools in Europe such as Antwerp's Conservatoire, the École Normale de musique de Paris, Geneve's Conservatoire, and Valencia's and Brussels's music academies. The special thing about these masterclasses is that the students do not pay. International masterclasses can be extremely expensive and therefore

---

18 Walker, 'Alumni Stories: Tal Walker'.
19 We are currently exploring curating a concert or a series of events related to Gabriel Fauré's centenary (1924–2024) in London in 2024.

not accessible for some young pianists, and so we have decided that ticket sales, donations, contributions from the hosting school, the audience or other sources will cover the costs. Students can participate without breaking the bank.

Initiatives and Collaborations

Some of our past concerts have featured collaborations with visual artists, fashion designers, hair designers and dancers. In February 2020, we held a concert in *Museum De Reede*, which exhibits art by Edvard Munch, Félicien Rops and Francisco Goya. The concert began in a standard theatre setting with the performance of emerging artists. At the break, we asked our audience to come to a small reception downstairs and have a glass of wine, while we transformed the hall into a catwalk. This concert was a collaboration with a sustainable fashion designer, who creates textiles herself from recycled fabric. The concert focused on the music of Francis Poulenc, and the Paris of these years, which was a symbol of art, music, literature, cinema and fashion. In this period, *Les années folles*, international writers and artists were attracted to Paris to pursue and exhibit their art. Among the notable women in Paris of the time were Coco Chanel, Josephine Baker and Édith Piaf. Chanel's designs became the symbol of the emancipated woman. Our models were in fact dancers from the Royal Conservatoire of Antwerp – a small twist which made the connection with the music even greater. An international hairstylist designed the models' hair.

This concert was a representation of *Monsieur Croche*'s artistic vision. It was a surprising fusion of visual art, music, dance and fashion which were all tied together through the narrative surrounding Poulenc. The event proved complicated logistically, but the museum's staff was able to accommodate our needs through innovative solutions: for example, blocking a section of the exhibition space in order to transform it into a dressing room for the models. Many positive reactions from our listeners concluded that the evening was 'unique' and 'unforgettable'. Yet, some of the listeners testified that the narrow exhibition space provided limited visibility in a theatre setting, while fitting perfectly for a catwalk. Others complained that it was hard to focus on the music when the dancer-models roamed the space followed by the photographer; some added that it was almost impossible to see the piano with such a seating arrangement. Overall, the evening was considered a success by *Monsieur Croche*'s team (based on the satisfaction of the audience, the artists and the museum, as well as the excellent turnout).

Monsieur Croche's little nephew *Mini Croche* is our initiative of narrated concerts for children, which started in 2019. The idea was to make classical music concerts, which usually have serious, adult connotations, more accessible for children. We did so through storytelling, acting, and visual objects and images. During our first concert, our narrator told the story of *Babar the Little Elephant*, written by Jean de Brunhoff, in an interactive way, with dancing and acting, and with my accompaniment on the piano playing a piece composed by Francis Poulenc. Our narrator has also created his own text and story to the music of Debussy's *Children's Corner*, which was performed by a pianist. This was a fun concert for the children but also the adults accompanying them. So far, this project has taken place in schools such as *House of Music* and *Prince Dries* primary and ballet school in Antwerp, as well as part of *Maagdenuis*'s charity Christmas concert. Future productions will include Shakespeare's *A Midsummer Night's Dream* adapted for children and accompanied by Debussy's *Préludes* and Jacques Ibert's *Histoires*.

Our little non-profit organisation would not be what it is without its growing family of volunteers. As well as initiatives such as *Mini Croche*, was the digital concert named *Monsieur Croche Blijft Thuis* (*Monsieur Croche stays home* in Dutch), which took place during the first and second COVID-19 lockdowns. It was based on our past performances, with poetry, visual art and narration. Instead of distributing the video on social media, we decided to offer it to retirement homes and hospitals. We had a few wonderful partners, one of them, the *Ziekenhuis Netwerk Antwerpen*, whose patients enjoyed our concerts in their own way.

Even though the collaborations mentioned above were successful, unfortunately, not all envisioned collaborations were eventually realised. Due to financial constraints and the outbreak of COVID-19, a fully envisioned project together with the orchestra *Antwerpen Camerata* did not take place. The project *Debussy – Fauré: Dialogue* was supposed to bring the parallel and overlapping stories of Debussy and Fauré and their compositions into the spotlight. Some of the titles and inspirations for their compositions were published coincidentally (or not) at the same time.[20] Not only musical information was to be shared, but also more personal anecdotes, such as the fact that Fauré's lover, Emma Bardac, later became the wife of Debussy. We still hope to realise this, or another project together with *Antwerpen Camerata*. The orchestra believes that 'music belongs to everybody and [we] put all our passion and skill into making every single concert a unique experience', which is in line with *Monsieur Croche*'s vision.[21] The idea of two young and energetic organisations working together was very exciting and hopefully is still on the table.

Obstacles and Successes

Monsieur Croche did not survive five seasons without any challenges. In the beginning, our initiative received some resistance from art galleries and museums who preferred to remain a place for visual art alone. The first locations to be interested, *Valerie Traan* and *House Happaert*, caught the attention of other venues, who soon followed.[22] Some music institutions, concert halls and concert organisations did not appreciate a new initiative in town, while others were interested in collaborating with or promoting us. Today, *Monsieur Croche* enjoys a diversity of venues that appreciate our vision and professionalism, while new venues join the family every year as our hosts. During the pandemic, *Alliance Française d'Anvers* has honoured us with an artists' exchange and mutual promotion. A year later, *De Kathedraal*, Antwerp's monumental cathedral, invited *Monsieur Croche* to produce two of its concerts, during the *Festival César Franck in Antwerpen* bicentenary chamber music and organ music festival.

The logistics of transforming a non-conventional concert hall also proved to be difficult. Some venues were too cold in the winter, and others had challenging acoustics for the artists. We had to turn down venues where transporting a piano would be too difficult or expensive.

---

20 Jean-Michel Nectoux, 'Debussy et Fauré' in *Cahiers Debussy* (France: Centre de documentation Claude Debussy, 1979), pp. 13–30.
21 'Homepage' in *Antwerpen Camerata's Website* (Antwerp: 2020), https://www.antwerpencamerata.be
22 *House Happaert* unfortunately had to shut down for public initiatives in 2018 just before our first performance. Luckily, we were honoured to produce our very first performance in the celebrated art gallery *De Zwarte Panter* instead.

For one concert in the first season, we even ended up transporting chairs manually one by one from one location to another. With proper planning and expanding the network of partners, these tasks became easier and part of our routine. Undeniably, using a venue which was not intended for a musical performance might mean sacrificing some qualities such as optimal acoustics, comfortable seats or ideal lighting. Nonetheless, other qualities that are gained include an intimate space, proximity to the artists and an inspiring environment, among others.

An aspect that never becomes easier is promotion, which remains a challenge for any concert organisation. We started our first season completely unknown, handing out flyers in the streets. However, this proved to be unsustainable (both environmentally, physically and financially). Luckily the *Gazette van Antwerpen* newspaper decided to promote us in their culture column. We then decided to take a 'modern' approach and have gone digital. Together with *Studio Volt*, we created attractive promotion videos, which helped our crowdfunding campaign and our promotional reach. Social media platforms such as Instagram and Facebook proved to be useful in approaching a wider audience.

Finance was never an easy topic for *Monsieur Croche* as we did not receive subsidies. Since the venues are small, we can sell only a limited number of tickets for each concert. This small income goes directly to covering the artistic costs such as artists' wages, transportation and accommodation, as well as the performing rights when the music is not yet in the public domain. Organising a concert in an 'unconventional' concert hall is also not financially easy as it involves renting a piano, obtaining chairs, promotion and much more. To overcome this challenge, our first season was completely funded by a successful crowdfunding campaign. Our inner and outer circles agreed to donate various amounts which concluded with a successful campaign and more than €5,000. Looking back at the crowdfunding campaign, it was successful mostly thanks to our inner circles with a combination of integrating into it a pre-sale of our tickets. We quickly understood that relying on our family, friends and colleagues together with ticket sales alone is not a sustainable financial model.

In the following seasons, cuts, donations, small increases in ticket price, income from *Mini Croche* and benefit concerts all helped us to (almost) break even. Since 2020, *Monsieur Croche* has been able to cover its costs independently due to the generosity of loyal donors who contribute annually during an exclusive Christmas benefit concert. Our donors include some of our faithful listeners who responded to our offering (the programming, the artists and the concept) and hosted us in their houses while inviting their own circles. Despite the tension between exclusivity and inclusion, we feel that although this method of funding might be partially based on the old salon model, it is in line with our current values. These benefit concerts are indeed more exclusive; however, the same musical programme is shared with the broad public at a much more affordable price during our main events. These also provide an additional opportunity for our artists to perform, which means being paid for two performances of the same repertoire. The rest of the income from these concerts goes mostly to our artists in the main events.[23] Together with ticket sales and *Mini Croche*, we believe that we have come up with a more stable financial model that we hope to continue developing.

Whither *Monsieur Croche?* – Futuring Classical Music

After two years of the pandemic, we have learnt that we must remain flexible, agile and open to new ways of working. The future of *Monsieur Croche* is open: we seek to explore new programmes, exciting interdisciplinary combinations, surprising collaborations and always aspire to excellent music performances. Luckily, lesser-known composers, women composers, and extra-musically inspired compositions (those inspired by visual art, poetry, nature and literature) exist in abundance within the French repertoire of the nineteenth and twentieth centuries. Every year we discover new venues in Antwerp – it has been an adventure discovering each of their acoustics, their local audience and the atmosphere they convey. After including visual art, poetry and fashion during our concerts, we would like to introduce live visual creations (either painted live or projected in synchronisation with our music) and collaborate with actors and dancers. In 2022 we

---

23   Artists' salaries and artistic expenses (such as accommodation and transportation) are our biggest expenses.

included, for the first time, a pre-concert talk by a musicologist from the Royal College of Music in London.[24]

Improving our financial model is important to us. Being financially stable is crucial for *Monsieur Croche* to survive in the long term. As part of our goals and aims, we would like to stay affordable, but continue paying our artists properly. Some ideas include exporting our performances (or select pieces) to cultural centres; or performing the same programme more than once in various locations. We will continue offering donors access to our exclusive private events, offering private concerts and children's concerts, applying for subsidies and collaborating with other organisations.

'It is our strong belief that awareness, inclusion, and interaction are key elements in keeping classical music alive and relevant today'.[25] We will continue presenting concerts to the audience in an approachable, engaging, interdisciplinary, and unique way in non-conventional venues. We hope that creating small and local projects, which are intimate, diverse, inclusive in programming, approachable in presentation and financially affordable, together with outreach and social impact is the future of classical music. We wish to continue producing enjoyable concerts, keeping them 'young, relevant, and up-to-date while continuing a long and respectful tradition of music making'.[26]

References

Antwerpen Camerata (2020), https://www.antwerpencamerata.be

Bennett, Dawn and Jane Ginsborg, 'Audience reactions to the program notes of unfamiliar music', *Psychology of Music* 46:4 (2018), 588–605, https://doi.org/10.1177/0305735617721339

Chineke! Foundation (2021), https://www.chineke.org

---

24 Narrations, pre- and post-concert talks as well as conversation with the audience are encouraged by Pitts and Gross. These might help deepen the relationship with the audience and create an inclusive and meaningful experience. Stephanie Pitts and Jonathan Gross, '"Audience exchange": cultivating peer-to-peer dialogue at unfamiliar arts events', *Arts and the Market* 7:1 (2017), 65–79.
25 Monsieur Croche's website, http://www.monsieurcroche.be
26 Walker, 'Alumni Stories: Tal Walker'.

Curtin, Adrian and Adam Whittaker, 'Introduction: Representation in/of Classical Music', *Open Library of Humanities* 8:1 (2022), https://doi.org/10.16995/olh.8252

Debussy, Claude, *Monsieur Croche et autres écrits* (Paris: Éditions Gallimard, 1971).

Devlin, Graham and Judith Ackrill, *A Review of Orchestral Provision for Yorkshire* (London: Arts Council of England, 2005), https://webarchive.nationalarchives.gov.uk/ukgwa/20150205143656/http://www.artscouncil.org.uk/advice-and-guidance/browse-advice-and-guidance/a-review-of-orchestral-provision-for-yorkshire

Ewell, Philip, 'Music Theory and the White Racial Frame', *Music Theory Online* 26:2 (2020), https://doi.org/10.30535/mto.26.2.4

Johnson, Julian, *Who Needs Classical Music?: Cultural Choice and Musical Values* (Oxford: Oxford University Press, 2002).

La Maestra, http://www.lamaestra-aris.com

Monsieur Croche's Team, Strategy and Playbook (version 1.0, April 2020).

Monsieur Croche, http://www.monsieurcroche.be

Nectoux, Jean-Michel, 'Debussy et Fauré' in *Cahiers Debussy* (France: Centre de documentation Claude Debussy, 1979), pp. 13–30.

Parakilas, James, 'Classical Music as Popular Music', *The Journal of Musicology* 3:1 (1984), 1–18, https://doi.org/10.2307/763659

Ross, James, 'Music in the French Salon', in *French Music since Berlioz*, ed. by Richard Langham Smith and Caroline Potter (Aldershot: Ashgate, 2006), pp. 91–115.

Royal Conservatoire of Antwerp (Antwerp: 2018), https://www.ap-arts.be/en/news/alumni-stories-tal-walker

16. Strategies of Proximity: Breaking Away from the Standard Classical Concert

Folkert Uhde and Hans-Joachim Gögl

For quite some time, the classical music industry has been experiencing a phenomenon that is becoming increasingly obvious, particularly in the wake of the pandemic: there is an audience problem.[1] On average, audiences for classical music have been ageing and declining.

The pandemic has revealed that, in addition to demographic trends, there is a new, dangerous trend as well: many people are simply staying at home. At the time of writing, hardly anyone makes long-term plans anymore, subscription sales are falling dramatically, and the audience – if it comes – is largely impromptu and far fewer in number. Those who do attend feel a genuine need to listen to music. That said, the social framework has disappeared – no champagne reception, no socialising.

The pandemic has also made it clear that art and culture in general (and classical music in particular) do not enjoy a particularly high social status. No-one took to the streets to protest cancelled concerts; there were no mass demonstrations supporting freelance cultural workers, nor were there any large-scale fundraising campaigns to save freelance livelihoods. Instead, many music professionals who, until recently, were internationally successful, were forced to apply for unemployment benefits.

---

1   See, among others, Heiner Gembris and Jonas Menze, 'Zwischen Publikumsschwund und Publikumsentwicklung: Perspektiven für Musikberuf, Musikpädagogik und Kulturpolitik', in *Das Konzert II*, ed. Martin Tröndle (Bielefeld: Transcript Verlag, 2018).

Given the numerous sociological studies over the past fifteen years, the loss of social relevance and lack of audience development is hardly surprising. But in the cultural sector, it almost seems as if these realities have been successfully suppressed. Even the German Federal Agency for Civic Education estimates that cultural institutions can attract only 4.5 percent of the total population to their institutions. In other words, more than ninety-five percent do not come in the first place. Some studies are slightly more optimistic, but the statistics remain grim.

Such figures always refer to the totality of high-cultural institutions, i.e. opera, drama, dance, classical music and museums. There is no data for classical music alone. Nevertheless, case studies would most likely not improve this tally. In short, ninety-five percent of those visitors who theoretically could come to a concert never or seldom do. We need to keep reminding ourselves of that, even if it is painful and, above all, raises a storm of questions.

In 2019, the cultural scientist Martin Tröndle from Zeppelin University Friedrichshafen presented an extensive study on that ninety-five percent.[2] His book, *Non-Visitor Research*, paints a somewhat more differentiated picture of this hitherto largely under-researched segment of society. In total, 1,268 questionnaires filled out by students were evaluated, and those who explicitly avoided culture were invited to concerts, operas, and theatres and then interviewed.

The findings of this work are, on the one hand, surprising and encouraging, revealing that there is potential for new audiences to be found. On the other hand, the findings show how far removed we seem to be from these potential audiences. Firstly, the results show how thin the line is between those who attend concerts and those who do not. Many, it seems, would attend if they were invited, for example, by someone they knew well. An overwhelming forty-six percent say that the recommendation of a friend or someone they knew well provided the decisive impetus – regardless of whether this tip was received in the pub or via a social media channel. Feature articles, reputation and the name recognition of artists play almost no role.

---

2   Martin Tröndle, ed., *Nicht-Besucherforschung: Audience Development für Kultureinrichtungen* (Wiesbaden: Springer VS / Edition Würth Chair of Cultural Production, 2019). English translation available: *Non-Visitor Research* (London: Palgrave MacMillan, 2022).

Many, who in some cases had attended a classical concert for the first time, were surprised that so few of their prejudices had been confirmed: that they felt less bored and much less out of place, and that the audience and atmosphere were not at all what they had anticipated. In other words, their first time at a concert was a thoroughly positive experience, which is very encouraging.

According to the study, there is, overall, a greater potential for attracting new audiences for cultural institutions than many assume: about twenty percent of the group of 'infrequent' or 'not-yet' visitors can be won over, but only under certain conditions.

Martin Tröndle writes as a conclusion:

> The closer art is to people, the more likely they are to visit arts and culture organisations. *Proximity* must be understood here as a multidimensional concept: it implies proximity to art through socialisation in the parental home; one's field of study, which may allow one to repeatedly come into contact with artistic themes; knowledge about and personal reference to art; one's own artistic activities; and contact with art throughout one's school years and through later visits to arts and culture organisations.12 But it also implies proximity through one's musical tastes and leisure preferences as well as circle of friends.13 The closer art is to one's experienced reality of life, the more likely one is to visit arts and culture organisations.³

Martin Tröndle proposes this broad concept of *proximity* as a new dispositive for thinking about cultural offerings: 'It's not about breaking down barriers, but about building proximity.'⁴

If this concept is followed through, it would have far-reaching consequences for developing programmes in cultural institutions. Traditional audience development has always been based on the assumption that the 'product' is ready-made and needs to be communicated more effectively. Barriers are supposed to be broken down and hurdles overcome. People rarely question their own proud offerings. Communication and marketing are supposed to bring success.

But developing this proximity would mean adopting a completely new attitude as a cultural institution, an attitude that asks questions, listens and acts on impulses. Establishing contact with the audience should not start with the presentation of the finished program but with an open-ended development process that invites cooperation partners,

---

3   Ibid., p. 88.
4   Ibid., p. 89.

networks and potential audiences into a dialogue. Questions such as, 'What moves you right now?' 'Which performance situations and formats are suitable for this?' 'Which spaces can be used?' 'What fosters an experience, and what hinders it?' need to be posed.

When breaking down barriers, one is wedded to a venue and one's point of view. To build proximity, you have to initiate a process, approach others and become active. What consequences does this have for the identity of cultural institutions and, above all, for their organisers? What does programme development or 'curation' mean against this backdrop? And what other attitudes do cultural actors need to take for this process to be successful?

Montforter Zwischentöne and the Question of Relevance

Fig. 16.1 Zwischentoene Vision Rhinstadt by Matthias Dietrich © Montforter Zwischentöne. Image by Matthias Dietrich.

First and foremost, strategies of proximity need to take a new attitude when it comes to programme development: rather than barricading ourselves in an ivory tower, we need to reach out, network and connect. Rather than focusing on performers, celebrities, and musical works, we need to ask ourselves questions, search for new possibilities, and evaluate them. Rather than being representative, performances need to invite people to reflect: perceive the audience not as ticket consumers but as allies; reverse the sender-receiver principle again and again and replace it with permeability and reciprocity.

Only through this fundamentally changed development strategy can the question of relevance, which many overlook but is now being asked more and more loudly, be answered. Relevance is a very personal and individual decision: the provider cannot demand it; it can only be felt by the visitors.

For years, through our practical work at the Montforter Zwischentöne in Feldkirch (Vorarlberg, Austria), we have been developing cultural formats based on principles other than standard programmatic-interpretational offerings. The festival, which takes place annually in November, seizes on the period between All Souls' Day and Advent to address questions ranging from farewells to hopeful new beginnings. Strategies for transformational processes, both personal and social, are the focus of our program.

At the same time, we have been experimenting with new concert formats since the beginning of our artistic endeavours – an international development in which the festival is now regarded as a pioneer.[5] Trade publications, international teaching assignments and artistic cooperations, as well as the rise of the 'Hugo', Montforter Zwischentöne's 'International Competition for New Concert Formats', are proof of this. In just a few years, it has become the most prominent university forum for discussing the new performance practice of classical music in the German-speaking world. In 2021, student teams from around forty music universities in Austria, Germany and Switzerland participated.

With this, the Montforter Zwischentöne has the unique opportunity to run, on the one hand, a laboratory for new concert formats by international young artists and, at the same time, together with the festival, a platform for exploration, experimentation, and performance.

We have moved further away from the 'classical' concert and its focus on musical works, programmes or performers in the development process. Classical music still plays an important role, but the repertoire has broadened to include jazz, improvisation, contemporary and early music. Above all, improvisation has become increasingly important:

---

5   Irena Müller-Brozovic and Barabara Balba Weber, eds., *Das Konzertpublikum der Zukunft: Forschungsperspektiven, Praxisreflexionen und Verortungen im Spannungsfeld einer sich verändernden Gesellschaft* (Bielefeld: Transcript Verlag, 2021).

like a good orator speaking extemporaneously, the audience is more likely to eagerly follow a musician's reactive improvisation than, say, the fixed form of a Romantic sonata. At the moment of improvisation, all participants – including the audience – are fully present and become part of a unique process.

Of course, the audience should participate in a performance. But it should also be able to contribute to it as well. Every evening is a co-creation, and the level of attention that is being paid changes the character of the performance. Today we know from neuroscience that everyone in the hall interacts directly with each other in a physical way. And we are always surprised by how quickly audiences adapt to the unfamiliar settings we offer. Of course, this requires practical knowledge and important organisational skills. But basically, we experience the audience as being more curious, open and friendly than in the 'classical' structures.

Based on these experiences, we are proposing a 'strategy of proximity' as a new approach to developing cultural formats. Accordingly, our work always tries to start from the perspective of the audience or the impact potential. In terms of Hartmut Rosa's resonance theory, we see the 'concert' or 'event' as a potential sphere for the intensification of the way the individual 'relates to the world' (Rosa) as a kind of mediator.[6]

There are basically three possible topics or reference points (so to speak, 'sounding boards') to fulfil this mediator role:

OUTWARDS
WITHIN
THE LIVING ENVIRONMENT

1. OUTWARDS

OUTWARDS focuses on the interaction between the network surrounding us and us as individuals: how do we relate to our surroundings and regional communities, and what topics are taken into consideration? What is or is not important? How do we relate to them? What experiences are there in our immediate vicinity, and how can we use them? How can we re-collect individual experiences so that everyone can use them? How can we foster group identity and experience personal efficacy in the community through such processes?

---

[6] Harmut Rosa, *Resonanz: Eine Soziologie der Weltbeziehung* (Frankfurt: Suhrkamp, 2016).

How can we re-purpose spaces, give them new attributes, instil new experiences in them and still connect to the ones we have had there?

Below are two examples from our practical work to demonstrate how we grapple with some of these questions.

St. Matthew Passion (2019, Montforthaus Feldkirch)[7]

Fig. 16.2 Matthaeus Passion by Matthias Rhomberg © Montforter Zwischentöne. Image by Matthias Dietrich.

This was an oratorio and video installation for soloists, choir, orchestra, and historians.

'Then all the disciples deserted him and fled': The St. Matthew Passion by Johann Sebastian Bach is undoubtedly one of the great masterpieces of music history. As part of a festival focus on the theme 'resistance', we attempted to focus on two central thematic aspects of the work: what does personal responsibility mean to me? Where do I stand when it comes to participation or resistance? Would I resist the maelstrom of the majority, or do I allow myself to be incited and driven by fake news?

Death – its imminence – is the antithesis of the unreflective acceptance of the masses, and the primal fear of being left behind alone: 'If I am to

---

7   Musical direction: Benjamin Lack; Concept: Hans-Joachim Gögl, Folkert Uhde ; Video, direction and lighting: Folkert Uhde; Chamber Choir Feldkirch; Capella Stella Matutina.

depart one day, do not depart from me.' This chorale was sung twice in our performance, once on stage and a second time with the entire audience. The entrance to the concert hall was designed as an installation: video interviews with the orchestral musicians and choristers about their experiences of moral courage (or lack thereof) in everyday life. After the intermission, there was an interview session with historian Meinrad Pichler on civil courage and resistance during the National Socialist era in Vorarlberg: major historical events set in a local context.

A late afternoon to pause for thought, with great music about courage and fear and the human need to belong. A programme about everyday heroes and heroines who paid the price for keeping true to themselves and their values.

Here is an entirely different example: the next project took an exemplary approach to a local, hotly debated issue through an artistic experimental arrangement.

Vision Rheinstadt (Vision Rhine City)[8]

In a legal proceeding professionally conducted on stage, the question of the dissolution of all Vorarlberg Rhine Valley municipalities in favour of the establishment of a new collective city was at stake. The topic has been hotly debated in Vorarlberg for years. Was the concept of a collective city with a population of 250,000 a dream or a nightmare? One single administration instead of twenty-nine independent municipalities? All the best arguments for and against were exchanged. The witnesses were former mayors, architects, spatial planners, regional development experts. Pianist David Helbock provided musical commentary, and the audience, who took on the role of jurors, passed the verdict. In the end, the great surprise was the merging of municipalities and the founding of a city! A complex, approximately two-hour dramaturgy with elements of Pecha Kucha, pleas, cross-examinations, musical summaries and a summative vote by the audience. The performance was unrehearsed but instead had an intuitive, dense set of rules in the background, making it possible to create a complex, elegant interplay.

The highlight of the evening was the realisation that a cultural format can shape a debate that is so politically charged (and almost taboo) that it

---

8   Concept: Hans-Joachim Gögl with the collaboration of all participants. Montforter Zwischentöne 2017.

can be discussed in an exciting, informed, high-quality and humorously conciliatory manner. The improvisations of David Hellbock responded, commented upon and contrasted with the debate – and also provided time and space for the audience to reflect on the discussion.

Outpatient Clinic for Unsolvable Tasks[9]

Fig. 16.3 Outpatient Clinic © Montforter Zwischentöne. Image by Matthias Dietrich.

We are familiar with the city's current issues and are in constant dialogue with the development departments of Feldkirch. By doing so, we maintain contact with our most important sponsor and ensure the festival's relevance, thus repeatedly creating formats that relate to socio-political issues in the region. Another example is the conflict in Vorarlberg between nature conservancies and commercial enterprises that want to build in the green belt.

Citizens' initiatives and nature conservationists criticise these companies for overdeveloping the countryside, to which the companies counter that growth potential is being impeded. The conflict poses important questions and offers fertile ground for format development.

---

9   *Ambulanz* für *unlösbare Aufgaben* [Outpatient Clinic for Unsolvable Tasks]: A political choreography, with musicians and dancers from Spodium—Ensemble für Improvisationskunst, Montforter Zwischentöne. Basic concept: Hans-Joachim Gögl.

We aimed to see whether it was possible to use an artistic vocabulary to address this conflict in a way that would be fruitful for both sides. As a result, we created a kind of dance-musical family constellation, with improvised personifications of the opposing parties.

2. WITHIN

The aim here is to turn one's perspective around: rather than focusing on our interaction with the outside world, our own personal, individual development with the outside world is considered. The focus is on ourselves: What is missing in our lives, what issues have we avoided so far, what questions are we facing? Where do we find meaning? Which experiences could be enriching? What means do we need for this, and in what forms?

Among our most intense concert experiences on this topic was an evening as part of our thematic focus on 'dying – of letting go'.

Concerto for Hospice Companion and Cello[10]

Fig. 16.4 Concert for companion © Montforter Zwischentöne. Image by Matthias Dietrich.

---

10   *Konzert für Sterbebegleiter und Cello* [Concert for hospice companion and cello]: Concept/Format development: Hans-Joachim Gögl with Folkert Uhde. Realised in the context of the focus 'dying—about letting go' of the Montforter Zwischentöne, 2016.

A doctor, a priest, a relative and a hospice companion recount their experiences on a bare stage in the spotlight. In the audience is the cellist Peter Bruns, who reacts to these stories with spontaneously selected music from his repertoire by Bach and Reger, performed by heart, thereby creating an intense space to reflect on what was heard. The result is an almost liturgical order, unrehearsed as it often is, but with a precise timing and a coordinated dramaturgical framework of the four narratives in the background.

The Funeral[11]

Fig. 16.5 The Funeral © Montforter Zwischentöne. Image by Matthias Dietrich.

Another format has now developed into a permanent part of the series: The Funeral. Our living world is spinning faster and faster. What was cutting-edge yesterday – fashions, technologies, knowledge – is outdated today. But we hardly take time to reflect on these things, appreciate them and part ways. That is why we have developed a new ritual, modelled on the classical funeral ceremony, to say farewell through words and music.

---

11   *Die Beerdigung* [The Funeral]: Format development Hans-Joachim Gögl with Folkert Uhde, realised at the Montforter Zwischentönen 2020 and 2021.

The very elements of this format make up a powerful theme, which in our case denotes a term, a circumstance or a state. In this way we have already put to rest certitudes, privacy, leisure and distance. A philosopher delivers a eulogy on the respective theme, for which relevant texts are also selected. There is music before and between the eulogies. So far we invited a wide range of musicians for this format from Early Music, Classical String Trio and Vocal Ensemble to improvising musicians. Again, music is needed to give space for reflections and thoughts on the spoken word.

In the end, volunteers read out the intercessions written by the speakers. Every time, a different architectural firm creates a temporary interior design.

Love, Pray Tell, What Are You Doing? – Early Music and Oral History[12]

Fig. 16.6 Love, pray © Montforter Zwischentöne. Image by Matthias Dietrich.

---

12   *Liebe sag' was fängst du an?* [Love, pray tell, what are you doing?]: Format development Hans-Joachim Gögl with Folkert Uhde, realised at the Montforter Zwischentönen 2020 and 2021. Concept/format development: Hans-Joachim Gögl, Folkert Uhde, Mark Riklin; 'Liebe sag', was fängst du an?' Baroque love songs and video installation, Ensemble Age of Passions with Hille Perl and the soprano Dorothee Mields, Montforter Zwischentöne.

Another approach addresses the audience's biography and life stories. When we opened the Montforter Zwischentöne back in 2015, we focused on the theme 'anfangen—Über das Beginnen' (starting—About the beginning). While reflecting on such experiences, we, together with the artist Mark Riklin, hit upon the idea of how romantic relationships begin – those moments in our existence that are whimsical, sublime, banal, long-planned, spontaneous and funny, but always significant. In each family, and in every locality, there is an untapped treasure of extraordinary stories, and because of this we trained story collectors to track down these experiences among their circles of friends. The result was an exhibition in the foyer of the Montforthaus, where one could read these countless recollections before or after the concert.

From these, we then selected individual stories that participants had told us to camera and which we then placed in the context of baroque love songs by seventeenth-century composers like Philipp Heinrich Erlebach or Johann Krieger. Consequently, a live ensemble played music that addressed the same theme as the respective story. This created a visual layer in a concert where couples from the region – elderly, same-sex, long-divorced, or newly married – recounted their successful or failed stories of how love began.

At the end of the concert, a visitor came up to us and said, 'Early music was new music!'. It was only now that she realised for the first time that a song by Heinrich Albert from the seventeenth century thematised the same emotion as the story of the lovers who dialled the wrong number three times on the telephone two years ago and thus met.

3. THE LIVING ENVIRONMENT

A person's LIVING ENVIRONMENT – and how he or she confronts it – is related to one of the most frequently asked questions by non-attendees of cultural events: 'What has this got to do with me?' Here, the decisive factor is the constant search for new forms and formats that are in keeping with the present or adapted to deal with the present. Free, open forms, which are more likely to stem from the visual arts, are naturally more suitable here than the form of the civic concert, which has been handed down from the nineteenth century. Installation forms and the inclusion of public space, as well as digital formats, can be employed here. De-hierarchisation is also key: the active decision-making of the visitors, for example, who can freely choose the object and duration of the encounter, similar to an exhibition of visual art, is essential. We often combine different forms, ranging between lectures, concerts, art in public space and walks. In 2016, we realised a complex form of these different elements based on the theme 'Belief—between doubt and revelation'.

Credo - Six Concerts and Ten Encounters with Mystics[13]

Fig. 16.7 Credo Mutter Hildgard © Montforter Zwischentöne. Image by Matthias Dietrich.

The tour featured three different elements: in the large, empty hall of Montforthaus, there was a meditative pendulum installation by the Austrian light artist Erwin Redl. Two points of light at the end of the pendulum, approximately twelve metres long, danced across the floor with an amplitude of about fifteen metres. Live concerts from a nearby chapel were transmitted into this pendulum installation: violinist Midori Seiler and organist Christian Rieger played the fifteen-sonata cycle of the

---

13 *CREDO – Sechs Konzerte und zehn Begegnungen mit Mystikerinnen und Mystikern* (CREDO - Six concerts and ten encounters with mystics): Concept and format development: Hans-Joachim Gögl and Folkert Uhde, realised at the Montforter Zwischentönen, 2016.

Rosary Sonatas by Baroque composer Heinrich Ignaz Franz Biber. Their performance, spread throughout the day at the times of the medieval Liturgy of the Hours, could be heard by the audience either live in the chapel or in the focused, darkened atmosphere of the great hall with the light pendulum. The path between the two venues traversed a brightly-lit covered bridge that led over a stream. The interior of the bridge, which itself had become an installation, posed questions that invited the audience to respond and reflect for themselves during the short walk. Additional impulse lectures on various spiritual topics took place in the Montforthaus throughout the day, among others by the abbess and the head of a Buddhist monastery.

Salon Paula

Fig 16.8 Salon Paula © Montforter Zwischentöne. Image by Matthias Dietrich.

Our 'Salon Paula' series illustrates a simple aspect of proximity that is also in line with our objective. For these offsite concerts, staged at the kitchen table or in the living rooms of our audience's homes, we select soloists from the fields of music, science, art or mainstream culture. We pay the complete fee and anyone in Vorarlberg can apply to host such an event. The underlying idea is straightforward: the expert or musician comes to that person's home and provides half an hour of content or musical input; afterwards there is a chance for everyone to exchange thoughts and ideas. Friends and family are invited – it doesn't matter to us if there are five people or twenty-five – and we put up a poster in front of the entrance to welcome everyone. In attendance is an on-site artistic director, who goes over to the kitchen table of the student co-op, villa or social housing project and says, 'Welcome to the Montforter Zwischentönen,' thereby transgressing the barrier of the concert hall by privatising it.

Conclusion

Of course, the above examples taken from our work at the Montforter Zwischentöne over the past several years are just that – examples. Each demonstrates our underlying desire to establish a participatory link with audiences that, hopefully, achieves our objective of building proximity. And although the programmes described here have been tailored for our facilities and epitomise our vision of striving to create a sounding board for issues relevant to audiences in our region, they are by no means set in stone. One venue's success story may not work for another – there is no single formula, and yet the possibilities are limitless. One only needs imagination, as well as the courage to step down from the ivory tower of the 'classical' concert and listen to the needs of the public.

Of course, the beauty of this – of breaking away from the standard 'classical' concert – is that a clean slate appears suddenly before your eyes. No longer is it necessary to succumb to the pressure of wooing potential audiences by presenting the 'best' musicians with the 'best' programmes – elements that, once you have freed yourself of such constraints, make you realise that the classical concert can resemble a three-ring circus at times. Of course, we strive to offer high-calibre performances at the Montforter Zwischentöne with top-quality musicians, but more important is our desire to find points where music, art and culture can be employed to strike a nerve and resonate with topics and issues current in today's ever-changing society. Simply put, we are not interested in creating an institution that elevates music and culture to a podium. Such an approach, in our opinion, leads institutions down a dead-end street, one that has resulted in declining concert attendance figures in the first place.

But with that clean slate comes the need for concert organisers to accept a particular responsibility, too. One must be willing to take risks, try things out and potentially make mistakes. That said, however, such risks can be calculated in advance with good planning. Behind our closed doors, we regularly meet for brainstorming sessions that, through trial and error and a bit of imagination, attempt to take the pulse of the issues at stake in society and turn them into programmes that extend beyond being representative. At times the results may seem unconventional at first or even crazy. And yet, our experience – again to echo Tröndle – is that when our offerings truly 'speak' to the inner voice of our potential visitors and invite them to reflect, people become interested and are likely to attend. That, in a nutshell, is our guiding principle for our ongoing experiment at the Montforter Zwischentöne. We hope that the examples here provide insight and inspiration to think beyond the horizon.

Fig 16.9 Zwischentoene © Montforter Zwischentöne. Image by Matthias Dietrich.

Translation: Eric Lloyd Dorset

References

Müller-Brozovic, Irena and Barabara Balba Weber, eds., *Das Konzertpublikum der Zukunft: Forschungsperspektiven, Praxisreflexionen und Verortungen im Spannungsfeld einer sich verändernden Gesellschaft* (Bielefeld: Transcript Verlag, 2021).

Gembris, Heiner and Jonas Menze, 'Zwischen Publikumsschwund und Publikumsentwicklung: Perspektiven für Musikberuf, Musikpädagogik und Kulturpolitik', in *Das Konzert II*, ed. by Martin Tröndle (Bielefeld: Transcript Verlag, 2018), pp. 305-352, https://doi.org/10.1515/9783839443156-017

Rosa, Harmut, *Resonanz: Eine Soziologie der Weltbeziehung* (Frankfurt: Suhrkamp, 2016).

Tröndle, Martin, ed., *Nicht-Besucherforschung: Audience Development für Kultureinrichtungen* (Wiesbaden: Springer VS / Edition Würth Chair of Cultural Production, 2019).

17. Audiences of the Future – How Can Streamed Music Performance Replicate the Live Music Experience?

Michelle Phillips and Amanda E. Krause

Introduction

The COVID-19 pandemic created a crisis for the live music industry. It 'disrupted the spatial practice of music' around the world and resulted in long-term impacts on the live music sector, a sector which may subsequently need to consider health and safety in new ways (e.g. the need for social distancing) for years to come.[1]

In place of live music events, many artists and organisations around the world developed new methods of offering their content in an online format. Formats included performances that were livestreamed (broadcast) in real time, and performances that were recorded and then made available at a later date (accessed either 'live' whilst the recording was broadcast at a designated time, or available to access at any later point, akin to a YouTube video). For many artists and organisations, this was a new way of presenting content and, hence, the

---

[1] See Iain A. Taylor, Sarah Raine, and Craig Hamilton, 'COVID-19 and the UK Live Music Industry: A Crisis of Spatial Materiality', *The Journal of Media Art Study and Theory* 1:2 (2020), p. 219; Richard Florida and Michael Seman, 'Measuring COVID-19's Devastating Impact on America's Creative Economy', *Metropolitan Policy Program at Brookings, August* 32 (2020); Xin Gu, Nevin Domer, and Justin O'Connor, 'The Next Normal: Chinese Indie Music in a Post-COVID China', *Cultural Trends* 30:1 (2021), 63-74; M. Harris, J. Kreindler, A. El-Osta, T. Esko, and A. Majeed, 'Safe Management of Full-Capacity Live/Mass Events in COVID-19 Will Require Mathematical, Epidemiological and Economic Modelling', *Journal of the Royal Society of Medicine* 114:6 (2021), 290-294.

pandemic allowed audiences to engage with performances in an online environment for the first time (Rendell terms this 'pandemic media').[2] For example, the English National Opera, Vienna Philharmonic, Wigmore Hall and the Royal Northern College of Music (RNCM) (in their #LiveFromTheRNCM broadcast series) offered performances in a livestreamed or recorded-and-then-broadcast format during the various COVID-19-related lockdown periods.

Organisations that would usually have made artistic content available in person only (live), found themselves exploring new ways of continuing to share content. These online formats introduced multiple new considerations, such as the technical requirements for broadcasting live and the selection of relevant online platforms used to reach existing audiences. Other urgent questions concerned what audiences would want in their livestream experience, and whether they would even be interested in switching from live to online attendance. Mixed in with these questions are considerations around how an online experience might be similar or different to a live performance, whether people's motivations to attend these two different formats are similar, and how preferences for live and online attendance may differ depending on people's own characteristics, or individual differences.

Another important question facing organisations attempting to translate the live experience to an online one, is what a 'live' experience consists of, and what audiences might expect of this experience to be represented in online attendance. Furthermore, of those expectations, what elements of the live experience are possible to replicate online, and are there aspects that are simply not possible to maintain? There is evidence to support the value of 'liveness' in music performance,[3] but what this is, and whether it can be replicated in an online format, is currently little understood.

---

[2] James Rendell, 'Staying In, Rocking Out: Online Live Music Portal Shows During the Coronavirus Pandemic', *Convergence* 27:4 (2021), p. 1092.

[3] See e.g. Philip Auslander, *Liveness: Performance in a Mediatized Culture* (Abingdon, Oxon: Routledge, 2008); Steven C. Brown and Don Knox, 'Why Go to Pop Concerts? The Motivations Behind Live Music Attendance', *Musicae Scientiae* 21:3 (2017), 233–249; Michael Tsangaris, 'The Eternal Course of Live Music Views and Experiences of an Audience', in *The Future of Live Music* (New York, Bloomsbury, 2020).

Despite the pandemic and associated lockdowns having 'propelled many musicians into the livestreaming arena and the practice of livestreaming concerts',[4] there is at present little research to support decisions that organisations may make in terms of how they transfer a performance which would have usually been offered live to an online performance, and how they might evaluate factors which may be important in how they record and / or livestream (e.g. sound quality, camera angles). The study which is discussed in this chapter sought to address some of these questions. Namely, the data analysed and reported here sought to examine what people's motivations to attend live and livestreamed music *pre*-COVID-19 were, which format they preferred, and what they saw as the advantages and disadvantages of livestreamed music. The aim of asking these questions was to determine what people value in a live performance versus a livestreamed performance, in order for the findings to be available to, and relevant for, organisations considering whether to return to live music performance, or also continue to livestream some or all events. One of the main focuses of the chapter, as the data and findings are discussed, will be an examination of two factors – the notion of live music as a shared experience, and as being about fun or having a good time on a night out.

Current Study

An online survey was conducted with 281 members of the general public (average age: 35.89 years, all UK residents), who were invited to discuss their experiences of live and livestreamed music before and during the COVID-19 pandemic. They were recruited, and paid for their time, using the survey platform *Prolific*. Respondents were asked a series of questions regarding their preferred music genre, motivations to attend live and livestreamed performance, what they consider to be the advantages and disadvantages of attending performances online, and what they consider 'liveness' to mean.

---

4 Julia Haferkorn, Brian Kavanagh, and Samuel Leak, 'Livestreaming Music in the UK: Report for Musicians' (2021), https://eprints.mdx.ac.uk/33787/1/Livestreaming%20Music%20in%20the%20UK.pdf, p. 4.

Motivations to Attend Live and Livestreamed Performance Pre-Pandemic

Respondents, who listed mostly pop and rock music as their preferred music genre, gave the following main motivations for attending live and livestreamed music (these were selected form a list of options, and participants were invited to select all that applied to them).[5]

Top live responses:	Top livestreamed responses:
Having fun/ having a good night out	The quality of the band/ performer/ ensemble
Sharing an experience with my friends/ partner/ family	The sense of occasion
The quality of the band/ performer/ ensemble	Filling my free time in a meaningful/ enriching way
The sense of occasion	The sound quality in my home environment

From these lists of motivations, it can be seen that, whilst two factors are common between live and livestreamed performance attendance – 'the quality of the band / performer / ensemble' and 'the sense of occasion' – two factors in each list differ (underlined in the table above). Attendance at live performance often results from a desire to share an experience with friends, a partner or family, and to have fun, or have a good night out. In contrast, attendance at performances streamed online may be motivated by a wish to fill time in a meaningful and enriching way, and the sound quality in one's own home. From this it could be concluded that, whilst some attendance motivations are the same, there are also some that are fundamentally different. These data suggest that different people may choose to attend live or livestreamed performances based on different motivations, and these may be useful for organisations

---

5 The options were: Discovering more about the arts, sharing an experience with my friends/partner/family, experiencing thought-provoking art, having a strong emotional experience, losing myself in an arts experience, giving my support to an organisation whose values I believe in, feeling like I have experienced a unique event, having fun / having a good night out, filling my free time in a meaningful/ enriching way, being around people like me, the quality of the band/performer/ ensemble, the venue, the programme/set, the sound quality in a live environment / my home environment, the sense of occasion, other.

and performers to be aware of when planning and marketing live and livestreamed events. These data also provide some evidence that there may be particular aspects of live performance which motivate people to attend in person. The remainder of the chapter will examine these two factors – the notion of live music as a shared experience, and as being about fun or having a good time on a night out – in more detail, with reference both to existing research and thematic analysis of further data gathered in the survey discussed above.

Music as a Social Tool

A wealth of research testifies to the value of music as fostering a sense of social connectedness.[6] For example, Schäfer and Eerola surveyed the role that people felt that listening to music played for them, and found that music acted for some as a 'social surrogate' (i.e. music was used by listeners to feel a sense of being with other people, and could subsequently alleviate loneliness).[7] Music has been considered to be a valuable human communication system due to having indirect meaning, in contrast to language's direct meaning, enabling a musical exchange to be free from conflict, and music has been found to possess an important quality which might be termed 'floating intentionality'.[8] The role of music in the community, often in the form of community choirs, amateur ensembles, brass bands, karaoke events and music used to enhance health and wellbeing for not only the general public, but those living with Parkinson's or dementia, might legitimately be attributed

---

6   See e.g. Betty A. Bailey and Jane W. Davidson, 'Effects of Group Singing and Performance for Marginalized and Middle-Class Singers', *Psychology of Music* 33:3 (2005), 269-303; Amanda E. Krause, Jane W. Davidson, and Adrian C. North, 'Musical Activity and Well-Being: A New Quantitative Measurement Instrument', *Music Perception* 35:4 (2018), 454-474.

7   Katherina Schäfer and Eerola, Tuomas, 'How Listening to Music and Engagement with Other Media Provide a Sense of Belonging: An Exploratory Study of Social Surrogacy', *Psychology of Music* 48:2 (2020), 232-251, https://doi.org/10.1177/30575618795036. See also Amanda E. Krause, 'The Role and Impact of Radio Listening Practices in Older Adults' Everyday Lives', *Frontiers in Psychology* 11:603446 (2020); Katherina Schäfer, Suvi Saarikallio, and Tuomas Eerola, 'Music May Reduce Loneliness and Act as Social Surrogate for a Friend: Evidence from an Experimental Listening Study', *Music & Science* 3 (2020), 2059204320935709.

8   Ian Cross, 'Music and Communication in Music Psychology', *Psychology of Music* 42:6 (2014), 809–819.

to its power in bringing people together and fostering social cohesion (music has also been discussed in terms of indicating class distinction, and affiliation with specific groups, for example those identifying as 'punks').

Never has the positive impact of music been clearer than in research on music as a social tool during the last few years. Many studies examining the role of music listening during the COVID-19 pandemic have demonstrated not only an increase in the amount of time spent listening to music,[9] but also the use of listening to music to regulate mood, cope with stress and connect with other people.[10] Additional findings have shown that music, more than other activities and media

---

9   See e.g. Alberto Cabedo-Mas, Cristina Arriaga-Sanz, and Lidon Moliner-Miravet, 'Uses and Perceptions of Music in Times of COVID-19: A Spanish Population Survey', *Frontiers in Psychology* 11:606180 (2021); Emily Carlson, Johanna Wilson, Margarida Baltazar, Deniz Duman, Henna-Riika Peltola, Petri Toiviainen, and Suvi Saarikallio, 'The Role of Music in Everyday Life During the First Wave of the Coronavirus Pandemic: A Mixed-Methods Exploratory Study', *Frontiers in Psychology* 12:647756 (2021); Lauren K. Fink, Lindsay A. Warrenburg, Claire Howlin, William M. Randall, Niels C. Hansen, and Melanie Wald-Fuhrmann, 'Viral Tunes: Changes in Musical Behaviours and Interest in Coronamusic Predict Socio-Emotional Coping During COVID-19 Lockdown', *Humanities & Social Sciences Communications* 8:1 (2021), 1-11.

10 See e.g. Alberto Cabedo-Mas et al, 'Uses and Perceptions', 2021; Lauren K. Fink et al., 'Viral Tunes', 2021; Roni Granot, Daniel H. Spitz, Boaz R. Cherki, Psyche Loui, Renee Timmers, Rebecca S. Schaefer, Jonna K. Vuoskoski, ... Salomon Israel, '"Help! I Need Somebody": Music as a Global Resource for Obtaining Wellbeing Goals in Times of Crisis', *Frontiers in Psychology* 12:648013 (2021); Noah Henry, Diana Kayser, and Hauke Egermann, 'Music in Mood Regulation and Coping Orientations in Response to Covid-19 Lockdown Measures Within the United Kingdom', *Frontiers in Psychology* 12:647879 (2021); Pastora Martínez-Castilla, Isabel M. Gutiérrez-Blasco, Daniel H. Spitz, and Roni Granot, 'The Efficacy of Music for Emotional Wellbeing During the COVID-19 Lockdown in Spain: An Analysis of Personal and Context-Related Variables', *Frontiers in Psychology* 12:647837 (2021); Rosie Perkins, S. L. Kaye, B. B. Zammit, Adele Mason-Bertrand, Neta Spiro, and Aaron Williamon, 'How Arts Engagement Supported Social Connectedness During the First Year of the COVID-19 Pandemic in the UK: Findings from the HEartS Survey', *Public Health* 207:1208 (2022); Fabiana S. Ribeiro, João P. Araujo Lessa, Guilherme Delmolin, and Flávia H.Santos, 'Music Listening in Times of COVID-19 Outbreak: A Brazilian Study', *Frontiers in Psychology* 12:647473 (2021); Dianna Vidas, Joel L. Larwood, Nicole L. Nelson, and Genevieve A. Dingle, 'Music Listening as a Strategy for Managing COVID-19 Stress in First-Year University Students', *Frontiers in Psychology* 12:647065 (2021).

types, has supported emotional well-being and quality of life during COVID-19.[11]

Hansen et al. discuss media engagement habits during the COVID-19 pandemic, and moreover, the shift from audio- to video-based platforms.[12] Other studies have also explored experiences of livestreamed music during the pandemic. For example, Onderdijk, Swarbrick, Van Kerrebroeck, Mantei, Vuoskoski, Maes and Leman examined livestreamed experiences and what listeners valued in these, and found that social connectedness results from listeners feeling a sense of physical presence in a musical experience.[13] Indeed, this has been a noted feature of attending live music: that 'being there' to experience something 'unique' and 'special' is a primary motivator for attending live concerts.[14] As Earl noted, thanks to listening technologies, people do not have to attend live music to hear high-quality music they enjoy,[15] which suggests a social motivation to attend concerts. It is the concert experience, with considerations of the atmosphere, the uniqueness, the proximity to musicians, and opportunity to socialise with others sharing the experience – rather than the music itself – that underpins the reasons for seeking out live music opportunities.[16] While people engage with live music less than recorded music,[17] when asked about their favourite

---

11   Roni Granot et al., '"Help! I Need Somebody"', 2021; Amanda E. Krause, James Dimmock, Amanda L. Rebar, and Ben Jackson, 'Music Listening Predicted Improved Life Satisfaction in University Students During Early Stages of the COVID-19 Pandemic', *Frontiers in Psychology* 11:631033 (2021).

12   Niels C. Hansen, John M. G. Treider, Dana Swarbrick, Joshua S Bamford, Johanna Wilson, and Jonna K. Vuoskoski, 'A Crowd-Sourced Database of Coronamusic: Documenting Online Making and Sharing of Music During the COVID-19 Pandemic', *Frontiers in Psychology* 12:2377 (2021).

13   Kelsey E. Onderdijk, Dana Swarbrick, Bavo Van Kerrebroeck, Maximillian Mantei, Jonna K. Vuoskoski, Pieter-Jan Maes, and Marc Leman, 'Livestream Experiments: The Role of COVID-19, Agency, Presence, and Social Context in Facilitating Social Connectedness', *Frontiers in Psychology* 12:1741 (2021).

14   Steven C. Brown and Don Knox, 'Why Go to Pop Concerts?', 2017, p. 233; see also Jan Packer and Julie Ballantyne, 'The Impact of Music Festival Attendance on Young People's Psychological and Social Well-Being', *Psychology of Music* 39:2 (2011), 164–181.

15   Peter E. Earl, 'Simon's Travel Theorem and the Demand for Live Music', *Journal of Economic Psychology* 22 (2001), 335–358.

16   Steven C. Brown and Don Knox, 'Why Go to Pop Concerts?' (2017), 233-249.

17   Amanda E. Krause and Steven C. Brown, 'A Uses and Gratifications Approach to Considering the Music Formats that People use Most Often', *Psychology of Music* 49:3 (2021), 547-566.

format (selecting from live music, digital file, paid-for streaming, free streaming, physical and radio), a preference for live music has been noted.[18] While each format has associated uses and gratifications, Brown and Krause's findings reveal that live music still holds a special place for listeners: that it is a 'unique and organic form of entertainment'.[19] This is due to the social and emotional elements highlighted as reasons for preferring live music, which were not noted as reasons pertaining to the other formats.

What Is 'Liveness'?

Overwhelmingly, respondents to our survey reported they found the live music experience to be the more enjoyable type of music performance, compared to livestreamed attendance. As seen regarding the motivations above and in other data collected and analysed as part of this survey, reasons for wishing to attend live music include this being a shared experience (and opportunities to interact both with other audience members and performers) and having fun and a good night out. But what aspects of live music performance grant these experiences, and how can we translate these into factors that organisations can attempt to replicate if they do choose to offer previously live experiences in an online format?

Thematic analysis of survey respondents' answers to the question of what they consider 'liveness' to mean resulted in the following five themes:

Theme	Illustrative quotes
Interaction with audience and performers	'A crowd, along with the performer reacting in real time to a crowd. Not just [a] repeatable set'
Atmosphere / immersion	'Ambience, movement, atmosphere, emotion'

---

18 Steven C. Brown and Amanda E. Krause, 'Freedom of Choice: Examining Music Listening as a Function of Favorite Music Format', *Psychomusicology: Music, Mind, and Brain* 30:2 (2020), 88-102.
19 Ibid., p. 8.

Theme	Illustrative quotes
Being there in real life	'Being physically present in the same space as the band and other fans'
Sensory experiences	'Be[ing] able to watch other <u>peoples</u> [sic] reactions be[ing] able to feel the vibrations of the music'
Sharing the experience with other people	'The sense of "togetherness" with a whole bunch of people with the same taste'

The themes of 'Interaction with audience and performers' and 'sharing the experience with other people' testify to the desire to be with other people in the same space (a crowd), and the possibilities of interacting with others in the room. The themes 'Atmosphere / immersion', 'being there in real life' and 'sensory experiences' give more detail regarding factors that may be linked to the motivations to have fun, and to have a good night out, which were found in the data discussed above.

The survey on livestream experiences conducted by Haferkorn, Kavanagh and Leak in 2021 demonstrated that, overwhelmingly, audiences used the platforms Facebook and YouTube most often to access online content during the COVID-19 pandemic.[20] These platforms do not offer any particular features designed to impact atmosphere, sense of presence or sensory experience. However, perhaps future developments in effective livestreamed music might consider how best to facilitate these aspects of what listeners value in liveness. Such considerations might take into account the technology that listeners use to access livestreamed performance (and, for example, the resolution of audio and visual information), and how to optimise experiences on commonly used technology, as well as how to foster a sense of presence (perhaps by developing features such as Facebook's options to contribute emojis and comments during a livestream, which other listeners can see and respond to). Relatedly, work on music experiences in virtual reality (VR) and augmented reality (AR) may be particularly pertinent to future decisions about how to best present musical performances. Such technologies can distort the boundaries of

---

[20] Julia Haferkorn et al., 'Livestreaming' (2021).

live and mediated performance.[21] Developments in VR and AR speak to immersiveness, which may have significant implications for creating feelings of 'liveness.' Indeed, Onderdijk, Swarbrick, Van Kerrebroeck, Mantei, Vuoskoski, Maes and Leman found that VR did provide a sense of physical presence in their study of livestreamed experiences using VR headsets.[22] In this study, participants watched a YouTube stream of the performance filmed in 360 degrees, and, therefore, had a sense of being surrounded by the performance as they watched through the headset. Such technology may be intended to allow attendees to feel that they are inside a venue or performance space simply by wearing a VR headset in their own homes.

Advantages and Disadvantages of Livestreamed Performance

Respondents to the survey were asked what they saw as the advantages and disadvantages of livestreamed performance. The following themes resulted from thematic analyses of these two questions, and each set of themes is listed in order of the extent to which the theme was prominent in the data (the most prominent theme is at the top of each list).

What do you see as the advantages of attending a performance which is streamed online (compared to a live (in-person) performance)? Results of thematic analysis:

---

21 Charron Jean-Philippe, 'Music Audiences 3.0: Concert-Goers' Psychological Motivations at the Dawn of Virtual Reality', *Frontiers in Psychology* 8:800 (2017).
22 Kelsey E. Onderdijk et al., 'Livestream Experiments' (2021).

Theme	Sub-themes	Illustrative quotes
Convenience / easier engagement	- More comfortable (seating, access to food and drink, access to toilets, clothing) - Ease/convenience (can arrive and leave at will, less stressful) - Time saved (queuing for toilets, food and drink and parking, travelling, planning)	'Cheaper, easier, and don't have to make as much effort.'
Logistics	- Travel (saves time and money, parking, queues) - Weather considerations (avoiding bad weather, mud and rain) - Lower cost (cheaper, ticket prices, food and drinks, travel)	'Can watch in comfort of own home, cheaper, less time required as no travel involved.'

Theme	Sub-themes	Illustrative quotes
Accessibility	• Access to greater number of events (less risk of event being sold out, possibility of accessing events around the world) • Individual accessibility needs (parenting responsibilities, anxiety, illness, disability)	'You can see a performance that one has no hope of attending in person such as distance or costs.'
(Lack of) Social interaction	• Not being with other people / in large crowds	'No anxiety around being with other people in close proximity to each other and sharing conveniences etc.'
Health and safety	• Safety (COVID-19 risk, risk of other infections)	'Keeps you safe from COVID.'
Environment	• Better for the environment (more eco-friendly)	'Better for the environment.'
Quality of experience	• Better view of artist(s) (camera angles, closer view, guaranteed view)	'A better, close-up, view of the performers, too.'

Some of these themes and sub-themes support the data analysis discussed above; for example, social interaction appeared there as a motivation to attend live performance, but not livestreamed. However, this thematic analysis also underlines that, for some people, the opportunity *not* to be with others, or in a crowd, during the performance is an advantage to livestreamed performance. Given the findings discussed above regarding the importance of the social aspect of live events, it is worth bearing in mind that some audience members may actively seek to avoid such social interaction (e.g. people who experience social anxiety).

However, the thematic analysis also revealed important new themes, such as considerations around accessibility and environmental concerns. Such factors suggest that there may be specific individuals or demographics who may choose livestreamed performance over live performance in future. For example, if environmental concerns are a factor in how listeners choose to attend a performance, they may opt for livestreamed rather than live, in-person events. The 'safety' theme also suggests that there may be short-to-medium-term effects of the COVID-19 pandemic, and that performers and venues may need to consider what measures they keep in place (such as recommending the wearing of face masks) in the medium or even long term. Furthermore, this thematic analysis captures the important consideration that a wide practice of livestreaming may open up access to events around the world that audiences might not otherwise attend; the primary and sub-themes in the table above suggest that audiences feel that livestreaming means that more performances around the world are available to them, and that such engagement may better accommodate their own needs, such as disabilities, or caring responsibilities.

What do you see as the disadvantages of attending a performance which is streamed online (compared to a live (in person) performance? Results of thematic analysis:

Theme	Sub-themes	Illustrative quotes
Sensory experience	• Atmosphere (being in the moment, being captivated, vibe, energy, buzz, ambience) • Physicality of the live experience (dancing, sensory experiences, immersion)	'the sound, the atmosphere, the energy, the immediacy, the reality of an event right in front of you.'

Theme	Sub-themes	Illustrative quotes
Social interaction	• Social interaction (with performers and other audience members, sense of community, connection with other people)	'there isn't a feeling of belonging and sharing a unique experience with all those around you.'
Emotional response	• Emotional response (fun, excitement, mood, feelings, livestreamed experiences feeling lonely / solitary)	'Emotional experience is not as good.'
Quality of experience	• Different quality of experiences (livestream experience as inferior, not the same, not as memorable) • Sense of occasion (going out / leaving the house, chance to also enjoy eating and drinking at the venue)	'There's not the excitement of getting dressed up and going out for a "once in a lifetime" event.'

Theme	Sub-themes	Illustrative quotes
Logistics	• Technological considerations (sound quality, internet connection issues, home listening systems and technology)	'1. Camera dictates the audience's gaze. 2. Experience isn't as immersive. 3. Quality of stream isn't normally as good as in-person.'
	• Home environment (distractions at home, livestream experience as similar to watching television)	
	• Logistics (live music venue, travel considerations, cost of tickets)	

This thematic analysis further emphasises some of the findings of data discussed above, such as the importance of the atmosphere (a theme which arose in the data on what constitutes 'liveness'), the opportunity for social interaction (which appeared in both the data regarding 'liveness' and the motivations to attend live performance), and the physical sensations of the live experience (which also appeared in the themes concerning 'liveness'). Also, the quality of the sound, and the reliability of the internet signal, appeared as themes here, and sound quality was also listed as a motivation to attend online performances. Notable here is the theme of 'Emotional response'. This could be seen as linked to the motivation to have fun / have a good night out, which was seen in the analysis discussed above; however, it also stands on its own and speaks to an additional common motivation and response concerning musical involvement. These respondents felt that a disadvantage of a livestreamed experience was that different parts of the emotional experience were missing or lessened, such as the fun or excitement of the live event. Again, there are some themes here not evident in the results and data analysis discussed earlier in this chapter. For example, the considerations that a person's own home environment is relevant, and the extent to which there are distractions at home, or whether people simply enjoy a chance to leave the house.

Respondents perceived both the advantages and disadvantages of livestreamed performance to include considerations around social interaction, logistics and quality of experience. However, each analysis revealed different sub-themes, and respondents demonstrated that an aspect perceived as an advantage for one person may be perceived as a disadvantage for another (e.g., the social interaction theme). Most notable in the summary of these two thematic analyses is that they each have themes that are unique to that set of responses; the advantages of livestreamed performance include convenience and ease of engagement, accessibility, environment and health and safety, and the disadvantages include sensory experience and emotional response. It is perhaps these factors that organisations, performers and venues should bear in mind when planning whether performances are made available in person, online or in a hybrid format. For example, if a performance is only available in a livestreamed format, the impact on the environment and the links to accessibility might be emphasised, in order to appeal to audiences motivated by these considerations.

Conclusion

A music industry report published in May 2021, 'Livestreaming music in the UK', predicted that 'there is little doubt that the format [livestreaming] will continue to form part of the music industry post-COVID'.[23] Other industry experts and publications imagine a similar, permanent, change in the industry,[24] and many organisations have already established programme series which offer their events in both live and livestreamed performances (e.g. Wigmore Hall).

The study discussed in this chapter suggests that audiences do have some similar, and some different, motivations concerning whether they

---

23 Julia Haferkorn et al., 'Livestreaming' (2021), p. 50.
24 See e.g. Hattie Collins, 'Once Lockdown Lifts, Will the Music Industry be Changed Forever?', *Vogue*, 7 May 2020, https://www.vogue.co.uk/arts-and-lifestyle/article/music-industry-recovery

attend live or livestreamed performance. Live performance may be more about having fun, and a good night out, sharing an experience with others, and the emotional experience of an in-person event. Livestreamed performance attendance may result from a desire to fill time in a meaningful way, or the sound quality on a home listening system. People's concepts of liveness include factors linked to their motivations to attend in person, such as the opportunity for interaction. However, liveness is also felt to be about the atmosphere and sense of immersion, being physically present, and having sensory experiences.

In terms of the advantages and disadvantages of live and livestreamed performance, some of the responses here have common primary themes, such as logistics, social interaction (or lack of) and factors which impact on the quality of the experience. However, the sub-themes for these are often very different; for example, the logistics theme for the advantages of livestreamed performance includes travel, whereas the thematic analysis of the disadvantages reveals sub-themes around the quality of internet connections and the home environment. Moreover, advantages of livestreamed performance may include considerations such as accessibility, impact on the environment and health and safety, which are not perceived to be advantages offered by in-person attendance. Parts of the experience that may be special to live event attendance might include the emotional response to such an event and the opportunity to share an experience.

There are multiple implications that may be derived from the survey findings discussed above for performers and organisers of music events. For example, if there is a desire to create a sense of 'liveness' in an online event, facilitating social interaction during the performance (perhaps by audience members being able to share comments or emojis as they watch) may be important. However, music industry stakeholders should also bear in mind that there may not be a need to replicate 'liveness' in a livestreamed event, as factors such as accessibility, sound quality and logistics (e.g. travel), and environmental concerns play a role in whether audiences choose to attend online, and indeed some prefer not to have to interact socially.

In light of this changed industry, and new forms by which audiences can experience music performance, it is vital that we understand what might motivate listeners to attend online performance. If organisations intend this option to be chosen by listeners instead of in-person attendance, there is a need to understand which of the factors that people value in the live music experience might be replicable online. Future research might seek to explore the response to live and livestreamed experiences using other methods (e.g. physiological, neurological), and might also further examine whether specific groups of people might prefer one or the other form of attendance, and whether this changes in specific circumstances or for different events. There is also a chance for music venues, performers and event organisers to learn from other industries, for example, opera, ballet and theatre companies were already broadcasting performances live to cinemas pre-pandemic, for audiences to access locally, in real time. Also, the sports industry has a well-established format of broadcasting live events to bars and homes; communities and sports fans often gather to watch together, creating their own sense of a shared experience as they watch, and sense of occasion. However, research around the digital transmission of such events conducted pre-COVID-19 suggests that similar challenges remain to those discussed in this current chapter, for example, 'despite improvements in digital technology, traditional theatre and broadcasted theatre are two different experiences, not substitutes'[25] and that experiences of live, compared to broadcast sports events, may result in differences in audience members' recall and levels of arousal.[26] Nonetheless, such examples of activity in other disciplines demonstrates there are opportunities to develop new, varied methods of creating some of the factors that people value in live music performance, such as the chance to interact with other people, and to feel a sense of immersion (for example, in a surround-sound cinema environment).

At the time of writing, live music performance has returned around the world, and numbers of performances are at an almost pre-pandemic level. Audience numbers are slowly returning to pre-pandemic levels, and it is expected that the live music industry will recover fully (albeit

---

[25] Daniela Mueser and Peter Vlachos, 'Almost Like Being There? A Conceptualisation of Live-Streaming Theatre, *International Journal of Event and Festival Management* 9:2 (2018), 183.

[26] François Anthony Carrillat, Alain d'Astous, François Bellavance, and François Eid, 'On 'Being There': A Comparison of the Effectiveness of Sporting Event Sponsorship Among Direct and Indirect Audiences', *European Journal of Marketing* 49:3-4 (2015).

some venues do still recommend face masks and cases of COVID-19 are not uncommon). However, some performers, organisations and venues continue to livestream performance, often alongside offering live attendance at events. For example, when the iconic 'Koko' venue in Camden, London reopened in Spring 2022 following fire damage, the rebuild included built-in facilities to livestream their live music events.[27] It seems that the question of whether livestreaming music events that are also offered live will become a permanent feature of the music industry post-pandemic is still an open one.

References

Auslander, Philip, *Liveness: Performance in a Mediatized Culture* (Abingdon, Oxon: Routledge, 2008), https://doi.org/10.4324/9781003031314

Bailey, Betty A., and Davidson, Jane W., 'Effects of Group Singing and Performance for Marginalized and Middle-Class Singers', *Psychology of Music* 33:3 (2005), 269-303, https://doi.org/10.1177/0305735605053734

BBC News, 'Koko: Historic Camden Music Venue to Reopen After Fire', 21 October 2021, https://www.bbc.co.uk/news/uk-england-london-58992508

Brown, Steven C., and Knox, Don, 'Why Go to Pop Concerts? The Motivations Behind Live Music Attendance', *Musicae Scientiae* 21:3 (2017), 233-249, https://doi.org/10.1177/1029864916650719

Brown, Steven C., and Krause, Amanda E., 'Freedom of Choice: Examining Music Listening as a Function of Favorite Music Format', *Psychomusicology: Music, Mind, and Brain* 30:2 (2020), 88-102, http://dx.doi.org/10.1037/pmu0000254.

Cabedo-Mas, Alberto, Arriaga-Sanz, Cristina, and Moliner-Miravet, Lidon, 'Uses and Perceptions of Music in Times of COVID-19: A Spanish Population Survey', *Frontiers in Psychology* 11 (2021), https://doi.org/10.3389/fpsyg.2020.606180

Carlson, Emily, Wilson, Johanna, Baltazar, Margarida, Duman, Deniz, Peltola, Henna-Riikka, Toiviainen, Petri, and Saarikallio, Suvi, 'The Role of Music in Everyday Life During the First Wave of the Coronavirus Pandemic: A Mixed-Methods Exploratory Study',

---

27 BBC News, 'Koko: Historic Camden Music Venue to Reopen After Fire', 21 October 2021, https://www.bbc.co.uk/news/uk-england-london-58992508

Frontiers in Psychology 12 (2021), https://doi.org/10.3389/fpsyg.2021.647756.

Carrillat, François Anthony, d'Astous, Alain, Bellavance, François, & Eid, François, 'On "Being There": A Comparison of the Effectiveness of Sporting Event Sponsorship Among Direct and Indirect Audiences', *European Journal of Marketing* 49:3-4 (2015), 621-642, https://doi.org/10.1108/EJM-03-2013-0156

Charron Jean-Philippe, 'Music Audiences 3.0: Concert-Goers' Psychological Motivations at the Dawn of Virtual Reality', *Frontiers in Psychology* 8:800 (2017), https://doi.org/10.3389/fpsyg.2017.00800

Collins, Hattie, 'Once Lockdown Lifts, Will the Music Industry be Changed Forever?', *Vogue*, 7 May 2020, https://www.vogue.co.uk/arts-and-lifestyle/article/music-industry-recovery

Cross, Ian, 'Music and Communication in Music Psychology', *Psychology of Music* 42:6 (2014), 809-819, https://doi.org/10.1177/0305735614543968

Earl, Peter E., 'Simon's Travel Theorem and the Demand for Live Music', *Journal of Economic Psychology* 22 (2001), 335–358, https://doi.org/10.1016/S0167-4870(01)00037-X

Fink, Lauren K., Warrenburg, Lindsay A., Howlin, Claire, Randall, William M., Hansen, Niels C., and Wald-Fuhrmann, Melanie, 'Viral Tunes: Changes in Musical Behaviours and Interest in Coronamusic Predict Socio-Emotional Coping During COVID-19 Lockdown', *Humanities & Social Sciences Communications* 8:1 (2021), 1-11, https://doi.org/10.1057/s41599-021-00858-y

Florida, Richard, and Seman, Michael, 'Measuring COVID-19's Devastating Impact on America's Creative Economy', *Metropolitan Policy Program at Brookings*, August 32 (2020).

Granot, Roni, Spitz, Daniel H., Cherki, Boaz R., Loui, Psyche, Timmers, Renee, Schaefer, Rebecca S., Vuokoski, Jonna K., Israel, Salomon, '"Help! I Need Somebody": Music as a Global Resource for Obtaining Wellbeing Goals in Times of Crisis', *Frontiers in Psychology* 12 (2021), https://doi.org/10.3389/fpsyg.2021.648013

Gu, Xin, Domer, Nevin, and O'Connor, Justin, 'The Next Normal: Chinese Indie Music in a Post-COVID China', *Cultural Trends* 30:1 (2021), 63-74, https://doi.org/10.1080/09548963.2020.1846122

Haferkorn, Julia, Kavanagh, Brian, and Leak, Samuel, 'Livestreaming Music in the UK: Report for Musicians' (2021), https://eprints.mdx.ac.uk/33787/1/Livestreaming%20Music%20in%20the%20UK.pdf

Hansen, Niels C., Treider, John M. G., Swarbrick, Dana, Bamford, Joshua S., Wilson, Johanna, and Vuoskoski, Jonna K., 'A Crowd-Sourced Database of Coronamusic: Documenting Online Making and Sharing of Music During the COVID-19 Pandemic', *Frontiers in Psychology* 12:2377 (2021), https://doi.org/10.3389/fpsyg.2021.684083

Harris, M., Kreindler, J., El-Osta, A., Esko, T., and Majeed, A., 'Safe Management of Full-Capacity Live/Mass Events in COVID-19 Will Require Mathematical, Epidemiological and Economic Modelling', *Journal of the Royal Society of Medicine* 114:6 (2021), 290-294, https://doi.org/10.1177/01410768211007759

Henry, Noah, Kayser, Diana, and Egermann, Hauke, 'Music in Mood Regulation and Coping Orientations in Response to Covid-19 Lockdown Measures Within the United Kingdom', *Frontiers in Psychology* 12 (2021), https://doi.org/10.3389/fpsyg.2021.647879

Krause, Amanda E., 'The Role and Impact of Radio Listening Practices in Older Adults' Everyday Lives', *Frontiers in Psychology* 11 (2020), https://doi.org/10.3389/fpsyg.2020.603446

Krause, Amanda E., and Brown, Steven C., 'A Uses and Gratifications Approach to Considering the Music Formats that People use Most Often', *Psychology of Music* 49:3 (2021), 547-566, https://doi.org/10.1177/0305735619880608

Krause, Amanda E., Davidson, Jane W., and North, Adrian C., 'Musical Activity and Well-Being: A New Quantitative Measurement Instrument', *Music Perception* 35:4 (2018), 454-474, https://doi.org/10.1525/MP/2018.35.4.454

Krause, Amanda E., Dimmock, James, Rebar, Amanda L., and Jackson, Ben, 'Music Listening Predicted Improved Life Satisfaction in University Students During Early Stages of the COVID-19 Pandemic', *Frontiers in Psychology* 11 (2021), https://doi.org/10.3389/fpsyg.2020.631033

Martínez-Castilla, Pastora, Gutiérrez-Blasco, Isabel M., Spitz, Daniel H., and Granot, Roni, 'The Efficacy of Music for Emotional Wellbeing During the COVID-19 Lockdown in Spain: An Analysis of Personal and Context-Related Variables', *Frontiers in Psychology* 12 (2021), https://doi.org/10.3389/fpsyg.2021.647837

Mueser, Daniela, & Vlachos, Peter, 'Almost Like Being There? A Conceptualisation of Live-Streaming Theatre', *International Journal of Event and Festival Management* 9:2 (2018), 183-203, http://dx.doi.org/10.1108/IJEFM-05-2018-0030

Onderdijk, Kelsey E., Swarbrick, Dana, Van Kerrebroeck, Bavo, Mantei, Maximillian, Vuoskoski, Jonna K., Maes, Pieter-Jan, and

Leman, Marc, 'Livestream Experiments: The Role of COVID-19, Agency, Presence, and Social Context in Facilitating Social Connectedness', *Frontiers in Psychology* 12:1741 (2021), https://doi.org/10.3389/fpsyg.2021.647929

Packer, Jan, and Ballantyne, Julie, 'The Impact of Music Festival Attendance on Young People's Psychological and Social Well-Being', *Psychology of Music* 39:2 (2011), 164–181, https://doi.org/10.1177/0305735610372611

Perkins, Rosie, Kaye, S. L., Zammit, B. B., Mason-Bertrand, Adele, Spiro, Neta, and Williamon, Aaron, 'How Arts Engagement Supported Social Connectedness During the First Year of the COVID-19 Pandemic in the UK: Findings from the HEartS Survey', *Public Health* 207:1208 (2022), https://doi.org/10.1186/s12889-021-11233-6

Rendell, James, 'Staying In, Rocking Out: Online Live Music Portal Shows During the Coronavirus Pandemic', *Convergence* 27:4 (2021), 1092-1111, https://doi.org/10.1177/1354856520976451

Ribeiro, Fabiana S., Araujo Lessa, João P., Delmolin, Guilherme, and Santos, Flávia H., 'Music Listening in Times of COVID-19 Outbreak: A Brazilian Study', *Frontiers in Psychology* 12 (2021), https://doi.org/10.3389/fpsyg.2021.647473

Schäfer, Katherina, and Eerola, Tuomas, 'How Listening to Music and Engagement with Other Media Provide a Sense of Belonging: An Exploratory Study of Social Surrogacy', *Psychology of Music* 48:2 (2020), 232-251, https://doi.org/10.1177/30575618795036

Schäfer, Katherina, Saarikallio, Suvi, and Eerola, Tuomas, 'Music May Reduce Loneliness and Act as Social Surrogate for a Friend: Evidence from an Experimental Listening Study', *Music & Science* 3 (2020), https://doi.org/10.1177/2059204320935709

Taylor, Iain A., Raine, Sarah, and Hamilton, Craig, 'COVID-19 and the UK Live Music Industry: A Crisis of Spatial Materiality', *The Journal of Media Art Study and Theory* 1:2 (2020), 219-241.

Tsangaris, Michael, 'The Eternal Course of Live Music Views and Experiences of an Audience', in *The Future of Live Music* (New York: Bloomsbury, 2020), pp. 197-208, http://dx.doi.org/10.5040/9781501355905.0022

Vidas, Dianna, Larwood, Joel L., Nelson, Nicole L., and Dingle, Genevieve A., 'Music Listening as a Strategy for Managing COVID-19 Stress in First-Year University Students', *Frontiers in Psychology* 12 (2021), https://doi.org/10.3389/fpsyg.2021.647065

18. Artificial Intelligence and the Symphony Orchestra

Robert Laidlow

Introduction: The Age of Artificial Intelligence

It is a cold day in December 2020. It is almost a year since British orchestras, and most others around the world, packed up their instruments for the unexpected and unwelcome hiatus caused by the pandemic. I am working in my study on music for orchestra and artificial intelligence (AI); or perhaps, I am working with artificial intelligence on a study for orchestra. To my left is my grandmother's old upright piano, missing the top two notes and the tuning slightly wonky (the tuner was not available to come in the brief period between national lockdowns). To my right my computer is teaching itself to write music, though it doesn't *know* it is writing music. It doesn't know what a sound is. In front of me the window is open. The computer's graphics card, essential for AI algorithms, produces more than enough heat for the little study and the quiet of the woods through the window is only broken by the continual whirr of cooling fans.

When the computer is off, I am no less plugged into a world of AI. It serves me advertisements for upcoming concerts it has learned that I like.[1] It changes the directions on my satnav based on live information from other drivers' phones. It summarises an article I cannot be bothered

---

1 Emmanuel Mogaji, Sunday Olaleye, & Dandison Ukpabi, 'Using AI to Personalise Emotionally Appealing Advertisement', in *Digital and Social Media Marketing*, ed. by N. P. Rana, E. L. Slade, G. P. Sahu, H. Kizgin, N. Singh, B. Dey, A. Gutierrez, & Y. K. Dwivedi (Cham: Springer, 2020), pp. 137-150.

to read, corrects the grammar in an email I send before I have had my morning coffee, recommends new films for me to watch.[2] In short, it is everywhere, but more importantly it is, or could be, *anywhere*.[3] That is the reality of a world that increasingly relies on algorithms to command the hidden infrastructures that support our society.

The effects of hidden AI are not always good, or even intentional. In contrast to those examples already mentioned, we have also seen recently that AI can accidentally replicate harmful biases, with recent cases including discrimination against women in the workplace, failure to recognise ethnic minorities in passport recognition software, and the automatic promotion of extremist social media groups to those already at risk of radicalisation.[4]

As a technology, AI also forms an integral part of wider issues that encompass many other technologies and social questions. The proposed 'metaverse', hypothesised to synthesise physical and digital experience seamlessly, relies upon AI in concord with other advanced technologies such as augmented reality and wearable technology.[5] Many researchers are focussed on AI as an essential tool to mitigate climate change,

---

[2] Johann Lau, 'Google Maps 101: How AI helps predict traffic and determine routes', The Keyword, 3 September 2020, https://blog.google/products/maps/google-maps-101-how-ai-helps-predict-traffic-and-determine-routes/; Mico Tatalovic, 'AI writing bots are about to revolutionise science journalism: we must shape how this is done', *Journal of Science Communication* 17:1 (2018); Laksnoria Karyuatry., 'Grammarly as a Tool to Improve Students' Writing Quality: Free Online-Proofreader across the Boundaries', *JSSH (Jurnal Sains Sosial Dan Humaniora)* 2:1 (2018), 83–89; Carlos A. Gomez-Uribe & Neil Hunt 'The Netflix Recommender System', *ACM Transactions on Management Information Systems (TMIS)* 6:4 (2015).

[3] Geoff Cox & Morton Riis, '(Micro)Politics of Algorithmic Music', in *The Oxford Handbook of Algorithmic Music*, ed. by A. McLean & R. Dean (Oxford: Oxford University Press 2018), pp. 603–626.

[4] Jeffrey Dastin, 'Amazon Scraps Secret AI Recruiting Tool that Showed Bias against Women', in *Ethics of Data and Analytics* ed. by K. Martin (Boca Raton: Auerbach Publications, 2022), pp. 296–299; Leslie, David, 'Understanding Bias in Facial Recognition Technologies', *SSRN Electronic Journal* (2020); Hao, Karen, *He got Facebook hooked on AI. Now he can't fix its misinformation addiction* (MIT Technology Review, 2021), https://www.technologyreview.com/2021/03/11/1020600/facebook-responsible-ai-misinformation/

[5] Lik-Hang Lee, Tristan Braud, Pengyuan Zhou, Lin Wang, Dianlei Xu, Zijun Lin, Abhishek Kumar, Carlos Bermejo, Pan Hui, *All One Needs to Know about Metaverse: A Complete Survey on Technological Singularity, Virtual Ecosystem, and Research Agenda* (2021), https://doi.org/10.48550/arxiv.2110.05352

mobilising it alongside more well-known political and social arguments.[6] Climate change is the principal example of what Timothy Morton calls a 'hyperobject': an idea so abstract and vast that it is difficult or impossible for any individual to grapple it in its entirety.[7] Like the case of climate change, it is entirely plausible that AI, which can absorb and analyse truly vast quantities of data, will become a critical tool in understanding other hyperobjects – and may become a hyperobject itself.

In short, I believe the relationship between humans and technology has never been more important, nor more complex. I share this view with others: increasingly there has been a push for closer scrutiny of AI as the techno-utopian vision of a wholly fair, omnibenevolent, quasi-magical algorithm has been disrupted and dismantled. AI is a powerful, exciting, and malleable technology, and it is here to stay. Society has always probed ideas, ideologies and technologies, and art has always been one tool in our arsenal to do so. Music is my way of making sense of these hidden technologies, my chosen method to expose and highlight issues that arise from AI, whether we know it is there or not.

Even taking that for granted, however, I am often asked: 'why classical music?' or 'why the orchestra?'. What relationship does, or can, AI have with the symphony orchestra? These are good questions, and at first glance it may appear that the two have little in common. Dig a little deeper, however, and one finds there exists a kinship between the AI and orchestra, in all its guises as ensemble, community, institution and historical concept. Having said that, I do not imply that other types of music do not share this relationship with AI, nor that classical music and the orchestra is the best type of music to explore the relationship; it is simply my way of doing so.

The relationship is more than one-way: it is not simply using orchestral music as a vessel to comment on a society dependent on AI. AI can, in return, offer the orchestra new perspectives, technologies and approaches to music-making that did not exist even a decade ago, even at the same time as certain actors within the music industry work towards

---

6   Josh Cowls, Andreas Tsamados, Mariarosaria Taddeo, & Luciano Floridi, 'The AI gambit: leveraging artificial intelligence to combat climate change—opportunities, challenges, and recommendations' in *AI and Society* 1 (2021), 1–25.

7   Timothy Morton., *Hyperobjects: Philosophy and Ecology after the End of the World* (Minneapolis: University of Minnesota Press, 2013).

replacing human musicians with indistinguishable AI performances. AI is both dangerous and full of potential, both good and bad, both hidden behind-the-scenes and on full display as a corporate buzzword. It has these dualities that are both alluring to artists and highly relevant to the orchestra, which is also, I would argue, partially reliant on a foundation of dualities and contradictions. Three particular dualities have stood out to me as important for discourse around designing and understanding AI, which are also areas to which musicians and orchestral institutions already give a great deal of thought. I have termed these:

1. Future and Past
2. Fake and Real
3. System and Secret

Each of these dualities is the focus of an individual movement of my piece *Silicon*, written for the BBC Philharmonic Orchestra as part of my doctoral research at the Centre for Practice & Research in Science & Music at the Royal Northern College of Music, Manchester UK. Through this chapter, I hope to offer an artistic reflection and provocation on the utility of the symphony orchestra as an investigative tool into the technology that is changing our world, as well as a case study of *Silicon*, showing how these abstract ideas might be transformed into music. This case study will also discuss the exciting creative possibilities available when incorporating this technology into a live performance: this is music both *about* AI and *using* AI.

I will give a brief explanation of exactly what I mean by AI, because the term is unhelpfully broad. After this, I will ground my own artistic work and research amongst other fields that it relates to. Outside of fiction and clickbait internet articles, AI in a research context usually means the design of algorithms that, through statistical methods, can 'learn' how to mimic human intelligence. Most AI is designed to excel at one specific task, not to have any form of *general* intelligence (the term for this field of research is AGI). There are several approaches one might take to designing an algorithm, depending on the task, but over the last decade much research focus has been on the development of machine-learning algorithms.[8] Most interaction between art and

---

8   Terry Sejnowski, *The Deep Learning Revolution* (Cambridge, M.A.: MIT Press, 2018).

AI currently uses machine learning, and for this chapter the terms AI and machine learning can be regarded as interchangeable. Machine-learning algorithms 'learn' from a dataset (in this chapter, the dataset will most often be music of some sort), encoding the rules they learn into a digital 'model'. This model will then be used to carry out the AI's task, be that writing music or directing traffic. Machine learning can be both 'supervised', where a computer programmer provides positive or negative feedback on the results, usually directing towards a desired result, or 'unsupervised', where the algorithm is left totally on its own to learn. It is difficult to speak about AI algorithms, especially regarding their decision-making process, without risking some level of anthropomorphism. For the avoidance of doubt, I want to make it clear that none of these algorithms 'think' or in any way can make conscious decisions as we would understand them.

There are many composers using algorithms in their music and the algorithmic music field is a lively and fascinating area of practice-based research.[9] There is a rich history of musicians engaging specifically with classical music utilising algorithms, from twentieth-century composers such as Iannis Xenakis[10] and Karlheinz Stockhausen, to musician-programmers such as Francois Pachet,[11] stretching back to the earliest pioneers in the field of what would become computer science, including Ada Lovelace. However, these algorithms are generally coded top-down, which means the composer/programmer has had complete control over the creation of the algorithm. Even if the composer leaves in elements of randomness or instability, this remains a creative decision they have made. By definition, this is not an AI algorithm, which in some way teaches itself and can subsequently make decisions responding to new information based on what it has previously learned. Since AI technology is relatively nascent, the area of the orchestra and AI remains an exciting and comparatively untapped field, with space for many perspectives and artistic approaches.

---

9   *The Oxford Handbook of Algorithmic Music*, ed. by Alex McLean, & Roger T. Dean (Oxford: Oxford University Press, 2018).
10 Iannis Xenakis, *Formalized Music* (Bloomington, I.N.: Indiana University Press, 1971).
11 Francois Pachet, 'The Continuator: Musical Interaction with Style', *Journal of New Music Research* 32:3 (2010), 333-341, http://dx.doi.org/10.1076/jnmr.32.3.333.16861

By contrast, there is fascinating AI being developed by computer scientists that relate to music (music-related AI), though these tools are not always primarily intended to be used by composers. Often, music-related AI's purpose is to emulate existing music as accurately as possible, using music as a yardstick through which we can audibly measure the progress of the machine-learning field as a whole. Of course, there are several inspiring exceptions, including the work of Google Magenta, which releases intuitive AI tools for use by amateur and professional musicians in the studio, the Wekinator, which explores AI as a way to control digital instruments, PRiSM's reimplementation of SampleRNN, which many composers have used in recent years to generate electronics tracks for new pieces, and recent work from IRCAM such as the RAVE algorithm.[12]

Future and Past (*Silicon Mind*)

The first duality to be discussed is the relationship between the future and the past. Specifically, this relationship is one of legitimacy: how does the past legitimise the future? In the field of music-related AI, this relationship is often implied through the data and evaluation methods frequently employed to judge the success of AI. Here I will focus on AI that *generates* music.

AI needs data to learn from and, in the case of music, that data usually comes either in the form of audio files or sheet music. In both cases, AI cannot create music out of nothing, it needs to learn from music that already exists. When coding generative AI, researchers usually use existing music both as a dataset from which the AI learns the rules of music and also as a yardstick against which to judge the quality of the AI's outputs. Marcus du Sautoy writes that 'Bach is the composer most composers begin [learning] with, but he is the composer most computers

---

12   On the Wekinator see: Rebecca Fiebrink, & Perry R. Cook, 'The Wekinator: a system for real-time, interactive machine learning in music', *The 11th International Society for Music Information Retrieval Conference* (2010), http://code.google.com/p/wekinator/; for further discussion of PRiSM see: Christopher Melen, 'PRiSM-SampleRNN', *RNCM PRiSM* (2019), https://www.rncm.ac.uk/research/research-centres-rncm/prism/prism-collaborations/prism-samplernn/

begin with too',[13] and indeed Bach is often the choice of dataset and generation for much recent research.[14] The more indistinguishable from Bach, the more successful the AI is deemed to be. This might lead to the impression that one of the main uses of generative AI could be to complete unfinished pieces by dead composers, as indeed we have seen in recent years with AI 'completions' of Beethoven and Schubert.[15] Relatedly, several recent AI algorithms outside of academia have been developed that automatically generate music for soundtracks or other media uses.[16] Crucially, these are designed to replace composers who write this music, not necessarily to create more interesting music. Once again, AI needs to sound like what already exists as much as possible, in this case to avoid the costs of human labour.

This leaves us in the situation that this technology, which promises the future, is consistently looking to the past to prove its legitimacy. Of course, there are exceptions to this rule, as some researchers do place genuine novelty and creativity at the heart of their research. Overall, however, it is easier for AI to function in this way because currently the dominant AI methodology is machine learning, which relies on existing data. I worry that such a relationship between past and future has the potential to hamper innovation. As this technology becomes more prevalent, it will become even more essential to have the skills to use it for more interesting and creative purposes than simple repetition and recreation.

This is where the orchestra comes in. The performance of established music is perhaps the genre's defining trait, evident in the programming

---

13 Marcus du Sautoy, *The Creativity Code: Art and Innovation in the Age of AI* (Cambridge, M.A.: Fourth Estate 2020).
14 Gaëtan Hadjeres, François Pachet, & Frank Nielsen, 'DeepBach: a Steerable Model for Bach Chorales Generation' in *Proceedings of the 34th International Conference on Machine Learning* (2017); Raymond Whorley, & Robin Laney, 'Generating Subjects for Pieces in the Style of Bach's Two-Part Inventions' in *Proceedings of the 2020 Joint Conference on AI Music Creativity* (2021); Alexander Fang, Alisa Liu, Prem Seetharaman, & Bryan Pardo *Bach or Mock? A Grading Function for Chorales in the Style of J. S. Bach* (2020), ArXiv:2006.13329 [Cs.SD].
15 Jason Goodyer, *How an artificial intelligence finished Beethoven's last symphony*, (Science Focus, 2021), https://www.sciencefocus.com/news/ai-beethovens-symphony/
16 Robert Langkjær-Bain, 'Five ways data is transforming music' in *Significance* 15:1 (2018), 20–23; AIVA, *AIVA - The AI composing emotional soundtrack music* (AIVA), https://www.aiva.ai/.

of the vast majority of symphony orchestras.[17] Why do we do this? In my view, it is because we believe that ideas from the past can have something to say in the present – something beyond merely being a benchmark by which to judge technical progress. We never try to merely recreate. Conversely, modern composers often use references to older music, or different genres of music, to make exciting and fascinating musical arguments (e.g. Michael Gordon's *Rewriting Beethoven's Seventh Symphony* or Sky Macklay's *Many Many Cadences*).

Silicon's first movement, *Mind*, is scored for a classical orchestra with a few additional instruments. There are no electronics: the relationship between orchestra and AI is realised solely through the live performers. It is the longest movement of *Silicon* at around fifteen minutes. Through it, I explore Future and Past in two specific ways:

By using an AI designed to imitate composers to push orchestral music into new places.

By creating a piece that might make sense to a theoretical, far-future AI mind.

The AI I chose to use for this piece is called MuseNet.[18] MuseNet, developed by OpenAI, produces MIDI data (i.e. sheet music) and has been trained on a very large dataset of music throughout history. This allows it to imitate a wide range of styles, including my own (though I did not use this functionality while composing *Silicon*). I have developed familiarity with its interface and quirks through using it in several projects over the last few years.

MuseNet works by providing the trained model with some music (a 'prompt') and giving it some basic instructions of how to continue writing the piece (a 'response'). For this movement, I instructed MuseNet to continue it in the style of Mozart. This suited the classical orchestra, and relates to the use of the sonata form in this movement, which will be discussed later. I would provide MuseNet with prompts in short score and sift through the many possible responses it generated.

---

17 Donne, *Women In Music, 2019-2020 - Donne, Women in Music Research* (Donne 2020), https://donne-uk.org/2019-2020/; Mark Gotham, 'Coherence in Concert Programming: A View from the U.K.', in *IRASM* 45:2 (2014), 293–309.
18 Christine Payne, 'MuseNet' in *OpenAI* (2019).

In contrast to an approach aiming to show how well the algorithm learned, where I might have chosen to keep responses I thought sounded like Mozart, I instead elected to retain the responses which I found unusual, uncanny, obsessive and – in a word – bizarre. I was fascinated by these responses, because it was clear that MuseNet understood them to be just as stylistically accurate as the responses that really did sound like Mozart. It felt like there was a strange, almost alien, methodology at work under the surface, which to me was far more interesting than a computer showing it can learn rules we already know concerning harmony, counterpoint and voice-leading. Perhaps the learning machine had discovered a deeper 'style' that underpins this music, which does not necessarily relate to the surface-level features of the music.

Selecting which to retain was a creative act in this work, in which I was rejecting the idea of 'best' and instead comparing each generation on their own merits according to my own subjective criteria. In general, I was drawn to responses that introduced a fundamental change in some parameter, for example substantially altering the harmonic rate, introducing completely novel melodic material, or repeating material in an unexpected way. After choosing a response, I might compose the next few bars, or sometimes simply give that response as the prompt for the next iteration of MuseNet to work with. In this way, the work goes down a unique rabbit-hole that I couldn't have planned on my own. This is one of the joys of working with AI – it can introduce an element of spontaneity to work that you can't account for, like a voice from another world. Analysing the responses can also be quite illuminating, and in these responses I was particularly taken by MuseNet's approach to repeated material, which is very polarised. Often material is stated once and never repeated or developed. Equally often, material will be obsessed over for an extremely long period. Sometimes it does repeat phrases in a way we would associate with classical music (such as composing a four-bar phrase and repeating it with an ending in the dominant rather than the tonic). This shows the AI did, or could, learn how repeats are used stylistically, but that it made the decision *not* to do this. I found these approaches to repeated material very inspiring and developed them throughout *Silicon*.

In my second area of exploration, I investigated what music of the future might sound like if an AI wrote music intended for other computers, not humans. Even when informed by real AI research, this remains very speculative and there are many areas this might affect. However, I was particularly taken by the way that AI algorithms consider time. The notion of general algorithmic time is one that already has strong parallels with music. Rohrhuber's argument that 'algorithmic methods suggest a break with the idea of time as an immediate grounding' is based upon the idea that an algorithm defines its own time through unfolding its pre-programmed computations, or steps, in a specific order.[19] Time 'begins' with the first step and 'ends' when the algorithm is complete. It does not necessarily matter how long, in actual time, these steps take. This perspective chimes with some orchestral music. We can imagine a sonata form or the four movements of a traditional symphony as a type of algorithmic time, where it is more informative to understand the relationship of the internal sections that unfold in a specific order (e.g. exposition – development – recapitulation, or sonata – rondo – finale), than it is to count how many seconds have passed in actual time. That is not to say that this is the only way of viewing musical time, which is a complex phenomenon – or even that, on its own, algorithmic time is a sufficient method of understanding musical time. It was to me, however, a new perspective on how algorithms, as a concept, can relate to classical music. *Silicon Mind* is in a warped sonata form, partly to explore this connection.

Musical time has more specific connections with AI algorithms. AI learns from audio data like WAV files, or from symbolic data like MIDI files. Whether audio or MIDI, for AI training purposes this data can be transformed into an image, such as a spectrograph or a MIDI roll.[20] Images do not exist in time, they are static. It's only when we tell the machine-learning algorithm to play that image from left to right that the dimension of time suddenly originates. But if a machine was creating music for itself, in a theoretical future where machines exist that enjoy listening to music for its own sake, musical time probably wouldn't need

---

19 Julian Rohrhuber, 'Algorithmic Music and the Philosophy of Time', in *The Oxford Handbook of Algorithmic Music*, ed. by A. McLean & R. Dean (Oxford: Oxford University Press 2018), pp. 17–40.
20 Carykh, *AI Evolves to Compose 3 Hours of Jazz!* [video], YouTube, 5 July 2017, https://youtu.be/nA3YOFUCn4U

to work in the way we experience it. The image-music could be enjoyed all at once, top-to-bottom, right-to-left or the traditional start-to-end.

To enact this in *Silicon Mind*, I created several axes of reflection across the piece. On either side of these axes, we hear the same music both forwards and backwards. This is not only retrograding rhythms and pitches, but also the timbre, decay and attack of the sound. If we imagine reading a spectrograph backwards (right-to-left) the entire sound is in reverse. Realising this with only the physical instruments of the orchestra presented an enjoyable challenge: reversing the sound of the vibraphone, for example, requires the percussionist to first bow the note to produce a sustained note, before striking and damping the note with a mallet. In this way we hear decay followed by attack followed by silence. Returning to the sonata form idea, I composed the two subjects as a contrasting pair: where one is heard forwards, the other is heard backwards, synchronising at the end of the movement.

MuseNet can be instructed to create any number of responses to a prompt, which will all be created simultaneously, and each will be different. This also fed into the approach to musical time during *Silicon Mind*. Several times while composing, I added one MuseNet response before rewinding back to the start of that phrase to use another, creating a sonification of constant progress through many iterations of the same task – the core tenet of machine-learning AI.

Fake and Real (*Silicon Body*)

One of the biggest concerns raised by AI concerns authenticity. In recent years we have become familiar with AI's capacity for creating believable fakes. This technology is used to automatically generate stories that resemble human-written news and by social media giants to encourage engagement, with the dissemination and promotion of fake news stories a known by-product.[21] It is now a regular occurrence to see AI algorithms used to create fake videos showing public figures in unfavourable light and it has also been used in movies to allow deceased actors to appear

---

21 Patrick Wang, Rafael Angarita, & Ilaria Renna, 'Is this the Era of Misinformation yet: Combining Social Bots and Fake News to Deceive the Masses', in *The Web Conference 2018 - Companion of the World Wide Web Conference, WWW 2018* (2018), 1557–1561.

in new releases (e.g. Peter Cushing and Carrie Fisher in *Rogue One: A Star Wars Story*) or to de-age live ones.[22] This kind of technology is often colloquially called deepfake, but the technical term for this field is Style Transfer.

We are now becoming used to questioning the provenance of believable-looking sources in a way that we were not even at the turn of this century. I believe this question of authenticity will be one that defines society over the next generation, and even if the identification of human-made or AI-made content were resolved. Real is not the same as authentic, and this is especially clear in the creative fields. An AI might generate *real* music in the style of Mozart (as discussed), but this music might not feel *authentic* to all listeners. Authenticity is a much more subjective question than truth or untruth. Here, the orchestra, and classical music more generally, can offer a perspective.

Classical musicians are familiar with questions of authenticity. Discussions and disagreements emerging around, for example, performing Bach on the modern piano,[23] using vibrato in eighteenth-century symphonies,[24] or casting singers of colour to sing operatic roles representing minority groups can be viewed, at least partially, as questions of authenticity.[25] Though this is not exclusive to this musical genre alone, it remains true that classical musicians are plugged in to whether music feels authentic, in addition to what it sounds or looks like on the surface. A music that deliberately grapples with fake and real is already in a good place to survive the onslaught of a deepfake society.

This leads to the questions that are at the foundation of the second orchestral movement, *Silicon Body*. What exactly is fake music? And does fake or inauthentic music become any more authentic when performed by an orchestra, by real people? Perhaps most importantly, I wanted

---

22   Johnny Botha, & Heloise Pieterse, 'Fake News and Deepfakes: A Dangerous Threat for 21st Century Information Security', in *ICCWS 2020 15th International Conference on Cyber Warfare and Security* ed. by B. K. Payne & H. Wu (2020), pp. 57–66; Alexi Sargeant, *The Undeath of Cinema* (The New Atlantis, 2017), https://www.thenewatlantis.com/publications/the-undeath-of-cinema

23   Aron Edidin, 'Playing Bach His Way: Historical Authenticity, Personal Authenticity, and the Performance of Classical Music', *Journal of Aesthetic Education* 32:4 (1998), 79.

24   Roger Norrington, 'The sound orchestras make', *Early Music* 32:1 (2004), 2–6.

25   Naomi André, Karen M. Bryan, & Eric Saylor in *Blackness in Opera* (Urbana: University of Illinois Press, 2012).

to hear what this deepfake technology actually sounds like. I wanted to embed an instrument that uses AI deepfake technology within the orchestra, to be played by an orchestral musician, as a kind of model for how orchestras might be constituted in the age of AI.

One research paper that particularly interested me showcasing deepfake technology is called 'Everybody Dance Now'.[26] It demonstrates taking a video of a dancer (Source), an image of a second person (Target), and the use of AI to make the Target appear to move like the Source. To do this, it strips the Source video down to a basic set of moving points and lines, abstractly representing the human body. With this distilled from the Source, the AI then rebuilds the video, this time with the Target fleshing out the skeletal nodes. I found it fascinating the way that computer vision 'sees' people fundamentally differently to how we see people, and also perhaps a little unnerving. An answer to what fake music might sound like lay, for me, in the relationship between the surface – the Target – and the hidden layers – the Source.

Silicon Body has a Source, a layer of music I composed that sits underneath the whole piece. It's a skeletal musical framework, made up of mathematical patterns of pitches and rhythms moving in cycles. This musical Source is not performed by a regular orchestral instrument, but instead by a digital instrument called DDSP (Differential Digital Signal Processing)[27] developed by Google Magenta. DDSP is a Style Transfer instrument that works in a similar way to the earlier dancer example, except that the Source and Target are audio-based rather than video-based. We can play any sound into DDSP and instruct it to transfer that sound's harmonic content into any other timbre using AI. This can be very convincing, but it can also be rather uncanny: a sound that is nearly right, but not quite. It is also possible to push the instrument outside of its intended comfort zone to create exciting new timbres through AI. Embedding new AI instruments within the ensemble was creatively interesting and engaging, and there is much more work to be done in this field.

---

26   Caroline Chan, Shiry Ginosar, Tinghui Zhou, & Alexei A. Efros, 'Everybody Dance Now' in *Proceedings of the IEEE/CVF International Conference on Computer Vision (ICCV)* (2019), 5933–5942.

27   Jesse Engel, Lamtharn Hantrakul, Chenjie Gu, & Adam Roberts, *DDSP: Differentiable Digital Signal Processing* (2020), https://doi.org/10.48550/arxiv.2001.04643

On top of this Source are superimposed three Target styles of music that are performed by the orchestral instruments. Inspired by 'Everybody Dance Now', these three styles are based on different types of dance music: big-band jazz, electronic and folk. Continuing the idea of reference to traditional orchestral music, this also makes *Silicon*'s second movement a kind of dance movement, to follow the first warped sonata form. While each of these dance styles sounds completely different on the surface, they are each controlled by the Source instrument. As the piece progresses, the three Targets are rotated faster and faster, until they reach a breaking point and the Source is revealed finally on its own. The music is meant to sound fun, uncanny and sinister, reflecting the many uses of deepfake technology.

System and Secret (*Silicon Soul*)

Both case-study algorithms discussed so far, MuseNet and DDSP, are partly interesting due to their imperfections. Both do not always do what might have originally been intended, and in not doing so they reveal interesting artefacts, processes and obsessions of AI. For many artists, these artefacts are one of the main reasons to use AI in the creative process, and the uncanny or strange is actively sought out.

Let us now imagine the inverse as a thought experiment, which will lead to the third duality: System and Secret. Our thought-experiment algorithm has no artefacts, and it can achieve whatever musical task we set it. It can analyse any amount of data, unrestricted by hardware limitations, and can produce new data (i.e. music) trivially quickly. It can produce sound indistinguishable from human musicians in any genre, historical period or ensemble. It can even produce entirely new music by combining existing music in novel ways or identifying gaps in its dataset that have never been exploited. It is, in a word, perfect. But is it music?

Across society there is a trend to understand any problem as inherently solvable by data. Here I draw upon the work of Federico Campagna, especially his book *Technic and Magic*,[28] but also more

---

28   Federico Campagna, *Technic and Magic* (London: Bloomsbury Academic, 2018), https://doi.org/10.5040/9781350044005

widely upon recent public policy decisions in the UK and abroad. The implication, in the field of music-related AI, is that with enough data and computer resources, an AI does not only produce something that *sounds* like music, but that it *is* music, that is, that there is nothing that constitutes music that exists outside of data. Given a sufficiently sophisticated system, creating meaningful music is trivial.

But would people accept this music, or do we require some kind of secret ingredient in order to feel a genuine connection with art? We do not know the answer to this question because AI has not yet reached the fluency of our thought experiment, but it is reasonable to imagine that it will some day. And if we take the view that there is more to music than computer data can communicate, what is that secret? Does it exist inherently within the music, or can this secret be imagined or imposed by the audience? Will AI research, in its dogged pursuit of a systematic understanding of the world, help us understand what the secret of music is?

This question is already under active consideration from a wide range of artists and scholars. Campagna argues that embracing a worldview he terms 'magic', informed by elements of spiritualism, mysticism and religion, can help alleviate the difficulties, both personal and social, inherent in a worldview reliant on data. Similarly, the authors of the *Atlas of Anomalous AI* explicitly state their aim to 're-mythologise AI in a way that reveals the roots of the technological project in spiritual practices, institutions and frameworks'.[29] Composer and academic George E. Lewis, when explaining why he is interested in teaching computers how to improvise music, describes a view of improvisation as 'something essential, fundamental to the human spirit', before going on to assert that attempting to teach computers to improvise 'can teach us how to live in a world marked by agency, indeterminacy, analysis of conditions, and the apparent ineffability of choice'.[30] The question of what the secret is, and how computers and data might help us understand it, has as many answers as answerers.

---

29 Ben Vickers, & K. Allado-McDowell, 'Introduction', in *Atlas of Anomalous AI*, ed. by B. Vickers & K. Allado-McDowell (London: Ignota Books 2021).

30 George E. Lewis, 'Why Do We Want Our Computers to Improvise?', in *The Oxford Handbook of Algorithmic Music*, ed. by A. McLean & R. Dean (Oxford: Oxford University Press 2018), pp. 123–130.

I set out to provide one response, if not an answer, to this difficult question by examining it through the lens of orchestral music. I wondered why audiences still go to see the orchestra today. As the COVID-19 pandemic has shown, it is perfectly possible to livestream performances to tune into from home, and there are even sample libraries – frequently used for video game, movie and TV soundtracks – that allow us to emulate the orchestral sound without needing any humans at all. What is its secret that compels people to physically come and watch humans make these sounds live?

For me personally, it is in understanding an orchestral performance not primarily as an act of creating sound, but rather as an act of community shared between musicians and audience. For the third movement of *Silicon, Silicon Soul*, I wanted to experiment with including AI inside such a framework. This means not just providing notes to be interpreted, or brought to life, by human musicians – like *Silicon Mind* – nor providing a fixed, uncanny perspective against the human members of the orchestra – like *Silicon Body* – but understanding AI as an integral part of the orchestra's communal act.

For this movement, I used an AI called PRiSM-SampleRNN. PRiSM-SampleRNN is an audio-based AI that learns to create new sounds from a dataset of existing sound. It produces the raw audio – both 'notes' and timbre, making it different to MuseNet and DDSP which both require human performers somewhere in the realisation. The version of PRiSM-SampleRNN I used was released by PRiSM in 2020.[31] One method I explored for integrating AI into the community of the orchestra was to make the AI personal to *that* orchestra. I trained PRiSM-SampleRNN on recordings of the BBC Philharmonic exclusively. This means that whatever it learned about music, it has learned from analysing that orchestra alone. In performance, the results of this training will be heard alongside the BBC Philharmonic – like an apprentice performing alongside a master. In this instance AI is used as a tool to increase the personalisation and site-specific nature of a piece, rather than as a tool to make general rules about music. It is in service of defining what the nature of *this* ensemble is, and the audience is challenged to make their

---

31 Christopher Melen, 'PRiSM SampleRNN', *RNCM PRiSM* (2019), https://www.rncm.ac.uk/research/research-centres-rncm/prism/prism-collaborations/prism-samplernn/

own decisions about the differences in sound between the physical orchestra in front of them and its AI doppelganger.

There was also literal integration of the AI sound with the orchestral sounds. Unlike the use of DDSP in *Silicon Body*, where the distinction between orchestra and AI is visually and audibly apparent, I wanted the overall sound of this movement to be an indivisible unit where AI and human sounds seamlessly merged. To achieve this, I requested that the PRiSM-SampleRNN audio be dispersed amongst many audio monitors, instead of the more standard stereo pair, and that these monitors be hidden amongst and underneath the orchestral players. To complement this, the compositional dialogue between orchestra and AI was considered on a spectrum throughout the movement, where at one end the two are totally overlapping in musical material, while at the other they make separate musical arguments. This brings to mind questions of human-computer interactivity and interdependency, an area I look forward to other artists and myself exploring with even more sophisticated tools in the future as technology develops.

Conclusions and the Future

Having set out how I have recently used AI in my work, I will briefly discuss the overall effect on my compositional craft and outlook that using this technology has had. These are beyond the general benefits, which should not be understated, of learning to code and of incorporating complex electronics into my music.

My music has always been driven by an interest in structure and musical time. Working with AI has driven this interest in new directions. Most prominent is the role of spontaneity within the compositional process. When working with algorithms such as MuseNet or PRiSM-SampleRNN, it is not possible to plan exactly the form of a work in advance, because it is not possible to control those algorithms' generations. I have therefore adopted a balance between spontaneity and structure in my work, which has (in my opinion) been for the better. Even on a small, moment-by-moment scale, there is very little control over specific details (for example, the timbre of a PRiSM-SampleRNN generation). Rather than forcing this AI-generated material into a pre-set idea, I have found myself listening to what this material *is*, and how I might either heighten or obscure that essence. In turn, this has informed my approach to working with human performers too. Working with AI has made me consider the role of the human performer a great deal. AI does not (currently) generate particularly idiomatic parts for performers, which has caused me to consider the roles of playable and awkward music, particularly regarding the idea of authenticity in classical music.

Perhaps the greatest effect AI has had on my compositional process is in its treatment of the basic elements of music. When I sit down and analyse its approach to, say, repeated material (as discussed), tuning, rhythm, time or harmony, I find that it is subtly yet fundamentally different to approaches I am familiar with. As a composer, it is easy to get caught up in fine details of musical elements. These remain interesting, but working with AI has opened my eyes to the benefits of searching out a paradigm shift. Much of my recent non-AI compositional work, for example, has been focussed on exploring new forms of tuning, which I became interested in through analysing AI-material.

If I have described a possible future relationship between the orchestra and AI, then what are the concrete steps that might lead us along this path? Some areas for further development, based on this chapter's discussion, will be highlighted. In terms of making AI algorithms more generally useful for musicians themselves, the most obvious point is that of user interface. Many AI algorithms are interfaced with through Python, a coding language that few musicians are comfortable with. Creating a graphical interface that requires no coding, as exemplified by Google Magenta, will be the most important step to encourage more musicians to experiment with this technology. As further AI instruments are developed, the orchestra and other performing ensembles might take an active role in facilitating experimentation with these new technologies. While I used DDSP for its timbral and metaphorical advantages in *Silicon Body*, I think that a major benefit that AI instruments will bring to classical music is accessibility. AI has been shown to be proficient at learning its users' gestures and actions (e.g. your phone recognises your face and no-one else's), and this opens up the real possibility of utilising AI to create adaptive instruments for people whose physical impairments might preclude the practice of traditional instruments.

The composition of *Silicon Mind* highlighted the fact that current AI generates music from start-to-finish. A more useful compositional tool might be an AI that can generate music back-to-front, or perhaps bridge two materials that a composer provides. This has been achieved on a small scale through algorithms such as CocoNet,[32] where the user provides a melody which is harmonised by AI in the style of Bach. Many composers do not write their pieces from start to finish, so future AI intended to be helpful for composers should take this into account.

It is now the winter of 2022, and the work on *Silicon* for orchestral and artificial intelligence is finished. This chapter has used it as a backdrop and anchor to explore three relatively abstract dualities shared between AI and classical music, and to transform these dualities into something audible. It also showed three different ways AI can be employed as a technology within the orchestral texture itself, playing the role of composer (MuseNet), instrument (DDSP) and performer (PRiSM-SampleRNN). I hope that through experimentation like this, the orchestra can remain at the forefront of instrumental and compositional exploration, as it did in the days of Berlioz and Wagner.

Three dualities, and three technological use-cases of AI within the orchestra, barely scratch the surface of the potential relationship here, and my biggest hope is that this chapter has caused readers to consider other ways AI might be a useful concern for the orchestra and classical music more generally. My experience and interests using AI within the orchestra are biased towards the way that I operate as a composer, and so I hope to see other composers' substantially varied takes on this technology in the coming years. This chapter has been quite speculative, and I am sure that while some concerns described here might end up as dead ends, there will also be unforeseen questions emerging from this technology.

My own work has been supported by several institutions, which has placed me in the fortunate position of being able to seek out the positive elements of AI that can help me attain my artistic goals. As stated at the beginning of this chapter, however, this technology can be used in many ways, not all of them positive. AI has profound implications for the future of labour. In classical music, this question could be posed as: who might be replaced by AI? Already film composers utilise high-quality

---

32   Cheng-Zhi Anna Huang, Tim Cooijmans, Adam Roberts, Aaron Courville, & Douglas Eck, 'Counterpoint by Convolution' in *Proceedings of the 18th International Society for Music Information Retrieval Conference, ISMIR 2017* (2019), 211–218.

sample libraries which have, by and large, replaced live musicians for much of their work. Will composers be replaced by AI algorithms next? What kinds of music will audiences accept as being written by AI, and which will they demand should be written by humans? Will it be mandatory to announce whether music is AI- or human-composed, to avoid hoodwinking the public? These are not yet questions that have been tested, but may well feature in future discourse.

There is also the question of access. Currently, AI is prohibitively difficult to use both in terms of expertise and resources. Until more AI tools are open-source, or at least made affordable to use, it is difficult to see this technology becoming widespread. This would preclude its use in most educational contexts, an area that I believe AI has much to offer (i.e. assisting a student composer in mixing their music, or recommending several different paths for the music to take from a given moment).

Audiences and programmers of classical music might find both positives and negatives stemming from this technology. On the one hand, it might provide novel and exciting programmes (for example, the 2019 Cheltenham Science Festival used AI to suggest the titles of talks, which were then programmed). On the other, considering where AI-generated music might fit into the classical music programming model might require a radical rethink of how seasons and individual events are put together. This is not to mention the power of AI as a marketing tool: institutions that are slow to incorporate AI may be left behind compared to rivals using advanced AI to attract audiences.

Ultimately, I am sure that AI is here to stay, like the printing press, computer and internet before it. It already touches upon much of our society, whether we know it or not, and its expansion is only likely to continue in the future. It is partly through the work of artists that we might further understand its place in our world.

References

AIVA, *AIVA—The AI composing emotional soundtrack music* (AIVA), https://www.aiva.ai/

André, N. A., Bryan, K. M., & Saylor, E., *Blackness in Opera* (Urbana: University of Illinois Press, 2012).

Botha, Johnny, & Pieterse, Heloise, 'Fake News and Deepfakes: A Dangerous Threat for 21st Century Information Security', in *Proceedings of the 15th International Conference on Cyber Warfare and Security, ICCWS 2020*, ed. by B. K. Payne & H. Wu (2020), pp. 57–66.

Campagna, Federico, *Technic and Magic* (London: Bloomsbury Academic, 2018), https://doi.org/10.5040/9781350044005

Carykh, *AI Evolves to Compose 3 Hours of Jazz!*, YouTube, 5 July 2017, https://youtu.be/nA3YOFUCn4U" https://youtu.be/nA3YOFUCn4U

Chan, C., Ginosar, S., Zhou, T., & Efros, A. A., 'Everybody Dance Now', *Proceedings of the IEEE/CVF International Conference on Computer Vision (ICCV)* (2019), 5933–5942.

Cowls, J., Tsamados, A., Taddeo, M., & Floridi, L., 'The AI gambit: leveraging artificial intelligence to combat climate change—opportunities, challenges, and recommendations', *AI and Society* 1 (2021), 1–25, https://doi.org/10.1007/s00146-021-01294-x

Cox, Geoff, & Riis, Morton, '(Micro)Politics of Algorithmic Music', in *The Oxford Handbook of Algorithmic Music*, ed. by A. McLean & R. Dean (Oxford: Oxford University Press 2018), pp. 603–626, https://doi.org/10.1093/oxfordhb/9780190226992.001.0001

Dastin, Jeffrey, 'Amazon Scraps Secret AI Recruiting Tool that Showed Bias against Women', in *Ethics of Data and Analytics*, ed. by K. Martin (Boca Raton: Auerbach Publications, 2022), pp. 296–299.

Donne, Women In Music, 2019-2020—Donne, Women in Music Research (Donne 2020), https://donne-uk.org/2019-2020/

du Sautoy, Marcus, *The Creativity Code: Art and Innovation in the Age of AI* (Cambridge, M.A.: Fourth Estate, 2020).

Edidin, Aron, 'Playing Bach His Way: Historical Authenticity, Personal Authenticity, and the Performance of Classical Music', *Journal of Aesthetic Education* 32:4 (1998), 79, https://doi.org/10.2307/3333387

Engel, J., Hantrakul, L., Gu, C., & Roberts, A., *DDSP: Differentiable Digital Signal Processing* (2020), https://doi.org/10.48550/arxiv.2001.04643

Fang, A., Liu, A., Seetharaman, P., & Pardo, B., *Bach or Mock? A Grading Function for Chorales in the Style of J. S. Bach* (2020), ArXiv:2006.13329 [Cs.SD].

Fiebrink, Rebecca, & Cook, Perry R., 'The Wekinator: a system for real-time, interactive machine learning in music', *The 11th International Society for Music Information Retrieval Conference* (2010), http://code.google.com/p/wekinator/

Gomez-Uribe, Carlos A., & Hunt, Neil, 'The Netflix Recommender System', *ACM Transactions on Management Information Systems (TMIS)* 6:4 (2015).

Goodyer, Jason, 'How an artificial intelligence finished Beethoven's last symphony', *Science Focus*, 14 October 2021, https://www.sciencefocus.com/news/ai-beethovens-symphony/

Gotham, Mark, 'Coherence in Concert Programming: A View from the U.K.', *IRASM* 45:2 (2014), 293–309.

Hadjeres, G. Pachet, F., Nielsen, F., 'DeepBach: a Steerable Model for Bach Chorales Generation', *Proceedings of the 34th International Conference on Machine Learning* (2017). https://proceedings.mlr.press/v70/kim17a.html.

Hao, Karen, 'He got Facebook hooked on AI. Now he can't fix its misinformation addiction', *MIT Technology Review*, 11 March 2021, https://www.technologyreview.com/2021/03/11/1020600/facebook-responsible-ai-misinformation/

Huang, C. Z. A., Cooijmans, T., Roberts, A., Courville, A., & Eck, D., 'Counterpoint by Convolution', *Proceedings of the 18th International Society for Music Information Retrieval Conference, ISMIR 2017* (2019), 211–218, https://doi.org/10.48550/arXiv.1903.07227

Karyuatry, Laksnoria, 'Grammarly as a Tool to Improve Students' Writing Quality: Free Online-Proofreader across the Boundaries', *JSSH (Jurnal Sains Sosial Dan Humaniora)* 2:1 (2018), 83–89, http://dx.doi.org/10.30595/jssh.v2i1.2297

Langkjær-Bain, Robert, 'Five ways data is transforming music', *Significance* 15:1 (2018), 20–23, https://doi.org/10.1111/j.1740-9713.2018.01106.x

Lau, Johann, 'Google Maps 101: How AI helps predict traffic and determine routes', *Google: The Keyword*, 3 September 2020, https://blog.google/products/maps/

google-maps-101-how-ai-helps-predict-traffic-and-determine-routes/

Lee, L.-H., Braud, T., Zhou, P., Wang, L., Xu, D., Lin, Z., Kumar, A., Bermejo, C., & Hui, P., *All One Needs to Know about Metaverse: A Complete Survey on Technological Singularity, Virtual Ecosystem, and Research Agenda*, arXiv:2110.05352 [cs.CY] (2021), https://doi.org/10.48550/arxiv.2110.05352

Leslie, David, 'Understanding Bias in Facial Recognition Technologies', Zenodo (2020), https://doi.org/10.5281/zenodo.4050457

Lewis, George E., 'Why Do We Want Our Computers to Improvise?', in *The Oxford Handbook of Algorithmic Music*, ed. by A. McLean & R. Dean (Oxford: Oxford University Press, 2018), pp. 123–130.

McLean, Alex, & Dean, Roger T., *The Oxford Handbook of Algorithmic Music* (Oxford: Oxford University Press, 2018).

Melen, Christopher, 'PRiSM SampleRNN', *RNCM PRiSM* (2019), https://www.rncm.ac.uk/research/research-centres-rncm/prism/prism-collaborations/prism-samplernn/

Mogaji, Emmanuel, Olaleye, Sunday, & Ukpabi, Dandison, 'Using AI to Personalise Emotionally Appealing Advertisement', in *Digital and Social Media Marketing*, ed. by N. P. Rana, E. L. Slade, G. P. Sahu, H. Kizgin, N. Singh, B. Dey, A. Gutierrez, & Y. K. Dwivedi (Cham: Springer, 2020), pp. 137-150, https://doi.org/10.1007/978-3-030-24374-6_10

Morton, Timothy, *Hyperobjects: Philosophy and Ecology after the End of the World* (Minneapolis: University of Minnesota Press, 2013).

Norrington, Roger, 'The sound orchestras make', *Early Music* 32:1 (2004), 2–6, https://doi.org/10.1093/earlyj/32.1.2

Payne, Christine, 'MuseNet', *OpenAI* (2019), https://openai.com/research/musenet

Rohrhuber, Julian, 'Algorithmic Music and the Philosophy of Time', in *The Oxford Handbook of Algorithmic Music*, ed. by A. McLean & R. Dean (Oxford University Press 2018), pp. 17–40, https://doi.org/10.1093/oxfordhb/9780190226992.001.0001

Sargeant, Alexi, *The Undeath of Cinema* (The New Atlantis, 2017), https://www.thenewatlantis.com/publications/the-undeath-of-cinema

Sejnowski, Terry, *The Deep Learning Revolution* (Cambridge, M.A.: MIT Press, 2018).

Tatalovic, Mico, 'AI writing bots are about to revolutionise science journalism: we must shape how this is done', *Journal of Science*

Communication 17:1 (2018), https://doi.org/10.22323/2.17010501

Vickers, Ben, & Allado-McDowell, K., 'Introduction', in *Atlas of Anomalous AI*, ed. by B. Vickers & K. Allado-McDowell (London: Ignota Books, 2021), pp. 9-29.

Wang, P., Angarita, R., & Renna, I., 'Is this the Era of Misinformation yet: Combining Social Bots and Fake News to Deceive the Masses', *The Web Conference 2018—Companion of the World Wide Web Conference, WWW 2018* (2018), 1557–1561, http://dx.doi.org/10.1145/3184558.3191610

Whorley, Raymond, & Laney, Robin, 'Generating Subjects for Pieces in the Style of Bach's Two-Part Inventions', *Proceedings of the 2020 Joint Conference on AI Music Creativity*, KTH Royal Institute of Technology2021), https://doi.org/10.30746/978-91-519-5560-5.

19. Ghosts of the Hidden Layer

Jennifer Walshe

The following was originally delivered as a talk at the Darmstädter Ferienkurse in 2018.

Today I'm going to talk about the voice, language and artificial intelligence. We're going to cover a lot of ground, but at the end we should all end up in the same place.

1.

 Abstract sound, mixture of static and wind-like sounds. Duration: 0:16.
https://hdl.handle.net/20.500.12434/6227db0e

1st Audio: Dadabots © Jennifer Walshe.

I don't have a voice. I have many, many voices. My voice – this biological structure located in my body, an apparatus which usually functions in close collaboration with technology – is the staging area for everything I've ever heard and everywhere I've ever lived. There is infinite material to draw on, in infinitely different ways.

    We all grapple with the plethora of voices that have made their mark on ours. We're told the goal is to find "our" voice. But this polyphony, this confusion, is what interests me. I don't want to choose.

    I listen to and collect voices constantly. Recording, notating, jotting down times as I watch a video so I can go back and memorise voices.

    A lot of my work deals with negotiating and editing this huge archive of material. The first piece I ever wrote for my voice, *as mo cheann*, was concerned with investigating all the vocal sounds I could make along a vertical physical axis, projecting from the space above my head to below my feet. I've made pieces for my voice which represent the connections between the thousands of pop song samples in my brain; I've made pieces which are the result of hours upon hours of listening to animal, insect and frog sounds; pieces for which recordings of DNA microarray machines, underwater volcanoes and the toilets on the International Space Station form an aural score.

Because I love voices, I love language. I view language as a subset of what a voice does. I am fascinated by how language functions off- and online. I love slang and argot technical language; I love newly invented words. Through language, voices give a vivid snapshot of the times we live in. Times filled with collarbone strobing, meta predators and procrastibaking. Hate-watching, nootropics and dumpster fires. Manbabies, co-sleepers and e-liquids. I read these words on the page and they bounce into life in my head as voices.

Aside from the extremely rich sound world the voice can be implicated in, I'm fascinated by the voice because it provides an aperture through which the world comes rushing in. The Thai artist Larry Achiampong states that 'Our lives are political because our bodies are.' I would extend this statement and say our lives are political because our voices are. Gender, sexuality, ability, class, ethnicity, nationality – we read them all in the voice. The voice is a node where culture, politics, history and technology can be unpacked.

2.

 Peaceful melody with choral accompaniment. Duration: 0:37.
https://hdl.handle.net/20.500.12434/342be800

2nd Audio: EMRALDIA 'Llac Centre Suite' (excerpt) – Celtorwave track
© Jennifer Walshe.

19. *Ghosts of the Hidden Layer*

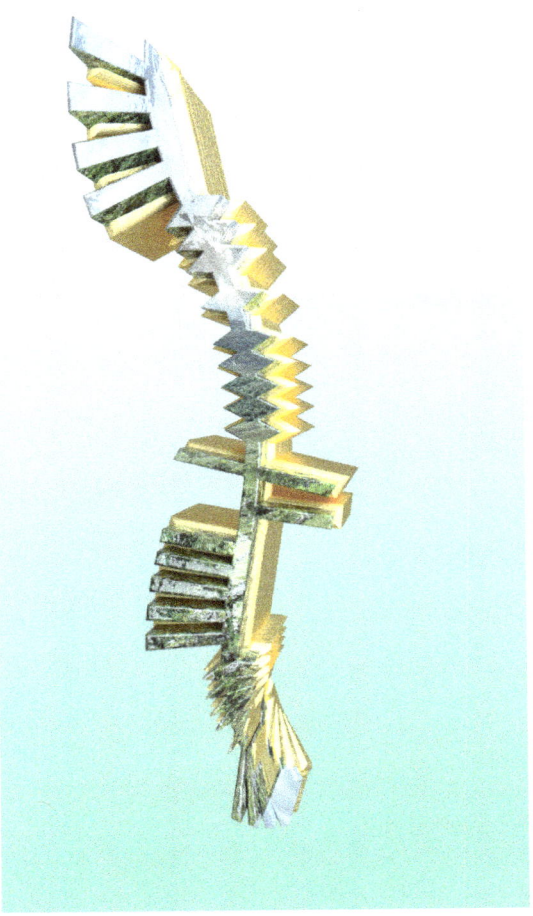

Fig. 19.1 Celtorwave by Tom Kemp @ Jennifer Walshe.

In January 2015 I launched a project called Historical Documents of the Irish Avant-Garde, also known as Aisteach. For this project, I worked in collaboration with a wide number of people to create a fictional history of Irish avant-garde music, stretching from the mid-1830s to 1985. Many of the materials related to this project are housed at aisteach.org, the website of the Aisteach Foundation, a fictional organisation which is positioned as 'the avant-garde archive of Ireland.' The site contains hours of music, numerous articles, scores, documents and historical ephemera. Every detail of this project was composed, written and designed with the utmost care and attention to detail. It's a serious exercise in speculative composition, fiction and world-building. In Aisteach, Irishness becomes a medium. Aisteach creates an uncanny space, where we write our ancestors into being in the hopes of being able to summon their voices and listen to them.

Fig. 19.2 Aisteach © Jennifer Walshe.

Aisteach includes many different musics, many personae[1]. The subliminal tapes and films of Outsider artist Caoimhín Breathnach, my dear great-uncle; The Guinness Dadaists, staging sound poetry performances in the brewery at St James's Gate; Sr Anselme, a nun living in an enclosed order, immersed in long-form organ improvisations; Roisín Madigan O'Reilly, the radio enthusiast performing with ionosphere and landscape; Dunne's Dérives, the notorious queer performance nights featuring members of the Radical Faerie movement.

Aisteach is an on-going project. It continually spills over into the offline world in the form of concerts, film screenings, exhibitions, radio shows.

Two of Aisteach's most respected fellow travellers include Afrofuturism and Hauntology. Hauntology in particular seems like

---

1   For further reading about the musics and personae, see aisteach.org.

an obvious native choice for Irish-based art, embedded as we are in superstition, nostalgia and the occult. But Hauntology functions differently in Ireland – Aisteach is haunted by a past which suppressed, marginalised and erased many voices. Aisteach is not interested in fetishising this past. The crackle on the recordings is not there for cosy retro warmth or nostalgia for the rare oul' times – it's sand on the lens, grit between the tape heads, violently hacking history to urge us to create a better future. And a better future means being alert and responsible to the present.

At the moment I'm preparing a new Aisteach exhibition.[2] We're working on Celtorwave, an Irish version of the online subculture Vaporwave; we're collecting water from holy wells for a holy water cocktail bar; we're building an artificial intelligence system that writes Irish myths.

3.

 Generated sound with Walshe's voice of static-like whistling sound.
Duration: 0:18.
https://hdl.handle.net/20.500.12434/fb0d7fd8

3rd Audio: Jennifer Walshe's voice generated by Dadabots, Epoch 6
© Jennifer Walshe.

On September 11th 2001, the American-Canadian science fiction author William Gibson was at home, drinking coffee, when he heard of the attacks on the World Trade Center. He describes how he 'ran upstairs, turned on CNN and that was it. "All bets are off!" my inner science-fiction radar screamed. "Cannot compute from available data."'

When the attacks happened, Gibson was one hundred pages into writing a new novel. Weeks after the attacks, as Gibson tried to get back to work, he realized his work in progress 'had become a story that took place in an alternate time track, in which September 11th hadn't happened.' He had to rework the novel completely.

---

2   Jennifer Walshe, *The Journal of Music* (2023), https://journalofmusic.com/subject/jennifer-walshe

Gibson is one of my favourite authors, and in June 2016 and again in November I wondered what he was doing. How many pages he had to rip up. How many plotlines he had to rework.

This is what I'm interested in – making work which is concerned with the world that we're living in. Work which thinks deeply about and through the human and non-human beings in this world and the universe beyond it. Work that is so enmeshed with and affected by the world that it cannot help but change in response to it.

Gibson says the approach to doing this is to use the sci-fi toolkit, to use 'science fiction oven mitts to handle the hot casserole' of the times we live in.[3] Because our world is utterly strange, utterly more bizarre, layered and textured than any science fiction scenario or imaginary future could be. And a huge part of that strangeness is because we are overwhelmed, dominated and enmeshed with technology.

4.

 Walshe's synthesised voice saying, "If I was dying and I had a turtleneck on, he tells me, with my last dying breath, I would take the turtleneck off and try to throw it as far away from my body as possible." Duration: 0:09. https://hdl.handle.net/20.500.12434/e913fb49

4th Audio: Elon Musk quote spoken by version 1 of Walshe's synthesised voice
© Jennifer Walshe.

The concept of the 'uncanny valley' was first described by the Japanese robotics professor Masahiro Mori in the journal *Energy* in 1970.[4] Mori's paper deals with the challenges facing designers of prosthetic limbs and robots. Mori describes a graph with two axes – affinity and human likeness. Mori's model describes how we feel little affinity with industrial robots which in no way resemble people, versus feeling huge affinity with healthy humans.

---

3 Douglas Gorney, 'William Gibson and the Future of the Future' in *The Atlantic* (2010), https://www.theatlantic.com/entertainment/archive/2010/09/william-gibson-and-the-future-of-the-future/62863/
4 Masahiro Mori, 'The Uncanny Valley: The Original Essay by Masahiro Mori' in Spectrum (2012) https://spectrum.ieee.org/the-uncanny-valley

Between these two extremes, we find the uncanny valley. As robots, or any other representations of humans, such as dolls or puppets, come to more closely resemble humans, we feel increasing levels of affinity, until we come to the uncanny valley, at which point humans become completely freaked out. The uncanny valley is inhabited by corpses, zombies, prosthetic limbs and robots who are 'almost human' or 'barely human.' For Mori, as we enter the uncanny valley there is an abrupt shift from empathy to revulsion.

Mori theorises that the sense of eeriness we feel in the uncanny valley is without a doubt 'an integral part of our instinct for self-preservation.' Mori encourages the building of 'an accurate map of the uncanny valley, so through robotics research we can come to understand what makes us human.' His goal is a compassionate one – by understanding the uncanny valley, designers can make better prosthetic limbs; prosthetics which will put their users and the people around them at ease.

Japanese robotics professor Hiroshi Ishiguro designed the android Geminoid to look exactly like him, going so far as to implant some of his own hair in the Geminoid's head.

Developing realistic-sounding voices and coupling these with realistic-looking movements is one of the greatest challenges facing robotics. The Geminoid has a speaker in its chest. Ishiguro speaks into a microphone, and his voice is relayed through the speaker as the Geminoid approximates the mouth movements implied by the speech. This is where the illusion starts to fade most rapidly.

The Otonaroid, another of Ishiguro's robots, is on display at the Museum of Emerging Technology in Tokyo. When I visit, I speak to her, and her voice comes out of a speaker on the wall behind her as she gestures independently. It is confusing and disorienting. When I pet Paro, the robotic therapy seal, and it purrs back to me, I can feel the parts of its body where its speaker is located. It is both the same and also entirely different to petting a live, purring cat.

5.

When I was eleven, my father worked for IBM.[5] He took my sister and I to an event for the children of IBM employees. This event was extremely exciting, because IBM had hired a Hollywood actor to come and provide entertainment for the kids. The actor IBM hired was the actor Michael Winslow, known as 'The Man of 10,000 Sound Effects'. Winslow is famous for his stunning ability to mimic sounds with his voice. He played the character of Larvell Jones in all seven of the Police Academy movies.[6] I sat spellbound as Winslow used his VOICE to make the sounds of telephones, engines, sirens and tape recorders. He was amazing. I witnessed a human using their voice to disrupt, confuse and explode notions of embodiment, of what the voice and the body are.

Winslow was a master of extended vocal techniques. But there was one sound he could not do. Winslow could not do an Irish accent. We witnessed him fail that day. But he was no less a hero to me.

Irish people have grown used to seeing people crucify the Irish accent. Tom Cruise in *Far & Away*.[7] Ryan O'Neal in *Barry Lyndon*. There is a circle in hell, a neon green, shamrock-encrusted Irish pub in Sunnyside, where Seán Connery is condemned to eternally do dialogue from *Darby O'Gill & the Little People*.[8] But not only did we grow up watching people failing to do Irish accents in television programs and films; we also saw it happening on the news.

Between 1988 and 1994 the British government under Margaret Thatcher banned the broadcast of the voices of members of Sinn Féin and other Irish republican and loyalist groups. This meant that broadcasters could show footage of someone such as Gerry Adams speaking, but they

---

5   Céad Míle Fáilte – Welcome to Ed Walshe's Kayak Site. http://homepage.eircom.net/~sizler/index.html
6   Movieclips, *Police Academy (1984) – Larvell Jones, M.D. Scene (1/9)*, movie clip, YouTube, June 19, 2019, https://youtu.be/6OKt2CZ4ULE?si=D-KBfCV9gL5xb9_g
7   Movieclips, *Far and Away (4/0) Movie CLIP – Say You Like My Hat!*, movie clip, YouTube, June 16, 2011, https://youtu.be/eKrEVWGTuRg?si=PDHmHoDHpjLjVEmu
8   Bmoviereviews *Darby O'Gill and the Little People – Sean Connery's Leprechaun Dream*, movie clip, YouTube, June 30, 2010, https://youtu.be/--DYI9wTtAs?si=Chbl3nRSBY5QfANg

could not broadcast the sound of his voice. Broadcasters got around the restrictions by hiring Irish actors to 're-voice' the original voices.

There were many approaches to the re-voicings – some actors over-acted in an attempt to get political points across; others attempted to be neutral; some journalists asked the actors to deliberately speak out of sync, to highlight the absurdity of the restriction.

Irish actor Stephen Rea, who was nominated for an Academy Award for his role in *The Crying Game*, re-voiced both Gerry Adams and Martin McGuinness. The process gave Rea powers that went way beyond traditional voice-acting – Rea has described how he tried to make Adams and McGuinness's messages as clear as possible by editing their speech during the re-voicing process, eliminating the hesitations, umms and aahs of the original. The irony is stunning – by choosing to literally silence the voices of republican and loyalist groups, the British government enabled a situation where world-class actors had the power to polish extremist voices and make them more eloquent.

What was happening, in cognitive terms, when we watched Martin McGuinness on TV? Whose voice was speaking when we saw his lips move? Was it Martin McGuinness? An actor deliberately speaking out of sync? Was it New & Improved Martin McGuinness, courtesy of Stephen Rea? Was it Margaret Thatcher, the prime minister who introduced the ban? The uncanny valley explodes into the political realm.

6.

The virtual digital assistant market is projected to be worth $15.8 billion by 2021. As voice interaction is central to virtual digital assistants, all of the major tech companies are currently investing huge sums in voice technology – Amazon alone have created a $100 million Alexa fund. The thirty-six percent of the world's population who own smartphones have access to virtual assistants such as Siri, Google Assistant, Cortana, Samsung S Voice.

Voice assistants like Siri or Cortana use concatenative text to speech – they sew together fragments from pre-existing recordings of human speech. Concatenative text to speech relies on huge databases – each individual voice is the result of one person spending days recording thousands of words. It sounds somewhat natural, but has its limits – the database will not contain recordings of every word in current use, and switching to a new voice means recording an entirely new database.

The holy grail of voice synthesis is natural-sounding speech that does not require huge databases of recordings. Voices that can be expressed as models in code, models that can be modified with infinite flexibility.

In 2017, a group of researchers from MILA, the machine-learning lab at the University of Montreal in Canada, launched a company called Lyrebird (since absorbed by Descript).[9] Lyrebird creates artificial voices. Using recordings of a person's voice, Lyrebird creates a 'vocal avatar' of that person. The recordings are not sampled – they are analysed by neural networks. Lyrebird's system learns to generate entirely new words – words that the original person may never have spoken in real life.

As soon as Lyrebird releases a beta version, I make a wide range of vocal avatars. Natural Jenny. Dubliner.J+. Jenpoint1000. I pump in text I've collected over the years. Ultimately, though, my feeling is of frustration. The rhythmic patterns of the voices are always the same. When I try to create a vocal avatar with radically different vocal cadence it crashes the system. I can hear a soft buzz whirring through every recording.

Let me be clear – Lyrebird is a huge technical accomplishment. But ultimately Lyrebird is not weird enough for me. I feel like I'm seeing brochures for the watered-down tourist section of the uncanny valley. I want the real thing.

Lyrebird named their company after the Australian lyrebird, a creature known for its stunning ability to mimic sounds. Lyrebirds have been heard making the sounds not only of other birds and animals, but also human voices, camera shutters and car engines. They do this extremely convincingly. Why do lyrebirds make these sounds? What do they think they're communicating when they reproduce the sound of a chainsaw? What do I think I'm communicating when I make animal sounds with my voice, which I do in so many of my pieces? I find the uncanny more readily in the biological lyrebird than the digital one. In

---

9   Masahiro Mori, 'The Uncanny Valley: The Original Essay by Masahiro Mori' in Spectrum (2012) https://spectrum.ieee.org/the-uncanny-valley

the tragedy of a wild creature imitating the sound of machinery that's cutting down trees in the forest it inhabits.

But this broader listening is where so much meaning resides. If the Broadcast Ban were to happen now, I could imagine the BBC hiring Lyrebird or Google to make a pristine model of Gerry Adams's voice. They would bypass the producers, the actors, all those messy humans who directly intervened in the re-voicing process. How would we listen to this voice? What would we hear? What would its politics be? And would we even hear the message, or simply be struck by the technological achievement? Would the most salient part of the voice be the cosy relationship between the state and the tech companies which dominate our lives?

7.

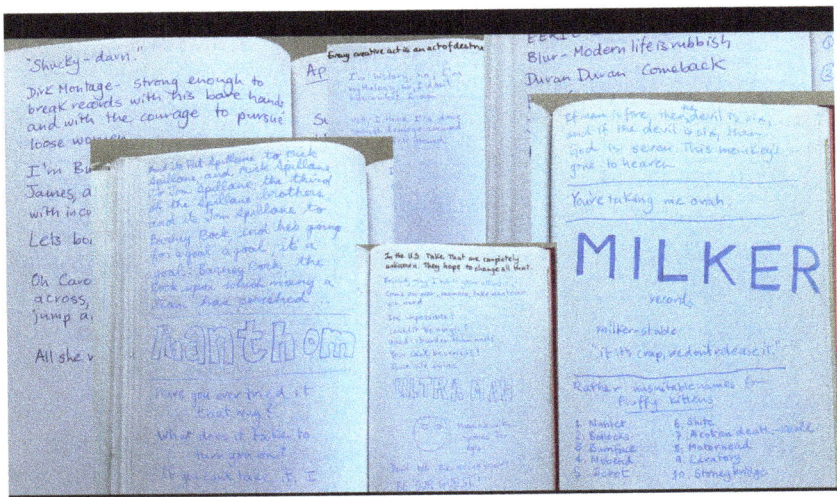

Fig. 19.3 Notebooks © Jennifer Walshe.

Fig 19.4 Book is book © Jennifer Walshe.

Since I was a child, I have collected text in notebooks. I didn't know of the tradition of commonplace books or about literary works like *The Pillow Book* when I started doing this. I just didn't want to lose anything – stories, poetry and songs I wrote, jokes my friends told, conversations I witnessed or simply overheard, lines from films or TV shows, text from books and magazines.

I started writing these notebooks by hand, but these days I collect everything on Evernote across all my devices. Every few months I edit the files, send them off to a print-on-demand service, then wait excitedly for the next volume to arrive in the post. I call this archive BOOK IS BOOK. When I'm composing, these books are close to hand. When I improvise using text, I use the books in the same way a DJ uses records.

Over the last few years, BOOK IS BOOK has been used as the input for various machine-learning projects. Bob Sturm and Oded Ben Tal, two composers and machine-learning specialists based in London, fed it into their neural network Folk-rnn.[10] Folk-rnn was originally developed to write folk songs, but also work for text generation. The output is

---

10   folkRNN, https://folkrnn.org/

exactly what I wanted – bizarre, with shades of Early English, *Finnegan's Wake* and Gertrude Stein:

> Tumpet. Not be to strowded voice this singo to food so your befire to days. action and say enouginies. To be the cingle from milodaticls get preference to could, ever this experience 3 isfortation, melity, if I parky to before is redelf winter, you've becomited specalised into a meculate activaticially

With output like this, my job is to commit. To sell it as if I understand it innately, and through that process gain a new understanding of what text and the voice can mean. The reality is that the second I read the text, it starts to infer, imply, even demand its vocal treatment. And that is a process driven by both myself and the neural network that produced it.

But this is the point – I'm interested in AI because I would like to experience not just artificial intelligence but also alien intelligence. Brand new artistic vocabularies, systems of logic and syntax, completely fresh structures and dramaturgies.

My role as an artist is to pay very close attention to the output of an AI, trying to understand and interpret this output as a document from the future, blueprints for a piece which I try to reverse-engineer in the present.

 Sound poetry and vocal work by Jennifer Walshe. Duration: 0:38.
https://hdl.handle.net/20.500.12434/437a7854

5th Audio: THEY GO PEOPLE & PERSON (excerpt) by Jennifer Walshe.

8.

I love text scores, but I've found much of contemporary text score practice frustrating for a long time. In many scores, the vocabulary, the syntax, even the verb choices have remained static since the 1960s. For many of the composers of these scores, this simplicity is precise and apt. But I feel strongly that text scores are the most democratic, efficient, powerful form of notation, and yet we're stuck aping the linguistic style of the Fluxus period.

I feel we're missing out on a rich engagement if we fail to let text scores be affected by the language of the times we live in. I want text scores that are warped by Twitter and Flarf, bustling with words from

Merriam-Webster's Time Traveller, experimenting with language in the way Ben Marcus and Claudia Rankine do. If, as Donna Haraway says, 'Grammar is politics by other means', why not take the opportunity to interfere?

My early text scores were concerned with trying to push the limits of what a text score could do by turning it into highly technical language dealing with esoteric procedures. These experiments culminated in a large-scale score titled *The Observation of Hibernalian Law*. The work consists of a book, objects, diagrams and schematics.

In recent years I've been using the web to produce scores, trying to witness how the ecosystems of different social media platforms affects how a score is made and the sounds it might produce. I've made text-score projects on Snapchat, YikYak and numerous projects on Twitter.[11] These works aren't made for conceptual LOLs, they're serious attempts to welcome contemporary technology and language to the text score. The language in many of these scores was produced by feeding pre-existing text scores into Markov Chain Generators, by crossbreeding text scores and Weird Twitter accounts.

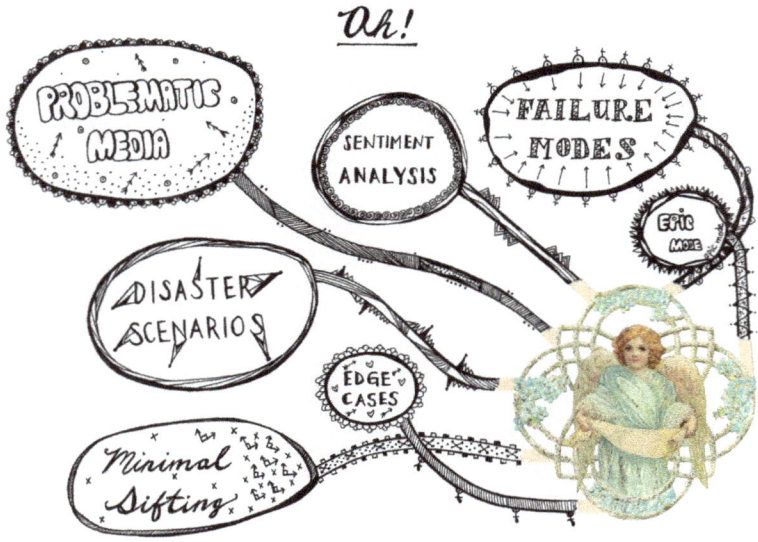

Fig 19.5. YOUR WORK IS OXYGEN FOR THE FUTURE (excerpt) by Jennifer Walshe. ÓJennifer Walshe.

---

11   TextScores is Emerege [@SuperSuperThank], https://twitter.com/SuperSuperThank

Syntax and grammar are disrupted here, and that is the point. I've done multiple performances of these scores, and both the experience of engaging with the score and the results produced are different to other text scores I've worked with.

Markov Chain Generators have their limits, however, and the advent of Deep Learning brings new possibilities. Over the last year I've been working to create a neural network which can write text scores. We're in the middle of the laborious process of taking folders full of PDFs, TIFFs, JPGs and DOCs and transcribing them. This is the grunt work of machine learning – cleaning up and formatting thousands of words of text scores to create a master .txt file of everything we can get our hands on.

Even at this level, a lot of decisions have to be made that will affect the output. What do we do with formatting? With blank lines and paragraph breaks? With fonts and italics and words in bold? What if the text score was designed to be a badge? A t-shirt? A mug? My machine-learning friends tell me that we will eventually get to the point where I'll just throw the folder at the network and it will know what to do. Unfortunately we're not there yet.

Beyond the formatting issues, we have to think about the corpus of text which will be used to train the model. This corpus is not the input – it's used simply to get the network to understand what language is. Many of the researchers I've talked to who make networks to generate text use the Bible as their corpus. I can understand. The Bible is in the public domain, it is easily available as an appropriately formatted file. But think about it lads, just for a second.

I spend hours making a corpus comprised of books by early feminists and Gothic writers. Mary Wollstonecraft. Mary Shelley. Edgar Allen Poe. Anne Radcliffe. It runs for several hours and then crashes the system.

Nonetheless, we are already getting outputs heavy with the directives of Fluxus:

> Get a girlfriend! Go to bed everyday and get out in the class. Call yasmin and eat a bit. Speak Chinese! Put your weight on the table at the brig. Take your best friends and get rid of the throne. Tell them you are an idiot. Wake up a banknote and the love for you, and 100%. See concert that i'm very beard. Look after your daddy. Talk about lunch. Keep playin'!

9.

In 2016, Deep Mind, the artificial intelligence division of Google, released WaveNet, a generative model for raw audio.[12] A WaveNet is a convolutional neural network that can model any type of audio. It does this on a sample-by-sample basis. Given that audio recordings typically have at least 16,000 samples per second, the computation involved is significant.

Deep Mind's original blog post shows the structure of a WaveNet. Like any neural network, data enters, moves through hidden layers (this schematic shows three – in reality they could be higher in number), and then an output is produced.

The hidden layers are what interest me here. Machine learning borrows the concept of the neural network from biology. The neural networks in our brains have hidden layers. For example, the networks in our brains relating to sight contain layers of neurons that receive direct input from the world in the form of photons hitting our eyeballs. This input then travels through a series of hidden layers which identify the most salient aspects of what we're seeing, before rendering what we are seeing into a 3D whole.

The Nobel-winning physicist Frank Wilczek describes how 'Hidden layers embody...the idea of emergence. Each hidden layer neuron has a template. It becomes activated, and sends signals of its own to the next layer, precisely when the pattern of information it's receiving from the preceding layer matches (within some tolerance) that template...the neuron defines, and thus creates, a new emergent concept.'

This blows my mind. Hidden layers of calculations. Neurons buried in vast amounts of code, creating and defining emergent concepts. And us, we puny humans, getting to witness new forms of thinking. New forms of art.

---

12 'WaveNet: A generative model for raw audio' in *Google Deep Mind* (8 September 2016), https://www.deepmind.com/blog/wavenet-a-generative-model-for-raw-audio

10.

Generative deep neural networks such as WaveNets can be used to generate any audio – text, voices, music, sound, you name it. It simply depends on what the model is trained on. Think of it like this: a sculptor takes a block of marble, and carves away everything that is not necessary to produce a sculpture of a horse. A generative deep neural network takes a block of white noise, and carves out everything that is not necessary to make the sound of a horse.

In his famous essay 'The Grain of the Voice' Roland Barthes writes how 'the "grain is the body in the voice as it sings, the hand as it writes, the limb as it performs.... I shall not judge a performance according to the rules of interpretation... but according to the image of the body given me."' Where is the grain in these recordings? Who does it belong to? How are we to judge something that has no body?

I was stunned when I first heard the WaveNet examples. I've learned to reproduce these examples with my voice and have used my versions in pieces such as IS IT COOL TO TRY HARD NOW?. I have listened to these examples many, many times. I can hear fragments of a language beyond anything humans speak. I can hear breathing and mouth sounds. I can hear evidence of a biology the machine will never possess. And I know that regardless of its lack of biology, the voice will be read as having gender, ethnicity, class, ability, sexuality. The voice will be judged.

The process of listening to the output of a neural network and trying to embody those results; the experience of trying to take sounds produced by code and feel my way into their logic – for me, that is part of the texture of being a person, of being a composer in 2018.

11.

 Generated sound with Walshe's voice of sounds like hard typing, mumbling, singing, and breathing. Duration: 0:22.
https://hdl.handle.net/20.500.12434/b9367366

6th Audio: Jennifer Walshe's voice, generated by Dadabots, Epoch 27.

CJ Carr and Zack Zukowski, who operate under the name Dadabots, use machine learning to create what they call artificial artists.[13] They use a modified version of the recurrent neural network SampleRNN to do this (SampleRNN itself was developed in response to WaveNet). CJ and Zack take pre-existing music and use it to train their network, which outputs 'new' albums by bands such as the Beatles and Dillinger Escape Plan.

I send CJ and Zack a link to a folder of recordings of my voice. A few weeks later, they send me back a link to a folder containing 341 sound files. 341 sound files of their network learning to sound like me. Hours and hours of material.

Listening to the files is a surreal experience. You should know—you've been listening to them over the course of this talk. I find the initial files hilarious—series of long notes, the network warming up in the same way a musician would. As I work my way through the files, they evolve and improve. I can hear myself, and it's both uncanny and completely natural. The hidden layers have coughed up all sorts of tasty stuff, and I begin to hear certain habits and vocal tics in a new light. I start to hear my voice through the lens of the network.

12.

 Generated sound with Walshe's voice, unrecognizable sounds and breathing. Duration: 0:26.
https://hdl.handle.net/20.500.12434/6421b917

7th Audio: Jennifer Walshe's voice, generated by Dadabots, Epoch 39.

As a performer, my voice operates closely in collaboration with technology. It has been this way ever since I was seven years old and used my First Holy Communion money to buy a tape recorder. It's rare for me to perform without a microphone, and I'm used to the idea that when I'm performing, my voice exists as multiple overlapping voices, some of which the sound engineer has more control over than me. There are the resonating chambers inside my head; there is my monitor; and there is the PA.

---

13 Neural networks in *Dadabots*, https://dadabots.com/

I'm used to my voice being sampled, vocoded, autotuned, layered with effects. I sing through SM58s and Neumanns, through homemade microphones attached to drum kits. I sing into wax cylinder machines and through exponential horns. I do battle with Max/MSP. I put contact microphones on my throat; I allow the Science Gallery in Dublin to send a transnasal camera down my throat to film my vocal cords. Would I have been a singer, one hundred years ago? Probably, but a very different one. Perhaps, a very frustrated one.

My voice evolved through free improvisation – I have never had any vocal training beyond the discipline I impose on myself as an improviser. The free improvisation duo is one of the dearest relationships to me. The people I've played with the most – Tony Conrad, Panos Ghikas and Tomomi Adachi – are like family members. My strange brothers.

At the moment I'm working on ULTRACHUNK, a collaboration with the artist and machine-learning specialist Memo Akten.[14] I sit in front of my laptop and film myself improvising. Memo uses these recordings to train a convolutional neural network called Grannma (Granular Neural Music & Audio). I think about what it means to improvise for an artificial intelligence system. Who is listening, and how? The goal is that Grannma will be able to produce both audio and video in collaboration with me in a performance situation. No midi, no sampling – a network synthesizing my voice, live. We will witness Grannma learning to see, and learning to listen, live. I'll grapple with performing with a network whose results I cannot predict. A new, strange sibling, both of us together in the uncanny valley on stage.

13.

Walshe's synthesized voice saying "But do I actually want to download all that data. I mean there is a lot of dumb things in a passive aggressive likes and what if they logged all the times my grandma used my account to look at my cousin's profile pics to see if she was not lying about being pregnant." Duration: 0:14.
https://hdl.handle.net/20.500.12434/022b25a7

8th Audio: Dubliner quote spoken by version 2 of Walshe's synthesised voice.

---

14 Memo Akten, Selected Projects in *Memo*, https://www.memo.tv/works/#selected-works

In *The Voice in Cinema*, film theorist Michel Chion describes how when we hear a voice in a film soundtrack and 'cannot yet connect it to a face – we get a special being, a kind of talking and acting shadow to which we attach the name *acousmêtre*.' Chion discusses what he terms the 'complete *acousmêtre*, the one who is not-yet-seen, but who remains liable to appear in the visual field at any moment.' The moment of appearance of the body belonging to the voice results in 'de-acousmatization' a process which is 'like a deflowering.' Chion attributes awesome powers to the *acousmêtre* – 'the ability to be everywhere, to see all, to know all, and to have complete power.' He compares the *acousmêtre* to the voice of God, to the voices of our mothers we heard in the womb before we were born.

The voices that emerge from machine-learning systems, voices that will never be seen, voices without bodies or homes – Chion's theory of the *acousmêtre* suggests one way to think about them. And as after a prolonged voiceover in a film, I start to wonder when the voice's body will appear, and what it will look like.

14.

 Generated sound with Walshe's voice of unrecognizable sounds, moments of static like sounds, breathing and some vocalization.
Duration: 0:36.
https://hdl.handle.net/20.500.12434/6eba0fe6

9th Audio: Jennifer Walshe's voice, generated by Dadabots, Epoch 40.

When I was a student, I was taught neat narratives about the development of Western music. The historical inevitability of serialism, the emancipation of the dissonance, the liberation of noise. In terms of the larger picture, we are about to leave all of this in the dust. I am convinced that not only the development of the music, but life in the twenty-first century will be primarily marked by how we engage with, respond to and think about AI. If we care about the world, if we're curious about human and non-human beings, art and consciousness, we need to be thinking about AI. We have a long way to go, but we can see glimpses of the future already in the world around us – autonomous vehicles, machine-learning-aided cancer diagnosis, neural networks making accurate predictions of schizophrenia onset, high-frequency trading, gene editing.

What does AI mean for music? Everything. I'm convinced that within fifteen to forty years, machines will be able to write music, in many genres, which is indistinguishable from that written by humans. Well-defined genres with clear rules will be the first to be automated - film music, music for games, advertising music, many genres of pop songs. The machines will write this music more quickly, and more cheaply, than humans ever will. A lot of musicians will be out of work.

Over the next forty years, AI will completely change the way music is made and who it's made by. AI will change the reasons why music is made, and will make us question what the function of music and music-making is. Let me be clear – I don't think humans will ever stop making music. And I think a great deal of music in the future will be made without AI. The challenge of the future will be deciding what it means to make music when the machines can. We will have to think about what it means to make music when, in many cases, the machines will be able to make music of a far higher standard than many humans can.

By engaging with AI, we look at the world in its entirety. We continue asking the questions asked by musicians like the League of Automatic Music Composers, by George Lewis and Voyager.[15] We see how Bach chorales written almost 300 years ago are used by one of the most powerful corporations in the history of the world to train neural networks. We get to be ethnomusicologists romping through the Wild West section of the uncanny valley.

We are all involved, we are all enmeshed, we are all implicated in the development of AI, regardless of whether we code or not, regardless of whether we ever make a piece of music using AI. Every second of every day, our behaviour provides the data for machine-learning systems to train on. We foot the bill for the hardware necessary to do some of these computations – for example, most smartphones now contain dedicated chips for machine learning. Our interactions with our phones – and by that I mean our every waking moment – provides training data for

---

15   League of Automatic Music Composers (2023), https://www.dramonline.org/labels/league-of-automatic-music-composers
    Claude Nobbs, 'George E. Lewis – Voyager Duo 4' clip, YouTube (Aug 3, 2015) https://www.youtube.com/watch?v=hO47LiHsFtc

neural chips on our phones, data that drives the creation of AI at the corporate level. And of course, the AI that develops at the corporate level will be the intellectual property of the corporation. And the AI at the corporate level will define the structure of all of our futures. Every single challenge facing us as a species can either be faced successfully or exacerbated by how we engage with AI.

I am not a computer scientist. I'm a composer who is living in the twenty-first century and trying to think it through. I'm both sublimely excited and blackly horrified about what is coming. I'm trying to give you a sense of how I view the world, and where I think things are going, because that psychological space is where my art comes from. It's a magical space, that is by turns speculative, uncanny and hidden, but most of all deeply embedded in the here and now of the world.

Where do we go from here? AI. What is coming next? AI. What a time to be alive.

Darmstadt, 25 July 2018.

List of Illustrations

Fig. 1.1	Score of Incredible Distance.
Fig. 1.2	Iconic Wester Hailes sound: Birdsong © Laura Baxter.
Fig. 5.1	Lore Lixenberg, The Voice Party election flyer for the 2019 UK Election (2019) © Lore Lixenberg.
Fig. 5.2	Frederic Acquaviva, The Election Night Count, Hackney Britannia Centre © Lore Lixenberg (2019).
Fig. 5.3	Jeremy Richardson, Election window banner design © Lore Lixenberg.
Fig. 5.4	Frederic Acquaviva Election night: 3am exhaustion with the obligatory flask of hot whisky todd © Lore Lixenberg (2019).
Fig. 5.5	Lore Lixenberg, The Voice Party Election street poster Berlin (2017) © Lore Lixenberg.
Fig. 13.1	Anri Sala, table of wind descriptions: quotes from James Bell's journal and their translation into rhythmic patterns used in The Last Resort (2017). © Anri Sala VG Bild-Kunst, Bonn c/o Pictoright Amsterdam 2023.
Fig. 13.2	Wolfgang Amadeus Mozart, Clarinet Concerto in A major (1791), Adagio, beginning of 2nd theme, mm. 17-20, CC BY-SA 4.0.
Fig. 13.3	Anri Sala, excerpt from the score of The Last Resort: Based on Mozart's Clarinet Concerto in A major, Adagio, mm. 17-23 © Anri Sala VG Bild-Kunst, Bonn c/o Pictoright Amsterdam 2023.
Fig. 13.4	Anri Sala, The Last Resort (2017), installation and live performance, Garage Museum for Contemporary Art, Moscow. © Ivan Erofeev, Anton Donikov.
Fig. 13.5	The soloist, located above the orchestra. Anri Sala, The Last Resort (2017), installation and live performance, Garage Museum for Contemporary Art, Moscow. © Ivan Erofeev, Anton Donikov.
Fig. 13.6	Left: Anri Sala, The Present Moment (In D) (2014), Haus der Kunst, Munich. © Jens Weber. Right: Physical layout of speakers and projection of The Present Moment (in D) at Haus der Kunst.

Fig. 13.7	Anri Sala, installation view of The Present Moment (In D) (2014), video projection added in the last phase of the revised music. Haus der Kunst, Munich. © Jens Weber.
Fig. 13.8	Anri Sala, The Present Moment (In D) (2014), Haus der Kunst, Munich © Anri Sala.
Fig. 13.9	Igor Stravinsky, mm. 11-15 from the Elegy for Solo Viola, score used by Anri Sala for the film If and Only If (2018) © Anri Sala VG Bild-Kunst, Bonn c/o Pictoright Amsterdam 2023.
Fig. 13.10	Anri Sala, If and Only If (2017) the exhibition AS YOU GO (2019), Castello di Rivoli Museum of Contemporary Art, Turin © The author, 23 April, 2019.
Fig. 13.11	Anri Sala, If and Only If (2018) the exhibition AS YOU GO (2019), Castello di Rivoli Museum of Contemporary Art, Turin © The author, 23 April, 2019.
Fig. 16.1	Zwischentoene Vision Rhinstadt by Matthias Dietrich © Montforter Zwischentöne. Image by Matthias Dietrich.
Fig. 16.2	Matthaeus Passion by Matthias Rhomberg © Montforter Zwischentöne. Image by Matthias Dietrich.
Fig. 16.3	Outpatient Clinic © Montforter Zwischentöne. Image by Matthias Dietrich.
Fig. 16.4	Concert for companion © Montforter Zwischentöne. Image by Matthias Dietrich.
Fig. 16.5	The Funeral © Montforter Zwischentöne. Image by Matthias Dietrich.
Fig. 16.6	Love, pray © Montforter Zwischentöne. Image by Matthias Dietrich.
Fig. 16.7	Credo Mutter Hildgard © Montforter Zwischentöne. Image by Matthias Dietrich.
Fig 16.8	Salon Paula © Montforter Zwischentöne. Image by Matthias Dietrich.
Fig 16.9	Zwischentoene © Montforter Zwischentöne. Image by Matthias Dietrich.
Fig. 19.1	Celtorwave by Tom Kemp @ Jennifer Walshe.
Fig. 19.2	Aisteach © Jennifer Walshe.
Fig. 19.3	Notebooks © Jennifer Walshe.
Fig 19.4	Book is book © Jennifer Walshe.
Fig 19.5	YOUR WORK IS OXYGEN FOR THE FUTURE (excerpt) by Jennifer Walshe. ÓJennifer Walshe.

List of Audio Files

1st Audio: Dadabots © Jennifer Walshe.
2nd Audio: EMRALDIA 'Llac Centre Suite' (excerpt) – Celtorwave track © Jennifer Walshe.
3rd Audio: Jennifer Walshe's voice generated by Dadabots, Epoch 6 © Jennifer Walshe.
4th Audio: Elon Musk quote spoken by version 1 of Walshe's synthesised voice © Jennifer Walshe.
5th Audio: THEY GO PEOPLE & PERSON (excerpt) by Jennifer Walshe.
6th Audio: Jennifer Walshe's voice, generated by Dadabots, Epoch 27.
7th Audio: Jennifer Walshe's voice, generated by Dadabots, Epoch 39.
8th Audio: Dubliner quote spoken by version 2 of Walshe's synthesised voice.
9th Audio: Jennifer Walshe's voice, generated by Dadabots, Epoch 40.

Index

Abels, Michael 84
Afrofuturism 84–87, 382
Albania 254, 258
Albert, Heinrich 327
archive 43, 231, 233, 237–247, 379, 381, 390
Artful Participation project 241
artificial intelligence (AI) 10, 21, 95, 100, 129, 355–374, 379, 383, 391, 394, 397–400
Asian 42
Association of British Orchestras 189
audience(s) 1, 6, 8, 10, 13, 16, 18–20, 32, 38, 53, 63, 70–71, 83, 85, 88, 103, 106, 116–120, 129, 131, 143, 154, 158, 163–164, 167–168, 171, 173, 177, 181–183, 186, 188–193, 195–201, 206, 208–211, 214, 220–223, 241–243, 245, 254–255, 262–263, 273, 277–278, 280–288, 290–291, 293, 300–309, 311–313, 315–320, 322–323, 325, 327, 329–330, 334, 340–341, 344–350, 369–370, 374
Australia 255–256

Bach, Johann Sebastian 158, 216, 277, 321, 325, 360–361, 366, 373, 399
BAME (Black, Asian and Minority Ethnic) 32, 44–45
BBC Philharmonic Orchestra 358, 370
Belgium 20, 219, 306
Biber, Heinrich Ignaz Franz 329
Black 42, 44, 49, 81–88
Black Administrators of Opera 81–82, 86
Black Music Action Coalition 86

Black Opera Alliance 81, 86
Black Opera Research Network 86
Black Orchestral Network 86
Blacktivism 17, 81
Blanchard, Terrance 83
Boekman Foundation 178–179
Brexit 92, 101, 131
Brussels Philharmonic Orchestra 212

Chineke! Foundation 303
Chineke! Orchestra 32
climate change 8, 177, 179–180, 206–207, 356–357
Codarts 32
Columbia University 30, 38
Conservatorium Maastricht 233, 243
corrective critiques 49–50, 52
COVID-19 pandemic 9–10, 70, 92, 95, 105, 109–110, 127, 132, 168, 182, 192, 197, 214, 277, 280, 283, 307, 309, 333–335, 338–339, 341, 344–345, 350–351, 370
Creative Carbon Scotland 180, 189
Creative Scotland 189

Darmström, Cecilia 183
Davis, Anthony 84
Davis, Nathan 84
Debussy, Claude 158, 299, 306, 309–310
Denmark 43
Differential Digital Signal Processing (DDSP) 367–368, 370–373
diversification 1, 38, 45, 247, 303
Documenta 37–38

Donaueschinger Musiktage 38, 44
DONNE Foundation 42
Drake Music Scotland 63, 69

Edinburgh, University of 35, 283
ELIA 30–31
English National Opera 334
Ensemble Modern 38
environmental impact 183–184, 206–211, 214–223
Enwezor, Okwui 37, 267
ethnographic research 161, 233, 243, 281
Euskadi Symphony orchestra 209

Fair Access Principles 17, 60–64, 73–74, 76
Finland 19, 154, 180–181
Finnish Lahti Symphony Orchestra 178
Flanders Symphony Orchestra 207, 220
Germany 19, 44, 65, 178, 180, 184–186, 192–194, 197, 199–200, 219, 265, 319
Giddens, Rhiannon 84
Gottstein, Björn 38
Green Events 219
Green Music Initiative 219
Green Track Ghent 219, 221
Grouse, Matthew 291

Hauntology 382–383
healthcare 10, 18, 78, 154–157, 163, 167–168, 170–173
Hermes Ensemble 282, 290
higher music education 9, 31, 38, 156, 163–164, 170, 172–173
Historical Documents of the Irish Avant-Garde (Aisteach) 381–383

Ireland 180, 381, 383, 386–387
Irish Ministry of Culture 180
Irishness 382
Italy 75

Julie's Bicycle 207, 219–221

Kaldor Public Art Projects 255
Keychange 17, 50–53, 59–60, 65–67, 72

Kinshasa symphony 32
Kliphuis, Tim 180

Lahti Symphony Orchestra 19, 178, 181, 184
League of American Orchestras 82
liveness 10, 21, 334–335, 340–342, 347, 349
Locatelli, Pietro 288
London Contemporary Music Festival 195
Lyrebird 388–389

Maastricht Centre for the Innovation of Classical Music 3, 30, 110, 178, 241, 243, 281
Madagascar 185
MaerzMusik festival 43, 53–54
Manchester Collective 17, 104, 109–110, 117–119
Manhattan School of Music 132, 139
Meaningful Music in Healthcare (MiMiC) 18, 153, 156–168, 170–172
Menefield, William 84
Metropolitan Opera (MET) 83
Montforter Zwischentöne 318–319, 321, 323–331
Mozart, Wolfgang Amadeus 199, 256–262, 362–363, 366
Munich Philharmonic 185
MuseNet 362–363, 365, 368, 370–371, 373
museum problem 2, 13, 15, 19–20, 192, 199, 229–230, 237, 247, 253, 274
Music Foundation (PRSF) 63, 65, 67
Musikcentrum Öst 65
Musikvermittlung 196

Netherlands 3, 10, 161, 163, 178–180, 219, 241
Nevis Ensemble 19, 22, 178, 181, 187
Norway 44, 219

Opera North Projects 63
Orchester des Wandels 19, 178, 181, 184, 186

Philharmonia Orchestra 17, 104, 109–110
Philzuid 3, 241

Prince Claus Conservatoire 157
PRiSM-SampleRNN 370–371, 373

radical critiques 41, 49–50, 53, 55
Ragland, Dave 84
Reeperbahn Festival 65
Rotterdam 32
Royal Conservatoire of Scotland 35, 73
Royal Danish Academy of Music 131
Royal Flemish Opera 307
Royal Liverpool Philharmonic Orchestra 207, 220
Royal Northern College of Music (RNCM) 334
Royal Scottish Academy 33

Sage Gateshead 63
Sala, Anri 20, 253–274
Schoenberg, Arnold 266–268, 270
Scotland 17, 19, 22, 30, 35, 60, 63, 69–70, 73, 101, 178, 180, 187–190, 280, 283
Scottish Chamber Orchestra (SCO) 30, 33–34
Scottish Classical Music Green Guide 189
Scottish Classical Sustainability Group 189
Scottish Ensemble 282, 288
Sibelius, Jean 181
Sound and Music 17, 59–61, 64–65, 70
SoundCloud 95. *See also* streaming platforms
Sound Festival 63, 285, 287

Sphinx organisation 32
Stollery, Pete 283, 285, 287
Stravinsky, Igor 15, 258, 270–271
streaming platforms 92, 214. *See also* SoundCloud
Studio for New Music ensemble 263
sustainability 8–9, 13, 19, 72, 120, 131, 135, 173, 178–180, 185–188, 190, 196, 205–207, 209–213, 216–223, 308, 311
Sweden 43
Symphony Orchestra of Madrid 209

Tanglewood's Festival of Contemporary Music 38
Tchaikovsky, Pyotr Ilyich 199, 258
Thompson, Joel 84
Twaalfhoven, Merlijn van 180
Tŷ Cerdd-Music Centre Wales 63

uncanny valley 384–385, 387–388, 397, 399
United Kingdom (UK) 59, 190, 280, 335
Unlimited 63

Vienna Philharmonic 334
Vienna, University of Music and Performing Arts 131
Voice Party, the 17, 91–92, 94–101

Werktreue 47
Westdeutscher Rundfunk 194
Whiteside, Matthew 282

Zeppelin University Friedrichshafen 316

About the Team

Alessandra Tosi was the managing editor for this book.

Lucy Barnes copy-edited this book, and compiled the index.

Jeevanjot Kaur Nagpal designed the cover. The cover was produced in InDesign using the Fontin font.

Cameron Craig typeset the book in InDesign and produced the paperback and hardback editions. The text font is Tex Gyre Pagella and the heading font is Californian FB.

Cameron also produced the PDF, EPUB, XML and HTML editions. The conversion was performed with open-source software and other tools freely available on our GitHub page at https://github.com/OpenBookPublishers.

This book has been anonymously peer-reviewed by experts in their field. We thank them for their invaluable help.

This book need not end here...

Share

All our books — including the one you have just read — are free to access online so that students, researchers and members of the public who can't afford a printed edition will have access to the same ideas. This title will be accessed online by hundreds of readers each month across the globe: why not share the link so that someone you know is one of them?

This book and additional content is available at:
https://doi.org/10.11647/OBP.0353

Donate

Open Book Publishers is an award-winning, scholar-led, not-for-profit press making knowledge freely available one book at a time. We don't charge authors to publish with us: instead, our work is supported by our library members and by donations from people who believe that research shouldn't be locked behind paywalls.

Why not join them in freeing knowledge by supporting us:
https://www.openbookpublishers.com/support-us

Follow @OpenBookPublish

Read more at the Open Book Publishers BLOG

You may also be interested in:

Classical Music
Contemporary Perspectives and Challenges
Edited by Michael Beckerman and Paul Boghossian

https://doi.org/10.11647/obp.0242

Annunciations
Sacred Music for the Twenty-First Century
Edited by George Corbett

https://doi.org/10.11647/obp.0172

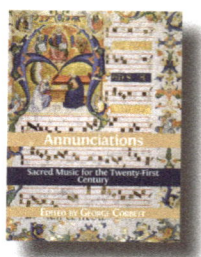

Rethinking Social Action through Music
The Search for Coexistence and Citizenship in Medellín's Music Schools
Geoffrey Baker

https://doi.org/10.11647/obp.0243

www.ingramcontent.com/pod-product-compliance
Lightning Source LLC
Chambersburg PA
CBHW041732300426

44116CB00019B/2960